T IS once again a tremendous privilege to extend a very wa... to this, the 1993/94 edition of The Scottish Football League... This is the 14th edition of a publication that is now firmly r... ...ttish football's premier reference book and as you will have already ...ticed, I am delighted that the book is once again sponsored after a one ...r absence, with Tartan Special having agreed to commit itself to ...nsoring the title for this season. Over the years, Scottish Brewers have ...n actively involved in sponsoring various aspects of our national game ...d I am certain that they will continue to enjoy the benefits from their ...nsorship of this very prestigious publication.

...he 1992/93 season proved to be ...ntful to say the least, both on and off ...park and I have no doubts that the ...nts during the course of this season ...not prove any less dramatic as the ...s, weeks and months unfold. Off the ...d of play, I think that it would be fair ...omment, however, that events last ...son proved to be somewhat difficult ...this organisation. These events have ...n well documented by the various ...tors of the media, however, ...withstanding the various arguments ...counter arguments which took ...ce, I firmly believe that following the ...ision taken at our Annual General ...eting in May of this year to alter the ...cture to four divisions of ten clubs, ...Scottish Football League has grown ...h in strength and in stature and ...mately, this will prove beneficial for ...League in particular and our game in ...eral.

...On the park, last season provided ...ny memorable highlights, particularly ...u were a Rangers' supporter, ...ough I have no doubts that all ...tball fans will have their own special ...ments to savour. Certainly most of ...glory last season belonged to the ...x club and their achievements in ...ning the domestic treble, especially ...ne highly charged competitive ...ironment of modern day football and ...demands that it now places on ...vers, deserves special praise. ...lowever, even more significant were ...r magnificent performances during ...course of last season's European Cup ...npetition. To play in ten ties, ...uding six games in the much ...licised Champions' League stage, all ...inst top quality opposition and

remain undefeated, was a tremendous feat and although they narrowly missed out in gaining a place in the European Cup Final, their players, management, directors and supporters deserve a special mention for not only being a great credit to their club, but for also enhancing the Scottish game at a time when it has attracted criticism from various quarters.

Away from the glamour of the European stage and back on the domestic front, congratulations to both Raith Rovers and Kilmarnock in gaining promotion to the Premier Division. The Kirkcaldy club dominated the First Division last season and contrary to the views of many critics, continued to get better as the season unfolded and won the title with plenty to spare. On the other hand, Kilmarnock were involved in a real dogfight with Dunfermline Athletic right up until the very last game of the season. However, it is great to see a club, which has a very proud history, but have not enjoyed much success lately, playing again at the highest level.

Events in the Second Division were no less dramatic and although Clyde won the Championship with a week to spare, the second promotion place went to the very last kick of the ball... literally. A last minute penalty ensured that Brechin City and not Stranraer would be playing in the First Division this season, however, sympathy must be extended to the Stair Park club, who, despite a last day 5-2 victory, ultimately lost out on goal difference.

As I have already mentioned, Rangers in winning the treble won both the Skol Cup and the Tennents Scottish Cup and congratulations must also be extended

to Hamilton Academical for retaining the B & Q Cup for a second successive season, when they defeated Morton 3-2 in a highly entertaining Final at Love Street, Paisley. Certainly, this tournament has steadily grown in popularity and is now eagerly awaited by players, officials and fans of the clubs in the First and Second Divisions.

The preparation of the Review requires a tremendous amount of time and effort and I would like to extend my particular thanks to the following:-

David C. Thomson (Editor)

All other staff of The Scottish Football League

The 38 Member Clubs

Messrs. George Ashton (Sportapic) and Alan Elliott

Our Contributors

Sports Projects Ltd and, in particular, Bernard Gallagher, Trevor Hartley and Nadine Goldingay.

As I have already mentioned, the 1993/94 season will prove vital in many areas, none more so than the actual structure of the League. As you will be aware, from the commencement of season 1994/95, two new Associate Member Clubs will be admitted, resulting in a set-up of four divisions of ten clubs. To assist fans in understanding how this new set-up will come about and how it will operate, a detailed summary is contained elsewhere in this publication. With all of the various movements that will take place between each division, a very exciting and dramatic season is guaranteed.

ENJOY THE SEASON!

YULE CRAIG
PRESIDENT,
THE SCOTTISH FOOTBALL LEAGUE

Scottish Football League Management Committee, Season 1993/94

J. Y. Craig J.P., C.A (President), J. Clydesdale (Vice-President), G. J. Fulston (Treasurer), J. K. Kelly, R. C. Ogilvie, D. B. Smith, I. R. Donald, R. A. Paxton, J. Wilson, D. McK. MacIntyre, J. W. Baxter, J. McGoogan LL.B.

FIVE IN A ROW!

RANGERS may not quite have turned the 44 game Premier Division marathon into a sprint last season - but the focussed way the Ibrox men lifted their fifth successive title would have won the total approval of Linford Christie.

From the moment they came off the blocks with a 1-0 win over St. Johnstone at Ibrox on 1st August, there was scarcely a moment when Walter Smith's men failed to justify the bookies installing them as odds-on favourites to take the Championship again.

Ally McCoist ensured the flag-unfurling party went with a bang, slotting in the only goal of the game 10 minutes from time.

The Scotland striker was starting out where he had left off the previous season and was to enjoy another fabulous campaign.

Aberdeen and Celtic, the sides expected to provide most resistance to Rangers' domination, matched their good start.

Duncan Shearer, an expensive close season recruit from Blackburn Rovers, gave Aberdeen fans a taste of what was to come when he rattled in a double as the Dons defeated Hibs 3-0 at Pittodrie on opening day.

Celtic negotiated the extremely tough hurdle of a visit to Tynecastle, a late own goal from Craig Levein earning Liam Brady's men a hard-earned 1-0 win over Hearts.

When the Dons and Celtic shared the points at Pittodrie the following midweek, while Rangers were beating Airdrie 2-0 at Ibrox, the League table suddenly had a familiar look to it with the reigning

Champions on top. But hope for the chasing pack sprang eternal on 15th August, when Rangers travelled to Tayside to face Simon Stainrod's Dundee side.

Against all expectations, the Den Park men won an extraordinary contest 4-3 to leave a stunned Rangers in fourth place in the Premier Division behind Celtic, Aberdeen and Hearts.

Stainrod afterwards called on more teams to ask the questions of Rangers defence which his men had done - but few others proved up to the task. Still, the title race enjoyed an even more competitive look the following week as Rangers came from behind at Ibrox when the first 'Old Firm' clash of the season was drawn 1-1.

The Champions slipped down a further place to fifth as Dundee

United also stated their early challenge as they jumped into the leading group. August ended with two goals from Duncan Ferguson helping United beat Falkirk 2-0 to go to the top of the table.

However, the most significant result of the afternoon came at Ibrox where Rangers had trailed Aberdeen 1-0 at half-time. The second 45 minutes saw the Light Blues produce arguably their finest football of the season as they stormed to a 3-1 win which lifted them into second place.

On Tuesday, 1st September, it was Hearts turn to enjoy pole position when they beat Dundee 3-1 at Dens Park. It was purely temporary. Just 24 hours later, a stunning hat-trick from McCoist inspired Rangers to a 4-1 win over Motherwell at Fir Park. They were back at the top of the pile and did not relinquish the position again.

Come the end of September, Rangers had chalked up impressive victories over Hearts (2-0) and Dundee United (4-0) to leave the challenge of those two clubs seriously damaged.

One month further on, with the Skol Cup and a place in the Second Round of the European Cup also clinched, Rangers held a comfortable looking four point lead over nearest rivals Celtic.

However, the Parkhead men's chase was severely dented on 7th November when Ian Durrant grabbed the only goal of a torrid 'Old Firm' showdown at Celtic Park.

By the turn of the year, it was from the north that the only credible challenge to Rangers emerged. With new boy Shearer in free-scoring form, Aberdeen had mounted a determined bid to ensure the title race ran all the way to the finish line.

Willie Miller's side produced some magnificent football and victims included Partick Thistle (7-0), Hearts (6-2) and Airdrie (7-0) as Shearer was ably supported by fellow front men Eoin Jess, Scott Booth and Mixu Paatelainen.

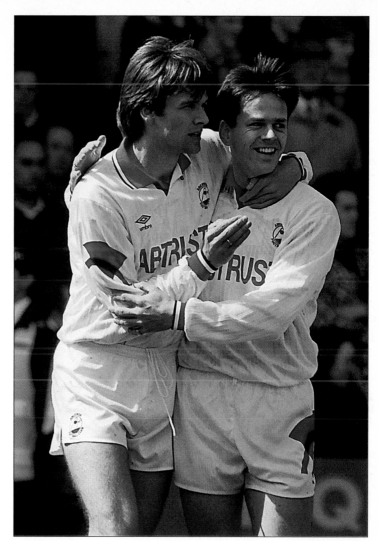

Aberdeen's Theo Ten Caat (left) and Scott Booth

Ally McCoist scored his 50th League and Cup goal against Dundee.

At the end of January, despite Aberdeen's impressive form, Rangers had unerringly continued to win and they held a five-point lead at the top.

Tuesday, 2nd February was D-Day for the Dons as Walter Smith's side came to Pittodrie. Victory for the home side would blow the title race wide open once more.

Miller could hardly have asked more of his side. They outplayed Rangers for long spells of the game but their hearts were broken by inspirational goalkeeping from Andy Goram.

Thirteen minutes into the second half, Mark Hateley notched the game's only goal with a magnificent header and Rangers grip on the Championship was tighter than ever.

By the end of February, Rangers had surged 11 points clear but, to their credit, Aberdeen refused to concede anything until it was mathematically impossible for them to catch up.

Astonishingly, since that early defeat at Dens Park, Rangers had put together a run of 29 unbeaten Premier Division matches which saw them drop a mere five points.

Against the backdrop of a fabulous European Cup campaign, it was a stunning level of consistency and one which left the rest gasping in awe.

Rangers finally tasted defeat again at Parkhead on 20th March losing 2-1 to Celtic. When Aberdeen visited Ibrox ten days later, the gap between themselves and Rangers had been whittled back to seven points.

However, any lingering hopes of a dramatic late charge from the Dons were dashed when they lost 2-0 at Ibrox.

Formalities were finally completed at Broomfield on Saturday, 1st May. Rangers needed just a point to clinch the title but went one better, Gary McSwegan scoring the only goal against

relegation haunted Airdrie.

The final table saw Rangers finish nine points ahead of Aberdeen with Celtic a further four points adrift in third place, at least enough to comfortably earn them a UEFA Cup place.

Dundee United earned a European return by finishing fourth, three points ahead of Hearts who were later granted an extra UEFA Cup slot courtesy of a match fixing scandal in Poland.

At the other end of the table, there had often been more drama and excitement than provided by the title chasers.

In the end, Falkirk and Airdrie took the drop into the First Division but only after a tremendous battle which left Partick Thistle, Motherwell and Dundee all very relieved sides come the end of the season.

STEPHEN HALLIDAY,
(Scottish Daily Express)

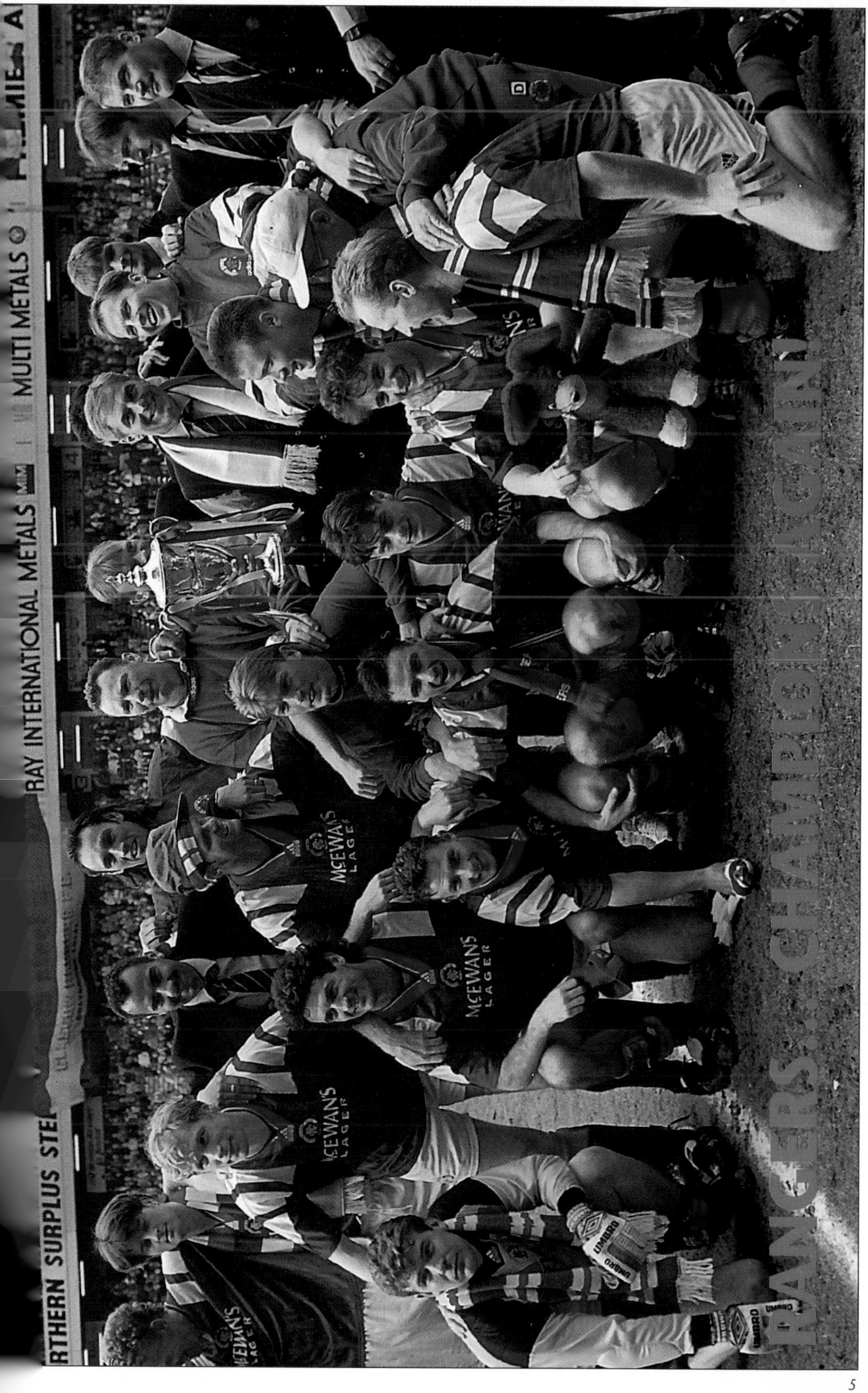
RANGERS... CHAMPIONS AGAIN!
MULTI METALS
McEWAN'S LAGER

ABERDEEN

Pittodrie Stadium
Pittodrie Street
Aberdeen AB2 1QH

Chairman
Richard M. Donald
Vice-Chairman
Ian R. Donald
Directors
Denis J. Miller;
Gordon A. Buchan
Manager
William Miller MBE
Secretary
Ian J. Taggart
Commercial Executive
David Johnston
Telephones
Ground/Ticket Office
(0224) 632328
Commercial Executive
(0224) 630944
Fax (0224) 644173
Donsline (0898) 121551
Club Shop (0224) 593866
Club Shop
c/o Crombie Sports
23 Bridge Street, Aberdeen
and Ticket Office
c/o Aberdeen FC
Pittodrie Stadium, Aberdeen
Official Supporters Club
Association Secretary
Mrs. Susan Scott,
32 Earns Heugh Crescent,
Cove, Aberdeen AB1 4RU.
Team Captain
Alex McLeish
Club Sponsor
A-Fab

LIST OF PLAYERS 1993-94

Name	Date of Birth	Place of Birth	Date of Signing	Height	Weight	Previous Club
Adams, Derek	25/06/75	Glasgow	05/09/91	5-10	10.12	Deeside
Aitken, Robert Sime	24/11/58	Irvine	27/06/92	6-0	13.0	St. Mirren
Bett, James	25/11/59	Hamilton	26/06/85	5-11.5	13.4	Lokeren
Booth, Scott	16/12/71	Aberdeen	28/07/88	5-9	11.10	Deeside B.C.
Connor, Robert	04/08/60	Kilmarnock	15/08/86	5-11	11.4	Dundee
Cooper, Neil	12/08/58	Aberdeen	23/09/91	5-11	12.7	Hibernian
Ferguson, Graeme	03/03/71	Stirling	09/07/87	5-10	11.10	Gairdoch United
Gibson, Andrew	02/02/69	Dechmont	24/12/88	5-9.5	11.10	Stirling Albion
Gilbert, Kenneth	08/03/75	Aberdeen	07/06/91	5-6.5	11.4	East End "A"
Grant, Brian	19/06/64	Bannockburn	15/08/84	5-9	11.2	Stirling Albion
Hick, Martin Allan	16/05/74	Paisley	11/09/92	5-11	11.10	Eastercraigs
Irvine, Brian Alexander	24/05/65	Bellshill	19/07/85	6-2.5	13.7	Falkirk
Jess, Eoin	13/12/70	Aberdeen	13/11/87	5-9.5	11.6	Rangers
Kane, Paul James	20/06/65	Edinburgh	22/11/91	5-9.5	11.0	Oldham Athletic
MacRonald, Colin William	22/08/73	Aberdeen	08/08/90	5-7.5	10.0	Deeside Boys Club
McKimmie, Stewart	27/10/62	Aberdeen	12/12/83	5-8	11.4	Dundee
McLeish, Alexander	21/01/59	Glasgow	11/03/77	6-1.5	13.4	Glasgow Utd
Miller, Joseph	08/12/67	Glasgow	30/07/93	5.8	9.12	Celtic
Milne, Colin Richard	23/10/74	Aberdeen	11/06/91	6-0	10.11	Albion Rangers
Milne, John	25/04/69	Montrose	07/07/92	6-3.5	15.2	Dartmouth College
Nisbet, Iain	11/05/74	Bellshill	18/05/91	5-9	10.2	Ayr United B.C.
Paatelainen, Mika-Matti P.	03/02/67	Helsinki	31/03/92	6-0	14.0	Dundee United
Reeley, Derek	26/12/74	Glasgow	08/08/91	5-8	10.7	"S" Form
Richardson, Lee	12/03/69	Halifax	16/09/92	5-10	12.0	Blackburn Rovers
Robertson, Hugh Scott	19/03/75	Aberdeen	24/08/93	5-9	12.7	Lewis United
Roddie, Andrew Robert	04/11/71	Glasgow	16/04/88	5-10.5	11.6	Glasgow United
Shearer, Duncan	28/08/62	Fort William	09/07/92	6-0	13.8	Blackburn Rovers
Smith, Gary	25/03/71	Glasgow	06/08/91	6-0	11.10	Falkirk
Snelders, Theodorus G.A.	07/12/63	Westervoort	22/07/88	6-2	14.12	F.C. Twente
Stillie, Derek	03/12/73	Irvine	03/05/91	6-0	11.10	Notts County
Ten Caat, Pieter Theodoor	08/12/64	Scheveld	27/07/91	5-11	11.10	Groningen
Thomson, Scott Munro	29/01/72	Aberdeen	05/11/91	5-10	11.10	Brechin City
Watson, Graham	11/09/70	St. Andrews	24/12/86	5-9.5	11.6	Deeside B.C.
Watt, Michael	27/11/70	Aberdeen	02/07/87	6-1	12.6	Cove Rangers U 18s
Winnie, David	26/10/66	Glasgow	22/11/90	6.1	12.7	St. Mirren
Wright, Stephen	27/08/71	Bellshill	28/11/87	5-10.5	11.2	Eastercraigs

CLUB FIXTURES 1993-94

Date	Opponent	Venue	Date	Opponent	Venue	Date	Opponent	Venue
Aug 4	League Cup 1		Oct 24	League Cup Final		Feb 12	Raith Rovers	H
Aug 7	Dundee United	A	Oct 30	Dundee	H	Feb 19	SFA Cup 4	
Aug 11	League Cup 2		Nov 6	St. Johnstone	A	Feb 26	Motherwell	A
Aug 14	Kilmarnock	H	Nov 9	Celtic	H	Mar 5	Heart of	
Aug 21	Dundee	A	Nov 13	Motherwell	H		Midlothian	H
Aug 25	League Cup 3		Nov 20	Raith Rovers	A	Mar 12	Partick Thistle	A
Aug 28	St. Johnstone	H	Nov 27	Hibernian	H	Mar 19	Kilmarnock	A
Sept 1	League Cup 4		Dec 1	Rangers	A	Mar 26	Dundee United	H
Sept 4	Celtic	A	Dec. 4	Heart of		Mar 29	Hibernian	H
Sept 11	Hibernian	A		Midlothian	A	Apr 2	Rangers	A
Sept 18	Rangers	H	Dec 11	Partick Thistle	H	Apr 9	Raith Rovers	A
Sept 22	League Cup S/F		Dec 18	Kilmarnock	H	Apr 16	Motherwell	H
Sept 25	Raith Rovers	H	Dec 27	Dundee United	A	Apr 23	Partick Thistle	H
Oct. 2	Motherwell	A	Jan 1	Dundee	A	Apr 27	Heart of	
Oct 5	Heart of		Jan. 8	St. Johnstone	H		Midlothian	A
	Midlothian	H	Jan 15	Celtic	A	Apr 30	Dundee	H
Oct 9	Partick Thistle	A	Jan 22	Rangers	H	May 7	St. Johnstone	A
Oct 16	Kilmarnock	A	Jan 29	SFA Cup 3		May 14	Celtic	H
Oct 23	Dundee United	H	Feb 5	Hibernian	A	May 21	SFA Cup Final	

MILESTONES
Year of Formation: 1903
Most Capped Player: Alex McLeish (77)
Most League Points in a Season:
64 (Premier Division – 1992-93 (44 games)
Most League goals scored by a player in a Season: Benny Yorston (38) 1929/30
Record Attendance: 45,061 v Hearts, 13/3/54
Record Victory: 13–0 v Peterhead, Scottish Cup 9/2/23
Record Defeat: 0–8 v Celtic, Division 1, 30/1/65

SEASON TICKET INFORMATION
Seated
Main Stand Centre Adult £225
Wing Stand Adult...£210
South Stand Adult £160
Merkland Stand Parent and Juvenile £200
Merkland Stand Juveniles/OAPs £60
Richard Donald Stand £210/185/160

LEAGUE ADMISSION PRICES
Seated
Main Stand Adult £12
South Stand Home Support £8
South Stand East (Visitors) – Adults.................£8.50
                                 – Juveniles/OAPs £3.50
Merkland Stand Adult £7
                     – Juveniles/OAPs £3.50
Richard Donald Stand £8

Registered Strip:	Shirt - Red, Shorts - Red, Stockings - Red
Change Strip:	Shirt - Navy with Gold Stripes, Shorts - Navy with Gold Trim, Stockings - Navy with Gold Trim

CLUB FACTFILE 1992/93... RESULTS... APPEARANCES... SCORERS

The DONS

Date	Venue	Opponents	Result	Snelders T.	Wright S.	Winnie D.	Aitken R.	Irvine B.	Smith G.	Mason P.	Bett J.	Booth S.	Shearer D.	Paatelainen M.-M.	Jess E.	McKimmie S.	Ferguson G.	Roddie A.	Kane P.	Thomson S.	Grant B.	McLeish A.	Ten Caat T.	Richardson L.	Watt M.	Connor R.	Gibson A.
Aug 1	H	Hibernian	3-0	1	2	3	4	5	6	7	8	9^{1}	10^{2}	11	12												
5	H	Celtic	1-1	1	2	3	4	5	6	7	8	9	10^{1}	11	12												
8	A	Falkirk	1-0	1	12	3	4^{1}	5	6	7	8		10	11	9	2											
15	A	Motherwell	1-2	1	8	3	4	5	6	7			10	11	9^{1}	2	12	14									
22	A	Dundee	2-1	1	3	12		5	6		8		10^{1}	11^{1}	9	2				7	14						
29	A	Rangers	1-3	1	3	12	4^{1}	5	6	7			10	11	9	2				8	14						
Sept 2	H	Airdrieonians	0-0	1	3	10	4	5	6	7				11	9	2				14		8					
12	A	Heart of Midlothian	0-1	1	14	3	4	5	6	12	8		10	11	9	2					7						
19	A	Partick Thistle	2-0	1	2	3			6	7			10	11^{1}	9							4^{1}	5	8	14		
26	A	St. Johnstone	3-0		2	3			6	12			10^{2}	11^{1}	9					7		4	5	14	8	1	
Oct 3	H	Dundee United	0-1	1	2	3		5	6	12			10	11	9			14		4				7	8		
7	A	Hibernian	3-1	1	2	3		5	6	7			10^{1}	11	9^{2}			14	12	4					8		
17	A	Falkirk	3-1	1	2	3	7		6	12			14^{1}	10^{1}	11^{1}	9^{1}				4	5				8		
31	A	Airdrieonians	2-1	1	2	3		5	6		8		10^{1}	11	9			12		4					7		
Nov 7	A	Dundee	2-1	1	2	3		5	6	12	8		10^{1}	11	9					4					7^{1}		
11	H	Motherwell	2-0	1	2	3		5	6	12	8		10^{1}	11	9					4^{1}					7		
24	A	Partick Thistle	7-0	1	2		5	6		11^{1}	8	14^{1}	10^{3}		9^{1}				12^{1}		4	3		7		
28	H	Heart of Midlothian	6-2	1	2		5^{1}	6		11^{1}	8	14^{1}	10^{3}		9				12		4	3		7		
Dec 2	A	Celtic	2-2	1	2		5	6	11	8	10				9^{1}			14	12^{1}		4	3		7		
5	H	St. Johnstone	3-0	1	2		5^{1}	6	11^{1}	8	9				10^{1}						4	3		7		
12	H	Dundee United	2-2	1	2		5^{1}	6	11	8	10				9^{1}			12			4	3		7		
19	H	Hibernian	2-0	1	2	14	5	6	11	8	10^{1}				9			12			4	3		7^{1}		
26	H	Motherwell	2-0	1		2	5^{1}	6	11	8	10				9^{1}			14			4	3		7		
Jan 2	H	Dundee	0-0	1		2	5	6	11	8	10				9						4	3		7		
16	H	Airdrieonians	7-0	1	2	12	5^{1}	3	8				10^{1}	11^{4}	9^{1}			14			4	6		7		
30	A	Falkirk	4-1	1	2	12	5	3	8		8^{1}		10^{1}		9^{2}			14			4	6		7		
Feb 2	H	Rangers	0-1	1	2		5	3	11			8	12	10	9			14			4	6		7		
13	H	Celtic	1-1	1	2	3	8	5				14	10	11^{1}	9						4	6		7		
20	A	St. Johnstone	2-0		2	12	5	3	8		14^{1}		10	11	9^{1}						4	6		7	1	
24	H	Dundee United	0-0		2	4	5	3	8		14		10	11	9							6		7		
Mar 2	H	Partick Thistle	1-0	1	2	12	5	3	14		8		10	11^{1}	9						4	6		7		
9	A	Hibernian	2-1	1	2	8	5	3					10	11^{1}				14	12^{1}		4	6		7	9	
13	H	Falkirk	2-2	1	2	3	8	5					10^{1}	11				14^{1}	7		4	6		9		
20	A	Dundee	2-1	1	2		8	5	3	14			9^{1}	12	11^{1}		6			7		4			10		
27	A	Motherwell	1-0	1	2				3	8		9^{1}		11			6	14			4	5	10	7		
30	A	Rangers	0-2	1			2		3	8		9	10	11			6	14	4			5	12	7		
Apr 10	A	Airdrieonians	1-1	1			12	5	3	8		9	10^{1}	11			2	14	4			6		7		
17	H	Heart of Midlothian	3-2	1			4	5	3		8^{1}	9	10^{1}	11^{1}			2	14				6	7			
20	H	Partick Thistle	3-1	1				5	3	9	8	14	10	11^{2}			2		4^{1}			6	7			12
May 1	A	Celtic	0-1	1			4	5		7		14	10	11			2		12	8		6	9			3
5	A	Heart of Midlothian	2-1				4	5		7		9	10^{1}	11^{1}			2			8		6	12	1		3
8	H	St. Johnstone	1-1	1	2	12	5	6	8		9^{1}	10	11				4					14	7			3
12	H	Rangers	1-0	1	2	12	5	6	8		9	10^{1}					4					11	7			3
15	A	Dundee United	4-1	1	2	12	5	6	8		9^{2}				14		4				7^{1}		11			3 10^{1}
TOTAL FULL APPEARANCES				41	34	18	18	39	40	31	17	21	32	33	28	14	1	13		29	27	11	28	3	5	1
TOTAL SUB APPEARANCES					(2)	(3)	(8)			(8)		(8)	(2)		(3)		(1)	(10)	(14)	(2)			(4)	(1)		(1)
TOTAL GOALS SCORED						2		5		4		13	22	16	12					2	4		3		2	1

*Small figures denote goalscorers † denotes opponent's own goal

---

PITTODRIE STREET
GOLF ROAD

HOW TO GET THERE

Buses: The following buses all depart from the city centre to within a hundred yards of the ground. Nos. 1, 2, 3, 4 and 11.

Trains: The main Aberdeen station is in the centre of the city and the above buses will then take fans to the ground.

Cars: Motor Vehicles coming from the city centre should travel along Union Street, then turn into King Street and the park will be on your right, about half a mile further on.

Parking on Beach Boulevard, King Street and Golf Road.

Celtic Park, 95 Kerrydale Street, Glasgow, G40 3RE.

Chairman
J. Kevin Kelly
Deputy Chairman
David D. Smith
Directors
John C. McGinn;
James M. Farrell, M.A. LL.B.;
Christopher D. White, B.A., C.A.
Thomas J. Grant;
Michael Kelly, C.B.E., O.ST.J., JP., B.SC.
(ECON.), PH.D., LL.D., D.L., F.C.I.M.
Manager

Secretary
Christopher D. White, B.A. C.A.
Commercial Manager
John McGuire
Telephones
Ground (041) 556 2611
Ticket Office (041) 551 8654
Comm. Manager (041) 556 2611
Fax (041) 551 8106
Telex 931 2100437 BW

Club Shops
18/20 Kerrydale Street,
Glasgow, G40 3RE.
Tel. 041-554-4231 (9.00 a.m.
to 5.00 p.m. Mon–Sat) and 40
Dundas Street, Glasgow, G1
2AQ. Tel. 041-332-2727 (9.00
a.m. to 5.00 p.m. Mon–Sat)

Official Supporters Club
Celtic Supporters Association,
1524 London Road, Glasgow,
G40 3RJ.

Team Captain
Paul McStay

Club Sponsor
C.R. Smith

CELTIC

LIST OF PLAYERS 1993-94

Name	Date of Birth	Place of Birth	Date of Signing	Height	Weight	Previous Club
Bonner, Patrick Joseph	24/05/60	Donegal	20/06/78	6-2	13.1	Keadue Rovers
Boyd, Thomas	24/11/65	Glasgow	06/02/92	5-11	11.4	Chelsea
Byrne, Paul Peter	13/06/72	Dublin	26/05/93	5-11	13.0	Bangor
Carberry, Garrett	01/11/75	Glasgow	27/05/93	5-11	10.7	Celtic B.C.
Collins, John Angus Paul	31/01/68	Galashiels	13/07/90	5-7	10.10	Hibernian
Creaney, Gerard Thomas	13/04/70	Coatbridge	15/05/87	5-10	10.7	Celtic B.C.
Dolan, William Thomas	28/11/72	Glasgow	10/05/91	5-9	11.9	Giffnock North A.F.C.
Donnelly, Simon	01/12/74	Glasgow	27/05/93	5-9	10.12	Celtic B.C.
Galloway, Michael	30/05/65	Oswestry	16/06/89	6-0	13.0	Heart of Midlothian
Gillespie, Gary Thomson	05/07/60	Bonnybridge	15/08/91	6-3	13.0	Liverpool
Grant, Peter	30/08/65	Bellshill	27/07/82	5-9	10.3	Celtic B.C.
Gray, Stuart	18/12/73	Harrogate	07/07/92	5-11	11.0	Giffnock North A.F.C.
Hay, Christopher Drummond	28/08/74	Glasgow	27/05/93	5-11	11.7	Giffnock North A.F.C.
Kerr, Stewart	13/11/74	Bellshill	27/05/93	6-2	13.0	Celtic B.C.
Mackay, Malcolm George	19/02/72	Bellshill	06/08/93	6.1	11.7	Queen's Park
Marshall, Gordon G.B.	19/04/64	Edinburgh	12/08/91	6-2	12.0	Falkirk
McAdam, Thomas Ian	09/04/54	Glasgow	13/07/93	6-0	12.9	Airdrieonians
McAvennie, Francis	22/11/59	Glasgow	06/01/93	5.11	11.7	South China
McGinlay, Patrick David	30/05/67	Glasgow	30/07/93	5.10	11.10	Hibernian
McLaughlin, Brian	14/05/74	Bellshill	07/07/92	5-4	8.7	Giffnock North A.F.C.
McNally Mark	10/03/71	Motherwell	15/05/87	5-9	10.7	Celtic B.C.
McQuilken, James	03/10/74	Glasgow	31/03/93	5-9	10.7	Giffnock North A.F.C.
McStay, Paul Michael Lyons	22/10/64	Hamilton	20/02/81	5-10	10.7	Celtic B.C.
McStay, Raymond	16/05/70	Hamilton	15/05/87	5-11	11.0	Celtic B.C.
Melly, Nigel Seamus M.	13/10/71	Derry	06/09/91	6-4	13.3	Derry City
Mowbray, Anthony M.	22/11/63	Saltburn	08/11/91	6-1	13.2	Middlesbrough
Nicholas, Charles	30/12/61	Glasgow	09/07/90	5-9	11.0	Aberdeen
O'Neil, Brian	06/09/72	Paisley	10/07/91	6-1	12.4	Porirua Viard United
Payton, Andrew Paul	23/10/67	Burnley	14/08/92	5-10	11.7	Middlesbrough
Slavin, James	18/01/75	Lanark	24/12/92	6-2	14.0	Giffnock North A.F.C.
Smith, Barry Martin	19/02/74	Paisley	21/06/91	5-10	12.0	Giffnock North A.F.C.
Vata, Rudi	13/02/69	Schroder	18/08/92	6-1	12.5	Dinamo Tirana
Wdowczyk, Dariusz	25/09/62	Warsaw	17/11/89	5-11	11.11	Legia Warsaw

CLUB FIXTURES 1993-94

Date	Opponent	Venue	Date	Opponent	Venue	Date	Opponent	Venue
Aug 4	League Cup 1		Oct 24	League Cup Final		Feb 12	Heart of	
Aug 7	Motherwell	A	Oct 30	Rangers	A		Midlothian	A
Aug 11	League Cup 2		Nov 6	**Partick Thistle**	H	Feb 19	SFA Cup 4	
Aug. 14	**Hibernian**	H	Nov 9	Aberdeen	A	Feb 26	**Kilmarnock**	H
Aug 21	**Rangers**	H	Nov 13	Kilmarnock	A	Mar 5	St. Johnstone	A
Aug 25	League Cup 3		Nov 20	**Heart of**		Mar 12	**Dundee**	H
Aug 28	Partick Thistle	A		**Midlothian**	H	Mar 19	Hibernian	A
Sept 1	League Cup 4		Nov 27	**Raith Rovers**	H	Mar 26	**Motherwell**	H
Sept 4	**Aberdeen**	H	Nov 30	Dundee United	A	Mar 30	**Raith Rovers**	H
Sept 11	Raith Rovers	A	Dec 4	**St. Johnstone**	H	Apr 2	Dundee United	A
Sept 18	**Dundee United**	H	Dec 11	Dundee	A	Apr 9	**Heart of**	
Sept 22	League Cup S/F		Dec 18	**Hibernian**	H		**Midlothian**	H
Sept 25	Heart of		Dec 27	Motherwell	A	Apr 16	Kilmarnock	A
	Midlothian	A	Jan 1	**Rangers**	H	Apr 23	Dundee	A
Oct 2	**Kilmarnock**	H	Jan 8	Partick Thistle	A	Apr 27	**St. Johnstone**	H
Oct 6	St. Johnstone	A	Jan 15	**Aberdeen**	H	Apr 30	Rangers	A
Oct 9	**Dundee**	H	Jan 22	**Dundee United**	H	May 7	**Partick Thistle**	H
Oct 16	Hibernian	A	Jan 29	SFA Cup 3		May 14	Aberdeen	A
Oct 23	**Motherwell**	H	Feb 5	Raith Rovers	A	May 21	SFA Cup Final	

MILESTONES
Year of Formation: 1888
Most Capped Player: Paul McStay (67)
Most League Points in a Season:
72 (Premier Division) - 1987/88
Most League goals scored by a player in a Season: Jimmy McGrory (50) Season 1935/36
Record Attendance: 92,000 v Rangers, 1/1/38
Record Victory: 11-0 v Dundee, Division 1, 26/10/1895
Record Defeat: 0-8 v Motherwell, Division 1, 30/4/37

Registered Strip: Shirt - Green and White Hoops, Shorts - White, Stockings - White with Green Trim

Change Strip: Shirt - Jade and Black Vertical Stripes, Shorts - Black with Jade Trim, Stockings - Black with Jade Trim

CLUB FACTFILE 1992/93... RESULTS... APPEARANCES... SCORERS

The BHOYS

Date	Venue	Opponents	Result	Marshall G.	Morris C.	Boyd T.	Wdowczyk D.	Mowbray A.	Gillespie G.	O'Neil B.	McStay P.	Creaney G.	Nicholas C.	Collins J.	Coyne T.	Miller J.	Whyte D.	Galloway M.	Payton A.	Grant P.	McNally M.	Slater S.	Fulton S.	Bonner P.	Vata R.	McCarrison D.	McAvennie F.	Smith B.	McQuilken J.	Gray S.
Aug 1	A	Heart of Midlothian	†1-0	1	2	3	4	5	6	7	8	9	10	11	12	13														
5	A	Aberdeen	1-1	1	2	3	4	5	6	7	8	9[1]	10	11	12		13													
8	H	Motherwell	1-1	1	2	3	4	5[1]	6	7	8	9	10	11	12	13														
15	H	Dundee United	2-0	1		2	3		5	6	13	8	10[2]	11	12	7		4	9											
22	A	Rangers	1-1	1		2			5		13	8	9[1]	11		7		3	10	4	6	12								
29	A	Airdrieonians	1-1	1		2	3		5		8		10	11		7			9[1]	4		12								
Sept 2	H	St. Johnstone	3-1	1		2	3		5	4	8		10[1]	11[2]				6	9	13	7	12								
12	H	Hibernian	2-3	1		2	3[1]		5	4	8[1]		10	11			12	6	9		7									
19	A	Falkirk	5-4			2	3[1]	5	6		8		10[2]	11[1]				9[1]	4	13	7			1						
26	A	Partick Thistle	1-2			3			5	6	8		10	11	12		13	9[1]	4	2	7			1						
Oct 3	A	Dundee	1-0			3			5		8		10	11				6[1]	12	4	2	9	13	1	7					
7	H	Heart of Midlothian	1-1			3			5		8		10	11		7[1]		6	12	4	2	9		1						
17	A	Motherwell	3-1			3			5	13	8		10	11		7[1]		6[1]	12	4[1]	2	9		1						
24	H	Airdrieonians	2-0			3			5		8[1]	12		11[1]		7		6	10	4	2	9		1	13					
31	A	St. Johnstone	0-0			3			5	6	8		10	11		7		2	12	4		9		1						
Nov 7	H	Rangers	0-1			7	3		5	6	13	8	10	12	11			2		4		9		1						
11	A	Dundee United	1-1			7	3		5	6	13	8	10	12[1]	11			2		4		9		1						
21	A	Falkirk	3-2			2	3	5[1]		6	4[1]	8	9[1]	10	11			12			7			1	13					
28	A	Hibernian	2-1			3		6	5		4[2]	8	9	10	11			12	2		7			1	13					
Dec 2	H	Aberdeen	2-2			3		6	5	7		8	10	11				12	4	2	9[1]			1	13[1]					
5	A	Partick Thistle	3-2			3			5		8	12[1]	10	11				9[1]	4[1]	2	7			1	6					
12	H	Dundee	1-0			2			6		8		10	3				9[1]	4	5	11	13	1	7	12					
19	H	Heart of Midlothian	0-1			3		5	6		8	12		11		13		9	4	2	10	1	7							
26	H	Dundee United	0-1			3		5			8	10	6			7		4	9	12	2	11		1	13					
Jan 2	A	Rangers	0-1			3		5			13	8	10	6		7		4	9	12	2	11		1						
23	A	Airdrieonians	1-0			3			5		8	12		11	10[1]			6			2	7		1	4		9			
30	A	Motherwell	1-1			3			5		8[1]			11	10			6	12		2	7		1	4		9			
Feb 3	H	St. Johnstone	5-1			3	5[1]				8		12	11[1]	10[2]			6	13		2	7		1	4		9[1]			
13	A	Aberdeen	1-1			2	3			4	8			11	10			6	12[1]		5	7		1	13		9			
20	H	Partick Thistle	0-0			2	3			4	8			11	10			6	12		5	7		1			9			
23	A	Dundee	1-0			2	3				8			11	12			6	10[1]		5	7		1			9			
27	A	Falkirk	3-0			2	3				8			11				6	10[2]	4	5			1	7		9[1]			
Mar 10	H	Heart of Midlothian	1-0			2	3				8			11	12			6	10[1]	4	5	7		1			9			
16	H	Hibernian	2-1			2	3				8			11				6	10[2]	4	5	7		1			9			
20	H	Rangers	2-1			2	3				8			11[1]				6	10[1]	4	5	7		1			9			
27	A	Dundee United	3-2			2	3				8			10	11[1]			6[1]		4	5	7		1	12		9[1]			
Apr 3	A	Motherwell	0-2			2	3		6		8			10	11			12		4	5	7		1			9			
6	H	Airdrieonians	4-0			6	3				8			10	11[1]			12		4	5	7[1]		1	2[1]		9[1]	13		
10	A	St. Johnstone	1-1			3			5	6	8			10	11			12		4		7		1	2		9	13		
17	A	Hibernian	1-3			3			5	6	8			10[1]	11			12		4		7		1	2		9	13		
20	H	Falkirk	1-0								8			10	11			12	6		4	7		1	5		9[1]		2	3
May 1	H	Aberdeen	1-0	1		3									12			6	10	4		7	8		5		9[1]	2		11
8	H	Partick Thistle	1-0	1		3	13				8			11		7		6			10	4	5				9[1]	2		
15	H	Dundee	2-0	1		3	5				8[1]	10		11				6	13		7	4					9[1]	2		
TOTAL FULL APPEARANCES				11	3	42	24	26	18	11	43	23	12	43	5	10	29	19	27	25	37	3	33	15	19	4	1	1		
TOTAL SUB APPEARANCES					(1)			(6)		(3)	(4)		(5)	(13)	(1)		(1)	(10)		(4)	(2)	(2)	(3)		(7)	(1)		(2)	
TOTAL GOALS SCORED						3	2			3	4	9	2	8	3	2		3	13	2			2			2	9		

Small figures denote goalscorers † denotes opponent's own goal

---

CELTIC PARK

Capacity 49,856 (Seated 12,924, Standing 36,810)

Pitch Dimensions 112 yds x 74 yds.

Disabled Facilities Sections for 122 disabled supporters exists in the North Enclosure opposite the Stand. Details on application.

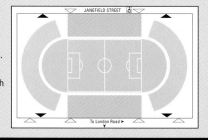

HOW TO GET THERE

Buses: The following buses all leave from the city centre and pass within 50 yards of the ground. Nos. 61, 62 and 64.

Trains: There is a frequent train service from Glasgow Central Low Level station to Bridgeton Cross Station and this is only a ten minute walk from the ground.

Cars: From the city centre, motor vehicles should travel along London Road and this will take you to the ground. Parking space is available in front of the Main Stand (restricted access) and also on the vacant ground adjacent to the park.

DUNDEE

Dens Park Stadium,
Sandeman Street,
Dundee, DD3 7JY

Chairman
Ronald N. Dixon
Vice-Chairman
Malcolm Reid
Managing Director
Robert R.F. Paterson
Directors
Robert W. Hynd, John F. Black
Director of Football Operations
Simon Stainrod
Player/Manager
James Duffy
Secretary
Andrew P. Drummond
LL.B (HONS) DIP, L.P., N.P.
Commercial Manager
June Webster

Telephones
Ground/Ticket Office/Commercial
Manager (0382) 826104
Fax (0382) 832284
Club Shop (0382) 823422

Club Shop
Unit 71 Forum Centre,
Dundee. Open Mon. to Sat.
9.00 a.m. - 5.30 p.m.

Team Captain
Dusan Vrto

LIST OF PLAYERS 1993-94

Name	Date of Birth	Place of Birth	Date of Signing	Height	Weight	Previous Club
Adamczuk, Dariusz	21/10/69	Stettin	20/08/93	5-10	12.0	Eintracht Frankfurt
Bain, Kevin	19/09/72	Kirkcaldy	28/06/89	6-0	11.9	Abbey Star
Christie, Martin Peter	07/11/71	Edinburgh	31/03/92	5-6	10.4	South China Athletic
Czachowski, Piotr	07/11/66	Warsaw	22/09/93	5-10	11.9	Legia Warsaw
David, Lionel	28/09/66	Nantes	06/08/93	6.1	12.7	La Roche Sur Yon
Dinnie, Alan	14/05/63	Glasgow	10/11/89	5-10	11.0	Partick Thistle
Dodds, William	05/02/69	New Cumnock	28/07/89	5-8	10.10	Chelsea
Duffy, James	27/04/59	Glasgow	22/05/92	5-10	11.11	Partick Thistle
Farningham, Raymond Paul	10/04/61	Dundee	03/09/93	5.8	11.5	Partick Thistle
Frail, Stephen	10/08/69	Glasgow	10/08/85	5-9	10.9	Possilpark Y.M.
Mathers, Paul	17/01/70	Aberdeen	06/10/86	5-11	10.7	Sunnybank "A"
McCann, Neil Docherty	11/08/74	Greenock	14/05/92	5-10	10.0	Port Glasgow B.C.
McGowan, Jamie	05/12/70	Morecambe	31/07/92	6-0	11.1	Morecambe
McKeown, Gary	19/10/70	Oxford	31/07/92	5-10.5	11.8	Arsenal
McMartin, Grant	31/12/70	Linlithgow	30/12/88	5-10	10.0	Dunipace Jnrs
McQuillan, John	20/07/70	Stranraer	18/08/87	5-10	10.7	Stranraer
Mobilio, Domenic	14/01/69	Vancouver	01/10/93	5-11	12.3	Vancouver 86'ers
Paterson, Garry	10/11/69	Dunfermline	21/08/92	6-4	13.10	Lochore Welfare
Pittman, Stephen Lee	18/07/67	Wilson, North Carolina	06/11/92	5.10	12.0	Fort Lauderdale Strikers
Ristic, Dragutin	05/08/64	Pula, Yugoslavia	10/09/93	6-0	12.7	Benevento Sporting
Ritchie, Paul Michael	25/01/69	St. Andrews	29/02/92	5-11	12.0	Brechin City
Stainrod, Simon Allan	01/02/59	Sheffield	06/02/92	6-0	13.0	Falkirk
Tannock, Gordon	11/06/74	Kilmaurs	14/05/92	5-11	10.10	Bellfield B.C.
Thompson, Barry Crawford	12/07/75	Glasgow	13/08/93	6-1	12.5	Aviemore Thistle
Tosh, Paul James	18/10/73	Arbroath	04/08/93	6-0	11.10	Arbroath
Vrto, Dusan	29/10/65	Banksa Stiavnica	07/08/92	6-0	10.12	Banik Ostrava
Wieghorst, Morten	25/02/71	Glostrup	02/12/92	6-3	14.0	Lyngby

MILESTONES
Year of Formation: 1893
Most Capped Player: Alex Hamilton (24)
Most League goals scored by a player in a Season: Alan Gilzean (52) Season 1963/64
Record Attendance: 43,024 v Rangers, 1953
Record Victory: 10-0 v Fraserburgh, 1931; v Alloa, 1947; v Dunfermline Athletic, 1947; v Queen of the South, 1962
Record Defeat: 0-11 v Celtic, Division 1, 26/10/1895

CLUB FIXTURES 1993-94

Date	Opponent	Venue	Date	Opponent	Venue	Date	Opponent	Venue
Aug 4	League Cup 1		Oct 24	League Cup Final		Feb 12	St. Johnstone	A
Aug 7	Kilmarnock	A	Oct 30	Aberdeen	A	Feb 19	SFA Cup 4	
Aug 11	League Cup 2		Nov 6	**Hibernian**	**H**	Feb 26	**Heart of**	
Aug 14	**Motherwell**	**H**	Nov 10	Rangers	A		**Midlothian**	**H**
Aug 21	**Aberdeen**	**H**	Nov 13	Heart of		Mar 5	**Partick Thistle**	**H**
Aug 25	League Cup 3			Midlothian	A	Mar 12	Celtic	A
Aug 28	Hibernian	A	Nov 20	**St. Johnstone**	**H**	Mar 19	Motherwell	A
Sept 1	League Cup 4		Nov 27	**Dundee United**	**H**	Mar 26	**Kilmarnock**	**H**
Sept 4	**Rangers**	**H**	Dec 1	Raith Rovers	A	Mar 29	**Dundee United**	**H**
Sept 11	Dundee United	A	Dec 4	Partick Thistle	A	Apr 2	Raith Rovers	A
Sept 18	**Raith Rovers**	**H**	Dec 11	**Celtic**	**H**	Apr 9	**St. Johnstone**	**H**
Sept 22	League Cup S/F		Dec 18	**Motherwell**	**H**	Apr 16	Heart of	
Sept 25	St. Johnstone	A	Dec 27	Kilmarnock	A		Midlothian	A
Oct 2	**Heart of**		Jan 1	**Aberdeen**	**H**	Apr 23	**Celtic**	**H**
	Midlothian	**H**	Jan 8	Hibernian	A	Apr 26	Partick Thistle	A
Oct 5	**Partick Thistle**	**H**	Jan 15	**Rangers**	**H**	Apr 30	Aberdeen	A
Oct 9	Celtic	A	Jan 22	**Raith Rovers**	**H**	May 7	**Hibernian**	**H**
Oct 16	Motherwell	A	Jan 29	SFA Cup 3		May 14	Rangers	A
Oct 23	**Kilmarnock**	**H**	Feb 5	Dundee United	A	May 21	SFA Cup Final	

Registered Strip: Shirt - Navy Blue with White/Red/Navy/White Horizontal Chest Stripes, Shorts - White with Navy Blue Side Panels with 4 Horizontal Stripes - White/Red/Navy/White, Stockings - White with Navy Blue and Red Tops

Change Strip: Shirt - White with Navy/Red/White/Navy Horizontal Chest Stripes, Shorts - Navy Blue with White Side Panels with 4 Horizontal Stripes - Navy/Red/White/Navy, Stockings - White with Navy Blue and Red Stripe on Turnover

CLUB FACTFILE 1992/93... RESULTS... APPEARANCES... SCORERS

The DARK BLUES

Date	Venue	Opponents	Result	Leighton J.	Dinnie A.	Campbell S.	Duffy J.	McGowan J.	McKeown G.	Ritchie P.	McMartin G.	Gilzean I.	Dodds W.	Rix G.	Gallagher E.	Den Bieman I.	Beedie S.	Vrto D.	Ratcliffe K.	Paterson G.	Campbell D.	Stainrod S.	McQuillan J.	Mathers P.	Bain K.	Dow A.	Kiwomya A.	Christie M.	Pittman S.	Wieghorst M.	West C.	McCann N.	David L.	Frail S.	Armstrong L.
Aug 1	H	Falkirk	1-2	1	2	3	4	5	6	7	8	9	10	11[1]		14																			
4	H	St. Johnstone	1-1	1	2[1]	3	4	5	6		12	9	10	11				7		8															
8	A	Airdrieonians	0-0	1	2	3	4	5	6			9	10	11		14		7	12	8															
15	H	Rangers	4-3	1	2		4	5				9[1]	10[2]	11				7[1]	3	8	6														
22	A	Aberdeen	1-2	1			5	4					10	11				7	3	8	6	9[1]	12			14									
29	A	Partick Thistle	3-6	1	2		4	5				9[1]	10[2]	11				7		8	3		14		12										
Sept 1	H	Heart of Midlothian	1-3		2	6	4	5				9	10[1]	11				7		8	3	14	12	1											
12	H	Motherwell	2-1		2	3	4		6				10[1]	11				9	5	8[1]			7	1											
19	A	Dundee United	1-0		2	3	4		6				9	10[1]				7	12	8			11	1	5										
26	A	Partick Thistle	0-0		2	3	4		6				9	10				7	12	8			11	1	5	14									
Oct 3	H	Celtic	0-1		2	3	4		6				9	10				7	12	8			11	1	5	14									
10	A	Falkirk	2-2		2	3	4		6				9	10[1]				7[1]	12	8			11	1	5	14									
17	H	Airdrieonians	2-0		2	3	4		6[1]				12	10[1]				7	11	8				1	5	9									
24	H	Partick Thistle	0-2		2	3	4		6				12	10				7	11	8				1	5	9									
31	A	Heart of Midlothian	0-1		2		4						10	9	7	3	8	14	12	11				1	5	6									
Nov 7	H	Aberdeen	1-2		2		4	8					10[1]	9	7	6				11				1	5		12	3							
11	A	Rangers	1-3		2	3	4	5	11				9	10	7[1]		8		12			14	6	1											
21	A	Dundee United	1-3		2	3	4	5	11				14	10[1]	7	12	8					9	6	1											
28	A	Motherwell	3-1		2		5			4	9[2]	10			8		12	7	14[1]	11	1		6				3								
Dec 2	A	St. Johnstone	4-4		2		5				9	10[2]			8		12	7	14	11	1		6				3[1]	4[1]							
5	H	Hibernian	1-1	1	2						9	10			7		12	14[1]	11			5	6				3	4							
12	H	Celtic	0-1		2		5				9	10			7		8	14	11	1			6				3	4	12						
19	H	Falkirk	2-1		2		4			7		10[1]			8		9[1]	5	1			11					3	6							
26	H	Rangers	1-3	1	2		5				14	10			8		6	9[1]	7			12	11				3	4							
Jan 2	A	Aberdeen	0-0		2		5				9	10		12	8		14	7		1			6	11			3	4							
27	A	Partick Thistle	0-2				5	7		12	10	14		9	8			2		1			6	11			3	4							
30	A	Airdrieonians	†2-2		2		5				9	10	11	7	8	14[1]		1		6				12			3	4							
Feb 3	H	Heart of Midlothian	1-0				5	6[1]	11	7		10			8		9	2	1	4							3		14						
13	H	St. Johnstone	1-0				5	7			10				8		9[1]	2	1	6				14			3	4	11						
20	A	Hibernian	3-1			3	5	7			10				8		9[1]	2	1	6				12[1]	14[1]			4	11						
23	H	Celtic	0-1				5	7			10	14			8		9	2	1	6							3	4	12						
27	A	Dundee United	0-1				5	7			10			9	8			2	1	6				14	11		3	4	12						
Mar 6	H	Motherwell	1-1				5			7	10	11[1]			8		9	2	1	6				12			3	4							
10	A	Falkirk	0-1				5	7			10	11			8		9	2	1	6				14			3	4	12						
13	H	Airdrieonians	1-1				5				10[1]				8		4	14	2	1	11	6	12				3			7					
20	H	Aberdeen	1-2				5			7	10				8		12	9[1]	2	1	6	11					3	4							
27	A	Rangers	0-3					5		7	10			9				2	1	6	12						3	4	11	8					
Apr 3	H	Partick Thistle	0-1					5	4	7	10	11			9				1	6					3	12			14	8	2				
10	A	Heart of Midlothian	0-0			3	5			11	7	14	10		9				1	6						12		4		8	2				
17	A	Motherwell	2-1			3	5			11	7[1]	12	10[1]		9				1	6						14		4		8	2				
20	H	Dundee United	0-4			3	5			11	7	12	10		9				1	6						14		4		8	2				
May 1	A	St. Johnstone	1-1			3	5			10	7[1]	9			6				1					14		11		4		8	2				
8	H	Hibernian	3-1			3	5			10	7[1]	9[1]			6				1					14		11		4[1]		8	2				
15	A	Celtic	0-2			3	5			10	7	14			6				1					11	12			4		8	2		9		
TOTAL FULL APPEARANCES				8	26	20	39	21	20	17	2	17	41	12	2	23	8	32	4	11	2	10	27	36	24	8	11	1	20	22	2	2	8	7	1
TOTAL SUB APPEARANCES							(2)	(1)	(7)			(2)	(2)	(1)	(6)					(9)	(2)	(10)	(2)			(6)	(10)	(2)		(1)	(5)	(1)		
TOTAL GOALS SCORED					1			1	1	3		5	16	2		3		1		2		7				1	1		1	2					

*Small figures denote goalscorers † denotes opponent's own goal

---

DENS PARK

Capacity 16,276 (Seated 10,976, Standing 5,300)

Pitch Dimensions 110 yds x 72 yds.

Disabled Facilities East End of Stand Enclosure.

HOW TO GET THERE

Buses: There is a frequent service of buses from the city centre. Nos 1A and 1B leave from Albert Square and Nos. 18, 19 and 21 leave from Commercial Street.

Trains: Trains from all over the country pass through the mainline Dundee station and fans can then proceed to the ground by the above buses from stops situated close to the station.

Cars: Cars may be parked in the local streets adjacent to the ground.

DUNDEE UNITED

Tannadice Park,
Tannadice Street,
Dundee, DD3 7JW

Chairman/Managing Director
James Y. McLean
Vice-Chairman
Douglas B. Smith
Directors
George F. Fox;
Alistair B. Robertson;
William M. Littlejohn
Manager
Ivan Golac
Secretary
Miss Priti Trivedi
Commercial Manager
Bobby Brown

Telephones
Ground (0382) 833166
Fax (0382) 89398
Commercial (0382) 832202
Club Shop (0382) 822352

Club Shop
Dundee United Souvenir
Shop, Forum Centre, Dundee
- Open 9.00 a.m. to 5.30 p.m.
(Mon-Sat). Souvenir shops are
also situated within the
ground and are open on
match days.

Team Captain
Maurice Malpas

LIST OF PLAYERS 1993-94

Name	Date of Birth	Place of Birth	Date of Signing	Height	Weight	Previous Club
Agnew, Steven	07/10/75	Irvine	02/10/92	5-7	10.4	Hamilton Thistle
Benvie, Gregor William	22/08/72	Dundee	20/06/89	5-9	10.8	Sporting Club '85
Biggart, Kevin	10/11/73	Kilmarnock	17/10/91	5-8.5	11.1	Muirend Amateurs
Bollan, Gary	24/03/73	Dundee	20/06/89	5-11.5	12.6	Fairmuir B.C.
Bowman, David	10/03/64	Turnbridge Wells	21/05/86	5-10	11.4	Coventry City
Brewster, Craig James	13/12/66	Dundee	05/08/93	5.11	10.7	Raith Rovers
Buchan, Scott Duncan	22/12/75	Aberdeen	24/06/93	5-11	11.2	Banks of Dee "A"
Cargill, Andrew	02/09/75	Dundee	25/03/93	5-6	10.4	Downfield Juniors
Clark, John	22/09/64	Edinburgh	27/07/81	6-0	14.1	"S" Form
Clark, Patrick	13/03/74	Hamilton	31/10/90	5-11	11.1	Hamilton Thistle
Cleland Alexander	10/12/70	Glasgow	18/06/87	5-8.5	11.1	"S" Form
Connolly, Patrick	25/06/70	Glasgow	02/08/86	5-8.5	10.6	"S" Form
Conville Edward	02/04/73	Carnwath	07/08/90	6-0	11.5	Campsie Black Watch
Crabbe, Scott	12/08/68	Edinburgh	03/10/92	5-7	11.0	Heart of Midlothian
Dailly, Christian Eduard	23/10/73	Dundee	02/08/90	6-0	12.5	"S" Form
Devlin, Neill	24/10/75	Kilmarnock	01/06/92	5-7.5	10.6	Bellfield B.C.
Garden, Stuart Robertson	10/02/72	Dundee	01/03/93	5-11	12.0	Dundee North End
Hannah, David	04/08/74	Coatbridge	04/09/91	5-11	11.3	Hamilton Thistle
Johnson, Ian Grant	24/03/72	Dundee	07/09/90	5-11	10.9	Broughty Ferry
Lindsay, John	17/03/73	Dundee	20/06/89	5-7.5	10.0	Dee Club
Main, Alan David	05/12/67	Elgin	25/11/86	5-11.5	13.0	Elgin City
Malpas, Maurice D.R.	03/08/62	Dunfermline	14/08/79	5-8	11.5	"S" Form
McBain, Roy Adam	07/11/74	Aberdeen	14/04/92	5-10.5	11.1	Dyce B.C.
McInally, James Edward	19/02/64	Glasgow	21/05/86	5-8.5	11.7	Coventry City
McKenna, Gerard	02/02/77	Bellshill	29/05/93	5-8	10.9	Dundee United B.C.
McKinlay, William	22/04/69	Glasgow	24/06/85	5-9	11.1	Hamilton Thistle
McLaren, Andrew	05/06/73	Glasgow	20/06/89	5-10	11.7	Rangers B.C.
McMillan, Thomas	08/08/72	Falkirk	20/06/89	5-10.5	11.0	Grahamston B.C.
Myers, Chris	01/04/69	Yeovil	05/08/93	5-10	12.0	Torquay United
Narey, David	21/06/56	Dundee	11/05/73	6-0	12.8	"S" Form
O'Neil, John	06/07/71	Bellshill	28/07/88	5-7	10.9	Fir Park B.C.
Perry, Mark George	07/02/71	Aberdeen	09/08/88	6-1	12.8	Cove Rangers
Prior, Peter	07/10/73	Glasgow	04/09/91	5-7.5	11.3	Clydebank B.C.
Sturrock, Paul Whitehead	10/10/56	Ellon	15/05/74	5-8.5	12.2	Bankfoot
Tighe, Martin	11/06/76	Bellshill	29/05/93	5-9	11.0	Strathbrock Juveniles
Van de Kamp, Guido	08/02/64	Den Bosch	27/07/91	6-2.5	12.8	BVV Den Bosch
Van Der Hoorn, Freddy	12/10/63	Den Bosch	03/08/89	5-11.5	12.6	BVV Den Bosch
Welsh, Brian	23/02/69	Edinburgh	24/06/85	6-2	13.7	Tynecastle B.C.
Winters, Robert	04/11/74	East Kilbride	11/01/92	5-9	11.1	Muirend Amateurs

---

MILESTONES
Year of Formation: 1923 (1909 as Dundee Hibs)
Most Capped Player: Maurice Malpas (55)
Most League Points in a Season:
60 (Premier Division – 1986/87)
Most League goals scored by a player in a Season: John Coyle (41) 1955/56
Record Attendance: 28,000 v Barcelona, 16/11/66
Record Victory: 14–0 v Nithsdale Wanderers, Scottish Cup 17/1/31
Record Defeat: 1-12 v Motherwell, Div. 2, 23/1/54

CLUB FIXTURES 1993-94

Date	Opponent	Venue
Aug 4	*League Cup 1*	
Aug 7	**Aberdeen**	H
Aug 11	*League Cup 2*	
Aug 14	Partick Thistle	A
Aug 21	St. Johnstone	A
Aug 25	*League Cup 3*	
Aug 28	**Heart of Midlothian**	H
Sept 1	*League Cup 4*	
Sept 4	Raith Rovers	A
Sept 11	**Dundee**	H
Sept 18	Celtic	A
Sept 22	*League Cup S/F*	
Sept 25	**Motherwell**	H
Oct 2	Hibernian	A
Oct 5	Kilmarnock	A
Oct 9	**Rangers**	H
Oct 16	**Partick Thistle**	H
Oct 23	Aberdeen	A
Oct 24	*League Cup Final*	
Oct 30	**St. Johnstone**	H
Nov 6	Heart of Midlothian	A
Nov 9	**Raith Rovers**	H
Nov 13	**Hibernian**	H
Nov 20	Motherwell	A
Nov 27	Dundee	A
Nov 30	**Celtic**	H
Dec 4	**Kilmarnock**	H
Dec 11	Rangers	A
Dec 18	Partick Thistle	A
Dec 27	**Aberdeen**	H
Jan 1	St. Johnstone	A
Jan 8	**Heart of Midlothian**	H
Jan 15	Raith Rovers	A
Jan 22	Celtic	A
Jan 29	*SFA Cup 3*	
Feb 5	**Dundee**	H
Feb 12	**Motherwell**	H
Feb 19	*SFA Cup 4*	
Feb 26	Hibernian	A
Mar 5	Kilmarnock	A
Mar 12	**Rangers**	H
Mar 19	**Partick Thistle**	H
Mar 26	Aberdeen	A
Mar 29	Dundee	A
Apr 2	**Celtic**	H
Apr 9	Motherwell	A
Apr 16	**Hibernian**	H
Apr 23	Rangers	A
Apr 26	**Kilmarnock**	H
Apr 30	**St. Johnstone**	H
May 7	Heart of Midlothian	A
May 14	**Raith Rovers**	H
May 21	*SFA Cup Final*	

SEASON TICKET INFORMATION
Seated
George Fox Stand
Top Tier   Adult £250
            Juvenile/OAP £150
Lower Tier Adult £135
            Juvenile/OAP......................£70
Family Section 1 Adult & 1 Juvenile £150
Standing   Adult £110
            Juvenile/OAP................................£55

LEAGUE ADMISSION PRICES
Seated
George Fox Stand
Top Tier   Adult £10
            Juvenile/OAP £6
Lower Tier Adult £8
            Juvenile/OAP £4
South Stand (Away Supporters)
            Adult £10
            Juvenile/OAPs......................£6
Family Section 1 Adult & 1 Juvenile £12
            Each Additional Juvenile................£4
Standing   Adult £6
            Juvenile/OAP......................£4
            Students/Unemployed (home fans only)
            - must bring matriculation card/UB40 ....£4

Registered Strip: Shirt - Tangerine with Two Black Shoulder Stripes Edged with White and Black Collar, Shorts - Black with Tangerine & White Stripes, Stockings - Tangerine with Black Hoops

Change Strip: Shirt - White and Grey with Black Collar, Shorts - Black with Grey, White and Tangerine Side Stripes, Stockings - Black with White and Tangerine Hoops

The TERRORS

Date	Venue	Opponents	Result	Main A.	Clark J.	Malpas M.	McKinlay W.	Van Der Hoorn F.	Narey D.	O'Neil J.	Johnson I.G.	Cleland A.	Ferguson D.	Bollan G.	Connolly P.	McInally J.	Ferreyra V.	Welsh B.	Bowman D.	McLaren A.	Dailly C.	Crabbe S.	O'Neill M.	Krivokapic M.	Perry M.	Hannah D.	Van De Kamp G.
Aug 1	A	Motherwell	1-0	1	2	3	4	5	6	7	8	9	10^1	11	12												
5	A	Partick Thistle	1-0	1	2	3	4	5	6	7	8	9	10	11	12^1	14											
8	H	Heart of Midlothian	1-1	1	2	3	4	5	6	7	8	9	10^1	11		14											
15	H	Celtic	0-2	1	2	3	4	5	6	7	8	14	10	11	9	12											
22	H	St. Johnstone	2-1	1	2	3	4	14		7^1	8	9	10		11^1	5			6								
29	H	Falkirk	2-0	1	2	3		5		7	8	9	10^2		12	4		11	6	14							
Sept 2	A	Hibernian	1-2	1	2	3		5	6	7	8	9	10		11^1	4	12	14									
12	A	Airdrieonians	2-1	1	2	3		5	6	7	8	9	10^2		11	4	12										
19	H	Dundee	0-1	1	2	3		5	6	7	8	9	10		11	4	12	14									
26	H	Rangers	0-4	1	2	3	4	5	6	7	8	9		11	12				14	10							
Oct 3	A	Aberdeen	1-0	1	2	3	7	5			11		6		10^1	4	14		8			9					
7	H	Motherwell	1-1	1	2	3	7	5			11	12	6		10	4	14^1		8			9					
17	H	Heart of Midlothian	0-1	1	2	3	7	5			14	12	6		10	4		11	8			9					
24	A	Falkirk	1-1	1	2	3	8	5	6				10		11	4^1	14			7		9					
31	H	Hibernian	1-0	1	2	3		5	6				10		14	4^1		11	8	7		9					
Nov 7	A	St. Johnstone	0-2	1	2	3		5	6				10		12	4	14	11	8	7		9					
11	H	Celtic	†1-1	1	9	3	8	5	6				10		11	4	14			12		7		2			
21	A	Dundee	3-1	1	9^1	3	8	5	6	7			10^1		11^1	4	14			12				2			
28	H	Airdrieonians	0-0	1	9	3	8	5	6	7			10			4	14	11		12				2			
Dec 1	H	Partick Thistle	2-1	1		3			6	7^1			10		11	4^1			8			9		2			
12	A	Aberdeen	2-2	1		3	12^1	5	6	7			10			4	14					9^1	8	2	11		
26	A	Celtic	1-0	1	12	3	7	5	6		8		10^1			4	14					9		2	11		
Jan 2	H	St. Johnstone	1-2	1	12	3	7	5	6				10			4	14					9^1	8	2	11		
5	A	Rangers	2-3	1	14	3	7	5			8		10			4			6^1			9		2	11^1		
16	H	Hibernian	1-2	1	5	3	8	5	6	2	7	12	10			4^1						9			11		
23	H	Falkirk	2-1	1	5	3	8		6	7			10^1	12		4						9^1		11	2		
30	H	Heart of Midlothian	0-1	1	5	3	4		6	7	8		10	11					2			9			12		
Feb 2	A	Motherwell	0-2	1	5	3	8	6		7			10	11		4					14	9			2		
13	A	Partick Thistle	4-0	1	5	3	8	6				10^1			11^2	4						7^1	9		2	14	
20	H	Rangers	0-0	1	5	3	8	6					10	11		4						7	9		2		
24	A	Aberdeen	0-0	1	5	3	8	6					10	11		4					12	7	9		2		
27	H	Dundee	1-0	1	5	3	8	6				12	10^1	11		4						7	9		2		
Mar 6	A	Airdrieonians	3-1	1	5^1	3	8	6					10^1	11^1		4						7	9		2	14	
9	H	Motherwell	0-0	1	5	3	9		6			12	10	11		4						7	8		2		
13	A	Heart of Midlothian	0-1	1	5	3	8	6					10	11		14	4			12		7	9		2		
20	A	St. Johnstone	4-1	1	5	3	8	6				12^1	10	11		4^1						7	9^1		2	14	
27	A	Celtic	2-3	1	5	3		6				12	10	11^1		4					14	7	9		2		
Apr 3	A	Falkirk	2-1	1	5	3	4	2	6		14	8^1	12	10		11^1						7	9				
13	H	Hibernian	0-3		5	3	4	2	6		8	7		11		10					12	9			14		1
17	H	Airdrieonians	3-0	1		8	5	7				3^1	11^1			6	4				9^1	10		2	14		
20	A	Dundee	4-0	1		8	5	7				3^1	11^1			6	4			14	9^2	12	10				
May 1	H	Partick Thistle	3-1	1		8	5	2				7	3		11^2	14	6	4			9	12	10^1				
8	A	Rangers	0-1	1	6	8	5	2				7	14	11	3	4					9	12	10				
15	H	Aberdeen	1-4	1	2	8	5					3	11	7	6	4					9^1	12	10	14			
TOTAL FULL APPEARANCES				43	35	37	35	31	27	21	15	21	30	12	32	27	3	15	18	4	8	22	22	8	17		1
TOTAL SUB APPEARANCES					(2)		(1)	(1)	(1)	(7)	(2)	(3)			(3)	(10)	(6)	(4)		(6)	(1)	(6)	(5)	(3)		(1)	(5)
TOTAL GOALS SCORED						2	1			3	1		12	3	16	5		1				4	4		2		1

Small figures denote goalscorers † denotes opponent's own goal

TANNADICE PARK

Capacity 14,163 (Seated 7,675, Standing 6,488)

Pitch Dimensions
110 yds x 72 yds.

Disabled Facilities Lower Tier - George Fox Stand - Cover for home supporters only on request.

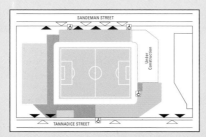

HOW TO GET THERE

Buses: The following buses leave from the city centre at frequent intervals. Nos. 18, 19 and 21 from Commercial Street and No. 20 from Reform Street.
Trains: Trains from all over the country pass through the main Dundee station and fans can then proceed to the ground by the above bus services from stops situated within walking distance of the station.
Cars: There is parking in the streets adjacent to the ground.

HEART OF MIDLOTHIAN

Tynecastle Park, Gorgie Road,
Edinburgh, EH11 2NL.

Chairman
A. Wallace Mercer
Vice-Chairman
Pilmar Smith
Directors
Leslie W. Porteous;
James Clydesdale, M.SC., M.C.I.O.B.;
Colin G. Wilson.
Manager
Alexander Clark
Secretary
Leslie W. Porteous
Commercial Manager
Charles Burnett

Telephones
Ground (031) 337 6132
Fax (031) 346-0699
Telex 72694
Ticket Office (031) 337 9011
Information (031) 346 8556
Commercial (031) 337 9011
Fax (031) 346 8974
Club Shop (031) 346 8511

Club Shop
Heart of Midlothian Sport
& Leisure, Tynecastle Park,
McLeod Street, Edinburgh.
Open 9.30 a.m. - 5.30 p.m.
Mon. to Sat. and match days.

Official Supporters Club
Heart of Midlothian
Federation, Alex Jones,
9 George Crescent, Loanhead.

Team Captain
Craig Levein

Club Sponsor
Strongbow

LIST OF PLAYERS 1993-94

Name	Date of Birth	Place of Birth	Date of Signing	Height	Weight	Previous Club
Berry, Neil	06/04/63	Edinburgh	05/12/84	6-0	12.0	Bolton Wanderers
Boothroyd, Adrian Neil	08/02/71	Bradford	11/12/92	5.9	11.5	Bristol Rovers
Bradley, Mark	10/08/76	Glasgow	31/07/92	5-4	9.9	Highbury B.C.
Callaghan, Stuart	20/07/76	Calderbank	03/08/92	5-6	9.13	Blantyre B.C.
Cameron, Mark Anthony	16/05/70	Paisley	30/05/92	5-7	11.5	Dalry Thistle
Clark, Alexander	28/10/56	Airdrie	24/04/90	6-0	12.7	Dunfermline Athletic
Colquhoun, John Mark	14/07/63	Stirling	27/07/93	5-7	10.0	Sunderland
Duncan, Grant	04/04/77	Edinburgh	25/08/93	5-6	10.6	Hutchison Vale B.C.
Fashanu, Justin Soni	19/02/62	London	20/07/93	6-1	14.1	Trelleborg
Ferguson, Ian	05/08/68	Dunfermline	09/10/91	6-1	12.0	Raith Rovers
Foster, Wayne Paul	11/09/63	Tyldesley	11/08/86	5-10	11.11	Preston North End
Harrison, Thomas Edward	22/01/74	Edinburgh	25/04/90	5-9	11.7	Salvesen B.C.
Hogg, Graeme James	17/06/64	Aberdeen	23/08/91	6-1	12.12	Portsmouth
Johnston, Allan	14/12/73	Glasgow	23/06/90	5-9	10.11	Tynecastle Boys Club
Johnston, Maurice Thomas	13/04/63	Glasgow	20/10/93	5-10	11.0	Everton
Leitch, Donald Scott	06/10/69	Motherwell	06/08/93	5-9	11.4	Dunfermline Athletic
Levein, Craig William	22/10/64	Dunfermline	25/11/83	6-0	12.12	Cowdenbeath
Locke, Gary	16/06/75	Edinburgh	31/07/92	5-10	11.3	Whitehill Welfare
Mackay, Gary	23/01/64	Edinburgh	16/06/80	5-9	11.5	Salvesen B.C.
Mauchlen, Alister Henry	29/06/60	West Kilbride	09/07/92	5-7	11.7	Leicester City
McKenzie, Roderick	08/08/75	Bellshill	06/08/93	6-0	11.9	Mill United
McKinlay, Thomas Valley	03/12/64	Glasgow	07/12/88	5-7	11.9	Dundee
McLaren, Alan James	04/01/71	Edinburgh	04/07/87	5-11	12.7	Cavalry Park
McManus, Allan William	17/11/74	Paisley	03/08/92	5-11	11.3	Links United
Millar, John	08/12/66	Bellshill	26/07/91	5-8	12.3	Blackburn Rovers
Murie, David	02/08/76	Edinburgh	31/07/92	5-8	10.5	Tynecastle B.C.
Murray, Grant Robert	29/08/75	Edinburgh	31/07/92	5-8.5	11.8	Hutchison Vale B.C.
Ritchie, Paul Simon	21/08/75	Kirkcaldy	31/07/92	5-10	11.10	Links United
Robertson, John Grant	02/10/64	Edinburgh	09/12/88	5-7	11.2	Newcastle United
Sharples, John Benjamin	26/01/73	Bury	26/07/91	6-1	12.8	Manchester United
Smith, Henry George	10/03/56	Lanark	05/08/81	6-2	12.0	Leeds United
Thomas, Kevin Roderick	25/04/75	Edinburgh	31/07/92	5-10.5	12.3	Links United
Walker, Colin	16/04/77	Edinburgh	10/06/93	5-6	11.1	Dalkeith Thistle B.C.
Walker, Joseph Nicol	29/09/62	Aberdeen	23/08/89	6-2.5	12.12	Rangers
Weatherston, Paul James	22/09/74	Edinburgh	31/07/92	5-8	10.1	Hutchison Vale B.C.
Weir, James McIntosh	15/06/69	Motherwell	15/08/93	6-1	12.2	Hamilton Academical
Whittaker, Brian	23/09/56	Glasgow	14/08/93	6-0	11.9	Falkirk
Wright, George	22/12/69	South Africa	04/07/87	5-7	11.5	Hutchison Vale B.C.

CLUB FIXTURES 1993-94

Date	Opponent	Venue	Date	Opponent	Venue	Date	Opponent	Venue
Aug 4	League Cup 1		Oct 30	Hibernian	A	Feb 26	Dundee	A
Aug 7	Rangers	A	Nov 6	**Dundee United**	**H**	Mar 5	Aberdeen	A
Aug 11	League Cup 2		Nov 9	Partick Thistle	A	Mar 12	**St. Johnstone**	**H**
Aug 14	**Raith Rovers**	**H**	Nov 13	**Dundee**	**H**	Mar 19	Raith Rovers	A
Aug 21	**Hibernian**	**H**	Nov 20	Celtic	A	Mar 26	**Rangers**	**H**
Aug 25	League Cup 3		Nov 27	**Motherwell**	**H**	Mar 30	**Motherwell**	**H**
Aug 28	Dundee United	A	Nov 30	Kilmarnock	A	Apr 2	Kilmarnock	A
Sept 1	League Cup 4		Dec 4	**Aberdeen**	**H**	Apr 9	Celtic	A
Sept 4	**Partick Thistle**	**H**	Dec 11	St. Johnstone	A	Apr 16	**Dundee**	**H**
Sept 11	Motherwell	A	Dec 18	**Raith Rovers**	**H**	Apr 23	St. Johnstone	A
Sept 18	**Kilmarnock**	**H**	Dec 27	Rangers	A	Apr 27	**Aberdeen**	**H**
Sept 22	League Cup S/F		Jan 1	**Hibernian**	**H**	Apr 30	Hibernian	A
Sept 25	**Celtic**	**H**	Jan 8	Dundee United	A	May 7	**Dundee United**	**H**
Oct 2	Dundee	A	Jan 15	**Partick Thistle**	**H**	May 14	Partick Thistle	A
Oct 5	Aberdeen	A	Jan 22	**Kilmarnock**	**H**	May 21	SFA Cup Final	
Oct 9	**St. Johnstone**	**H**	Jan 29	SFA Cup 3				
Oct 16	Raith Rovers	A	Feb 5	Motherwell	A			
Oct 23	**Rangers**	**H**	Feb 12	**Celtic**	**H**			
Oct 24	League Cup Final		Feb 19	SFA Cup 4				

MILESTONES
Year of Formation: 1874
Most Capped Player: Bobby Walker (29)
Most League Points in a Season:
63 (Premier Division – 1991/92)
Most League goals scored by a player in a Season: Barney Battles (44) 1930/31
Record Attendance: 53,496 v Rangers, 13/2/32
Record Victory: 18–0 v Vale of Lothian, Edinburgh Shield, 17/9/1887
Record Defeat: 1–8 v Vale of Leven, Scottish Cup, 1883

SEASON TICKET INFORMATION
Seated
Centre Stand	Adult	£225
Wing Stand	Adult	£200
	OAP	£150
Family Section	Adult	£150
	Juvenile	£75

Standing
Ground	Adult	£145
	Juvenile/OAP	£75

LEAGUE ADMISSION PRICES
Seated
Centre Stand	Adult	£9
Wing Stand	Adult	£8
Family Section	Adult	£6
	Juvenile/OAP	£3

Standing
Ground	Adult	£6
	Juvenile/OAP	£3

N.B. No concessions in all ticket games.

CLUB FACTFILE 1992/93... RESULTS... APPEARANCES... SCORERS

The JAM TARTS

Small figures denote goalscorers † denotes opponent's own goal

Date	Venue	Opponents	Result	Smith H.	McLaren A.	McKinlay T.	Levein C.	Mackay G.	Van De Ven P.	Crabbe S.	Mauchlen A.	Baird I.	Wright G.	Bannon E.	Hogg G.	Robertson J.	Snodin G.	Ferguson D.	Foster W.	Berry N.	Millar J.	Preston A.	Ferguson I.	Walker J.N.	Boothroyd A.	Thomas K.	Harrison T.	Johnston A.	Locke G.
Aug 1	H	Celtic	0-1	1	2	3	4	5	6	7	8	9	10	11	12	14													
5	H	Falkirk	3-0	1	2	3	4		6	14¹	8	9	10	11	5	7²	12												
8	A	Dundee United	1-1	1	2	3	4¹		6	12	10	9	14	11	5	7			8										
15	A	Partick Thistle	2-1	1	2	3	4		6¹	11	10	9¹			5	7			8	12									
22	A	Hibernian	0-0	1	2	3	4	5	6	12	10	9		14		7			8	11									
29	H	Motherwell	1-0	1		3	4	5	6			9	14		2	7	12		8	11	10¹								
Sept 1	A	Dundee	3-1	1		3	4¹	5	6			9			2	7¹			8¹	11	10								
12	H	Aberdeen	1-0	1		3	4	5	6			9			2	7¹	14		8	11									
19	A	Rangers	0-2	1		3	4	5	6	7	10	9			12	2	14		8	11									
26	A	Airdrieonians	0-1	1		3	4		6			9			5	12	2	7	8	11	10	14							
Oct 3	H	St. Johnstone	1-1	1	8	3	4		6	14		9			5	12	2	7¹		10		11							
7	H	Celtic	1-1	1		3	4		6		8	9			12		2	7		10		11¹							
17	H	Dundee United	1-0	1		3	4	5	6			9			12		2¹	7	14	8	10	11							
24	A	Motherwell	†3-1	1	2	3		5	6			9			4	7¹	14		8		10	11	12¹						
31	H	Dundee	1-0	1	2	3	4	5	6			9¹				7			8		10	11	12						
Nov 7	H	Hibernian	1-0	1	2	3	4	5	6		11	9¹				7	14		8		10	12							
10	A	Partick Thistle	1-1	1	2¹	3	4		6			9			5	7	14		8		10	11	12						
21	H	Rangers	1-1	1	2	3	4		6		11	9¹				7	14		8	5	10	12							
28	A	Aberdeen	2-6	1	2	3	4	5	6¹			9¹				7	14		8	11	10	12							
Dec 2	A	Falkirk	1-2	1	2		4	5	6			9				7¹	3		8	14	11	10							
5	H	Airdrieonians	1-3		2	3	4	5	6			9¹				7			8		10	12	11	1					
12	H	St. Johnstone	1-1		2	3	4	5	6							7			8		10	11	9¹	1		14			
19	H	Celtic	1-0		2	3	4	5	6							7			8	12	10	11	9¹	1		14			
26	H	Partick Thistle	1-1		2		4	5¹	6					12		7	3		8	9	10	11		1		14			
Jan 2	A	Hibernian	0-0		2		4	5	6		11	9				7	3		8		10	12		1					
20	A	St. Johnstone	2-0		2		4	5	6		10	9¹				7¹	3		8			11	12	1					
23	H	Motherwell	0-0		2		4	5	6		10	9				7	3		8	12		11		1					
30	A	Dundee United	1-0		2	14	4	5	6		10	9				7¹	3		8			11		1		12			
Feb 3	A	Dundee	0-1		2			5	6			9			4	7	3		8		10	11	12	1					
13	H	Falkirk	†3-1		2	3¹		5	6		10			14		7			8	4		11	9	1	12¹				
20	A	Airdrieonians	0-0		2	3		5	6		10			14		7		4	8			11	9	1					
27	A	Rangers	1-2		2	3		5	6					14	12	7		4			10¹	11	9	1					
Mar 10	A	Celtic	0-1		2	3		5	6			9		14		7		4			10	11	12	1					
13	H	Dundee United	1-0		2		4		6	14	9¹				12	5	7	3	8		10	11		1					
20	H	Hibernian	1-0		2		4		6	14		9			12	5	7¹	3	8		10	11		1					
27	A	Partick Thistle	1-1		2	14	4	5				9	8			7	3	6			10	11¹	12	1					
Apr 10	A	Dundee	0-0		2	3	4	5	6			9				7			8	14	10	11	12	1					
14	H	Rangers	2-3			3	4	5	6			9	11¹			7¹			8	2	10			1					
17	A	Aberdeen	2-3			3	4¹	5	6	1			11		2	7	14		8	10					12		9¹		
20	A	Motherwell	1-2	1	2		4	5			9¹		11		6	7	3		8		10	12							
May		Falkirk	0-6	1	2		4	5	6			9		11		7	3		8		10	12							
5	H	Aberdeen	1-2	1	5	3		10	6			9			2	11			8	7							14¹	4	
8	H	Airdrieonians	1-1	1	5	3	4	10							2	11			8	12							9	6	7¹
15	A	St. Johnstone	1-3	1		3		10	6						2	11			8	5			14		12		9	4¹	7
TOTAL FULL APPEARANCES				25	34	32	37	36	37	4	16	34	8	8	20	41	16	37	7	16	23	19	9	18	2	3	2		
TOTAL SUB APPEARANCES					(2)		(1)			(4)	(2)		(4)	(11)	(2)	(1)	(11)		(4)	(1)	(1)	(2)	(15)	(4)		(2)	(1)		(1)
TOTAL GOALS SCORED					1	1	3	2	1			9	1		2	11	1	1	1		2	4	2				1	1	1

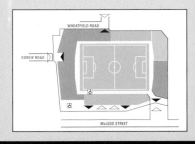

TYNECASTLE PARK

Capacity 25,177 (Seated 10,000, Standing 15,177)

Pitch Dimensions 110 yds x 74 yds.

Disabled Facilities Ten spaces (must be pre-booked) at South end of the Enclosure.

WHEATFIELD ROAD

GORGIE ROAD

McLEOD STREET

HOW TO GET THERE

Buses: A frequent service of buses leaves from the city centre, Nos. 1, 2, 3, 4, 33, 34, 35 and 44 all pass the ground.

Trains: Haymarket Station is about half a mile from the ground.

Cars: Car Parking facilities exist in the adjacent side streets in Robertson Avenue and also the Westfield area.

HIBERNIAN

LIST OF PLAYERS 1993-94

Easter Road Stadium,
Albion Road, Edinburgh,
EH7 5QG

Chairman
Douglas W. M. Cromb
Directors
Robert Huthersall;
Allan Munro;
Thomas J. O'Malley;
Kenneth McLean
Manager
Alexander MIller
Secretary
Cecil F. Graham, F.F.A.
Commercial Manager
Kenneth McLean

Telephones
Ground (031) 661 2159
Commercial (031) 661 2159
Fax (031) 659 6488
Ticket Office (031) 652 0630
Information Service 0898 121189

Club Shop
178A Easter Road, Edinburgh

Official Supporters Club
11 Sunnyside Lane,
Off Easter Road,
Edinburgh, EH7

Team Captain
Gordon Hunter

Club Sponsor
MacBean Protective Clothing

Name	Date of Birth	Place of Birth	Date of Signing	Height	Weight	Previous Club
Balmain, Kenneth J.A.	08/11/73	Bellshill	14/05/91	5-9	11.6	Eastercraigs B.C.
Bannon, Eamonn John	18/04/58	Edinburgh	02/09/93	5-9	11.11	Heart of Midlothian
Beaumont, David	10/12/63	Edinburgh	17/10/91	6-0	12.0	Luton Town
Brown, Stewart Anderson	08/10/75	Bangour	03/08/92	5-9	12.0	Hutchison Vale B.C.
Currie, Paul John	14/12/73	Edinburgh	14/05/91	5-9	10.8	Musselburgh Windsor
Dallas, Stephen	02/11/74	Glasgow	03/08/92	5-7	10.7	Duntocher B.C.
Dods, Darren	07/06/75	Edinburgh	03/08/92	6-1	12.10	Hutchison Vale B.C.
Donald, Graeme Still	14/04/74	Stirling	12/06/91	6-0	12.4	Gairdoch United
Evans, Gareth John	14/01/67	Coventry	06/02/88	5-7.5	11.0	Rotherham United
Farrell, David	29/10/69	Glasgow	12/08/88	5-9	11.11	Oxford United
Fellenger, David	06/06/69	Edinburgh	17/10/85	5-8	11.4	Hutchison Vale B.C.
Findlay, William McCall	29/08/70	Kilmarnock	13/06/87	5-10	12.2	Kilmarnock B.C.
Gardiner, Jason Stanley	30/10/73	Edinburgh	14/05/91	6-0	13.10	Salvesen Boys Club
Hamilton, Brian	05/08/67	Paisley	18/07/89	6-0	12.0	St. Mirren
Harper, Kevin Patrick	15/01/76	Oldham	03/08/92	5-6	10.9	Hutchison Vale B.C.
Hunter, Gordon	03/05/67	Wallyford	10/08/83	5-10	11.10	Musselburgh Windsor
Jackson, Christopher	29/10/73	Edinburgh	14/05/91	5-7	10.10	Salvesen Boys Club
Jackson, Darren	25/07/66	Edinburgh	14/07/92	5-10	10.1	Dundee United
Laidlaw, Douglas	17/01/76	Edinburgh	03/08/92	5-10	10.4	Hutchison Vale B.C.
Leighton, James	24/07/58	Johnstone	14/07/93	6-0	13.6	Dundee
Lennon, Daniel Joseph	06/04/69	Whitburn	09/10/85	5-5	10.8	Hutchison Vale B.C.
Love, Graeme	07/12/73	Bathgate	14/05/91	5-10	11.8	Salvesen Boys Club
McAllister, Kevin	08/11/62	Falkirk	29/07/93	5-5	11.0	Falkirk
McGraw, Mark Robertson	05/01/71	Rutherglen	14/02/90	5-11.5	11.2	Greenock Morton
McIntyre, Thomas	26/12/63	Bellshill	31/12/86	6-0	11.10	Aberdeen
Miller, Graeme	21/02/73	Glasgow	11/06/90	5-7	10.0	Tynecastle B.C.
Miller, William	01/11/69	Edinburgh	14/03/87	5-8	11.1	Edina Hibs B.C.
Mitchell, Graham	02/11/62	Glasgow	31/12/86	5-10	11.8	Hamilton Academical
Mitchell, Scott Cameron	18/04/76	Paisley	29/04/93	5-11	11.6	Duntocher B.C.
O'Neill, Michael A.M.	05/07/69	Portadown	20/08/93	5-11.5	11.3	Dundee United
Orr, Alan John	05/07/77	Vale of Leven	20/07/93	5-9	10.5	"S" Form
Reid, Christopher Thomas	04/11/71	Edinburgh	20/06/88	5-11	13.10	Hutchison Vale B.C.
Renwick, Michael	29/02/76	Edinburgh	03/08/92	5-9	10.5	Hutchison Vale B.C.
Riley, Paul	07/08/75	Edinburgh	03/08/92	5-7	9.11	Hutchison Vale B.C.
Tortolano, Joseph	06/04/66	Stirling	29/08/85	5-8	11.6	West Bromwich Albion
Tweed, Steven	08/08/72	Edinburgh	25/08/90	6-3	14.0	Hutchison Vale B.C.
Weir, Michael Graham	16/01/66	Edinburgh	14/01/88	5-4	10.3	Luton Town
Winter, Craig John	30/06/76	Dunfermline	03/09/92	5-9	10.0	Hutchison Vale B.C.
Wright, Keith	17/05/65	Edinburgh	01/08/91	5-11	12.4	Dundee

CLUB FIXTURES 1993-94

Date	Opponent	Venue
Aug 4	League Cup 1	
Aug 7	**Partick Thistle**	**H**
Aug 11	League Cup 2	
Aug 14	Celtic	A
Aug 21	Heart of Midlothian	A
Aug 25	League Cup 3	
Aug 28	**Dundee**	**H**
Sept 1	League Cup 4	
Sept 4	Kilmarnock	A
Sept 11	**Aberdeen**	**H**
Sept 18	St. Johnstone	A
Sept 22	League Cup S/F	
Sept 25	Rangers	A
Oct 2	**Dundee United**	**H**
Oct 5	**Raith Rovers**	**H**
Oct 9	Motherwell	A
Oct 16	**Celtic**	**H**
Oct 23	Partick Thistle	A

Date	Opponent	Venue
Oct 24	League Cup Final	
Oct 30	**Heart of Midlothian**	**H**
Nov 6	Dundee	A
Nov 9	**Kilmarnock**	**H**
Nov 13	Dundee United	A
Nov 20	**Rangers**	**H**
Nov 27	Aberdeen	A
Nov 30	**St. Johnstone**	**H**
Dec 4	Raith Rovers	A
Dec 11	**Motherwell**	**H**
Dec 18	Celtic	A
Dec 27	**Partick Thistle**	**H**
Jan 1	Heart of Midlothian	A
Jan 8	**Dundee**	**H**
Jan 15	Kilmarnock	A
Jan 22	St. Johnstone	A
Jan 29	SFA Cup 3	

Date	Opponent	Venue
Feb 5	**Aberdeen**	**H**
Feb 12	Rangers	A
Feb 19	SFA Cup 4	
Feb 26	**Dundee United**	**H**
Mar 5	**Raith Rovers**	**H**
Mar 12	Motherwell	A
Mar 19	**Celtic**	**H**
Mar 26	Partick Thistle	A
Mar 29	Aberdeen	A
Apr 2	**St. Johnstone**	**H**
Apr 9	**Rangers**	**H**
Apr 16	Dundee United	A
Apr 23	**Motherwell**	**H**
Apr 27	Raith Rovers	A
Apr 30	**Heart of Midlothian**	**H**
May 7	Dundee	A
May 14	**Kilmarnock**	**H**
May 21	SFA Cup Final	

MILESTONES
Year of Formation: 1875
Most Capped Player: Lawrie Reilly (38)
Most League Points in a Season:
57 (First Division – 1980/81)
Most League goals scored by a player in a Season: Joe Baker (42) 1959/60
Record Attendance: 65,860 v Hearts, 2/1/50
Record Victory: 22-1 v 42nd Highlanders, 3/9/1881
Record Defeat: 0-10 v Rangers, 24/12/1898

SEASON TICKET INFORMATION
Seated

Centre Stand	Adult	£195
	Juvenile/OAP	£150
Wing Stand	Adult	£165
	Juvenile/OAP	£120
Seated Enclosure	Adult	£130
	OAP	£90
	Juvenile	£40
Family Enclosure	Adult	£120
	First Child	£50
	Second Child	£40
Standing	Adult	£125
	Juvenile/OAP	£75

LEAGUE ADMISSION PRICES
Seated

Centre Stand	Adult	£9.50
Wing Stand	Adult	£8.50
Seated Enclosure	Adult	£7
	Juvenile/OAP	£4
Family Enclosure	Adult	£7
	Juvenile	£4
Standing	Adult	£7
	Juvenile/OAP	£4

No concessions in all ticket games v Celtic, Hearts & Rangers (No Juvenile/OAP gates)

Registered Strip:	Shirt - Green with White Sleeves, Shorts - White, Stockings - Green with White Turnover with Two Black Hoops
Change Strip:	Shirt - Purple with Green Collar/Cuffs, Shorts - Black, Stockings - Black with Purple Turnover with Two Green Hoops

The HIBEES

CLUB FACTFILE 1992/93... RESULTS... APPEARANCES... SCORERS

Player columns (left to right): Reid C., Orr N., Mitchell G., Beaumont D., McIntyre T., MacLeod M., Weir M., Hamilton B., Wright K., Jackson D., McGinlay P., Evans G., Miller W., Tortolano J., Milne C., Burridge J., Findlay W., Lennon D., Raynes S., McCraw M., Hunter G., Farrell D., Donald G., Fellenger D., Tweed S., Love G., Miller G., Jackson C.

Date	Venue	Opponents	Result	Appearances / Scorers (small figures denote goalscorers)
Aug 1	A	Aberdeen	0-3	Reid 1, Orr 2, Mitchell 3, Beaumont 4, McIntyre 5, MacLeod 6, Weir 7, Hamilton 8, Wright 9, Jackson D 10, McGinlay 11, Evans 12
Aug 4	A	Motherwell	2-1	Reid 1, Orr 2, Mitchell 3, Beaumont 4, McIntyre 5, MacLeod 6, Weir 7, Hamilton 8, Wright 9^1, Jackson D 10, McGinlay 11^1, Evans 12
Aug 8	H	Rangers	0-0	Reid 1, Mitchell 4, Beaumont 3, McIntyre 5, Weir 6, Hamilton 8, Wright 9, Jackson D 10, McGinlay 11, Evans 12, Tortolano 2, Milne 7, Findlay 14
Aug 15	H	Falkirk	1-2	Reid 1, Mitchell 4, Beaumont 3, McIntyre 5, MacLeod 6, Weir 14, Hamilton 8, Wright 9, McGinlay 7, Evans 11, Miller W 10, Tortolano 2, Milne 12^1
Aug 22	H	Heart of Midlothian	0-0	Mitchell 4, Beaumont 3, MacLeod 5, Weir 7, Hamilton 8, Wright 9, McGinlay 6, Evans 11, Miller W 10, Tortolano 2, Burridge 1, Findlay 14
Aug 29	A	St. Johnstone	1-1	Mitchell 4, Beaumont 3, McIntyre 5^1, Weir 7, Hamilton 8, Wright 9, McGinlay 6, Evans 11, Miller W 10, Burridge 2, Findlay 1, Lennon 14
Sept 2	H	Dundee United	2-1	Mitchell 4, Beaumont 3, McIntyre 5, Weir 7, Hamilton 8, Wright 9, McGinlay 6^1, Evans 11, Miller W 10, Tortolano 12^1, Burridge 2, Findlay 1, Lennon 14
Sept 12	A	Celtic	3-2	Mitchell 4, Beaumont 3, McIntyre 5, MacLeod 6, Weir 7, Hamilton 8, Wright 9^1, Jackson D 10^1, McGinlay 11, Evans 12^1, Miller W 2, Burridge 14, Findlay 1
Sept 19	H	Airdrieonians	†2-2	Mitchell 4, Beaumont 3, McIntyre 5, MacLeod 6, Weir 7^1, Wright 9, Jackson D 10, McGinlay 11, Evans 8, Miller W 2, Tortolano 12, Burridge 1, Findlay 14
Sept 26	H	Dundee	0-0	Mitchell 3, Beaumont 5, MacLeod 12, Hamilton 8, Wright 9, Jackson D 10, McGinlay 11, Evans 7, Miller W 2, Tortolano 6, Burridge 1, Hunter 4, Farrell 14
Oct 3	A	Partick Thistle	2-2	Mitchell 4, McIntyre 5, MacLeod 6, Weir 7^1, Hamilton 8, Wright 9, Jackson D 10^1, McGinlay 11, Miller W 2, Milne 3, Burridge 1
Oct 7	H	Aberdeen	1-3	Mitchell 4, Beaumont 3, McIntyre 5, Weir 7, Hamilton 8, Wright 9^1, Jackson D 10, McGinlay 11, Evans 12, Miller W 2, Milne 6, Burridge 1, Hunter 14
Oct 17	A	Rangers	0-1	Mitchell 3, McIntyre 5, MacLeod 6, Weir 7, Hamilton 4, Wright 9, Jackson D 10, McGinlay 11, Evans 8, Miller W 2, Burridge 1
Oct 24	H	St. Johnstone	3-1	Mitchell 3, McIntyre 5, MacLeod 6, Weir 7^1, Hamilton 4, Wright 9, Jackson D 10^2, McGinlay 11, Tortolano 2, Milne 8, Burridge 1, Hunter 14
Oct 31	A	Dundee United	0-1	Mitchell 4, MacLeod 5, Weir 6, Hamilton 7, Wright 8, Jackson D 9, McGinlay 11, Evans 10, Miller W 2, Milne 3, Burridge 1, Hunter 12
Nov 7	A	Heart of Midlothian	0-1	Mitchell 3, MacLeod 5, Weir 6, Hamilton 7, Wright 8, Jackson D 9, McGinlay 10, Evans 11, Miller W 12, Milne 2, Burridge 14, Hunter 1, Farrell 4
Nov 14	H	Falkirk	3-1	Mitchell 3, Weir 6, Hamilton 14^1, McGinlay 8, Evans 11, Miller W 7^1, Milne 2, Burridge 10^1, Hunter 1, Farrell 4, Donald 5, Fellenger 9
Nov 21	A	Airdrieonians	0-2	Mitchell 3, Beaumont 10, Weir 6, Wright 8, Jackson D 9, Miller W 7, Milne 2, Burridge 11, Hunter 1, Farrell 14, Donald 4, Fellenger 5, Tweed 12
Nov 28	H	Celtic	1-2	Mitchell 3, MacLeod 5, Weir 6, Hamilton 7, Jackson D 9, McGinlay 10^1, Evans 11, Miller W 12, Milne 2, Hunter 1, Farrell 8, Fellenger 4
Dec 1	H	Motherwell	2-2	Mitchell 3, MacLeod 5, Weir 6, Hamilton 7, Wright 14, Jackson D 9^1, McGinlay 10, Evans 11^1, Miller W 12, Milne 2, Hunter 4, Farrell 1, Donald 8
Dec 5	H	Dundee	1-1	Reid 4, Mitchell 3, MacLeod 5, Weir 12, Wright 8, Jackson D 9, McGinlay 10^1, Evans 11, Miller W 7, Milne 2, Burridge 1, Hunter 6
Dec 12	H	Partick Thistle	1-0	Reid 1, Mitchell 4, Beaumont 3, McIntyre 5, MacLeod 14, Weir 7, Hamilton 8, Jackson D 10^1, McGinlay 9, Milne 2, Findlay 11, Lennon 12, Hunter 6
Dec 19	A	Aberdeen	0-2	Reid 1, Mitchell 4, Beaumont 3, McIntyre 5, Weir 6, Hamilton 8, Wright 9, McGinlay 7, Evans 12, Miller W 11, Milne 2, Lennon 10, Hunter 14
Dec 26	H	Falkirk	3-3	Reid 1, McIntyre 5, Weir 6, Hamilton 8, Wright 9, McGinlay 7^1, Milne 2, Burridge 3, Findlay 10, Hunter 4, Farrell 14, Donald 12, Tweed 11^2
Jan 2	H	Heart of Midlothian	0-0	Reid 1, Orr 2, Mitchell 3, MacLeod 5, Weir 6, Hamilton 7, Wright 8, Jackson D 9, McGinlay 10, Evans 11, Hunter 4
Jan 16	H	Dundee United	2-1	Reid 1, Orr 2, Mitchell 3, MacLeod 5, Weir 6, Hamilton 7, Wright 8, Jackson D 10^1, McGinlay 11, Evans 12, Hunter 4, Tweed 14
Jan 23	A	St. Johnstone	0-2	Reid 1, Orr 2, Mitchell 3, MacLeod 5, Weir 6, Hamilton 7, Wright 8, Jackson D 9, McGinlay 10, Evans 11, Miller W 12, Tortolano 14, Hunter 4
Jan 30	H	Rangers	3-4	Reid 1, Orr 2, Mitchell 3, Weir 6, Hamilton 7, MacLeod 5, Wright 9, Jackson D 10^1, McGinlay 11^2, Evans 8, Tortolano 14, Hunter 4
Feb 13	A	Motherwell	0-0	Reid 1, Mitchell 3, Weir 6, Hamilton 7, Wright 9, McGinlay 11, Evans 10, Miller W 2, Tortolano 12, Hunter 4, Farrell 8, Tweed 14, Love 5
Feb 16	H	Partick Thistle	3-0	Reid 1, Mitchell 3, Weir 6, Hamilton 7^1, Wright 8, Jackson D 9, Evans 11^2, Miller W 12, Tortolano 14, Milne 10, Hunter 4, Farrell 2, Tweed 5
Feb 20	H	Dundee	1-3	Reid 1, Mitchell 3, Weir 6, Hamilton 7, Jackson D 9, Evans 11^1, Miller W 12, Tortolano 14, Milne 10, Burridge 8, Hunter 4, Farrell 2, Tweed 5
Feb 27	H	Airdrieonians	3-1	Orr 2, Mitchell 3, Weir 6, Hamilton 7, Wright 8, Jackson D 9, McGinlay 10^2, Evans 11^1, Miller W 12, Burridge 1, Hunter 4, Tweed 5
Mar 9	A	Aberdeen	1-2	Mitchell 3, Beaumont 4, Wright 8, Jackson D 9, McGinlay 10, Evans 11^1, Miller W 12, Findlay 6, Burridge 1, Hunter 7, Farrell 2, Tweed 5
Mar 13	A	Rangers	0-3	Mitchell 3, Wright 8, Jackson D 9, McGinlay 10, Evans 11, Miller W 12, Findlay 6, Burridge 1, Hunter 7, Farrell 4, Raynes 2, Love 14, Tweed 5
Mar 16	A	Celtic	1-2	Mitchell 3, Hamilton 7, Wright 8, Jackson D 9^1, McGinlay 10, Evans 11, Miller W 12, Tortolano 2, Milne 14, Burridge 1, Hunter 6, Farrell 4, Tweed 5
Mar 20	A	Heart of Midlothian	0-1	Mitchell 3, Hamilton 7, Wright 8, Jackson D 9, MacLeod 6, Evans 11, Miller W 10, Tortolano 2, Burridge 1, Hunter 4, Farrell 12, Tweed 5
Mar 27	A	Falkirk	1-1	Mitchell 3, Hamilton 7, Wright 8, Jackson D 9, McGinlay 10, Evans 11, Tortolano 2, Milne 6, Burridge 1, Hunter 12, Farrell 4, Tweed 5
Apr 6	H	St. Johnstone	2-2	Mitchell 3, MacLeod 6, Wright 8, Jackson D 9^1, McGinlay 10, Evans 11, Miller W 14^1, Tortolano 2, Milne 7, Burridge 1, Hunter 12, Farrell 4, Tweed 5
Apr 13	A	Dundee United	3-0	Mitchell 3, MacLeod 12, Wright 8, Jackson D 9^3, McGinlay 10, Evans 11, Milne 7, Tortolano 2, Milne 5, Burridge 1, Hunter 6, Farrell 4, Tweed 14
Apr 17	H	Celtic	3-1	Mitchell 3, MacLeod 12, Weir 14, Wright 8, Jackson D 9^1, McGinlay 10^1, Evans 11, Hamilton 7^1, Tortolano 2, Milne 5, Burridge 1, Hunter 6, Tweed 4
Apr 20	A	Airdrieonians	1-3	Mitchell 3, MacLeod 12, Wright 8, Jackson D 9, McGinlay 10, Evans 11^1, Hamilton 7, Tortolano 2, Milne 5, Burridge 1, Hunter 6, Tweed 4, Love 14
May 1	H	Motherwell	1-0	Mitchell 3, MacLeod 6^1, Wright 8, Jackson D 9, McGinlay 10, Evans 11, Hamilton 7, Tortolano 2, Milne 14, Burridge 1, Hunter 4, Tweed 5
May 8	A	Dundee	1-3	Reid 14, Mitchell 3, Hamilton 7, Wright 8, Jackson D 9, Evans 12, McGinlay 11, Milne 10^1, Tortolano 2, Burridge 1, Hunter 6, Tweed 4, Love 5
May 15	H	Partick Thistle	0-1	Mitchell 3, Hamilton 7, Jackson D 4, Wright 9, Evans 11, Milne 8, Tortolano 2, Burridge 1, Hunter 6, Tweed 12, Love 5, Miller G 3, 10, Jackson C 14

Player	Reid C.	Orr N.	Mitchell G.	Beaumont D.	McIntyre T.	MacLeod M.	Weir M.	Hamilton B.	Wright K.	Jackson D.	McGinlay P.	Evans G.	Miller W.	Tortolano J.	Milne C.	Burridge J.	Findlay W.	Lennon D.	Raynes S.	McCraw M.	Hunter G.	Farrell D.	Donald G.	Fellenger D.	Tweed S.	Love G.	Miller G.	Jackson C.
TOTAL FULL APPEARANCES	14	20	41	16	12	26	30	38	42	35	40	23	29	16	10	30	3	7	2	1	22	10	1	1	13	1	1	
TOTAL SUB APPEARANCES		(1)		(5)	(3)	(2)		(1)			(17)	(5)	(5)	(5)			(4)	(6)		(1)		(3)	(3)	(4)	(1)			(1)
TOTAL GOALS SCORED			1			5	1	11	13	10	6		3												2			

*Small figures denote goalscorers † denotes opponent's own goal

---

EASTER ROAD

Capacity 21,889 (Seated 6,299, Standing 15,590)

Pitch Dimensions 112 yds x 74 yds

Disabled facilities Area in South Seated Enclosure.

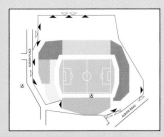

HOW TO GET THERE

Buses: The main bus station in the city is served by buses from all over the country and the following local buses departing from Princes Street all stop near the ground. Nos. 4, 15, 42 and 44.

Trains: Edinburgh Waverley Station is served by trains from all parts of the country and the above buses all stop near the ground.

Rugby Park,
Kilmarnock, KA1 2DP

Chairman
Robert Fleeting
Vice-Chairman
James H. Moffat
Directors
Mrs. Laurel J. Chadwick;
John Paton;
Ronald D. Hamilton
Player/Manager
Thomas Burns
Secretary
Kevin D. Collins

Commercial Manager
Denny Martin

Telephones
Ground/Commercial Manager/
Ticket Office (0563) 25184
Fax (0563) 22181
Club Shop (0563) 34210.

Club Shop
Killie Sports, 36 Bank Street,
Kilmarnock. Open Mon. to
Sat. 9.00 a.m. — 5.00 p.m.
Also portacabin at ground on
Match Days.

Official Supporters Club
c/o Rugby Park, Kilmarnock,
KA1 2DP

Team Captain
Raymond Montgomerie

Club Sponsor
A.T. Mays, Travel Agents

LIST OF PLAYERS 1993-94

Name	Date of Birth	Place of Birth	Date of Signing	Height	Weight	Previous Club
Black, Thomas	11/10/62	Lanark	08/11/91	5-8	10.12	St. Mirren
Brown, Thomas	01/04/68	Glasgow	27/08/93	5-7	10.0	Glenafton Athletic
Burns, Thomas	16/12/56	Glasgow	09/12/89	5-11	11.3	Celtic
Campbell, Calum	07/11/65	Erskine	31/03/91	6-1	12.0	Partick Thistle
Crainie, Daniel	24/05/62	Kilsyth	07/11/92	5-8	10.11	Airdrieonians
Flexney, Paul	18/01/65	Glasgow	16/12/88	6-1	11.12	Northampton Town
Gallacher, Iain Ronald	22/03/74	Irvine	03/12/91	5-9.5	10.9	Saltcoats Victoria
Geddes, Alexander Robert	12/08/60	Inverness	25/05/90	6-0	11.4	Dundee
Hamilton, Steven James	19/03/75	Baillieston	13/09/93	5-9	11.9	Troon Juniors
MacPherson, Angus Ian	11/10/68	Glasgow	10/06/86	5-11	10.4	Rangers
Matthews, Gary	15/03/70	Paisley	03/12/91	6-3.5	16.2	Saltcoats Victoria
McCarrison, Dugald	22/12/69	Lanark	26/02/93	5-11	10.7	Celtic
McCloy, Steven	28/04/75	Girvan	30/09/93	5-9	11.9	Craigmark Juniors
McCluskey, George M.C.J.	19/09/57	Hamilton	25/07/92	5-10.5	12.6	Hamilton Academical
McSkimming, Shaun P.	29/05/70	Stranraer	13/07/91	5-11	10.8	Dundee
Meldrum, Colin George	26/11/75	Kilmarnock	03/09/93	5-10.5	13.4	Kilwinning Rangers
Millen, Andrew Frank	10/06/65	Glasgow	04/08/93	5-11	11.2	Hamilton Academical
Mitchell, Alistair Robert	03/12/68	Kirkcaldy	05/07/91	5-7	11.0	East Fife
Montgomerie, S. Raymond	17/04/61	Irvine	12/08/88	5-8	11.7	Dumbarton
Paterson, Craig Stewart	02/10/59	South Queensferry	29/10/91	6-2.5	12.12	Motherwell
Porteous, Ian	21/11/64	Glasgow	31/01/92	5-7	10.6	Herfolge F.C. Denmark
Reilly, Mark	30/03/69	Bellshill	05/07/91	5-8	10.0	Motherwell
Roberts, Mark Kingsley	29/10/75	Irvine	07/02/92	5-9.5	9.10	Bellfield B.C.
Skilling, Mark James	06/10/72	Irvine	01/10/91	5-9.5	10.13	Saltcoats Victoria
Stark, William	01/12/56	Glasgow	03/08/92	6-1	11.11	Hamilton Academical
White, David	21/08/75	Cumnock	13/09/93	5-8	10.12	Cumnock
Williamson, Robert	13/08/61	Glasgow	15/11/90	5-7.5	12.9	Rotherham United
Wilson, Thomas Skinner	24/08/61	Paisley	14/11/92	5-8	9.7	Heart of Midlothian

MILESTONES
Year of Formation: 1869
Most Capped Player: Joe Nibloe (11)
Most League points in a Season:
58 (Division 2) - 1973/74
Most League goals scored by a player in a Season: Harry 'Peerie' Cunningham, Season 1927/28, and Andy Kerr, Season 1960/61 (34 each)
Record Attendance: 34,246 v Rangers, August 1963
Record Victory: 13-2 v Saltcoats, Scottish Cup, 12/9/1896
Record Defeat: 0-8 v Rangers and Hibernian, Division 1

CLUB FIXTURES 1992-93

Date	Opponent	Venue
Aug 4	*League Cup 1*	
Aug 7	**Dundee**	H
Aug 11	*League Cup 2*	
Aug 1	Aberdeen	A
Aug 21	**Motherwell**	H
Aug 25	*League Cup 3*	
Aug 28	Rangers	A
Sept 1	*League Cup 4*	
Sept 4	**Hibernian**	H
Sept 11	**St. Johnstone**	H
Sept 18	Heart of Midlothian	A
Sept 22	*League Cup S/F*	
Sept 25	**Partick Thistle**	H
Oct 2	Celtic	A
Oct 5	**Dundee United**	H
Oct 9	Raith Rovers	A
Oct 16	**Aberdeen**	H
Oct 23	Dundee	A
Oct 24	*League Cup Final*	
Oct 30	Motherwell	A
Nov 6	**Rangers**	H
Nov 9	Hibernian	A
Nov 13	**Celtic**	H
Nov 20	Partick Thistle	A
Nov 27	St. Johnstone	A
Nov 30	**Heart of Midlothian**	H
Dec 4	Dundee United	A
Dec 11	**Raith Rovers**	H
Dec 18	Aberdeen	A
Dec 27	**Dundee**	H
Jan 1	**Motherwell**	H
Jan 8	Rangers	A
Jan 15	**Hibernian**	H
Jan 22	Heart of Midlothian	A
Jan 29	*SFA Cup 3*	
Feb 5	**St. Johnstone**	H
Feb 12	**Partick Thistle**	H
Feb 19	*SFA Cup 4*	
Feb 26	Celtic	A
Mar 5	**Dundee United**	H
Mar 12	Raith Rovers	A
Mar 9	**Aberdeen**	H
Mar 26	Dundee	A
Mar 30	St. Johnstone	A
Apr 2	**Heart of Midlothian**	H
Apr 9	Partick Thistle	A
Apr 16	**Celtic**	H
Apr 23	**Raith Rovers**	H
Apr 26	Dundee United	A
Apr 30	Motherwell	A
May 7	**Rangers**	H
May 14	Hibernian	A
May 21	*SFA Cup Final*	

SEASON TICKET INFORMATION
Seated	Adult	£185
	Juvenile/OAP	£80
Family Enclosure	Adult	£140
	Juvenile	£45
	Each Additional Juvenile	£30
Standing	Adult	£125
	OAP	£65

LEAGUE ADMISSION PRICES
Seated	Adult	£9
	OAP	£4
Family Enclosure	Adult	£9
	Juvenile	£4
Standing	Adult	£6
	Juvenile/OAP	£3

Registered Strip: Shirt - White with Blue Trim, Shorts - Blue, Stockings - Blue

Change Strip: Shirt - Light Blue and Claret Design, Shorts - Light Blue, Stockings - Light Blue with Claret Bands

CLUB FACTFILE 1992/93... RESULTS... APPEARANCES... SCORERS

KILLIE

Date	Venue	Opponents	Result	Geddes R.	Burns H.	Black T.	Montgomerie R.	Paterson C.	MacPherson A.	Porteous I.	Skilling M.	Jack R.	Tait T.	Mitchell A.	Campbell C.	Reilly M.	Burns T.	Williamson R.	McSkimming S.	McCluskey G.	McStay W.	Furphy W.	Crainie D.	Wilson T.	Stark W.	Roberts M.	McCarrison D.
Aug 1	A	Morton	2-0	1	2	3	4	5	6	7	8	9¹	10	11¹	12												
Aug 4	A	Dumbarton	3-1	1	2	3	4	5¹	6	7	8	9¹	10¹	11	12	14											
Aug 8	H	Raith Rovers	1-1	1	2	3	4	5		7	8	9	10	11¹				6	14								
Aug 15	H	Dunfermline Athletic	0-1	1	2	3	4	5			8	9		11				6	7	10	14						
Aug 22	A	Ayr United	0-2	1	2	3	4	5			8	9		11	12			6	7	10	14						
Aug 29	H	Meadowbank Thistle	1-0	1		3	4	5	2	14	8						7	6	9¹	10	11						
Sept 5	A	Clydebank	1-1	1		3	4	5	2	14	8						7	6	9	10¹	11		12				
Sept 12	A	Stirling Albion	1-0	1			4	5	2		8	9¹				3	7	6		10	11						
Sept 19	H	St. Mirren	1-2	1			4	5	2		8	10		9	12	3	7	6	14¹	11							
Sept 26	H	Cowdenbeath	3-0	1			4	5	2	8¹		12¹				3	7	6	14	9¹	11				10		
Oct 3	A	Hamilton Academical	1-1	1			4	5	2	8¹		12				3	7	6		9	11				10		
Oct 10	A	Morton	3-0	1			4	5	2	14	8	12				3	7	6²		9	11				10¹		
Oct 17	H	Raith Rovers	1-1	1			4	5	2		8					3¹	7	6	14	9	11				10		
Oct 24	H	Clydebank	3-3	1			4	5	2		8					3	7	6		9	11¹				10²		
Oct 31	A	Meadowbank Thistle	1-1	1			4	5	2		8	12				3	7	6		9	11¹				10		
Nov 7	A	Dunfermline Athletic	0-2	1			4	5	2		8	12				3	7	6	14	9	11				10		
Nov 14	A	Ayr United	†3-0	1		3	4		8		5¹				12		7	6	9¹					2	10	11	
Nov 21	A	St. Mirren	1-0	1		3¹	4		8		5						7	6	9					2	10	11	
Nov 28	H	Stirling Albion	1-0	1			4		2		5¹	14		12	7	3		6	8	9					10	11	
Dec 1	H	Hamilton Academical	1-0	1			4		8¹		5	11			7	3		6	9					2	10	14	
Dec 5	A	Cowdenbeath	3-2	1			4		8¹		5	11¹			7	3¹		6	9					2	10		
Dec 19	A	Dumbarton	1-0	1			4	5	8			9		11			7¹	6	12	3			14	2	10		
Dec 26	H	Dunfermline Athletic	2-3	1			4	5	8			9		12	7	3¹		6	14					2	10¹	11	
Dec 29	A	Morton	0-2	1			4	5	8		12				7	3		6	9	11				2	10		
Jan 2	A	Ayr United	1-0	1			4	5	8		7¹						6	11	3	9				2	10		
Jan 16	A	Meadowbank Thistle	5-0	1			4	5	8¹		7¹			14			6	11¹	3	9²			12	2	10		
Jan 27	A	Hamilton Academical	2-1	1			4	5	8		7¹			14			6	11¹	3	9				2	10		
Jan 30	A	Raith Rovers	3-0	1			4	5	8		7²						6	11	3	9				2	10¹		
Feb 13	A	Dumbarton	0-1	1			4	5	8		7			9			6	11	3				14	2	10		
Feb 16	A	Clydebank	0-2	1			4	5	2		7			12	8		6	11	3	9					10		
Feb 20	H	Cowdenbeath	1-1	1	14	4		5			8	7		9	12¹		6	11	3					2	10		
Feb 27	A	St. Mirren	1-0	1	2		4	5			8						6	11	3	9¹					10		7
Mar 6	A	Stirling Albion	0-2	1	2		4	5			8			12		14	6	11	3	9					10		7
Mar 9	H	Morton	†2-2	1	2		4	5			8						6	11¹	3	9					10		7
Mar 13	A	Raith Rovers	0-2	1	2		4	5			8			7	12		6	11	3	9					10		
Mar 20	H	Ayr United	1-1	1			4	5			8¹			7			6	11	3	9				2	10		12
Mar 27	H	Dunfermline Athletic	2-2	1			4	5			7			8			6	11¹	12	3¹	9²			2	10		
Apr 3	A	Clydebank	6-0	1			4	5			7¹			8	14²		6	11	3¹	9²				2	10		
Apr 14	A	Meadowbank Thistle	1-1	1			4	5	12		8			7			6	11	3¹	9				2	10		14
Apr 17	H	Stirling Albion	3-0	1			4	5	2		8			7¹			6		3	9¹			14		10		11¹
Apr 24	H	St. Mirren	1-2	1			4	5	2		8			7¹			6	12	3	9			14		10		11
May 1	H	Dumbarton	1-0	1			4	5	2		8			7			6		3	9¹			12		10		11
May 8	A	Cowdenbeath	3-0	1			4	5	8¹					7			6		3	9			11¹	2	10¹		
May 15	H	Hamilton Academical	0-0	1			4	5	8		2			7			6		3	9			11		10		
TOTAL FULL APPEARANCES				44	9	10	42	21	39	17	40	11	5	26	13	18	39	26	35	29		1	3	18	28	4	6
TOTAL SUB APPEARANCES					(1)			(1)	(3)		(7)			(6)	(11)	(1)			(7)	(2)	(1)		(6)	(1)		(1)	(2)
TOTAL GOALS SCORED							1	5	6	4	5	1		6	4	3	2	6	5	11				1		3	1

Small figures denote goalscorers † denotes opponent's own goal

RUGBY PARK

Capacity 12,991 (Seated 3,141, Standing 9,850)

Pitch Dimensions 115 yds x 74 yds.

Disabled Facilities By prior arrangement with the Secretary.

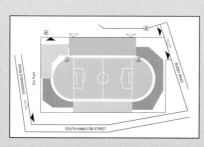

HOW TO GET THERE

Buses: The main bus station, which is served by services from all over the country, is ten minutes walk from the ground, but there are three local services which run from here to within a two minute walk of the park. These are the Kilmarnock–Saltcoats, Kilmarnock Ardrossan and Kilmarnock–Largs.

Trains: Kilmarnock Station is well served by trains from Glasgow and the West Coast, and the station is only a 15 minute walk from the ground.

Cars: Car parking is available in the club car park. Entry **only** from Dundonald Road. Visiting supporters enter **only** from Dundonald Road Entrance.

MOTHERWELL

Motherwell Football &
Athletic Club Ltd., Fir Park,
Firpark Street, Motherwell,
ML1 2QN.

Chairman
John C. Chapman, O.B.E., A.R.A.gS
Vice-Chairman
William H. Dickie, R.I.B.A.
Director
Thomas McLean
Manager
Thomas McLean
Secretary
Alan C. Dick
Commercial Manager
John Swinburne
Telephones
Ground (0698) 261437/8/9
Fax (0698) 276333
Ticket Office (0698) 261438
Information Service 0891 121553
Commercial (0698) 261437
Club Shop 0698 261438
Club Shop
Motherwell Football & Athletic
Club, Firpark Street,
Motherwell, ML1 2QN. Open
9.30 a.m. to 4.30 p.m. Mon. to
Fri. (Open Saturdays from 10.00
a.m. to 5.00 p.m. on first team
home match days only)
Official Supporters Club
c/o Fir Park, Firpark Street,
Motherwell, ML1 2QN.

Team Captain
Chris McCart

Club Sponsor
Motorola

LIST OF PLAYERS 1993-94

Name	Date of Birth	Place of Birth	Date of Signing	Height	Weight	Previous Club
Angus, Ian Allan	19/11/61	Glasgow	03/08/90	5-10	10.3	Dundee
Arnott, Douglas	05/08/61	Lanark	29/10/86	5-7	10.7	Pollok Juniors
Burns, Alexander	04/08/73	Bellshill	06/08/91	5-8	10.0	Shotts Bon-Accord
Cooper, David	25/02/56	Hamilton	11/08/89	5-8.5	12.5	Rangers
Denholm, Greg	05/10/76	Glasgow	19/08/93	6-1	10.12	Cumbernauld United
Dolan, James	22/02/69	Salsburgh	13/06/87	5-9	10.7	Motherwell B.C.
Dykstra, Sieb	20/10/66	Kerkrade	14/08/91	6-5	14.7	Hasselt K.S.C.
Ferguson, Paul	12/03/75	Dechmont	25/08/93	5-7	9.12	Stoneyburn United
Gourlay, Archibald M.	29/06/69	Greenock	31/03/92	5-10	11.7	Newcastle United
Griffin, James	01/01/67	Hamilton	24/06/85	5-8	11.4	Fir Park B.C.
Kirk, Stephen David	03/01/63	Kirkcaldy	23/05/86	5-11	11.4	East Fife
Krivokapic, Miodrag	06/09/59	Niksic Crna Gora	10/07/93	6-1	12.6	Dundee United
Kromheer, Elroy Patrick	15/01/70	Amsterdam	14/07/92	6-2	11.0	FC Volendam
Lambert, Paul	07/08/69	Glasgow	07/09/93	5-11	9.10	St. Mirren
Martin, Brian	24/02/63	Bellshill	14/11/91	6-0	13-0	St. Mirren
McCart, Christopher	17/04/67	Motherwell	19/12/84	5-11	10.5	Fir Park B.C.
McGrillen, Paul	19/08/71	Glasgow	14/04/90	5-8	10.5	Motherwell B.C.
McKinnon, Robert	31/07/66	Glasgow	08/01/92	5-10	11.12	Hartlepool United
McMillan, Stephen	19/01/76	Edinburgh	19/08/93	5-10	11.0	Troon Juniors
McSherry, Paul	11/09/74	Glasgow	04/09/93	5-11	10.4	Cumbernauld United
O'Donnell, Philip	25/03/72	Bellshill	30/06/90	5-10	10.5	Motherwell B.C.
O'Neill, Colin	14/06/63	Belfast	23/09/88	5-8	11.4	Portadown
Philliben, John	14/03/64	Stirling	05/09/86	5-11.5	12.7	Doncaster Rovers
Ritchie, Innes	24/08/73	Edinburgh	14/08/93	6-0	12.7	Bathgate Thistle
Ross, Ian	27/08/74	Broxburn	14/08/93	5-10	10.7	Bathgate Thistle
Shannon, Robert	20/04/66	Bellshill	21/07/93	5-11	11.8	Dunfermline Athletic
Shepstone, Paul	08/11/70	Coventry	18/06/92	5-9	10.3	Blackburn Rovers
Thomson, William Marshall	10/02/58	Linwood	10/07/91	6-2	12.3	Dundee United

MILESTONES
Year of Formation: 1886
Most Capped Player: George Stevenson (12)
Most League Points in a Season:
66 (Division 1 – 1931/32)
Most League goals scored by a player in a Season: William McFadyen (52) 1931/32
Record Attendance: 35,632 v Rangers, Scottish Cup, 12/3/52
Record Victory: 12-1 v Dundee United, Division 2, 23/1/54
Record Defeat: 0-8 v Aberdeen, Premier Division, 26/3/79

CLUB FIXTURES 1993-94

Date	Opponent	Venue	Date	Opponent	Venue	Date	Opponent	Venue
Aug 4	League Cup 1		Oct 24	League Cup Final		Feb 12	Dundee United	A
Aug 7	Celtic	H	Oct 30	Kilmarnock	H	Feb 19	SFA Cup 4	
Aug 11	League Cup 2		Nov 6	Raith Rovers	A	Feb 26	Aberdeen	H
Aug 14	Dundee	A	Nov 9	St. Johnstone	H	Mar 5	Rangers	A
Aug 21	Kilmarnock	A	Nov 13	Aberdeen	A	Mar 12	Hibernian	H
Aug 25	League Cup 3		Nov 20	Dundee United	H	Mar 19	Dundee	H
Aug 28	Raith Rovers	H	Nov 27	Heart of Midlothian	A	Mar 26	Celtic	A
Sept 1	League Cup 4		Nov 30	Partick Thistle	H	Mar 30	Heart of Midlothian	A
Sept 4	St. Johnstone	A	Dec 4	Rangers	H			
Sept 11	Heart of Midlothian	H	Dec 11	Hibernian	A	Apr 2	Partick Thistle	H
Sept 18	Partick Thistle	A	Dec 18	Dundee	A	Apr 9	Dundee United	H
Sept 22	League Cup S/F		Dec 27	Celtic	H	Apr 16	Aberdeen	A
Sept 25	Dundee United	A	Jan 1	Kilmarnock	A	Apr 23	Hibernian	A
Oct 2	Aberdeen	H	Jan 8	Raith Rovers	A	Apr 26	Rangers	H
Oct 9	Hibernian	H	Jan 15	St. Johnstone	A	Apr 30	Kilmarnock	H
Oct 16	Dundee	H	Jan 22	Partick Thistle	A	May 7	Raith Rovers	A
Oct 23	Celtic	A	Jan 29	SFA Cup 3		May 14	St. Johnstone	H
			Feb 5	Heart of Midlothian	H	May 21	SFA Cup Final	

SEASON TICKET INFORMATION
Seated

Main Stand (Members)	Adult	£165
	Juvenile/OAP	£100
East Stand	Adult	£125
	Juvenile/OAP	£65
Family Section	Parent & Juvenile	£185
	Every Additional Juvenile	£20
Standing	Adult	£125
	Juvenile/OAP	£65

LEAGUE ADMISSION PRICES
Seated

Main Stand (Members)	Adult	£9
	Juvenile/OAP	£5
East Stand	Adult	£7
	Juvenile/OAP	£3.50
South Stand (Visiting Support)	Adult	£8
	Juvenile/OAP	£4
Family Section	Parent & Juvenile	£10
	Every Additional Juvenile	£1
Standing	Adult	£7
	Juvenile/OAP	£3.50

Registered Strip: Shirt - Amber with Claret Chestband and Collar, Shorts - Claret, Stockings - Amber

Change Strip: Shirt - White with Claret Diagonal Flecked Stripes and Claret Collar, Shorts - White, Stockings - White

CLUB FACTFILE 1992/93... RESULTS... APPEARANCES... SCORERS

The WELL

Small figures denote goalscorers † denotes opponent's own goal

Date	Venue	Opponents	Result	Thomson W.	Sneddon A.	McKinnon R.	Simpson N.	Kromheer E.	Nijholt L.	Kirk S.	Martin B.	Arnott D.	Angus I.	Cooper D.	Ferguson I.	McLeod J.	Gardner J.	O'Donnell P.	Shepherd A.	McCart C.	Baker P.	Dykstra S.	Griffin J.	Bryce S.	Dolan J.	Philliben J.	Courtay A.	Shepstone P.	Verheul B.	McGrillen P.	Graham A.
Aug 1	H	Dundee United	0-1	1	2	3	4	5	6	7	8	9	10	11	14																
4	H	Hibernian	1-2	1	2	3	4	5	6	10¹	8	9		11		7	14														
8	A	Celtic	1-1	1	2	3	4	5	6	7¹	8	9	12	11		14		10													
15	H	Aberdeen	2-1	1	2	3	4	5		8	6	9¹	10¹	11	7					12											
22	H	Partick Thistle	2-2	1	2	3	4	5	6		8	9¹		11	7¹			10	14												
29	A	Heart of Midlothian	0-1	1		3			5	2	14	4	9	12	11	7		10	8	6											
Sept 2	H	Rangers	1-4	1	2	3			4	12	5	9¹		8	11	7		10		6	14										
12	A	Dundee	1-2	1		3			5	2	12	4	9	8	11	7		10¹		6											
19	H	St. Johnstone	3-3			3			5	8¹	4		6	11¹		12		10			9¹	1	2	7	14						
26	A	Falkirk	0-1			3			5	8		11	12	7		10	14	6	9	1	2		4								
Oct 3	H	Airdrieonians	2-0			3	4¹		2	14¹	12		11	9	7	10		6		1			8	5							
7	A	Dundee United	1-1	8	3	4		2	7	10	9		11			6¹	14	1		12	5										
17	H	Celtic	1-3	2	3			4	7	8	9	10	11			6¹	12	1		5	14										
24	H	Heart of Midlothian	1-3			3			2	8¹	5	9	10	11			6	12	1		4			7	14						
31	A	Rangers	2-4	2	3			4		5¹		10¹	11		14		6	9	1	8	12				7						
Nov 7	H	Partick Thistle	0-2	1		3			2	8	5	7	10	11			6	9		4	14				12						
11	A	Aberdeen	0-2	2	3	4	6	12		7	9	10	11		14			1	8		5										
24	A	St. Johnstone	0-2	2	3	4			14	6	7	8	11		12		10		9	1	5										
28	H	Dundee	1-3		3			8	2	7¹		11	9				6		1		4	5	14								
Dec 1	A	Hibernian	2-2				3	14¹	2	9	8	11	7¹			10		6		1	4	5									
5	H	Falkirk	3-1				3	7¹	2¹		8	11	9			10		6		1	4	12	5						14¹		
12	H	Airdrieonians	2-0				4	14	8	3	7¹	11	12	9		10¹		6		1	2		5								
26	H	Aberdeen	0-2					2	12	3	7	11	9			10		6		1	8	4	5								
Jan 2	A	Partick Thistle	1-0		3	8		2	7	4¹	9	14	11	12				6		1		10	5								
23	A	Heart of Midlothian	0-0			3		2	12	8	9	14	11		7	10		6		1		4	5								
30	A	Celtic	1-1	3				2	12	4		6¹	11		14	10			1	7	8	5								9	
Feb 2	H	Dundee United	2-0				6	14	2	7¹	4		11		9	10			1	3	8	5								12¹	
6	H	Airdrieonians	0-0			3		2	7	4	9		11			10			1	6	8	5								14	
13	H	Hibernian	0-0			3		2	7	4	9	12	11			10			1	6	8	5								14	
20	A	Falkirk	†3-1	6	3			2	7	4		8	11	14		10			1		12¹	5								9¹	
23	H	Rangers	0-4	6	3			2	12	4			11			10			1	8	14	5							7	9	
27	A	St. Johnstone	1-1		3		6		7	4			11	12					1	2	8¹	5							9	10	
Mar 6	A	Dundee	1-1		3		6			4	12		11				7	14	1	2¹	8	5							9	10	
9	A	Dundee United	0-0	3				7	4	9	8	11				10	6		1	2	14	5							12		
20	H	Partick Thistle	2-3		3			2	7¹	4	12		11			10	6		1	8		5							9¹		
27	A	Aberdeen	0-1		3			2	7	4	9	8	11			10	6		1		14	5							12		
Apr 3	H	Celtic	2-0		3				7¹	4	9	8	11¹			10	6		1	2		5							14		
10	A	Rangers	0-1		3			12	7	4	9	8	11			10	6		1	2		5							14		
17	H	Dundee	1-2		3				8	4	7	14	11			10	6		1	2		5							9¹		
20	H	Heart of Midlothian	2-1		3			2	12	4		7	11			10¹	6		1	8	14	5							9¹		
24	A	St. Johnstone	0-0		3			2	12	4	14	7	11			10	6		1	8		5							9		
May 1	A	Hibernian	0-1		3			2	12	4	9	7	11			10	6		1	8		5							14		
8	H	Falkirk	2-1		3			2	7	4	12¹	8	11			10	6¹		1	14		5							9		
15	A	Airdrieonians	2-1		3			12	4	14	8					10¹			1	2	7	5							11	9¹	
TOTAL FULL APPEARANCES				9	16	35	12	11	31	26	43	28	25	42	11	4	1	32	2	28	5	35	24	1	15	31	1		12		4
TOTAL SUB APPEARANCES					(1)	(3)	(14)	(1)	(5)	(6)	(1)	(4)	(6)	(2)		(3)	(1)	(4)		(1)	(10)			(2)			(1)	(10)		
TOTAL GOALS SCORED					1				10	3	6	3	2	2		4		3	1		1				2				6	1

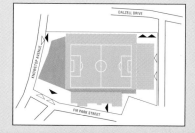

FIR PARK

Capacity 15,500 (Seated 11,500, Standing 4,000)

Pitch Dimensions 110 yds x 75 yds

Disabled Facilities Area in front of South West Enclosure. Prior arrangement must be made with the Secretary.

HOW TO GET THERE

Buses: Fir Park is less than a quarter of a mile from the main thoroughfare through the town and numerous buses serving Lanarkshire and Glasgow all pass along this road. De-bus at the Civic Centre.

Trains: Motherwell Station is a main-line station on the Glasgow–London (Euston) route, and the station is particularly well served by trains from numerous points throughout the Strathclyde Region. Motherwell station is a twenty minute walk from Fir Park, while the new station at Airbles is only fifteen minutes away.

Cars: Car Parking is only available in the many side streets around the ground. There is no major parking area close to Fir Park.

PARTICK THISTLE · 18 76

PARTICK THISTLE

Firhill Stadium, 80 Firhill Road, Glasgow, G20 7BA.

President
James R. Aitken
Chairman
James Oliver
Vice-Chairman
T. Brown McMaster
Directors
Angus MacSween;
Harry F. Scott; John Lambie;
Robert G.S. McCamley
Manager
John Lambie
Secretary
Robert W. Reid
General Manager
Jez Moxey

Telephones
Ground/Ticket Office
(041) 945 4811
Fax (041) 945 1525
Club Shop (041) 945 4811

Club Shop
c/o 90 Firhill Road, Glasgow,
G20 7AL. Open Tues-Fri
12.30-5.30pm and matchdays

Official Supporters Club
Ms Morag McHaffie,
99 Somerville Drive,
Glasgow G42 9BH.
Tel: (041) 632 3604

Team Captain
Willie Jamieson

Club Sponsor
Texstyle World

LIST OF PLAYERS 1993-94

Name	Date of Birth	Place of Birth	Date of Signing	Height	Weight	Previous Club
Britton, Gerard Joseph	20/10/70	Glasgow	05/08/92	6-1	11.0	Celtic
Budinauckas, Kevin	16/09/74	Bellshill	10/08/92	5-10	11.0	Armadale Thistle
Byrne, David Stuart	05/03/61	London	10/07/93	5-9	10.9	St. Johnstone
Cameron, Ian	24/08/66	Glasgow	30/07/92	5-9	10.4	Aberdeen
Clark, Martin John	13/10/68	Holytown	17/07/92	5-9	11.4	Mansfield Town
Craig, Albert Hughes	03/01/62	Glasgow	28/08/92	5-8	11.5	Dundee
Docherty, Stephen	18/02/76	Glasgow	25/08/93	5-8	10.10	Pollok Juniors
English, Isaac	12/11/71	Paisley	28/06/89	5-8	10.5	St. Mirren
Grant, Roderick John	16/09/66	Gloucester	14/07/93	5-11	11.0	Dunfermline Athletic
Jamieson, William George	27/04/63	Barnsley	21/09/92	5-11	12.0	Dundee
Kinnaird, Paul	11/11/66	Glasgow	02/07/93	5-8	11.11	Shrewsbury Town
Law, Robert	24/12/65	Bellshill	08/10/84	5-9.5	11.12	Stonehouse Violet
McGoldrick, Arthur	04/07/74	Glasgow	13/10/93	5-9	9.12	Campsie Black Watch
McKee, Kevin George	10/06/66	Edinburgh	10/07/93	5-8	11.11	Hamilton Academical
McKilligan, Neil	02/01/74	Falkirk	12/06/93	5-10	11.0	Southampton
Milne, Callum	27/08/65	Edinburgh	04/09/93	5-8.5	10.7	Hibernian
Murdoch, Andrew Gerard	20/07/68	Greenock	15/02/91	6-1	12.0	Celtic
Nelson, Craig Robert	28/05/71	Coatbridge	11/04/91	6-1	12.3	Cork City
O'Reilly, John Brady	10/10/74	Bellshill	31/12/90	6-0	12.5	"S" Form
Sharkey, Andrew Michael	30/11/76	Vale of Leven	13/07/93	5-11	10.2	Celtic
Shaw, George	10/02/69	Glasgow	11/06/91	5-7	10.9	St. Mirren
Smith, Thomas William	12/10/73	Glasgow	27/11/92	5-8.5	11.7	Cork City
Stirling, David Park	12/09/75	Bellshill	01/10/93	5-10	11.2	Armadale Thistle
Stirling, Jered	13/10/76	Stirling	29/09/93	6-0	11.6	St. Rochs
Taylor, Alexander	13/06/62	Baillieston	02/07/93	5-9.5	11.7	Falkirk
Tierney, Peter Grant	11/10/61	Falkirk	17/07/90	6-0.5	13.13	Dunfermline Athletic
Watson, Gregg	21/09/70	Glasgow	14/08/93	5-9.5	10.9	Aberdeen

CLUB FIXTURES 1993-94

Date	Opponent	Venue	Date	Opponent	Venue	Date	Opponent	Venue
Aug 4	League Cup 1		Oct 24	League Cup Final		Feb 5	Rangers	A
Aug 7	Hibernian	A	Oct 30	**Raith Rovers**	**H**	Feb 12	Kilmarnock	A
Aug 11	League Cup 2		Nov 6	Celtic	A	Feb 19	SFA Cup 4	
Aug 14	**Dundee United**	**H**	Nov 9	**Heart of**		Feb 26	**St. Johnstone**	**H**
Aug 21	Raith Rovers	A		**Midlothian**	**H**	Mar 5	Dundee	A
Aug 25	League Cup 3		Nov 13	St. Johnstone	A	Mar 12	**Aberdeen**	**H**
Aug 28	**Celtic**	**H**	Nov 20	**Kilmarnock**	**H**	Mar 19	Dundee United	A
Sept 1	League Cup 4		Nov 27	**Rangers**	**H**	Mar 26	**Hibernian**	**H**
Sept 4	Heart of		Nov 30	Motherwell	A	Mar 29	**Rangers**	**H**
	Midlothian	A	Dec 4	**Dundee**	**H**	Apr 2	Motherwell	A
Sept 11	Rangers	A	Dec 11	Aberdeen	A	Apr 9	**Kilmarnock**	**H**
Sept 18	**Motherwell**	**H**	Dec 18	**Dundee United**	**H**	Apr 16	St. Johnstone	A
Sept 22	League Cup S/F		Dec 27	Hibernian	A	Apr 23	Aberdeen	A
Sept 25	Kilmarnock	A	Jan 1	Raith Rovers	A	Apr 26	**Dundee**	**H**
Oct 2	**St. Johnstone**	**H**	Jan 8	**Celtic**	**H**	Apr 30	**Raith Rovers**	**H**
Oct 5	Dundee	A	Jan 15	Heart of		May 7	Celtic	A
Oct 9	**Aberdeen**	**H**		Midlothian	A	May 14	**Heart of**	
Oct 16	Dundee United	A	Jan 22	**Motherwell**	**H**		**Midlothian**	**H**
Oct 23	**Hibernian**	**H**	Jan 29	SFA Cup 3		May 21	SFA Cup Final	

MILESTONES
Year of Formation: 1876
Most Capped Player: Alan Rough (53)
Most League Points in a Season:
57 (First Division - 1991/92)
Most League goals scored by a player in a Season: Alec Hair (41) 1926/27
Record Attendance: 49,838 v Rangers, 18/2/22
Record Victory: 16-0 v Royal Albert, Scottish Cup, 17/1/31
Record Defeat: 0-10 v Queen's Park, Scottish Cup, 3/12/1881

SEASON TICKET INFORMATION

Seated	Adult	£180
	OAP	£100
	Juvenile	£60
Standing	Adult	£120
	OAP	£60
	Juvenile	£60

LEAGUE ADMISSION PRICES

Seated	Adult	£9
	OAP/Juvenile	£4
Standing	Adult	£6
	OAP/Juvenile	£3

Registered Strip:	Shirt - Red and Yellow Vertical Stripes with Black Shoulder Panel, Shorts - Black with One Red and Yellow Stripe, Stockings - Black
Change Strip:	Shirt - Black with Thin Red and Yellow Stripes, Shorts - Black with One Red and Yellow Stripe. Stockings - Black

CLUB FACTFILE 1992/93... RESULTS... APPEARANCES... SCORERS

The JAGS

Small figures denote goalscorers † denotes opponent's own goal

Date	Venue	Opponents	Result	Nelson C.	Law R.	McVicar D.	Chisholm G.	Tierney C.	Clark M.	McWalter M.	Peebles G.	McGlashan C.	Irons D.	Cameron I.	Shaw G.	Kinnaird P.	Britton G.	Farningham R.	McLaughlin P.	Craig A.	Jamieson W.	Johnston S.	Murdoch A.	English I.	Smith T.	Magee K.	Palin L.	Broddie J.	Taylor A.	McKilligan N.	Docherty S.
Aug 1	H	Airdrieonians	1-0	1	2	3	4	5	6	7	8	9	10¹	11	12	14															
5	H	Dundee United	0-1	1	2	3	4	5	6	7	8	9	10	11			12	14													
8	A	St. Johnstone	1-1	1	2	3	4	5	6		8	9¹	10	11			12	7	14												
15	A	Heart of Midlothian	1-2	1	2	3		5	4				10	11	7	14	9¹		8	6											
22	H	Motherwell	2-2	1	2	3	6	5		12	4		10	11¹	7¹			9	8												
29	H	Dundee	†6-3	1	2	3	6	5			4		10	11	7⁴			9	8		14										
Sept 5	A	Falkirk	1-0	1	2	3	6	5			4		10	11	7			9¹	8												
12	H	Rangers	1-4	1	2	3	4						10	11	7¹		6	9	8		12	5	14								
19	A	Aberdeen	0-2	1	2	3	6				4	12	10	11	7			9	8			5	14								
26	A	Celtic	2-1		2	4	14						10	6	7²	11	9	5	3	8				1							
Oct 3	H	Hibernian	2-2	1	2	3					14		10	6	7	11	9	4²	5	8	12										
10	A	Airdrieonians	2-2	1	2	3					12		10	6¹	7¹	11	9	4		8	5										
17	H	St. Johnstone	1-0	1	2	3					6		10		7	11	9	4¹		8	5										
24	A	Dundee	2-0	1	2	3					6		10	14¹	7	11	9	4		8	5¹										
31	H	Falkirk	1-2	1	2	3					14		10	6	7	11	9¹	4		8	5										
Nov 7	A	Motherwell	2-0			3			2				12	10	11	7	14	9	4	6	8¹	5¹			1						
10	H	Heart of Midlothian	1-1		8	3			2	14			10	11	7			9¹	4	6		5			1						
24	A	Aberdeen	0-7				5	2				12	6	11	7	10	9			3		4	8	1	14						
28	A	Rangers	0-3			3				7		11	10	12			14	9	2	6		5	4	1	8						
Dec 1	A	Dundee United	1-2			3							10	6		14	9¹	2	4		5	8	1	11	7						
5	H	Celtic	2-3	1	2	3							10	6	7	11	9	4²		8	5	14									
12	H	Hibernian	0-1	1	2	3					12		10	6	7	11	9	4	5	8											
19	A	Airdrieonians	1-1	1	2	3					9		10	6	7	11		4	5		8¹				14						
26	A	Heart of Midlothian	1-1	1	2	3							11	10	7			9¹	4	5	8		6		12	14					
Jan 2	H	Motherwell	0-1	1		3							11	10			7	9	2	4	8	14	6			12	5				
27	H	Dundee	2-0		2	3		5					10	6	7	11¹	9¹		4	8					1	12					
30	A	St. Johnstone	0-0		2	3		5					10	6	7	11	9		4	8			1								
Feb 2	A	Falkirk	2-4		2	3		5¹					12	10	6	7¹	11	9		4	8	14			1						
13	H	Dundee United	0-4			3		5	6		2	12		14	7		9		4	8			1					10	11		
16	H	Hibernian	0-3	1	2	3		5		11			10	6			9			8	4	14			12			7	3		
20	A	Celtic	0-0	1	2								10	6			9	8	4	7	5				12			11	3		
Mar 2	A	Aberdeen	0-1	1	2	3							14	10	6		9	8		4	5				12			7	11		
9	A	Airdrieonians	2-2	1	2	3							14	6¹	11¹	7	9	8		4	5							10			
13	A	St. Johnstone	†1-1	1	2	3							7	6	10		9	8		5	4		12		14			11			
20	A	Motherwell	3-2		2	3							10¹	6	11		9	8¹		14	5¹	4	1					7			
27	H	Heart of Midlothian	1-1			3							10	6	11	7	9	2¹			5	4	1	14				8			
Apr 3	A	Dundee	1-0			3							10	6	11¹	7			2	14	9	5	4	1	12			8			
10	H	Falkirk	0-1			3							10	6	11	7			2		5	4	1	9				8	14		
17	A	Rangers	1-3			3							10	6	11			9¹		2	4	7	5		1	12	14		8		
20	H	Aberdeen	1-3		2	3								6			9	8	4	10	5		1	11				7¹			
May 1	A	Dundee United	1-3		2	3								6	10		9¹	8	4	7	5		1						11	12	
4	H	Rangers	3-0	1	2			5¹					6	10	12		9¹	8¹	3	11	4								7		
8	H	Celtic	0-1	1	2			5					12	6	10	14	9	8	3	11	4								7		
15	A	Hibernian	1-0	1	3			5					12	6	10	7	9¹	8		4									11	2	14
TOTAL FULL APPEARANCES				27	34	38	8	16	8	7	8	12	43	38	28	14	39	35	22	26	26	11	17	3	2		5	6	8	3	
TOTAL SUB APPEARANCES					(1)				(5)	(1)	(10)		(3)	(3)	(6)	(1)	(2)	(1)	(3)	(3)	(4)		(10)		(5)			(2)	(1)	
TOTAL GOALS SCORED						2				2	2	5	10	1	12	8		1	3	1							1		

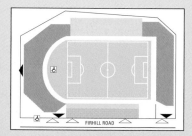

FIRHILL STADIUM
Capacity 19,243 (Seated ,813, Standing 16,430)
Pitch Dimensions
110 yds x 74 yds
Disabled Facilities
Covered Places available in North Enclosure.
0 wheelchair spectators,
0 attendants, 10 ambulant disabled. Telephone secretary in advance.

FIRHILL ROAD

HOW TO GET THERE
Trains: The nearest railway stations are Glasgow Queen Street and Glasgow Central and buses from the centre of the city pass within 100 yards of the ground.
Buses: The following buses from the city centre all pass close to the park. Nos. 1, 8, 18, 21, 21A, 57, 60, 61, 61B, 89 and 90 and the frequency of buses is just over 12 minutes.
Underground: The nearest GGPTE Underground station is St. George's Cross and supporters walking from here should pass through Cromwell Street into Maryhill Road and then walk up this road as far as Firhill Street. The ground is then on the right. The Kelvinbridge Underground Station is also not far from the park and supporters from here should walk along Great Western Road as far as Napiershall Street and then follow this into Maryhill Road.
Cars Car Parking is available at the north end of the ground.

RAITH ROVERS

Stark's Park, Pratt Street,
Kirkcaldy, Fife, KY1 1SA

Chairman
Peter J. Campsie

Vice-Chairman
William Shedden

Directors
Robert A. Paxton;
John Urquhart; Terry J. Watt

Player/Manager
James M. Nicholl

Secretary
Ms Susan Rankin

Commercial Manager
Peter Rodger

Telephones
Ground/Commercial/Club
Shop(0592) 263514
Fax (0592) 263514

Club Shop
Stark's Park, Pratt Street,
Kirkcaldy. Open during home
match days and 9.00 a.m. to
4.00 p.m. Mon. to Fri.

Official Supporters Club
c/o Fraser Hamilton, 22 Tower
Terrace, Kirkcaldy, Fife.

Team Captain
Peter Hetherston

Club Sponsor
Kelly Copiers

LIST OF PLAYERS 1993-94

Name	Date of Birth	Place of Birth	Date of Signing	Height	Weight	Previous Club
Broddle, Julian	01/11/64	Sheffield	14/07/93	5-9	12.8	Partick Thistle
Buchanan, Richard Lawson	16/11/76	Dunfermline	24/07/93	5-10	10.10	Rosyth Recreation
Buist, Mark	13/09/75	Kirkcaldy	20/07/93	6-0	11.12	Glenrothes Strollers
Cameron, Colin	23/10/72	Kirkcaldy	30/04/92	5-5.5	9.6	Sligo Rovers
Carson, Thomas	26/03/59	Alexandria	05/08/92	6-0	12.0	Dundee
Cochrane, Stewart	15/11/75	Dunfermline	18/08/93	5-9.5	11.0	Rosyth Recreation
Coyle, Ronald	04/08/64	Glasgow	08/01/88	5-11	12.9	Rochdale
Crawford, Stephen	09/01/74	Dunfermline	13/08/92	5-10	10.7	Rosyth Recreation
Dair, Jason	15/06/74	Dunfermline	03/07/91	5-11	10.8	Castlebridge
Dalziel, Gordon	16/03/62	Motherwell	25/02/87	5-10.5	10.13	East Stirlingshire
Dennis, Shaun	20/12/69	Kirkcaldy	03/08/88	6-1	13.7	Lochgelly Albert
Forrest, Gordon Iain	14/01/77	Dunfermline	21/07/93	5-6	8.2	Rosyth Recreation
Graham, Alastair	11/08/66	Glasgow	23/09/93	6-3	12.7	Motherwell
Hawke, Warren	20/09/70	Durham	03/08/93	5-10.5	11.4	Sunderland
Hetherston, Peter	06/11/64	Bellshill	17/10/91	5-9	10.7	Falkirk
Mackenzie, Alan	08/08/66	Edinburgh	16/08/91	5-8	9.2	Cowdenbeath
MacLeod, Ian Murdo	19/11/59	Glasgow	26/07/89	5-11	11.6	Falkirk
McBain, Steven John	11/10/75	Cardenden	29/09/92	5-4	8.9	Lochgelly Albert
McGeachie, George	05/02/59	Bothkennar	03/11/89	5-11.5	11.12	Dundee
McKinlay, Craig	19/10/76	Edinburgh	13/08/93	5-9.5	11.6	ICI Grangemouth
McMillan, Ian	09/06/76	Broxburn	31/03/93	5-10	11.4	Armadale Thistle
McNab, Gary	20/09/72	Dunfermline	14/08/92	6-0	11.5	Dundonald Bluebell
McStay, John	24/12/65	Larkhall	03/07/87	5-9.5	10.12	Motherwell
Mooney, Stephen	03/07/73	Vale of Leven	18/09/93	5-8	10.4	Airdrieonians
Nicholl, James Michael	20/12/56	Hamilton, Canada	27/11/90	5-10	11.10	Dunfermline Athletic
Potter, Brian	26/01/77	Dunfermline	13/08/93	5-10.5	11.4	Rosyth Recreation
Quinn, Mark	14/05/75	Broxburn	27/02/93	5-8	10.2	Strathbrock U18's
Raeside, Robert	07/07/72	South Africa	13/09/90	6-0	11.10	St. Andrews United
Robertson, Graham	02/11/76	Edinburgh	03/08/93	5-11	10.10	Balgonie Colts U16
Rowbotham, Jason	03/01/69	Cardiff	31/07/93	5-10	11.7	Plymouth Argyle
Sinclair, David	06/10/69	Dunfermline	11/02/92	5-11	12.10	Portadown
Thomson, Scott Yuill	08/11/66	Edinburgh	08/09/93	6-0	11.9	Forfar Athletic

MILESTONES
Year of Formation: 1883
Most Capped Player: David Morris (6)
Most League Points in a Season:
65 (First Division) - 1992/93
Most League goals scored by a player in a Season: Norman Heywood (42) Season 1937/38
Record Attendance: 31,306 v Hearts, Scottish Cup, 7/2/53
Record Victory: 10–1 v Coldstream, Scottish Cup, 13/2/54
Record Defeat: 2–11 v Morton, Division 2, 18/3/36

CLUB FIXTURES 1993-94

Date	Opponent	Venue	Date	Opponent	Venue	Date	Opponent	Venue
Aug 4	League Cup 1		Oct 23	St. Johnstone	A	Feb 5	**Celtic**	H
Aug 7	**St. Johnstone**	H	Oct 24	League Cup Final		Feb 12	Aberdeen	A
Aug 11	League Cup 2		Oct 30	Partick Thistle	A	Feb 19	SFA Cup 4	
Aug 14	Heart of Midlothian	A	Nov 6	**Motherwell**	H	Feb 26	**Rangers**	H
Aug 21	**Partick Thistle**	H	Nov 9	Dundee United	A	Mar 5	Hibernian	A
Aug 25	League Cup 3		Nov 13	Rangers	A	Mar 12	**Kilmarnock**	H
Aug 28	Motherwell	A	Nov 20	**Aberdeen**	H	Mar 19	**Heart of Midlothian**	H
Sept 1	League Cup 4		Nov 27	Celtic	A	Mar 26	St. Johnstone	A
Sept 4	**Dundee United**	H	Dec 1	**Dundee**	H	Mar 30	Celtic	A
Sept 11	**Celtic**	H	Dec 4	**Hibernian**	H	Apr 2	**Dundee**	H
Sept 18	Dundee	A	Dec 11	Kilmarnock	A	Apr 9	Aberdeen	A
Sept 22	League Cup S/F		Dec 18	Heart of Midlothian	A	Apr 16	Rangers	A
Sept 25	Aberdeen	A	Dec 27	**St. Johnstone**	H	Apr 23	Kilmarnock	A
Oct 2	**Rangers**	H	Jan 1	**Partick Thistle**	H	Apr 27	**Hibernian**	H
Oct 5	Hibernian	A	Jan 8	Motherwell	A	Apr 30	Partick Thistle	A
Oct 9	**Kilmarnock**	H	Jan 15	**Dundee United**	H	May 7	**Motherwell**	H
Oct 16	**Heart of Midlothian**	H	Jan 22	Dundee	A	May 14	Dundee United	A
			Jan 29	SFA Cup 3		May 21	SFA Cup Final	

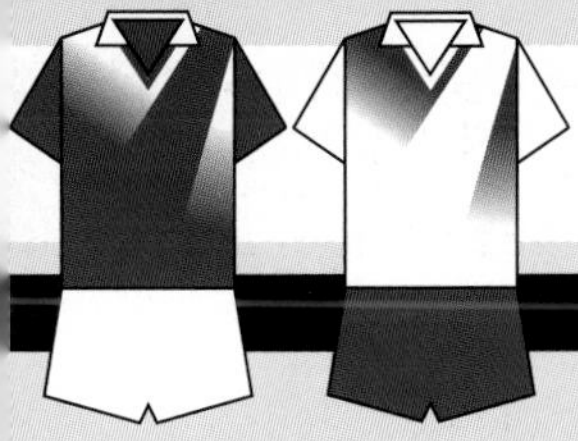

Registered Strip: Shirt - Navy Blue, Shorts - White, Stockings - Red
Change Strip: Shirt - White, Shorts - Blue, Stockings - White

CLUB FACTFILE 1992/93... RESULTS... APPEARANCES... SCORERS

The ROVERS

Date		Venue	Opponents	Result	Arthur G.	McStay J.	MacLeod I.	Coyle R.	Dennis S.	Sinclair D.	Nicholl J.	Dalziel G.	Hetherston P.	Brewster C.	Dair J.	MacKenzie A.	Thomson I.	Raeside R.	Carson T.	McGeachie G.	Williamson T.	Crawford S.	Cameron C.	Cusick J.
Aug	1	H	St. Mirren	7-0	1	2	3	4^{1}	5	6	7	8^{3}	9	10^{2}	11^{1}	12	14							
	4	H	Stirling Albion	0-0	1	2	3	4	5	6	7	8	9	10	11									
	8	A	Kilmarnock	1-1	1	2	3	4	5		7	8^{1}	9	10	11	12	14	6						
	15	H	Ayr United	1-0		2	3	4	5		6	8	9	10^{1}	11		7		1					
	22	A	Dunfermline Athletic	1-0		2	3	4	5		6	8	9	10	11	12	7^{1}		1	14				
	29	A	Dumbarton	2-1		2	3		5	14	4	8^{2}	9	10	11	12	7		1	6				
Sept	5	H	Hamilton Academical	2-1		2	3		5	14	4	8	9	10^{1}	11	12	7^{1}		1	6				
	12	H	Morton	2-1		2	3		5	12	4	8^{1}	9	10^{1}		11	7		1	6				
	19	A	Cowdenbeath	3-0		2	3		5	12	4	8^{3}	9	10		11	7		1	6				
	26	A	Meadowbank Thistle	2-0		2	3		5	12	4	8^{1}	9	10		11^{1}	7		1	6				
Oct	3	H	Clydebank	2-2		2^{1}	3		5		4	8^{1}	9	10		11	7		1	6	14			
	10	A	St. Mirren	1-1		2	3	4	5		7	8	9^{1}	10			11		1	6				
	17	H	Kilmarnock	1-1			3	4		7	2	8	9	10		12^{1}	11	5	1	6	14			
	24	A	Hamilton Academical	2-2		2	3	4		5	7	8^{1}	9	10^{1}		12	11		1	6				
	31	H	Dumbarton	4-1		2^{1}	3	4	5	12	7^{1}	8^{2}	9	10			11		1	6		14		
Nov	7	A	Ayr United	1-1		2	3	4	5	12	7	8	9	10^{1}			11		1	6		14		
	14	H	Dunfermline Athletic	1-0		2	3	4		6	7	8	9	10			14	5	1			11^{1}		
	21	H	Cowdenbeath	3-0		2	3	4		6	7	8^{2}	9^{1}	10				5	1			11		
	28	A	Morton	4-3		2	3	4		6	7	8^{2}	9^{1}	10^{1}			14	5	1			11		
Dec	1	A	Clydebank	0-3		2		4		6	7	8	9	10	14	12	3	5	1			11		
	5	H	Meadowbank Thistle	5-0		2^{1}		4		6	7^{1}	8^{1}	9	10^{1}		12^{1}	3		1	5		11		
	12	H	St. Mirren	3-1		2^{1}	14	4		5	7	8^{1}	9	10^{1}		12	3		1	6		11		
	26	H	Ayr United	1-1		2		4		6	7	8	9	10^{1}			3		1	5		11		
	29	A	Stirling Albion	3-0		2		4		6	7	8^{2}	9	10		12	3^{1}		1	5		11		
Jan	2	A	Dunfermline Athletic	0-0		2	3	4		6	7	8	9	10		12	11		1	5		14		
	26	H	Clydebank	4-2		2	3	4		5		8^{1}	9	10^{1}		12	6^{1}		1			11	7	
	30	A	Kilmarnock	0-3		2	3	4	5	6		8	9	10		12	11		1			14	7	
Feb	2	H	Hamilton Academical	1-1			2	4	5	6	7	8^{1}	9	10	11		3		1			14	12	
	6	A	Dumbarton	2-1		2	12	4	5	6	7	8^{1}	9	10^{1}		11	3		1			14		
	13	H	Stirling Albion	2-0	1		3^{1}	4	5	2		8	9	10			12			6		11^{1}	7	
	20	A	Meadowbank Thistle	1-1	1	2	3	4	5	11		8^{1}	9	10						6			7	
	27	A	Cowdenbeath	2-0	1	2	3	4	5	11		8^{1}	9	10			12			6			7^{1}	
Mar	6	H	Morton	2-0	1	2	3	4	5	11		8^{1}	9	10^{1}			12			6		14	7	
	10	A	St. Mirren	1-1	1	2	3^{1}	4	5	11	7	8	9	10						6				
	13	H	Kilmarnock	2-0	1	2	3	4	5	11	7	8^{1}	9	10^{1}		14				6			12	
	20	H	Dunfermline Athletic	2-0	1	2	3	4		5	7^{2}	8	9	10		12				6			11	
	27	A	Ayr United	0-0	1	2	3	4	5	11	7	8	9	10		12				6				
Apr	3	A	Hamilton Academical	2-2	1	2	3	4	5		7	8^{1}	9	10^{1}						6			11	
	10	H	Dumbarton	2-0	1	2	3	4	5		7	8	9	10^{2}	14			6				12	11	
	17	A	Morton	1-1	1	2	3		5		4	8	9	10^{1}	12			6				14	7	11
	24	H	Cowdenbeath	4-1	1	2			5		7	8^{2}	9^{1}	10^{1}	14		3	4		6			11	12
May	1	A	Stirling Albion	1-2	1	2		4	5^{1}		7	8	9	10	14		3			6			11	
	8	H	Meadowbank Thistle	†3-2	1	2			5		7	8	9	10^{2}	11		14	6		3		12	4	
	15	A	Clydebank	1-4		2^{1}		4	5		7	8	9	10	11	12	3		1	6			14	
TOTAL FULL APPEARANCES					17	41	34	35	31	25	38	44	44	44	10	5	26	10	27	29		10	13	1
TOTAL SUB APPEARANCES							(2)			(7)					(5)	(18)	(8)			(1)	(2)	(10)	(3)	(1)
TOTAL GOALS SCORED						5	2	1	1		4	33	4	22	1	3	4					3	1	

**Small figures denote goalscorers † denotes opponent's own goal*

STARK'S PARK

Capacity 8,159 (Seated 2,939, Standing 5,220)

Pitch Dimensions 113 yds x 69 yds.

Disabled Facilities By prior arrangement with the Secretary.

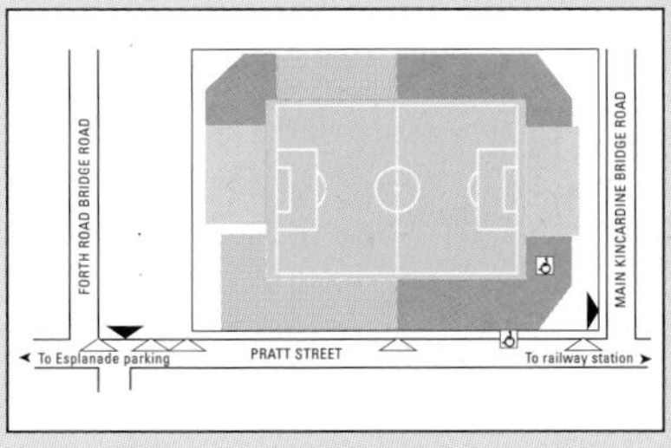

FORTH ROAD BRIDGE ROAD
MAIN KINCARDINE BRIDGE ROAD
PRATT STREET
◄ To Esplanade parking
To railway station ►

HOW TO GET THERE

Trains: Kirkcaldy railway station is served by trains from Dundee, Edinburgh and Glasgow (via Edinburgh) and the ground is within walking distance of the station.
Buses: The main bus station in Kirkcaldy is also within 15 minutes walking distance of the ground, but the Edinburgh, Dunfermline and Leven services pass close by the park.
Cars: Car parking is available in the Esplanade, which is on the south side of the ground, in Beveridge Park, which is on the north side of Stark's Road, and in ground adjacent to the railway station.

RANGERS

LIST OF PLAYERS 1993-94

Name	Date of Birth	Place of Birth	Date of Signing	Height	Weight	Previous Club
Ayton, Stuart	19/10/75	Glasgow	06/05/92	5-8	10.12	Rangers B.C.
Boyack, Steven	04/09/76	Edinburgh	01/07/93	5-10	10.7	Rangers B.C.
Brown, John	26/01/62	Stirling	15/01/88	5-11	11.2	Dundee
Cairns, Steven	06/10/76	Falkirk	01/07/93	6-2	12.2	Salveson B.C.
Caldwell, Andrew John	22/11/75	Belfast	09/09/93	5-10	11.8	Glasgow Perthshire
Caldwell, Neil	25/09/75	Glasgow	02/07/92	5-6	10.2	Rangers B.C.
Chisholm, Donald	08/11/75	Glasgow	02/07/92	6-1	11.8	West Park B.C.
Dair, Lee	28/05/77	Dunfermline	01/07/93	5-10	11.10	Rangers B.C.
Dickson, Alan	06/06/75	Paisley	14/10/91	5-10	11.6	Troon Juniors
Dodds, David	23/09/58	Dundee	01/09/89	5-11	11.5	Aberdeen
Durrant, Ian	29/10/66	Glasgow	27/07/84	5-8	9.7	Glasgow United
Ferguson, Duncan	27/12/71	Stirling	20/07/93	6-3	13.3	Dundee United
Ferguson, Ian	15/03/67	Glasgow	15/02/88	5-10	10.11	St. Mirren
Fotheringham, Kevin G.	13/08/75	Dunfermline	06/05/92	5-10	11.4	Rangers B.C.
Fraser, Mark Michael	20/02/75	Edinburgh	02/07/91	5-10	12.0	Lothian United
Galloway, Andrew	12/03/77	Glasgow	01/07/93	5-10	11.5	Rangers B.C.
Goram, Andrew Lewis	13/04/64	Bury	27/06/91	5-11	12.13	Hibernian
Gough, Charles Richard	05/04/62	Stockholm	02/10/87	6-0	11.12	Tottenham Hotspur
Hagen, David	05/05/73	Edinburgh	23/08/89	5-11	13.0	Grahamston B.C.
Hateley, Mark	07/11/61	Wallasey	19/07/90	6-2.5	13.0	A.S. Monaco
Huistra, Pieter	18/01/67	Goenga (Holland)	10/08/90	5-7	11.4	F.C. Twente Enschede
Inglis, Neil David	10/09/74	Glasgow	02/07/91	6-1	12.2	Rangers B.C.
Kerr, Roddy	04/05/77	Bellshill	09/07/93	5-8	9.7	"S" Form
Kerr, Ross H.	19/04/76	Hamilton	02/07/92	5-10	9.6	Mill United
Kouznetsov, Oleg	02/03/63	Kiev	09/10/90	6-2	12.8	Dinamo Kiev
Martin, John Paul	09/11/74	Lanark	02/07/91	5-7	10.1	Mill United
Maxwell, Alastair Espie	16/02/65	Hamilton	12/04/92	5-10	10.12	Motherwell
McCall, Stuart	10/06/64	Leeds	15/08/91	5-8	11.12	Everton
McCoist, Alistair	24/09/62	Bellshill	09/06/83	5-10	12.0	Sunderland
McCulloch, Scott A.J.	29/11/75	Irvine	02/07/92	5-11	11.12	Rangers B.C.
McGinty, Brian	10/12/76	East Kilbride	01/07/93	6-1	11.4	Rangers B.C.
McGregor, John Reid	05/01/63	Airdrie	20/03/91	5-11	12.8	Liverpool
McKnight, Paul	08/02/77	Belfast	05/08/93	5-7	11.4	St. Andrew's B.C.
McPherson, David	28/01/64	Paisley	04/06/92	6-3	11.11	Heart of Midlothian
Mikhailitchenko, Alexei	30/03/63	Kiev	05/07/91	6-2.5	13.3	UC Sampdoria SpA
Miller, Charles	18/03/76	Glasgow	02/07/92	5-9	10.8	Rangers B.C.
Moore, Craig Andrew	12/12/75	Canterbury, Australia	16/09/93	6-1	12.0	Australian Institute
Morrow, John	20/11/71	Belfast	29/07/88	5-7	10.0	Linfield
Murray, Neil	21/02/73	Bellshill	23/08/89	5-9	10.10	Rangers Amateurs F.C.
Nicholson, David	06/05/92	Coatbridge	06/05/92	5-10	10.0	Rangers B.C.
Nicholson, Iain	13/10/76	Glasgow	04/06/93	5-10	10.4	Rangers B.C.
Nisbet, Scott	30/01/68	Edinburgh	31/05/85	6-1	11.9	Salvesen B.C.
Patterson, Paul Joseph	30/07/75	Glasgow	02/07/92	5-10	9.1	Rangers B.C.
Pressley, Steven	11/10/73	Elgin	02/08/90	6-0	11.0	Inverkeithing B.C.
Rae, Derek	02/08/74	Glasgow	05/08/93	5-10	10.0	Rangers B.C.
Redpath, James	03/03/77	Belfast	05/08/93	5-10	12.3	St. Andrew's B.C.
Reid, Brian Robertson	15/06/70	Paisley	25/03/91	6-2	11.12	Greenock Morton
Robertson, Alexander	26/04/71	Edinburgh	29/02/88	5-9	10.7	"S" Form
Robertson, David	17/10/68	Aberdeen	02/07/91	5-11	11.0	Aberdeen
Robertson, Graham	17/09/76	Inverness	01/07/93	5-7	11.7	Rangers B.C.
Robertson, Joseph	12/04/77	Glasgow	01/07/93	5-8	11.5	Rangers B.C.
Robertson, Lee	25/08/73	Edinburgh	23/06/90	5-7	9.6	Salvesen B.C.
Scott, Colin	19/05/70	Glasgow	21/08/87	6-1	12.4	Dalry Thistle
Shanks, Craig	16/04/76	Coatbridge	02/07/92	6-2	11.8	Rangers B.C.
Shields, Greg	21/08/76	Falkirk	02/07/92	5-9	10.10	Rangers B.C.
Skillen, Robert	06/01/76	Belfast	15/07/92	5-6	10.2	Linfield
Steven, Trevor	21/09/63	Berwick-upon-Tweed	29/07/92	5-9	10.12	Olympique de Marseille
Stevens, Michael Gary	27/03/63	Barrow-in-Furness	19/07/88	5-11	12.7	Everton
Vinnicombe, Christopher	20/10/70	Exeter	03/11/89	5-8	10.10	Exeter City
Watson, Stephen	04/04/73	Liverpool	24/08/90	5-11	11.4	Maudsley
Wilson, Scott	19/03/77	Edinburgh	01/07/93	6-1	11.4	Rangers B.C.
Wishart, Fraser	01/03/65	Johnstone	27/07/93	5-8	10.0	Falkirk

CLUB FIXTURES 1993-94

Registered Strip:	Shirt - Royal Blue with White Shoulder Flashes and Red V-neck, Shorts - White, Stockings - Black with Red Tops
Change Strip:	Shirt - Orange and Navy Vertical Stripes, Shorts - Navy with Orange Stripes, Stockings - Navy with Three Horizontal Stripes

CLUB FACTFILE 1992/93... RESULTS... APPEARANCES... SCORERS

The GERS

Date	Venue	Opponents	Result	Goram A.	Nisbet S.	Robertson D.	Gough R.	McPherson D.	Brown J.	Durrant I.	McCall S.	McCoist A.	Hateley M.	Huistra P.	Rideout P.	Kouznetsov O.	Gordon D.	Mikhailitchenko A.	Steven T.	Maxwell A.	Ferguson I.	Spackman N.	Hagen D.	Robertson A.	Stevens G.	McSwegan G.	Pressley S.	Murray N.	Watson S.	Reid B.	Robertson L.
Aug 1	H	St. Johnstone	1-0	1	2	3	4	5	6	7	8	9^1	10	11	12	14															
4	H	Airdrieonians	2-0	1	2	3	4		6	14	8	9	10^1				5	7^1	11												
8	A	Hibernian	0-0	1	2	3	4	5	6	12	8	9	10					11	14	7											
15	A	Dundee	3-4		2	3	4	5	6	12	8	9^2	10					7	11				1	14^1							
22	A	Celtic	1-1	1		3	4	5	6	12^1	8	9	10	11				14	7												
29	H	Aberdeen	3-1	1		3	4	5		6	7^1		9^1		11			10^1			8	2									
Sept 2	A	Motherwell	4-1	1		3	4	5	6^1	7		9^3		11				10			8	2									
12	A	Partick Thistle	4-1	1		3	4^1	5^1	6	10	2^1	9	12^1	7				11			8										
19	H	Heart of Midlothian	2-0	1		3	4	5	6	10	2^1	9^1		11					7		8	14									
26	H	Dundee United	4-0	1	5	3			6		2	9^1	10	11^2			4		7^1		8	14									
Oct 3	H	Falkirk	4-0	1	2	3		5	6	12	7	9^4	10	11			4				8										
7	A	St. Johnstone	5-1	1	2	3		5		6	4	9^2	10^2	11				14	7		8^1										
17	H	Hibernian	1-0	1		3	4		6	9	12	14^1	10	11		2		5	7		8										
31	H	Motherwell	4-2	1		3		5	6^1		7	9^3		11		2	4	10			8			12							
Nov 7	A	Celtic	1-0	1		3	4	5	6	11^1	2	9	10	12			7	14			8										
11	H	Dundee	3-1	1		3		5	6	4	7	9^2	10^1	11			14				8			2							
21	H	Heart of Midlothian	1-1	1		3		5	6			9^1	10	11			4		7		8			2							
28	H	Partick Thistle	3-0	1		3		5^1	6		10			11			4		7^1		8			2	9^1						
Dec 1	A	Airdrieonians	1-1	1		3			6^1	4			10				12	11	7		8			2	9	5					
12	A	Falkirk	2-1	1		3		5	6	4	8	9^1	10^1				7	11						2							
19	H	St. Johnstone	2-0	1		3^1	4^1	5		6		8	9	10	11			7						2							
26	H	Dundee	3-1	1		3	4	5		11	6	9^1	10^2				14	7			8			2							
Jan 2	H	Celtic	1-0	1		3	4	5	6	11	2						9	14	7^1		8										
5	H	Dundee United	3-2	1		3	4	5	6		2^1	9^1	10^1	12				11	7		8										
30	A	Hibernian	4-3	1		3		5	6	12	8	9^1	10^2	14			4	11	7^1					2							
Feb 2	A	Aberdeen	1-0	1		3		5	6		8	9^1	10				4	11	7					2							
9	H	Falkirk	5-0	1		3^1	4			8		9^1	10^2	11^1		5			7^1					2							
13	H	Airdrieonians	2-2	1		3	4		6			9^2	10	11		5	14	8	7					12		2					
20	A	Dundee United	0-0	1		3	4	5			7	9	10	11					8					2		6					
23	A	Motherwell	4-0	1		3	4	5	6		2	9^1	10^2	11			12		7		8					14					
27	H	Heart of Midlothian	2-1	1	2	3^1		5	6		4	9^1	10	11			7	12			8					14					
Mar 10	A	St. Johnstone	1-1		2	3		5	6	12	8	9^1	10					11	7	1						4					
13	H	Hibernian	3-0			3		5	6	8	2	9^1	10^1				12			1		11^1				7	4				
20	A	Celtic	1-2	1	2	3		5	6	11	9	12	10^1					14	7					8			4				
27	H	Dundee	3-0			3	4	5	6		2^1	9^1	10	11			14	7	1	8^1							12				
30	H	Aberdeen	2-0	1		3	4	5	6		2	9^1	10	11			14	7		8^1							12				
Apr 10	H	Motherwell	1-0				4	5	6^1	14	2	9	10	11			7	1	8							3					
14	A	Heart of Midlothian	3-2					6	12	2^1		10^2	11			7	1	8					9	5	4	3					
17	H	Partick Thistle	3-1					6		2	10	11			7		1	8	11^1				9^2	5	4	3					
May 1	A	Airdrieonians	1-0	1		3	4	5	6		2		10	11				8					9^1	7							
4	A	Partick Thistle	0-3			4			6	8		10	11		5	7	14		1				9	2	3						
8	H	Dundee United	1-0	1		3	4	5	6	10				11^1		2	14	8	7		9	12									
12	A	Aberdeen	0-1				5	6	12				3	7	11		1	8	10	14	2				4	9					
15	A	Falkirk	2-1			3			4	8		10^1			7	11^1	1		12		9	6	2		5						
TOTAL FULL APPEARANCES				34	10	39	25	34	39	19	35	32	36	27		8	18	16	24	10	29	2	5	9	8	8	11	3	2	1
TOTAL SUB APPEARANCES										(11)	(1)	(2)	(1)	(3)	(1)	(1)	(4)	(13)		(1)		(3)	(2)		(1)		(5)			
TOTAL GOALS SCORED						3	2	2	4	3	5	34	21	4			1	3	5		4		2		4					

Small figures denote goalscorers † denotes opponent's own goal

---

IBROX STADIUM

Capacity 48,561 (Seated 41,561, Standing 7,000)
Pitch Dimensions 115 yds x 78 yds
Disabled Facilities Special area within stadium and also special toilet facilities provided. We also have a Rangers Disabled Supporters' Club. Contact: D. Currie, Secretary, Disabled Supporters' Club, c/o Ibrox Stadium, Glasgow, G51 2XD.

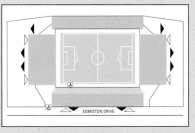

EDMISTON DRIVE

HOW TO GET THERE

Buses: The following buses all pass within 300 yards of the Stadium and can be boarded from the Glasgow city centre. Nos. 1, 4, 9A, 23, 23A, 52, 53, 53A, 54A, 54B, 89 and 91.
Underground: GGPTE Underground station is Ibrox, which is two minutes walk from the Stadium.
Cars: Motor Vehicles can head for the Stadium from the city centre by joining the M8 Motorway from Waterloo Street. Take the B768 turn-off for Govan. This will then take you to the ground. There are parking facilities available at the Albion Car Park.

ST. JOHNSTONE

McDiarmid Park, Crieff Road, Perth, PH1 2SJ.

Chairman
Geoffrey S. Brown
Directors
Douglas B. McIntyre;
Henry S. Ritchie;
David F. Sidey;
A. Stewart M. Duff.
Player/Manager
John McClelland
Secretary
A. Stewart M. Duff

Telephones
Ground (0738) 26961
Fax (0738) 25771
Ticket Office (0738) 26961
Commercial Department
(0738) 26961
Information Service
0891 121559

Club Shop
Mon-Fri Ticket Office at
Ground and Sat. Matchdays
Situated at South Stand

Official Supporters Club
c/o McDiarmid Park,
Crieff Road, Perth.

Team Captain
Andy Rhodes

Club Sponsor
The Famous Grouse

LIST OF PLAYERS 1993-94

Name	Date of Birth	Place of Birth	Date of Signing	Height	Weight	Previous Club
Anderson, Scott	23/04/75	Banff	28/08/92	6-0	11.7	Deveronvale
Budden, John Edward	17/07/71	Croydon	03/08/93	6-0	12.2	Crystal Palace
Buglione, Martin	19/06/68	London	30/03/93	6-1	11.9	Margate
Cherry, Paul Robert	14/10/64	Derby	02/07/88	6-0	11.7	Cowdenbeath
Cole, Anthony Richard	18/09/72	Gateshead	31/03/93	6-1	12.3	Middlesbrough
Curran, Henry	09/10/66	Glasgow	12/08/89	5-8	11.4	Dundee United
Davies, John	25/09/66	Glasgow	17/11/90	5-7	10.0	Clydebank
Deas, Paul Andrew	22/02/72	Perth	24/01/90	5-11	10.2	Kinnoull Jnrs
Donegan, John Francis J.	19/05/71	Cork	26/03/93	6-1	12.8	Millwall
Hamilton, Derek	09/08/76	Bellshill	22/09/93	6-0	12.1	East Kilbride Thistle
Inglis, John	16/10/66	Edinburgh	23/06/90	5-11	12.7	Meadowbank Thistle
Irons, David John	18/07/61	Glasgow	15/07/93	6-0	11.7	Partick Thistle
Maskrey, Stephen William	16/08/62	Edinburgh	12/06/87	5-6	10.0	Queen of the South
McAuley, Sean	23/06/72	Sheffield	22/04/92	6-0	11.7	Manchester United
McClelland, John	07/12/55	Belfast	15/07/92	6-2	13.9	Leeds United
McGinnis, Gary	21/10/63	Dundee	09/02/90	5-11	10.13	Dundee United
McGowne, Kevin	16/12/69	Kilmarnock	26/06/92	6-0	12.11	St. Mirren
McGuinness, Allan Kevin	07/06/76	Lanark	22/09/93	6-0	12.4	Scone Thistle
Miller, Scott	04/05/75	Glasgow	30/07/93	5-9	10.5	Possilpark YMCA
Moore, Allan	25/12/64	Glasgow	07/06/89	5-6	9.10	Heart of Midlothian
Morgan, Andrew Alan	10/12/74	Glasgow	19/11/91	5-7	10.9	Hutchison Vale B.C.
Ramsey, Paul	03/09/62	Derry	08/10/93	5-11	12.10	Cardiff City
Rhodes, Andrew Charles	23/08/64	Doncaster	02/07/92	6-1	14.0	Dunfermline Athletic
Robertson, Stephen	16/03/77	Glasgow	22/09/93	5-9	10.5	Scone Thistle
Scott, Philip Campbell	14/11/74	Perth	30/07/91	5-8	10.5	Scone Thistle
Torfason, Gudmundur	13/12/61	West Mann Islands	11/08/92	6-1	13.2	St. Mirren
Turner, Thomas Gibson	11/10/63	Johnstone	27/08/90	5-9	10.7	Greenock Morton
Wright, Paul Hamilton	17/08/67	East Kilbride	30/07/91	5-8	11.7	Hibernian
Young, Scott Robertson	05/04/77	Glasgow	22/09/93	5-8	8.10	West Park United

MILESTONES
Year of Formation: 1884
Most Capped Player: Sandy McLaren (5)
Most League Points in a Season:
59 (Second Division - 1987/88)
Most League goals scored by a player in a Season: Jimmy Benson (38) 1931/32
Record Attendance: 29,972 v Dundee, 10/2/51 (Muirton Park); 10,504 v Rangers, 30/10/90 (McDiarmid Park)
Record Victory: 8-1 v Partick Thistle, League Cup, 16/8/69
Record Defeat: 1-10 v Third Lanark, Scottish Cup, 24/1/03

CLUB FIXTURES 1993-94

Date	Opponent	Venue	Date	Opponent	Venue	Date	Opponent	Venue
Aug 4	League Cup 1		Oct 24	League Cup Final		Feb 12	**Dundee**	H
Aug 7	Raith Rovers	A	Oct 30	Dundee United	A	Feb 19	SFA Cup 4	
Aug 11	League Cup 2		Nov 6	**Aberdeen**	H	Feb 26	Partick Thistle	A
Aug 14	**Rangers**	H	Nov 9	Motherwell	A	Mar. 5	**Celtic**	H
Aug 21	**Dundee United**	H	Nov 13	**Partick Thistle**	H	Mar 12	Heart of	
Aug 25	League Cup 3		Nov 20	Dundee	A		Midlothian	A
Aug 28	Aberdeen	A	Nov 27	**Kilmarnock**	H	Mar 19	Rangers	A
Sept 1	League Cup 4		Nov 30	Hibernian	A	Mar 26	**Raith Rovers**	H
Sept 4	**Motherwell**	H	Dec 4	Celtic	A	Mar 30	**Kilmarnock**	H
Sept 11	Kilmarnock	A	Dec 11	**Heart of**		Apr 2	Hibernian	A
Sept 18	**Hibernian**	H		**Midlothian**	H	Apr 9	Dundee	A
Sept 22	League Cup S/F		Dec 18	**Rangers**	H	Apr 16	**Partick Thistle**	H
Sept 25	**Dundee**	H	Dec 27	Raith Rovers	A	Apr 23	**Heart of**	
Oct 2	Partick Thistle	A	Jan 1	**Dundee United**	H		**Midlothian**	H
Oct 6	**Celtic**	H	Jan 8	Aberdeen	A	Apr 27	Celtic	A
Oct 9	Heart of		Jan 15	**Motherwell**	H	Apr 30	Dundee United	A
	Midlothian	A	Jan 22	**Hibernian**	H	May 7	**Aberdeen**	H
Oct 16	Rangers	A	Jan 29	SFA Cup 3		May 14	Motherwell	A
Oct 23	**Raith Rovers**	H	Feb 5	Kilmarnock	A	May 21	SFA Cup Final	

SEASON TICKET INFORMATION
Seated

West Stand	Adult	£190
	Juvenile/OAP	£128
East Stand	Adult	£154
	Juvenile/OAP	£110
South Stand	Adult	£132
	Female/Juvenile/OAP	£48

LEAGUE ADMISSION PRICES
Seated

West Stand	Adult	£9
	Juvenile/OAP	£6
East Stand	Adult	£7
	Juvenile/OAP	£5
North Stand	Adult	£7
(Visitors)	Juvenile/OAP	£5
South Stand	Adult Male	£6
(Family Section)	Female/Juvenile/OAP	£2

Registered Strip:	Shirt - Royal Blue with White Trim, Shorts - White with Blue Trim, Stockings - Royal Blue with White Trim
Change Strip:	Shirt - White with Royal Blue and Yellow Trim, Shorts - Royal Blue with White and Yellow Trim, Stockings - White with Blue and Yellow Trim

The SAINTS

Date	Venue	Opponents	Result	Rhodes A.	Treanor M.	McAuley S.	Baltacha S.	Inglis J.	McClelland J.	Moore A.	Davies J.	Wright P.	McGinnis G.	Curran H.	Cherry P.	Maskrey S.	Turner T.	Redford I.	Torfason G.	McGowne K.	Arkins V.	Dunne L.	Deas P.	Scott P.	Sweeney P.	Byrne D.	Kinnaird P.	Cole A.	Buglione M.
Aug 1	A	Rangers	0-1	1	2	3	4	5	6	7	8	9	10	11	12	14													
4	A	Dundee	1-1	1	2	3	4	5	6	7	8	9	10	11^1			14	12											
8	H	Partick Thistle	1-1	1		3	2	5	6	7	12	9^1	4	11					10	8	14								
15	H	Airdrieonians	3-0	1		3	2	5	6	7		9^1	4	11^1			14			8	10^1								
22	A	Dundee United	1-2	1		3	2	5	6	7	12	9	4	11			14			8	10^1								
29	H	Hibernian	1-1	1		3	2	5	6	14		9^1	11	4			7		10	8	12								
Sept 2	A	Celtic	1-3	1	4	3	2	5	6	14		9^1	11	12			7		10	8									
12	H	Falkirk	3-2	1	12^1	3		5	6	7		9		11			14		10^1	8^1			2						
19	A	Motherwell	3-3	1		3		5	6	7^1	12	9^1	4	11^1					10	8			2						
26	H	Aberdeen	0-3	1	12	3	2	5	6	14		9	4	11			7		10	8									
Oct 3	A	Heart of Midlothian	1-1	1	2	3	4	5		14	7^1	9	6	11			12			8	10								
7	H	Rangers	1-5	1	2	3	4	5		14	7	9	6	11			12			8	10^1								
17	H	Partick Thistle	0-1	1	2	3	4	5		14	7	9	6	11						8	10								
24	A	Hibernian	1-3	1	2	3	4	5		14	7	9	6	11						8^1	10								
31	H	Celtic	0-0	1		3	4	5	6		7	9		11						8	10		2						
Nov 7	H	Dundee United	2-0	1		3	4	5	6		7	9^1		11			12			8	10^1		2						
14	A	Airdrieonians	2-0	1		3	4	5	6		7	9^2		11			12			8	10		2						
24	H	Motherwell	2-0	1		3	4	5	6	14	7	9		11^1						8	10		2						
28	A	Falkirk	2-2	1		3	4	5	6	14	7	9		11^1						8^1	10		2						
Dec 2	H	Dundee	4-4	1		3	4	5		14^1	7^1	9^2		11						8	10		2						6
5	A	Aberdeen	0-3	1		3	4	5		14	7	9		11						8	10		2						6
12	H	Heart of Midlothian	1-1	1		3	4	5		14	7	9^1		11						8	10		2						6
19	A	Rangers	0-2	1		6	4	5			7	9		11						8	10		2			3			
26	H	Airdrieonians	1-0	1		6	4	5		14	7	9		11			12			8	10^1		2			3			
Jan 2	A	Dundee United	2-1	1		3	4	5		14	7	9^1		11^1			12			8	10		2						6
20	A	Heart of Midlothian	0-2	1			4	5	6	14	7	9		11			12			8	10		2			3			
23	H	Hibernian	2-0	1			4	5	6		7	9		11						8^1	10		2			3^1			
30	H	Partick Thistle	0-0	1			4	5	6		7	9		11			12			8	10		2			3			
Feb 3	A	Celtic	1-5	1			4	5	6	14	7	9		11			12			8	10^1		2			3			
13	A	Dundee	0-1	1			4	5	6	14	7	9		11			12			8	10		2			3			
20	H	Aberdeen	0-2	1			4	5	6	14	7	9		11			12			8	10		2			3			
27	A	Motherwell	1-1	1			4	5	6	14	7	9		11^1			12			8	10		2			3			
Mar 10	H	Rangers	1-1	1			4	5	6	14	7	9^1		11			12			8	10		2			3			
13	A	Partick Thistle	1-1	1			4	5	6	14	7	9		11			12			8^1	10		2			3			
16	H	Falkirk	1-0	1			4^1	5	6	14	7	9		11						8	10		2			3			
20	H	Dundee United	1-4	1			4	5	6	14	7	9		11			12			8	10^1		2			3			
27	A	Airdrieonians	1-1	1			4^1	5	6	14	7	9		11			12			8	10		2			3			
Apr 6	A	Hibernian	2-2	1			4	5		14	7^1	9		11			12			8	10^1		2			3	6		
10	H	Celtic	1-1	1			4	5			7^1	9		11						8			2			3	6	10	
17	A	Falkirk	2-2	1			4^1	5		14	7^1	9		11						8	10		2			3		6	
24	H	Motherwell	0-0	1			4	5		12	7	9		11						8	10		2			3		6	
May 1	H	Dundee	1-1	1			4	5		12	7	9^1		11			14			8	10		2			3		6	
8	A	Aberdeen	1-1	1		12	4	5		14	7	9		11						8	10^1		2			3		6	
15	H	Heart of Midlothian	3-1	1			4^1	5	6	14	7	9^1		11						8	10^1		2			3		12	
TOTAL FULL APPEARANCES				44	7	24	25	39	25	17	33	42	26	32	12	3	25	12	9	25	24	4	25	2	2	12	2	7	6
TOTAL SUB APPEARANCES					(2)	(2)		(1)		(9)	(5)		(1)	(2)	(4)	(16)	(3)	(4)	(1)	(1)	(2)	(4)				(1)	(6)		(1)
TOTAL GOALS SCORED						1				3	4	14		8	1	2	1	2	4	1	6		2			1			2

Small figures denote goalscorers † denotes opponent's own goal

---

McDIARMID PARK

Capacity 10,721 (All Seated)

Pitch Dimensions 115 yds x 75 yds

Disabled Facilities Entrance via south end of West Stand and south end of East Stand. Visiting disabled fans should contact the club in advance.

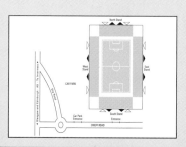

HOW TO GET THERE

Trains: Perth Station is well served by trains from all parts of the country. The station is about 40 minutes walk from the park.

Buses: Local services Nos. 1 and 2 pass near the ground. Both leave from Mill Street in the town centre.

Cars: The car park at the park holds 1,500 cars and 100 coaches. Vehicles should follow signs A9 to Inverness on Perth City by-pass, then follow "Football Stadium" signs at Inveralmond Roundabout South onto slip road adjacent to McDiarmid Park. Vehicle charges are £1.00 for cars and £5.00 for coaches.

The crowd scenes at Stark's Park said it all - Raith Rovers had clinched their first Championship in 44 years.

Two goals by hotshot Craig Brewster had been enough to beat Dumbarton, who had battled for an hour with ten men after central defender Paul Martin was red carded. The home fans swarmed on to the pitch to dance with their heroes in carnival style as Jimmy Nicholl's team were going into the Premier Division for the very first time.... and they did it with five games to spare in a new League points club record.

Raith had emerged quickly as solid front runners and stayed the course. As my racing friends would say - it was a one horse race. They were a revelation from the kick-off on the opening day of the season. An inspired 7-0 win over Jimmy Bone's St. Mirren side opened the floodgates to an impressive showing by the Kirkcaldy side throughout the remainder of the season. They were the team the others had to chase.

Jimmy Nicholl's side gained in confidence after an incredible start that saw them unbeaten in their first nineteen matches, but defeat eventually came their way by the unpredictable Clydebank, who became Raith's hoodoo side during the course of the season. The battling Bankies stopped their run with a 3-0 result on the first day of December at Kilbowie. Indeed, the Champions only beat the Bankies once in four matches, winning 4-2 at home on 26th January, 1993 and even then, they made life difficult for themselves surrendering a 2 goal lead before goals by Dalziel and Brewster eventually secured victory for the Kirkcaldy side. The other matches against the Bankies saw a share of the spoils on 3rd October, with both clubs sharing 4 goals and the final game of the season saw an inauspicious end to the Champions' League campaign losing 4-1.

RAITH RACE HOME

Raith skipper Peter Hetherston (left) and Player/Manager Jimmy Nicholl with the club's first Championship trophy in 44 years

In fact, Kilmarnock and Stirling Albion were the only other teams to win against the Stark's Park's men. Raith's strength was in midfield and up-front, but most importantly, as a team, they played as a collective unit.

Bossman Nicholl and captain Peter Hetherston were hard, productive and skilful, while Gordon Dalziel and Brewster were the deadly double act up-front. Hetherston, Dalziel and Brewster never missed a League game, while Nicholl's knee injury midway through the season kept him out of six matches. Gordon Dalziel, Dazza to his team-mates, rounded off a remarkable season with a testimonial match after a personal hat-trick of successes that went a long way to booking Raith's success. His personal roll of honour reads:

- First Division Player of the Year
- First Division Championship Medal
- Daily Record Silver Shot Award

"I'm really chuffed at getting the three, but the "Players" vote is special," said Gordon. "After all, this is a vote from my colleagues and the guys I play against. It's nice to be recognised by them, the professionals."

Raith's near-neighbours and rivals Dunfermline looked at times, to be the second Fife club to regain a place in the top division. But in a dog-fight with Kilmarnock, it was Tommy Burns' side that ultimately showed their "bottle" just at the right time.

The Pars had an horrendous final few weeks of the season, winning just five points in their last nine matches, which was just not good enough and enabled the Rugby Park side to overtake them in the final run-in. Killie however, also had their ups-and-downs, especially in those last few tense weeks, but in their last nine matches, they managed to pick up 12 points, although it was a last game decider, with both Kilmarnock and Dunfermline having a home fixture, which decided each club's fate.

Kilmarnock, a point in front, only drew 0-0 with Hamilton in a tense, nervy encounter, but it was good enough as Dunfermline stuttered once again at home and lost 2-1 to Morton. Tommy Burns declared afterwards, "This is the proudest moment of my football life. I know I've seen a lot in my time with Celtic, but this tops them all."

Nearest challengers were Jimmy Bone's St. Mirren, who gave his bright and talented youngsters a chance to mature. They take great credit for coming back so well following that horrendous defeat from Raith. Saints went 11 matches unbeaten before losing to Dumbarton at Boghead in October and remained in promotion contention until virtually the end of the season.

Iain Munro's Hamilton side flirted with the top four at various times during the season, but just didn't have it when the chips were down. However, winning the B & Q Cup for the second successive season provided ample compensation for the Douglas Park men.

Morton, Ayr United and Clydebank finished in the middle of the pack, out of the promotion scene, but clear of the relegation zone, although both the Honest Men and the Bankies flirted dangerously with the relegation dogfight for quite some time.

Meadowbank, having spent six seasons establishing themselves in the First Division, eventually succumbed to the fighting qualities of Stirling Albion, no doubt inspired by the move into their resplendent new Forthbank Stadium towards the end of the season. Dumbarton also managed to do just enough to avoid the big drop and this experience should stand them in good stead under the leadership of their new Manager, Murdo MacLeod. Unfortunately for Cowdenbeath, their stay in the middle division was short but certainly not sweet, winning a mere three games throughout the entire First Division programme.

Overall, the First Division was once again a very competitive and exciting affair with interest being maintained until the very final matches of the season.

DICK CURRIE
(Daily Record)

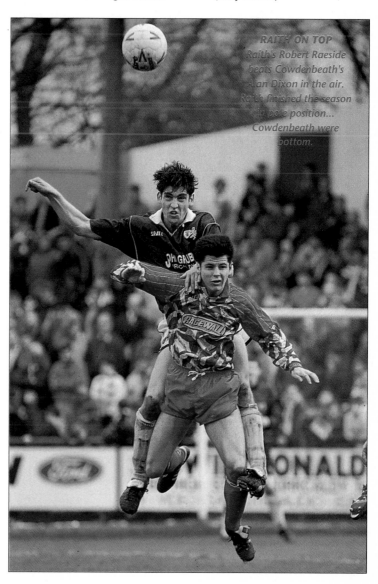

RAITH ON TOP
Raith's Robert Raeside beats Cowdenbeath's Alan Dixon in the air. Raith finished the season in pole position... Cowdenbeath were bottom.

AIRDRIEONIANS

Broomfield Park, Gartlea Road, Airdrie, ML6 9JL.

Chairman
George W. Peat, C.A.
Vice-Chairman
David W. Smith, C.ENG, M.I.C.E.
Directors
Joseph M. Rowan;
Douglas J. Watson;
Alexander P. Bryce
Manager
Alexander MacDonald
Secretary
George W. Peat, C.A.
Commercial Manager
Ally MacLeod
Telephones
Ground/Ticket Office/
Information Service
(0236) 762067
Commercial Manager
(0236) 769999
Fax (0236) 760698
Club Shop (0236) 747255

Club Shop
10 Forsyth Street, Airdrie,
ML6. Open Mon–Sat. 10.00
a.m. till 12.30 p.m. and 1.30
p.m. till 4.00 p.m.

Official Supporters Club
c/o David Johnstone, 16
Deveron Street, Coatbridge.

Team Captain
James Sandison
Club Sponsor
John C. Dalziel (Airdrie) Limited

LIST OF PLAYERS 1993-94

Name	Date of Birth	Place of Birth	Date of Signing	Height	Weight	Previous Club
Abercromby, Mark Henry	14/07/74	Glasgow	13/08/91	5-10	10.7	Eastercraigs A.F.C.
Balfour, Evan William	09/09/65	Edinburgh	12/05/89	5-11	12.6	Whitburn Juniors
Black, Kenneth George	29/11/63	Stenhousemuir	12/09/91	5-9	11.10	Portsmouth
Boyle, James	19/02/67	Glasgow	11/08/89	5-6	11.2	Queen's Park
Caesar, Gus Cassius	05/03/66	London	31/01/92	6-0	12.6	Bristol City
Davenport, Peter	24/03/61	Birkenhead	06/08/93	5-11	11.3	Sunderland
Dempsey, Samuel George	15/10/74	Bellshill	14/05/93	5-9	11.7	St. Mungo's B.C.
Ferguson, Iain John H.	04/08/62	Newarthill	14/09/93	5-9	10.7	Motherwell
Honor, Christian Robert	05/06/68	Bristol	10/08/91	5-10.5	12.2	Bristol City
Jack, Paul Dunn	15/05/65	Malaya	05/08/89	5-10	11.7	Arbroath
Kidd, Walter Joseph	10/03/58	Edinburgh	18/07/91	5-11	12.3	Heart of Midlothian
Kirkwood, David Stewart	27/08/67	St. Andrews	08/12/90	5-10	11.7	Heart of Midlothian
Lawrence, Alan	19/08/62	Edinburgh	31/03/89	5-7	10.0	Dundee
MacDonald, Nicholas John	27/11/73	Kirkintilloch	11/11/92	5-10	11.0	St. Mungo's B.C.
Martin, John Galloway King	27/10/58	Edinburgh	30/04/80	6-1	12.0	Tranent Jnrs
McCulloch, William	02/04/73	Baillieston	11/09/92	6-6	12.6	Rutherglen Glencairn
McIntyre, James	24/05/72	Alexandria	23/09/93	5-11	11.5	Bristol City
McVicar, Don Frederick	06/11/62	Perth	06/08/93	5-9	11.12	Partick Thistle
Reid, Wesley	10/09/68	London	20/03/92	5-9	11.4	Bradford City
Sandison, James William	22/06/65	Edinburgh	27/07/91	5-10.5	10.10	Heart of Midlothian
Smith, Andrew Mark	22/11/68	Aberdeen	09/08/90	6-1	12.7	Peterhead
Smith, Anthony	28/10/73	Bellshill	02/06/93	5-8	9.7	Heart of Midlothian
Stewart, Alexander	14/10/65	Bellshill	14/10/89	5-8	11.0	Kilmarnock
Tomnay, Derek Fraser	01/11/71	Glasgow	21/08/91	6-1	12.0	Heart of Midlothian
Wilson, Marvyn	01/12/73	Bellshill	22/07/92	5-7.5	10.0	Heart of Midlothian

CLUB FIXTURES 1993-94

Date	Opponent	Venue	Date	Opponent	Venue	Date	Opponent	Venue
Aug 4	League Cup 1		Oct 23	**Falkirk**	H	Jan 29	SFA Cup 3	
Aug 7	St. Mirren	A	Oct 24	League Cup Final		Feb 5	Falkirk	A
Aug 11	League Cup 2		Oct 30	Hamilton		Feb 12	**Ayr United**	H
Aug 14	**Brechin City**	H		Academical	A	Feb 19	SFA Cup 4	
Aug 21	**Hamilton**		Nov 6	**Dunfermline**		Feb 26	Dumbarton	A
	Academical	H		**Athletic**	H	Mar 5	**Stirling Albion**	H
Aug 25	League Cup 3		Nov 9	Greenock Morton	A	Mar 12	Clydebank	A
Aug 28	Dunfermline		Nov 13	Ayr United	A	Mar 19	Clyde	A
	Athletic	A	Nov 20	**Dumbarton**	H	Mar 26	**St. Mirren**	H
Sept 1	League Cup 4		Nov 27	**Clydebank**	H	Mar 29	Brechin City	A
Sept 4	**Greenock**		Dec 4	Stirling Albion	A	Apr 2	**Falkirk**	H
	Morton	H	Dec 11	Brechin City	A	Apr 9	Ayr United	A
Sept 11	Falkirk	A	Dec 18	**Clyde**	H	Apr 16	**Dumbarton**	H
Sept 14	**Clyde**	H	Dec 27	St. Mirren	A	Apr 23	Stirling Albion	A
Sept 18	**Stirling Albion**	H	Jan 1	**Hamilton**		Apr 26	**Clydebank**	H
Sept 22	League Cup S/F			**Academical**	H	Apr 30	Hamilton	
Sept 25	Clydebank	A	Jan 8	Dunfermline			Academical	A
Sept 28	Dumbarton	A		Athletic	A	May 7	**Dunfermline**	
Oct 2	**Ayr United**	H	Jan 15	**Greenock**			**Athletic**	H
Oct 9	**St. Mirren**	H		**Morton**	H	May 14	Greenock Morton	A
Oct 16	Clyde	A	Jan 22	**Brechin City**	H	May 21	SFA Cup Final	

MILESTONES
Year of Formation: 1878
Most Capped Player: Jimmy Crapnell (9)
Most League Points in a Season:
60 (Division 2) - 1973/74
Most League goals scored by a player in a Season: Hugh Baird (53) Season 1954/55
Record Attendance: 24,000 v Hearts, 8/3/52
Record Victory: 15–1 v Dundee Wanderers, Division 2, 1/12/1894
Record Defeat: 1–11 v Hibernian, Division 1, 24/10/59

SEASON TICKET INFORMATION

Seated	Adult	£125
	Juvenile/OAP	£80
Standing	Adult	£90
	Juvenile/OAP	£45

LEAGUE ADMISSION PRICES

Seated	Adult	£7
	Juvenile/OAP	£4.50
Standing	Adult	£5
	Juvenile/OAP	£2.50

Registered Strip: Shirt - White with Red Diamond, Shorts - Red, Stockings - Red
Change Strip: Shirt - Red with Black Collar, Shorts - Black, Stockings - Black

CLUB FACTFILE 1992/93... RESULTS... APPEARANCES... SCORERS

The DIAMONDS

Small figures denote goalscorers † denotes opponent's own goal

Date	Venue	Opponents	Result	Martin J.	Honor C.	Stewart A.	Jack P.	Caeser G.	Black K.	Boyle J.	Balfour E.	Lawrence A.	Coyle O.	Conn S.	Kidd W.	Reid W.	Sandison J.	Kirkwood D.	Smith A.	Wilson M.	Watson J.	Fashanu J.	Dick J.	McCulloch W.	Dempsey S.
Aug 1	A	Partick Thistle	0-1	1	2	3	4	5	6	7	8	9	10	11	12	14									
Aug 4	A	Rangers	0-2	1	2	3	11	5	6	7	8	9	10		12		4	14							
Aug 8	H	Dundee	0-0	1	2	3	11	5	6	7	8	9	10	14			4	12							
Aug 15	A	St. Johnstone	0-3	1	2	3	11	5	6	7	8	14	9				4	12							
Aug 22	H	Falkirk	2-0	1		3		5^1	6	7	8	10^1	11	9	2	14	4								
Aug 29	H	Celtic	1-1	1		3	11	5	6	7^1	8	9	10	14	2		4	12							
Sept 2	A	Aberdeen	0-0	1		3	11	5	6	7	8	9	10		2	14	4	12							
Sept 12	A	Dundee United	1-2	1	2	3		5	6	7	8	9	10	11^1			4	12							
Sept 19	A	Hibernian	2-2	1		3		5	6	7^2	8	9	10	11	2	14	4	12							
Sept 26	H	Heart of Midlothian	1-0	1		3		5	6	7	8	9	10	11^1	2	14	4	12							
Oct 3	A	Motherwell	0-2	1		3	11	5	6	7	8	9	10		2	14	4	12							
Oct 10	H	Partick Thistle	2-2	1		3		5	6	7	8	9	10	11^1	2		4^1	12							
Oct 17	H	Dundee	0-2	1		3		5	6	7	8	9	10	11	2	14	4								
Oct 24	A	Celtic	0-2	1		3		5	6	7	8	9	10	11	2	14	4								
Oct 31	H	Aberdeen	1-2	1		3		5	6	7	8^1	9	10	11	2	14	4								
Nov 7	A	Falkirk	1-5	1		3		5	6	7	8	9	10	11^1	2	14	4	12							
Nov 14	A	St. Johnstone	0-2	1	2	3		5	6	7	8	9	10	11		14	4	12							
Nov 21	H	Hibernian	2-0	1	2	3		5	6	7^1	8	9	10^1	11	12	14	4								
Nov 28	A	Dundee United	0-0	1	2	3		5	6	7	8	14	10	11	12		4								
Dec 1	H	Rangers	1-1	1	2	3		5	6	7^1	8	9	10	11		14	4	12							
Dec 5	H	Heart of Midlothian	3-1	1	2	3		5	6	7	8	9^1	10^1	11	12^1	14	4								
Dec 12	A	Motherwell	0-2	1	2	3		5	6	7	8	9	10	11	12	14	4								
Dec 19	A	Partick Thistle	1-1	1	2	3		5	6	7	8	9	10^1	11		14	4	12							
Dec 26	A	St. Johnstone	0-1	1	2	3		5	6	7	8	9	10	11		14	4	12							
Jan 2	A	Falkirk	0-1	1	2	3	11	5	6	7	8	9	10			14	4	12							
Jan 16	A	Aberdeen	0-7	1	2	3		5	6	7	8	9	10	11		14	4	12							
Jan 23	H	Celtic	0-1	1	2	3		5	6	7	8	9	10	11			4	12							
Jan 30	H	Dundee	2-2	1	2	3		5	6	7	8	9^1	10	11^1			4	12							
Feb 6	A	Motherwell	0-0	1	2	3		5	6	7	8	9	10	11	12		4								
Feb 13	A	Rangers	2-2	1	2	3			6	7	8	9	10^2	11	12		4				5	14			
Feb 20	H	Heart of Midlothian	0-0	1	2	3		5	6	7	8	9	10	11			4								
Feb 27	H	Hibernian	1-3	1	2	3		5	6^1	7	8	9	10	11	12	14	4								
Mar 6	H	Dundee United	1-3	1	2	3		5	6	7	8			11	12		4		10	14		9^1			
Mar 9	H	Partick Thistle	2-2		2	3		5^1	6	7	8			11^1	12		4		10			9	1		
Mar 13	A	Dundee	1-1	1	2	3		5	6	7				11			4		10^1		12	9			
Mar 20	H	Falkirk	1-0	1	2	3		5	6	7	8			11	12		4	14	10^1			9			
Mar 27	A	St. Johnstone	1-1	1	2	3		5	6	7	8			11^1	12		4		10			9			
Apr 6	A	Celtic	0-4	1	2	3		5	6	7	8			11			4				12	9			
Apr 10	H	Aberdeen	1-1	1	2	3		5	6	7	8			11			4		10		12	9^1			
Apr 17	A	Dundee United	0-3	1	2	3		5	6	7	8			11			4		10		14	9			
Apr 20	H	Hibernian	3-1	1	2	3^1		5	6	7	8			11	12		4	14	10			9^2			
May 1	H	Rangers	0-1	1	2	3		5	6	7	8			11	12	14	4		10			9			
May 8	A	Heart of Midlothian	1-1	1	2	3		5	6	7	8			11	14		4		10^1		12	9			
May 15	H	Motherwell	1-2	1	2	3		5	6	7	8			11			4		10			9^1			14
TOTAL FULL APPEARANCES				43	28	43	32	29	33	36	26	23	42	4	30	18	37	17	20	2	4	16	1		
TOTAL SUB APPEARANCES					(1)		(1)			(4)	(1)	(12)		(10)	(1)	(7)	(1)	(10)	(14)	(2)	(4)		(1)	(1)	
TOTAL GOALS SCORED					3		1	3	1	4	1	2	9					2	4			5			

BROOMFIELD PARK

Capacity 12,620 (Seated 1,300, standing 11,320)

Pitch Dimensions 112 yds x 67 yds

Disabled Facilities A small enclosure for disabled supporters has been erected. Visiting disabled fans should make prior arrangements with the secretary.

HOW TO GET THERE

Trains: Broomfield Park is a three-minute walk from Airdrie station. The town is well served by the electric service from Glasgow and there are usually four trains every hour from Glasgow Queen Street.

Buses: The Glasgow–Airdrie and Glasgow–Edinburgh (via Bathgate) buses run to Airdrie Bus Station, which is opposite the park.

Cars: Car Parking is available in the car park close to the ground and in the adjacent side streets.

AYR UNITED

Somerset Park, Tryfield Place,
Ayr, KA8 9NB.

Chairman
Donald McK. MacIntyre
Vice-Chairman
Donald R. Cameron
Directors
David J. Quayle, C.A.
David McKee
George H. Smith
William J. Barr
Player/Manager
George Burley
Secretary
David J. Quayle, C.A.
Assistant Secretary
Mrs Helen Nelson
Commercial Manager
Sandy Kerr

Telephones
Ground/Ticket Office
(0292) 263435
Fax (0292) 281314
Commercial/Club Shop
(0292) 280095

Club Shop
Ayr United Enterprises,
Tryfield Place, Ayr, KA8 9NB.
Open 9.00 a.m. – 3.30 p.m.
Mon–Fri and 1.00 p.m. – 3.00
p.m. on all first team match
days.

Official Supporters Club
c/o Ayr United, F.C.,
Somerset Park, Ayr, KA8 9NB

Team Captain
Malcolm Shotton

Club Sponsor
Sports Division

LIST OF PLAYERS 1993-94

Name	Date of Birth	Place of Birth	Date of Signing	Height	Weight	Previous Club
Agnew, Garry Hannah	27/01/71	Stranraer	02/08/91	5-10	12.7	Kilmarnock
Bryce, Steven	30/06/69	Shotts	23/02/93	5-8	10.7	Motherwell
Burley, George Elder	03/06/56	Cumnock	09/01/91	5-10	11.0	Motherwell
Burns, Hugh	13/12/65	Lanark	20/06/93	6-0	11.7	Kilmarnock
Carse, James	02/12/70	Barrhead	29/09/92	5-8	10.0	Annbank
Duncan, Cameron	04/08/65	Coatbridge	23/03/91	6-1	12.4	Partick Thistle
George, Duncan Henry	04/12/67	Paisley	29/03/91	5-10	10.7	Stranraer
Gribben, Kevin	30/08/75	Irvine	17/09/93	5-6	10.0	Aberdeen
Hood, Gregg	29/05/74	Bellshill	01/07/91	6.0	12.7	Ayr United B.C.
Howard, Nigel	06/10/70	Morecambe	08/11/91	6-0	13.8	Lancaster City
Jack, James Ross	21/03/59	Inverness	15/10/93	5-11	12.0	Montrose
Kennedy, David	07/10/66	Ayr	03/12/86	5-10	11.0	Minishant Amateurs
Lennox, Gary	06/12/69	Kilwinning	05/10/93	5-8	10.0	Derry City
Mair, Gordon	18/12/58	Bothwell	19/05/92	5-11	10.3	Clydebank
McClory, Ross	17/09/76	Kilwinning	03/06/93	5-11	11.1	Galston B.C.
McGivern, Samuel	09/10/63	Kilwinning	01/01/93	5-8	10.10	Falkirk
McGlashan, Colin	17/03/64	Perth	10/09/93	5-7	10.12	Partick Thistle
McQuilter, Ronald	24/12/70	Glasgow	21/07/93	6-1	12.7	Kilmarnock
Moore, Vincent	21/08/64	Scunthorpe	28/09/93	5-11	12.0	Stirling Albion
Robertson, Graeme W.T.	04/06/62	Dumfries	01/08/92	5-7	10.5	Partick Thistle
Scott, Barry	27/06/75	Irvine	01/06/93	5-7	10.10	Ayr United B.C.
Shotton, Malcolm	16/02/57	Newcastle	04/09/92	6-1	12.7	Hull City
Spence, William Waddell	20/07/66	Glasgow	07/09/92	6-2	13.7	Clydebank
Traynor, John Francis C.	10/12/66	Glasgow	07/11/91	5-10	11.0	Clydebank

MILESTONES
Year of Formation: 1910
Most Capped Player: Jim Nisbet (3)
Most League Points in a Season:
61 (Second Division - 1987/88)
**Most League goals scored by a player in a
Season:** Jimmy Smith (66) 1927/28
Record Attendance: 25,225 v Rangers, 13/9/69
Record Victory: 11-1 v Dumbarton, League Cup, 13/8/52
Record Defeat: 0-9 v Rangers, Heart of Midlothian,
Third Lanark - Division 1

CLUB FIXTURES 1993-94

Date	Opponent	Venue	Date	Opponent	Venue	Date	Opponent	Venue
Aug 4	League Cup 1		Oct 23	**Brechin City**	H	Feb 19	SFA Cup 4	
Aug 7	Clydebank	A	Oct 24	League Cup Final		Feb 26	**Greenock**	
Aug 11	League Cup 2		Oct 30	**Clyde**	H		**Morton**	H
Aug 14	**Stirling Albion**	H	Nov 6	Dumbarton	A	Mar 5	Hamilton	
Aug 21	Clyde	A	Nov 9	**St. Mirren**	H		Academical	A
Aug 25	League Cup 3		Nov 13	**Airdrieonians**	H	Mar 12	**Dunfermline**	
Aug 28	**Dumbarton**	H	Nov 20	Greenock Morton	A		**Athletic**	H
Sept 1	League Cup 4		Nov 27	Dunfermline		Mar 19	Falkirk	A
Sept 4	St. Mirren	A		Athletic	A	Mar 26	**Clydebank**	H
Sept 11	Brechin City	A	Dec 4	**Hamilton**		Mar 29	Stirling Albion	A
Sept 14	**Falkirk**	H		**Academical**	H	Apr 2	**Brechin City**	A
Sept 18	Hamilton		Dec 11	Stirling Albion	A	Apr 9	**Airdrieonians**	H
	Academical	A	Dec 18	**Falkirk**	H	Apr 16	Greenock Morton	A
Sept 22	League Cup S/F		Dec 27	Clydebank	A	Apr 23	**Hamilton**	
Sept 25	**Dunfermline**		Jan 1	Clyde	A		**Academical**	H
	Athletic	H	Jan 8	**Dumbarton**	H	Apr 27	Dunfermline	
Sept 28	**Greenock**		Jan 15	St. Mirren	A		Athletic	A
	Morton	H	Jan 22	**Stirling Albion**	H	Apr 30	**Clyde**	H
Oct 2	Airdrieonians	A	Jan 29	SFA Cup 3		May 7	Dumbarton	A
Oct 9	**Clydebank**	H	Feb 5	Brechin City	A	May 14	**St. Mirren**	H
Oct 16	Falkirk	A	Feb 12	Airdrieonians	A	May 21	SFA Cup Final	

SEASON TICKET INFORMATION
Seated
Centre Stand   Adult.....................................£135
    OAP £115
Wing Stand   Adult.....................................£115
    Juvenile/OAP......................£100
Family Stand   Adult/Juvenile £115
Standing
Ground/Enclosure   Adult.....................................£90
    Juvenile/OAP........................£50

LEAGUE ADMISSION PRICES
Seated
Main Stand   Adult...£7
Family Stand   Adult/Juvenile £7
    Each Additional Juvenile £1.50
Standing
Enclosure   Adult....................................£5.50
Ground   Adult.......................................£5
    Juvenile/OAP......................£2.50

Registered Strip:	Shirt - White with Black Sleeves and Collar, Shorts - Black with White Insert, Stockings - White with Black Top
Change Strip:	Shirt - Gold with Navy Blue Trim, Shorts - Navy Blue with Gold Insert, Stockings - Gold with Navy Blue Band

CLUB FACTFILE 1992/93... RESULTS... APPEARANCES... SCORERS

The HONEST MEN

Date	Venue	Opponents	Result	Duncan C.	Robertson G.	Agnew G.	Furphy W.	Howard N.	Kennedy D.	George D.	Walker T.	Graham A.	Gardner L.	Mair G.	McTurk A.	McLean P.	McVie G.	Traynor J.	Shaw G.	Shotton M.	Burley G.	Carse J.	Crews B.	Burke P.	McGuigan R.	Spence W.	Robertson S.	McGivern S.	Russell R.	Allan D.	Bryce S.	Scott B.	Hood G.
1	H	Dunfermline Athletic	1-1	1	2	3	4	5	6	7	8	9	10	11^{1}	12																		
4	H	Meadowbank Thistle	1-2	1	2	3^{1}	4	5		6		8	9	10	11	12	7																
8	A	Clydebank	1-1	1	6	3	4		2	10	8^{1}	9		11	12			5	7														
15	A	Raith Rovers	0-1	1	6		4	5	2	10	8	9		11				3	7	12													
22	H	Kilmarnock	2-0	1	6	3^{1}	4	5	2^{1}	10	8	9		11					7	12													
29	A	Hamilton Academical	1-1	1	6	3	4	5	2	10	8	9^{1}		14	11				7	12													
5	H	Morton	0-2	1	6	3		5	2	10	8	9		11				7	12	4													
12	H	Cowdenbeath	0-1	1	7	3			2	10	8	9		11			6		5	12	4												
19	A	Dumbarton	3-0	1	7	3		5	6		8	9^{1}		11	12^{1}			10^{1}		4	2												
26	A	St. Mirren	0-2	1	7	3		5	6			8	9	11	12			10		4	2												
3	H	Stirling Albion	2-1	1	7	3			6	10	8	9^{2}		11				5		4	2	12											
10	A	Dunfermline Athletic	3-1	1	7	3		5		6	8	9^{1}		11^{1}				10^{1}		4	2												
17	H	Clydebank	2-1	1	7	3		5		6	8	9		12^{1}	11			10^{1}		4	2			14									
24	A	Morton	1-2	1	7	3		5		6	8	9		11				10		4^{1}	2												
31	H	Hamilton Academical	0-0	1	7	3		5		6	8	9						10		4	2	12	14	14	11								
7	H	Raith Rovers	1-1	1	7			5		6	8^{1}	9		11				10		4	2		12		3								
14	A	Kilmarnock	0-3	1	7			5		6	8	9		11				3	2			12	10		14								
21	H	Dumbarton	5-3	1	7^{1}			5		6	8	9		11^{3}				14	10^{1}	4	2		3										
1	A	Stirling Albion	0-0	1	2	3		5		6	8	9		11	12			10		4			7										
5	H	St. Mirren	2-0	1	7	3		5		6	8^{1}	9^{1}		11				10^{1}		4	2												
8	A	Cowdenbeath	2-2	1	7	3		5		6	8	9^{1}		11				10^{1}		4	2			14									
12	H	Dunfermline Athletic	1-0	1	7	3		5	14	6	8	9^{1}		11				10		4	2		1										
19	A	Meadowbank Thistle	0-1	1	7			5	3	6	8	9		11				10		4	2	12				14							
26	A	Raith Rovers	1-1	1	7			5	14	6	8	9		11^{1}				10		4	2				3								
2	H	Kilmarnock	0-1	1	7			5	6		12	9		11				10		4	2					3	8						
26	H	Stirling Albion	2-2	1	12				6	7	9	11^{1}		5^{1}						4	2					3	8	10					
30	A	Clydebank	1-1	1	3			7	6	12	9	11						5		4	2						8	10^{1}					
9	H	Morton	0-0	1	3			7	6		9	11	12							4	2					14	8	10	5				
13	H	Meadowbank Thistle	1-0	1	3			7	6		9^{1}	11	10							4	2	14					8		5				
20	A	St. Mirren	0-1	1	3			7	10	6	9	11	14							4	2				12	3	8		5				
27	A	Dumbarton	0-2	1	3			7	6	8		12								4	2							9	10	5	11		
2	A	Hamilton Academical	3-1	1	3			7	6	8^{1}		12		10						4	2							5	9^{1}	11^{1}		
6	H	Cowdenbeath	3-1	1	3			12	6	8		14		10^{1}						4	2	7							9^{1}	11^{1}	5		
10	A	Dunfermline Athletic	1-1	1	3		4	10	6	8						7					2		7		1				9^{1}	11	5		
13	H	Clydebank	0-0	1	3			10	6	8				7						4	2		12					9	11	5			
20	A	Kilmarnock	1-1	1	3			7	6	8^{1}				10						4	2							9	11	5			
27	H	Raith Rovers	0-0	1	3			6		8				10						4	2	7						9	11	5			
3	A	Morton	0-1	1	3		4	6		8			7	10						4	2							9	11	5			
10	H	Hamilton Academical	1-0	1	7			6^{1}		8				3	10					4	2							9	11	5			
17	A	Cowdenbeath	1-0	1	3			6		7				4	10					2				8				9^{1}	11	5			
24	H	Dumbarton	0-0	2				7	6	12				3	10				4				1	8				9	11	5			
1	A	Meadowbank Thistle	1-0	1	3			7	6	8^{1}				10						4	2							9^{1}	11	5			
8	H	St. Mirren	†3-3	1	7			3	6	8				14	10					4	2							9	11^{1}	5^{1}			
15	A	Stirling Albion	1-1	1	3			7	6	8^{1}				10						4	2	11						9	12	5			
Apps				41	43	18	6	24	29	37	38	30	2	20	12	2	6	36	35	33	1	4	3	3	4	9	4	5	14	12	12		
Subs						(1)			(3)		(3)			(2)	(11)		(2)		(5)			(5)	(3)	(2)	(2)		(2)			(1)			
Goals					1	2			2		7	9		7	2			7		1									1	5	3	1	

SOMERSET PARK

Capacity 13,914 (Seated 1,498, Standing 12,420)

Pitch Dimensions 110 yds x 72 yds.

Disabled Facilities Enclosure and facilities for wheelchairs. Match commentary available for blind persons at first team matches.

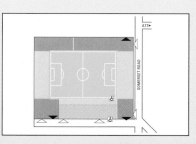

HOW TO GET THERE

Trains: There is a half hourly train service from Glasgow to either Ayr or Newton-on-Ayr. The ground is a ten minute walk from both stations.

Buses: There are several buses from the town centre with a frequency approximately every five minutes. Fans should board buses bound for Dalmilling, Whitletts or any bus passing Ayr Racecourse. The ground is only a ten minute walk from the town centre.

Cars: Car parking facilities are available at Craigie Park and at Ayr Racecourse.

BRECHIN CITY

Glebe Park, Brechin,
Angus, DD9 6BJ.

Chairman
Hugh A. Campbell Adamson
Vice-Chairman
David H. Birse
Directors
David H. Will
George C. Johnston
William C. Robertson
Martin Smith
I. Michael Holland
Honorary President
Ricardo Gallaccio
Player/Manager
Ian Redford
Secretary
George C. Johnston

Telephones
Ground (0356) 622856
Sec. Home (0356) 622942
Sec. Bus (0356) 624941
Sec. Bus. Fax (0356) 625371
Sec. Home Fax (0356) 622942

Club Shop
Glebe Park, Brechin, Angus,
DD9 6BJ. Open during home
match days.

Official Supporters Club
c/o Glebe Park, Brechin,
Angus, DD9 6BJ.

Team Captain
Bobby Brown

Club Sponsor
Stewart Milne Group

LIST OF PLAYERS 1993-94

Name	Date of Birth	Place of Birth	Date of Signing	Height	Weight	Previous Club
Alexander, Bruce	28/02/75	Dundee	10/09/93	5-10	10.8	Lochee Harp
Allan, Raymond George Kyle	05/05/55	Cowdenbeath	28/08/91	6-0	11.7	Forfar Athletic
Baillie, Richard Ketchen	06/06/68	Dunfermline	24/11/89	5-5.5	10.0	Cowdenbeath
Bell, Stuart Angus	07/02/69	Dundee	04/08/93	5-9	10.5	Dundee North End
Brand, Ralph	17/07/70	Dundee	10/08/91	5-9	10.3	Lochee United
Brown, Robert	11/11/59	Lincoln	10/01/85	5-10	11.4	Dundee North End
Cairney, Henry	01/09/61	Holytown	12/02/92	5-7	10.8	Stenhousemuir
Christie, Graeme	01/01/71	Dundee	04/08/93	6-1	11.0	Carnoustie Panmure
Conway, Francis Joseph	29/12/69	Dundee	25/11/89	5-11	11.4	Lochee Harp
Dallas, Andrew Fraser	26/08/73	Dundee	17/11/92	5-10	10.12	Dundee United "S" Form
Fisher, David John	23/08/73	Dundee	12/03/91	5-7	10.4	Lochmuir B.C.
Greig, Liam	26/09/72	Bellshill	06/10/93	5-8	10.10	Kilsyth Rangers
Hutchison, William George	22/10/72	Hong Kong	01/10/91	5-10	10.12	Jeanfield Swifts
Hutt, Graham John	29/03/61	Dunfermline	10/08/89	5-10	10.12	Cowdenbeath
Lawrie, David Ernest	09/04/65	Aberdeen	08/08/87	5-11	11.3	Aberdeen
Lees, Gordon	17/06/62	Dundee	30/07/85	5-9	10.6	Lochee United
Lorimer, Raymond	31/08/61	Glasgow	11/10/91	5-9	11.0	Forfar Athletic
McLaren, Paul	14/02/66	Bellshill	31/03/92	6-0	10.12	Berwick Rangers
McNeill, William John	12/03/67	Toronto	05/03/93	5-9	11.0	Meadowbank Thistle
Miller, Mark	10/04/69	Dundee	20/12/91	5-9	10.12	Riverside Athletic
Nicolson, Keith Derek	16/07/68	Perth	03/08/91	6-1	12.9	St. Johnstone
O'Brien, Paul Patrick	03/12/65	Glasgow	30/07/92	5-9	11.5	Dunfermline Athletic
Redford, Ian Petrie	05/04/60	Perth	05/08/93	5-11	11.9	St. Johnstone
Ross, Alexander Robert	01/08/63	Bellshill	31/12/91	6-0	9.7	Berwick Rangers
Scott, Walter Douglas	01/01/64	Dundee	28/07/83	5-9	10.7	Dundee
Vannett, Richard Alexander	20/01/73	Dundee	03/09/93	5-8	10.12	Kinnoull

CLUB FIXTURES 1993-94

Date	Opponent	Venue	Date	Opponent	Venue	Date	Opponent	Venue
Aug 4	League Cup 1		Oct 23	Ayr United	A	Feb 5	**Ayr United**	H
Aug 7	**Hamilton Academical**	H	Oct 24	League Cup Final		Feb 12	**Falkirk**	H
			Oct 30	Dunfermline Athletic	A	Feb 19	SFA Cup 4	
Aug 11	League Cup 2					Feb 26	St. Mirren	A
Aug 14	Airdrieonians	A	Nov 6	**Greenock Morton**	H	Mar 5	**Clydebank**	H
Aug 21	**Dunfermline Athletic**	H	Nov 9	Stirling Albion	A	Mar 12	Clyde	A
Aug 25	League Cup 3		Nov 13	Falkirk	A	Mar 19	**Dumbarton**	H
Aug 28	Greenock Morton	A	Nov 20	**St. Mirren**	H	Mar 26	Hamilton Academical	A
Sept 1	League Cup 4		Nov 27	**Clyde**	H			
Sept 4	**Stirling Albion**	H	Dec 4	Clydebank	A	Mar 29	**Airdrieonians**	H
Sept 11	**Ayr United**	H	Dec 11	**Airdrieonians**	H	Apr 2	Ayr United	A
Sept 14	Dumbarton	A	Dec 18	Dumbarton	A	Apr 9	Falkirk	A
Sept 18	**Clydebank**	H	Dec 27	**Hamilton Academical**	H	Apr 16	**St. Mirren**	H
Sept 22	League Cup S/F					Apr 23	Clydebank	A
Sept 25	Clyde	A	Jan 1	**Dunfermline Athletic**	H	Apr 26	**Clyde**	H
Sept 29	St. Mirren	A	Jan 8	Greenock Morton	A	Apr 30	Dunfermline Athletic	A
Oct 2	**Falkirk**	H	Jan 15	**Stirling Albion**	H			
Oct 9	Hamilton Academical	A	Jan 22	Airdrieonians	A	May 7	**Greenock Morton**	H
Oct 16	**Dumbarton**	H	Jan 29	SFA Cup 3		May 14	Stirling Albion	A
						May 21	SFA Cup Final	

MILESTONES
Year of Formation: 1906
Most League Points in a Season:
55 (Second Division) - 1982/83
Most League goals scored by a player in a Season: W. McIntosh (26) Season 1959/60
Record Attendance: 8,122 v Aberdeen, 3/2/73
Record Victory: 12-1 v Thornhill, Scottish Cup, 28/1/26
Record Defeat: 0-10 v Airdrie, Albion Rovers and Cowdenbeath, Division 2, 1937/38

SEASON TICKET INFORMATION
Seated	Adult	£100
	Parent/Juvenile (Under 12)	£110
	OAP	£55
Standing	Adult	£90
or Seated	Parent/Juvenile (Under 12)	£100
Enclosure	Juvenile	£45

LEAGUE ADMISSION PRICES
Seated	Adult	£7
	Juvenile/OAP	£4.50
Enclosure	Adult	£5
	Juvenile/OAP	£2.50
Standing	Adult	£5
	Juvenile/OAP	£2.50

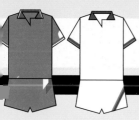

Registered Strip: Shirt - Red with Blue and White Shoulder Flashes, Shorts - Red with White Flash, Stockings - Red with Blue and White Stripes on Top

Change Strip: Shirt - White with Red and Blue Shoulder Flashes, Shorts - White with Red Flash, Stockings - White with Red and Blue Stripes at Top

The CITY

Small figures denote goalscorers   † denotes opponent's own goal

Date	Venue	Opponents	Result	Allan R.	McLaren P.	Cairney H.	Brown R.	McKillop A.	Hutt G.	Lees G.	Scott W.D.	Heggie A.	Miller M.	O'Brien P.	Lorimer R.	Ross A.	Brand R.	Thomson N.	Baillie R.	Fisher D.	Sexton P.	Conway F.	McNeill W.	Paterson I.
Aug 8	A	Arbroath	0-0	1	2	3	4	5	6	7	8	9	10	11	12	14								
15	H	Montrose	3-1	1	2	3	4	5	6[1]	7	8	9	10[1]	11	12	14[1]								
22	H	Berwick Rangers	5-1	1	2	3	4	5			8		10	11[1]	6[1]	9[1]	7[2]	14						
29	H	Albion Rovers	2-0	1	2	3	4	5			8	12[1]	10	11	6	9[1]	7	14						
Sept 5	H	Queen of the South	0-0	1	2	3	4	5			8	7	10	11	6	9	14	12						
12	A	Stranraer	1-1	1		3	4	5	6	7	8		10	11	2	9[1]	12	14						
19	H	Stenhousemuir	4-2	1	14	3	4	5	6	7[1]			10	12	11	2[1]	9[2]	8						
26	A	Alloa	2-3	1	4	3		5	6	7			10	12	11	2	9[2]	14	8					
Oct 3	H	East Stirlingshire	2-1	1	2	3	4	5			8	12	10	11	6	9	7[2]				14			
10	A	Queen's Park	2-1	1	2	3	4	5	12		8		10[2]	11	6	9	7							
17	H	East Fife	1-0	1	2	3	4	5		7	8		10[1]		6	9	12			11				
24	H	Clyde	2-1	1	2	3	4	5[1]	12		8	11	10		6	9[1]	7					14		
31	A	Forfar Athletic	1-0	1	2	3	4	5	14	12	8	11	10		6	9[1]	7							
Nov 7	H	Albion Rovers	4-1	1	2	3	4	5	12		8[1]	11	10[1]		6	9[1]	7[1]	14						
14	H	Queen of the South	3-0	1	2	3	4	5	12		8[1]	11[1]	10		6	9[1]	7	14						
21	H	Stenhousemuir	2-2	1	2	3	4	5	14		8	11[1]	10	9	6		7[1]							
28	A	Stranraer	0-0	1	2	3	4	5		7	8	12	10	11	6	9								
Dec 12	A	Arbroath	2-0	1	2	3	4	5		7	8		10		6	9[2]	11							
26	A	East Stirlingshire	0-0	1	2	3	4	5		7	8	14	10	11	6	9	12							
Jan 2	H	Montrose	2-0	1	2	3	4	5			8	12	10	11	6	9[2]	7				14			
30	H	Alloa	4-2	1	2	3	4	5	12		8		10[1]	11[1]	6	9[1]	7[1]				14			
Feb 2	H	Forfar Athletic	1-2	1	2	3	4	5	12		8		10	11	6	9[1]	7				14			
6	A	Berwick Rangers	2-0	1		3	4	5	2		8	14	10	11	6	9[2]	7							
9	A	East Fife	0-1	1		3	4	5	2		8	14	10	11	6	9	7							
13	H	Queen's Park	1-0	1		3	4	5			8	10[1]	7	14	6	9				11	2			
20	A	Arbroath	0-2	1		3	4	5			8	10	11	14	6	9	7				2	12		
23	A	Clyde	1-0	1	14	3	4	5	10	7	8	2	9	11[1]	6									
27	H	Montrose	0-0	1	10	3	4	5	8	7	12	2	9	11	6							14		
Mar 6	A	Queen of the South	2-1	1	2	3	4	5			8	7	12[1]		10	9	6						11[1]	
13	H	Stranraer	0-1	1	6	3	4	5		7	8		10		12	9					2	14	11	
20	A	Stenhousemuir	0-3	1	14	3	4	5		7	8	12	10		6	9					2	6	11	
27	H	Alloa	1-0	1		3	4	5		7			10	11	12	9[1]	6				2		8	14
Apr 3	H	Berwick Rangers	1-2	1		3	4	5		7			10	11	12[1]	9	6				2		8	14
10	H	East Stirlingshire	5-0	1	2	3	4	5	6		8		10[2]	9[1]	7	12					14		11[2]	
17	A	Queen's Park	0-1	1	2	3	4	5	6		8		10	9	7								11	
24	H	Forfar Athletic	0-1	1	2	3	4	5	6	14	8		10	9	7						12		11	
May 1	A	East Fife	2-1	1	2		4		6	14	8		10	12		9[1]	7[1]				3	5	11	
8	H	Albion Rovers	2-0	1	2	3			6	7	8		10[1]			9	12				4	5	11[1]	
15	A	Clyde	2-1	1	2	3	4		6	7	8		10[2]			9					5		11	
TOTAL FULL APPEARANCES				39	29	38	37	36	23	17	30	11	30	20	29	36	23	4	1	1		4	11	
TOTAL SUB APPEARANCES					(3)			(4)	(9)		(8)	(1)	(3)	(3)	(2)	(8)	(8)	(6)		(1)	(3)		(2)	
TOTAL GOALS SCORED								1	1	2	3	3	11	2	2	23	10					4		

GLEBE PARK

Capacity 3,960 (Seated 1,519, Standing 2,441)

Pitch Dimensions 110 yds x 67 yds.

Disabled Facilities Section of terracing designated for disabled supporters.

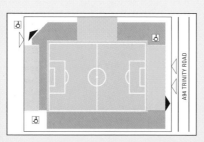

A94 TRINITY ROAD

HOW TO GET THERE

Trains: The nearest railway station is Montrose, which is eight miles away. There is a regular Inter-City service from all parts of the country and fans alighting at Montrose can then catch a connecting bus service to Brechin.

Buses: Brechin bus station is only a few hundred yards from the ground and buses on the Aberdeen–Dundee and Montrose–Edzell routes stop here.

Cars: Car parking is available in the Brechin City car park, which is capable of holding 50 vehicles. There are also a number of side streets which may be used for this purpose.

CLYDE

LIST OF PLAYERS 1993-94

Name	Date of Birth	Place of Birth	Date of Signing	Height	Weight	Previous Club
Bell, Douglas	05/09/59	Paisley	29/07/93	5-10.5	12.8	Portadown
Brown, James	21/10/74	Bellshill	09/07/93	6-0	10.0	Rangers
Clarke, Stephen	13/01/63	Coatbridge	10/07/89	5-7	11.9	Forfar Athletic
Dickson, John	23/12/69	Glasgow	07/08/92	5-5	9.7	Clydebank
Fridge, Leslie Francis	27/08/68	Inverness	11/08/93	5-11	11.10	St. Mirren
Knox, Keith	06/08/64	Stranraer	16/03/88	5-10	12.2	Stranraer
Malone, Paul	24/07/73	Bellshill	23/12/91	5-10	11.7	North Motherwell
McAulay, John	28/04/72	Glasgow	27/07/90	5-9	11.7	Clyde B.C.
McCarron, James	31/10/71	Glasgow	29/07/92	5-6	9.12	Aberdeen
McCheyne, Graeme	21/12/73	Bellshill	29/07/92	6-1	11.3	Dundee United
McConnell, Ian Paul	06/01/75	Glasgow	04/10/93	6-1	12.8	Derry City
McFarlane, Ross	06/12/61	Glasgow	30/06/83	5-8	12.0	Queen's Park
McGill, Daniel	07/07/71	Paisley	26/02/93	5-8	10.9	St. Mirren
Morrison, Stephen	15/08/61	St. Andrews	24/07/91	6-0	13.3	Dumbarton
Muir, Jack	08/02/75	Hamilton	14/10/93	5-10	10.10	Dunipace Juniors
Neill, Alan John	13/12/70	Baillieston	15/02/93	6-1	12.7	Bathgate Juniors
O'Neill, Martin	17/06/75	Glasgow	08/06/93	5-7.5	10.10	Clyde B.C.
Parks, Gordon John	19/11/72	Glasgow	18/08/92	5-9.5	10.7	Shettleston Juniors
Prunty, James	21/09/74	Bellshill	08/06/93	5-8.5	10.8	Clyde B.C.
Quinn, Kenneth	19/12/71	Glasgow	21/12/91	5-9	9.12	Possil Y.M.
Ronald, Paul	19/07/71	Glasgow	24/07/91	6.1	11.12	Campsie Black Watch
Sludden, John	29/12/64	Falkirk	29/07/93	5-10	10.10	Clydebank
Smith, James Richard	13/07/73	Stirling	18/08/92	5-5	10.9	St. Johnstone
Strain, Barry	04/08/71	Glasgow	18/08/92	5-11	12.7	Greenock Morton
Tennant, Stephen	22/10/66	Bellshill	09/08/91	5-8	11.7	Stirling Albion
Thompson, David Reid	28/05/62	Glasgow	16/01/90	6-0	13.6	Kilmarnock
Thomson, James	15/05/71	Stirling	09/08/91	6-1	12.7	Campsie Black Watch
Tierney, Paul	08/09/72	Bellshill	06/09/91	5-7	10.7	Anvil Amateurs
Wright, Andrew Matthew	21/12/73	Baillieston	11/08/93	5-9	11.0	Heart of Midlothian
Wylde, Gordon Thomas	12/11/64	Glasgow	04/08/93	5-9	12.12	Queen of the South

Douglas Park, Douglas Park Lane, Hamilton, ML3 0DF.

Chairman
John F. McBeth, F.R.I.C.S.
Directors
J. Sean Fallon; Robert B. Jack, M.A., LL.B., Harry McCall, B.A., C.ENG., M.I.C.E.
John D. Taylor A.I.B.
William B. Carmichael
Gerard W. Dunn
Honorary President
I.V. Paterson, C.B.E., D.L., J.P.
Manager
Alexander N. Smith
Secretary
John D. Taylor, A.I.B.
Commercial Manager
John Donnelly

Telephones
Ground (0698) 286103
(Match Days Only)
Office/Commercial (Monday to Friday) 041-221-7669
Fax 041-248-6193
Sec. Bus. 041-307-2078

Official Supporters Club
180 Main Street, Rutherglen.

Team Captain
Ross McFarlane

Club Sponsor
OKI

CLUB FIXTURES 1993-94

Date	Opponent	Venue	Date	Opponent	Venue	Date	Opponent	Venue
Aug 4	League Cup 1		Oct 23	Hamilton Academical	A	Feb 5	**Hamilton Academical**	H
Aug 7	**Greenock Morton**	H	Oct 24	League Cup Final		Feb 12	**Stirling Albion**	H
Aug 11	League Cup 2		Oct 30	Ayr United	A	Feb 19	SFA Cup 4	
Aug 14	Dumbarton	A	Nov 6	**Clydebank**	H	Feb 26	Falkirk	A
Aug 21	**Ayr United**	H	Nov 10	Dunfermline Athletic	A	Mar 5	St. Mirren	A
Aug 25	League Cup 3		Nov 13	Stirling Albion	A	Mar 12	**Brechin City**	H
Aug 28	Clydebank	A	Nov 20	**Falkirk**	H	Mar 19	**Airdrieonians**	H
Sept 1	League Cup 4		Nov 27	Brechin City	A	Mar 26	Greenock Morton	A
Sept 4	**Dunfermline Athletic**	H	Dec 4	**St. Mirren**	H	Mar 29	**Dumbarton**	H
Sept 11	**Hamilton Academical**	H	Dec 11	**Dumbarton**	H	Apr 2	Hamilton Academical	A
Sept 14	Airdrieonians	A	Dec 18	Airdrieonians	A	Apr 9	Stirling Albion	A
Sept 18	St. Mirren	A	Dec 27	**Greenock Morton**	H	Apr 16	**Falkirk**	H
Sept 22	League Cup S/F		Jan 1	**Ayr United**	H	Apr 23	**St. Mirren**	H
Sept 25	**Brechin City**	H	Jan 8	Clydebank	A	Apr 26	Brechin City	A
Sept 29	Falkirk	A	Jan 15	**Dunfermline Athletic**	H	Apr 30	Ayr United	A
Oct 2	**Stirling Albion**	H	Jan 22	Dumbarton	A	May 7	**Clydebank**	H
Oct 9	Greenock Morton	A	Jan 29	SFA Cup 3		May 14	Dunfermline Athletic	A
Oct 16	**Airdrieonians**	H				May 21	SFA Cup Final	

SEASON TICKET INFORMATION
Seated	Adult	£125
	Juvenile/OAP	£65
Standing	Adult	£95
	Juvenile/OAP	£45

LEAGUE ADMISSION PRICES
Seated	Adult	£6
	Juvenile/OAP	£3
Standing	Adult	£5
	Juvenile/OAP	£2.50

	Registered Strip:	Shirt - White with Black and Red Facings, Red and Black Striped Sleeves, Shorts - Black with Red and White Leg Band, Stockings - Black with Red and White Stripes
	Change Strip:	Shirt - Jade and Purple with Purple Collar, Shorts - Purple with White and Purple Leg band, Stockings - Jade

CLUB FACTFILE 1992/93... RESULTS... APPEARANCES... SCORERS

The BULLY WEE

Small figures denote goalscorers. † denotes opponent's own goal.

Player columns (left to right): Howie S., McFarlane R., Tennant S., Wylde G., Knox K., Thomson J., Thompson D., McCheyne G., McGarvey F., Clarke S., Ronald P., Quinn K., Speirs C., Morrison S., Dickson J., McCarron J., Mitchell J., Mallan S., Strain B., McAulay J., Watson E., McGill D., Neill A.

Date	Venue	Opponents	Result	Howie	McFarl.	Tennant	Wylde	Knox	Thomson	Thompson	McCheyne	McGarvey	Clarke	Ronald	Quinn	Speirs	Morrison	Dickson	McCarron	Mitchell	Mallan	Strain	McAulay	Watson	McGill	Neill
Aug 8	H	Albion Rovers	2-0	1	2	3	4	5	6	7	8	9	10[1]	11[1]	12	14										
Aug 15	A	East Stirlingshire	2-1	1	2	3	4	5	6	7	8	9[2]	10	11				12	14							
Aug 22	H	East Fife	2-2	1	2	3	4	5	6	7[1]	8	9	10	11				12[1]	14							
Aug 29	A	Alloa	5-1	1	2	3[1]	4	5	6[1]	7	8	9[1]	10[1]	11				12	14[1]							
Sept 5	H	Arbroath	2-0	1	2	3	4	5	6[1]	7	8	9	10	11				12[1]	14							
Sept 12	A	Queen's Park	6-1	1	2	3[1]	4	5	6	7[1]	8	9[1]	10[1]	11[1]				12[1]	14							
Sept 19	H	Forfar Athletic	0-0	1	2	3	4	5	6	7	8	9		11				10	12							
Sept 26	H	Stenhousemuir	0-0	1	2	3	4		6	7	8	9		11			5	10	14	12						
Oct 3	A	Queen of the South	1-3	1	2	3	14		6[1]	7	5		10	11			4	9	12	8						
Oct 10	H	Montrose	1-2	1	2			5	6	7	8	9	10		12[1]		11		14			4	3			
Oct 17	A	Stranraer	1-1	1				6	5		3	9	10[1]	7	11		4	12		8			2	14		
Oct 24	A	Brechin City	1-2	1	2			5	6		3	9	10	7	11		4	14		8			12[1]			
Oct 31	H	Berwick Rangers	2-0	1	2	3		5	6	7[1]		9	10[1]		12			14	11			4	8			
Nov 7	A	Alloa	1-1	1	2	3		5	6	7	12	9[1]	10		14				11			4	8			
Nov 14	A	Arbroath	1-1	1	2	3		5	6	7	8	9	10					14	11			4		12[1]		
Nov 21	A	Forfar Athletic	4-2	1	2	3		5		7[1]	8	9[1]	10[1]					14	6	12		4	11[1]			
Nov 28	H	Queen's Park	4-1	1	2	3		5		7[2]	8	9[2]			12			10	6			4	11		14	
Dec 12	H	Albion Rovers	2-1	1	2	3		5	6	7	8	9[1]			14			10[1]	12			4	11			
Jan 2	A	East Stirlingshire	5-1	1	2	3	5[1]	6				9[1]	8[1]		12			7	10	14			11[1]	4[1]		
Jan 16	H	Berwick Rangers	3-0	1	2	3		5	6	12	9		14[1]					8	7	10[1]		4	11[1]			
Jan 26	A	East Fife	1-1	1	2	3		5	6			9						8	7	10	12	4	11[1]	14		
Jan 30	A	Stenhousemuir	2-0	1	2	3		5	6			9[1]						8	7[1]	10	14	4	11	12		
Feb 6	H	Stranraer	0-0	1	3	2		5	6			12	9					8	7	10		4	11	14		
Feb 13	H	Montrose	2-1	1	3[1]	2		5	6	12[1]	8	9	10				14	7				4	11			
Feb 16	H	Queen of the South	2-1	1	2	3	5[1]	6	9	12	10[1]						14	7				4	11		8	
Feb 20	H	Queen's Park	2-3	1	2	3[1]	8	5	6	10[1]	9						14	7				4	11	12		
Feb 23	H	Brechin City	0-1	1	2	3		5	6	14	9	10						7	8	12		4	11			
Feb 27	A	East Fife	3-2	1	2	3		5	6		8	9[2]	4					14	10	11			12[1]		7	
Mar 6	A	Berwick Rangers	1-0	1	2	3		5	6			9[1]	10					12	4	8			11	14	7	
Mar 9	H	Arbroath	2-0	1	2	3		5	6			9						14	12	4	8		11[1]	10	7[1]	
Mar 20	A	Stranraer	1-1	1	2		3[1]	5	6	14		9	12					10	8			4	11		7	
Mar 27	A	East Stirlingshire	2-1	1	3	2	5[1]	6	14			9	12					10	8[1]			4	11		7	
Apr 3	A	Stenhousemuir	0-3	1	3	2	5			7		9	10					14	12	8		4	11			6
Apr 10	H	Montrose	2-1	1	3	2		5	6		8	9	10[2]					12	11	14		4			7	
Apr 17	H	Albion Rovers	4-0	1	3	4		5	6			9[1]	10	8			2[1]	12[1]	7[1]	14			11			
Apr 24	A	Alloa	1-1	1	3	4		5	6			9	10	7			2	12	8[1]				11	14		
May 1	A	Forfar Athletic	3-2	1	4	3		5	6			9[1]	10	8			2[1]	7	11[1]				12		14	
May 8	A	Queen of the South	3-2	1	2	3		5	6			9[1]	10[1]				4[1]	7	8				11	12	14	
May 15	H	Brechin City	1-2	1	2	3		5	6			10	8	12			4[1]	7	11				14		9	
TOTAL FULL APPEARANCES				39	31	35	17	37	36	19	19	33	26	15	6	1	15	13	24	9	1	24	20	1	7	1
TOTAL SUB APPEARANCES							(1)			(4)	(2)	(1)	(3)		(9)	(2)	(9)	(14)	(8)	(7)	(1)	(1)	(8)	(5)	(2)	
TOTAL GOALS SCORED						4	1	3	3	8		16	10	2	4		7	2	6	1			6	3	1	

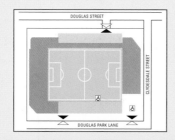

Stadium plan: DOUGLAS STREET / CLYDESDALE STREET / DOUGLAS PARK LANE

DOUGLAS PARK

Capacity 6,550 (Seated 1,580, Standing 4,970)

Pitch Dimensions 112 yds x 73 yds.

Disabled Facilities A section in front of the Presidents' Stand is reserved for disabled supporters. However, prior arrangement must be made with the Secretary.

HOW TO GET THERE

Buses: Hamilton Bus Station, which is located in Brandon Street is 10 minutes walk from the ground, and there are numerous services from all over the country which stop there.

Trains: Hamilton West Station is 100 yards from the ground and a frequent service of trains run from numerous points in the Strathclyde Region. Fans travelling from outside Strathclyde should travel to Glasgow Central Station (Low Level) and board a train from there.

Cars: Car Parking facilities exist for almost 1,000 vehicles just next to the ground (off Douglas Street). There is also a private parking area for Season Ticket holders only. Street parking around the ground is not permitted.

CLYDEBANK

Kilbowie Park, Arran Place,
Clydebank, G81 2PB.

Chairman
Charles A. Steedman
Managing Director
John S. Steedman C.B.E.
Directors
William Howat;
Ian C. Steedman, C.A.;
Colin L. Steedman, B.ACC., C.A.;
C. Graham Steedman;
James H. Heggie.
Coach
Brian Wright
Secretary
Ian C. Steedman, C.A.
Commercial Manager
David Curwood

Telephones
Ground (041) 952-2887
Commercial (041) 952-2887
Fax (041) 952 6948

Official Supporters Club
c/o Bankies Club, Kilbowie
Park, Clydebank.

Team Captain
Sean Sweeney

Club Sponsor
Wet Wet Wet

LIST OF PLAYERS 1993-94

Name	Date of Birth	Place of Birth	Date of Signing	Height	Weight	Previous Club
Crawford, Derek	18/06/74	Glasgow	05/07/93	5-8	10.0	Rangers
Crawford, Jonathen	14/10/69	Johnstone	26/04/89	6-1	12.7	Renfrew Juniors
Currie, Thomas	06/11/70	Vale of Leven	29/08/92	6-1	12.7	Shettleston Juniors
Eadie, Kenneth William	26/02/61	Paisley	16/01/88	5-10	11.8	Falkirk
Flannigan, Craig	11/02/73	Dumfries	13/03/92	5-6	10.2	Rangers
Harvey, Paul Edward	28/08/68	Glasgow	03/09/87	5-8	10.7	Manchester United
Hay, Graham Stuart	27/11/65	Falkirk	20/08/92	6-0	12.7	Stirling Albion
Henry, John	31/12/71	Vale of Leven	04/08/90	5-9	10.0	Clydebank B.C.
Jack, Stephen J.	27/03/71	Bellshill	28/05/92	5-11	10.0	Queen's Park
Lansdowne, Alan	08/04/70	Glasgow	13/06/89	5-11	11.4	Drumchapel Amateurs
Lee, Kevin Patrick	23/09/72	Glasgow	30/12/92	5-6	10.3	Kilbirnie Ladeside
Maher, John	18/12/66	Glasgow	27/06/85	5-11	11.7	Anniesland United
McIntosh, Martin	19/03/71	East Kilbride	17/08/91	6-2	12.0	St. Mirren
Monaghan, Allan	06/10/72	Glasgow	10/08/93	6-0	12.7	Rutherglen Glencairn
Murdoch, Scott McKenzie	27/02/69	Glasgow	22/10/92	5-7	10.7	St. Rochs
Nelson, Martin	09/05/67	Glasgow	10/08/93	5-7	10.4	Montrose
Smith, Shaun	13/04/71	Bangour	06/08/93	6-0	12.2	Alloa
Sweeney, Sean Brian	17/08/69	Glasgow	04/09/85	6-0	11.0	Clydebank B.C.
Thomson, Ian	24/09/65	Coatbridge	23/10/93	6-0	11.7	Raith Rovers
Treanor, Mark	01/04/62	Glasgow	03/08/93	6-0	11.0	Falkirk
Walker, John	12/12/73	Glasgow	31/07/93	5-9	11.6	Rangers
Wright, Brian Vincent	05/10/58	Glasgow	16/06/93	5-11	11.3	Queen of the South

CLUB FIXTURES 1993-94

Date	Opponent	Venue	Date	Opponent	Venue	Date	Opponent	Venue
Aug 4	League Cup 1		Oct 23	Greenock Morton	A	Feb 5	**Greenock**	
Aug 7	**Ayr United**	H	Oct 24	League Cup Final			**Morton**	H
Aug 11	League Cup 2		Oct 30	**Dumbarton**	H	Feb 12	**St. Mirren**	H
Aug 14	Dunfermline		Nov 6	Clyde	A	Feb 19	SFA Cup 4	
	Athletic	A	Nov 9	**Falkirk**	H	Feb 26	Stirling Albion	A
Aug 21	Dumbarton	A	Nov 13	St. Mirren	A	Mar 5	Brechin City	A
Aug 25	League Cup 3		Nov 20	**Stirling Albion**	H	Mar 12	**Airdrieonians**	H
Aug 28	**Clyde**	H	Nov 27	Airdrieonians	A	Mar 19	**Hamilton**	
Sept 1	League Cup 4		Dec 4	**Brechin City**	H		**Academical**	H
Sept 4	Falkirk	A	Dec 11	**Dunfermline**		Mar 26	Ayr United	A
Sept 11	**Greenock**			**Athletic**	H	Mar 29	**Dunfermline**	
	Morton	H	Dec 18	Hamilton			**Athletic**	H
Sept 15	Hamilton			Academical	A	Apr 2	Greenock Morton	A
	Academical	A	Dec 27	**Ayr United**	H	Apr 9	St. Mirren	A
Sept 18	Brechin City	A				Apr 16	**Stirling Albion**	H
Sept 22	League Cup S/F		Jan 1	Dumbarton	A	Apr 23	**Brechin City**	H
Sept 25	**Airdrieonians**	H	Jan 8	**Clyde**	H	Apr 26	Airdrieonians	A
Sept 28	Stirling Albion	A	Jan 15	Falkirk	A	Apr 30	**Dumbarton**	H
Oct 2	**St. Mirren**	H	Jan 22	Dunfermline		May 7	Clyde	A
Oct 9	Ayr United	A		Athletic	A	May 14	**Falkirk**	H
Oct 16	**Hamilton**		Jan 29	SFA Cup 3		May 21	SFA Cup Final	
	Academical	H						

Registered Strip:	Shirt - White with Black Collar and Red and Black Shoulder Flashings, Shorts - White with Red/Black Trim, Stockings - White with Red/Black Stripes
Change Strip:	Shirt - Purple with White Trim, Shorts - Purple with White Trim, Stockings - Purple with White Trim

CLUB FACTFILE 1992/93... RESULTS... APPEARANCES... SCORERS

The BANKIES

Date	Venue	Opponents	Result	Spence W.	Murray M	Crawford J.	Smith B.	Sweeney S.	McIntosh M.	Henry J.	Jack S.	Flannigan C.	Bryce T.	Henderson D.	Maher J.	Lansdowne A.	Harvey P.	Flannigan M.	Woods S.	Eadie K.	Wilson K.	Goldie P.	Hay G.	Barron D.	Currie T.	Smith L.	Murdoch S.	Brown T.	Sludden J.	Bowman G.
Aug 1	A	Cowdenbeath	3-3	1	2	3	4	5	6^1	7	8	9^1	10	11^1	12	14														
4	A	Morton	1-5	1	2	3	4	5	6			10	9	8^1	11	7	12	14												
8	H	Ayr United	1-1		2			5	3	7	6	10				14	4	8	1	9^1	11									
15	A	St. Mirren	0-0			4	12	5	3		6	10				7	14	8	1	9	11	2								
22	A	Dumbarton	0-1			4		5	3		8	10			12	14	7		1	9	11	2	6							
29	A	Dunfermline Athletic	3-1			4	12	5	3		8	11	14^1	10	2		7		1	9^2			6							
Sept 5	H	Kilmarnock	1-1		14^1			5	6		8	11	10		2	12			1	9	7		3	4						
12	A	Meadowbank Thistle	0-1		6			5			8	11	10	12	2	14	7		1	9			3	4						
19	H	Stirling Albion	4-1			12		5	6		8^1	11^1	10		2	14	7		1	9^2			3	4						
26	H	Hamilton Academical	3-1					5	6^1		8^1	11	10^1		2		7		1	9			3	4						
Oct 3	A	Raith Rovers	2-2			12		5	6		8	11	10^1		2		7		1	9^1	14		3	4						
10	H	Cowdenbeath	4-1			12		5^1	6		8^1	11	10^1		2		7		1	9^1	14		3	4						
17	H	Ayr United	1-2			12		5	6		8	11	10^1		2		7		1	9	14		3	4						
24	A	Kilmarnock	3-3			3		5	6		8	11	10^1		2	14	7^1		1	9^1				4						
31	H	Dunfermline Athletic	1-0			3		5	6		8	11	10		2	14	7^1		1	9				4						
Nov 7	A	St. Mirren	1-2			3		5	6		8^1	11	14		2		7		1	9	10			4						
14	A	Dumbarton	1-3			3		5	6		8	11	10		2	12	7		1	9	14^1			4						
21	H	Stirling Albion	1-0			12		5	3		8^1	11	10		2	14	7		1	9			6	4						
28	H	Meadowbank Thistle	0-0					5	3		8	11	10		2	14			1	9	7		6	4						
Dec 1	H	Raith Rovers	3-0					5	6^1		8^2	11	10		2		7		1	9			3	4						
8	A	Hamilton Academical	0-2					5	6		8	11	10	14	2	12	7		1	9			3	4						
12	A	Cowdenbeath	3-1			12		5	6		8	11	10^1		2	14	7^1		1	9^1			3	4						
19	H	Morton	2-2			3		5			8^1	11	10		2	12	7		1	9	14^1		6	4						
26	A	St. Mirren	2-3			3					8	11	10^1		2		7		1	9^1	14		6	4	5					
Jan 2	H	Dumbarton	3-1			12		5			8^2	11	10^1		2	14			1	9	7		3	4	6					
26	A	Raith Rovers	2-4					5	6		8	11	10^1				7		1	9	11^1		3	4	2					
30	H	Ayr United	1-1			12		5	6		8		2			14	7		1	9^1	11		3	4						
Feb 2	A	Dunfermline Athletic	0-2					5	3		8	11	10		2		7		1	9	14		6							
13	A	Morton	0-2					3	5		8	11	10		2		7		1	9			6	14	12		4			
16	A	Kilmarnock	2-0					3	5		8	12	10^1		2		7^1		1		11		6	14			4			9
20	A	Hamilton Academical	0-1					3	5		8	11	10		2		7		1	9			6	4	12		14			
27	H	Stirling Albion	1-1					3	5		8	11	10		2	14	7		1	9^1			6	4	12					
Mar 9	H	Cowdenbeath	5-0			12		5^1	3^1	6	8^1	10				14	7^1		1	9^1	11			4			2			
13	A	Ayr United	0-0		6			14	10	9					2		7		1	11	5		3	4			8			
20	A	Dumbarton	2-0					5		6	8	9	10^1		2		7		1		11	14	3^1	12			4			
27	H	St. Mirren	0-3					5		9	8	11	10		2		7		1	12	3	14	6	4						
31	H	Meadowbank Thistle	1-0					5	3		8	11	10		8	14	7		1	9^1				6	4	2				
Apr 3	A	Kilmarnock	0-6					5		6	8	10	12		2		7		1	9		3		4			11			
10	H	Dunfermline Athletic	1-1					5		8	6	10^1	11		2	14	7		1	9	12			4						3
17	H	Meadowbank Thistle	3-1					5		8	11	10^3			2	12	7		1	9			3				6		4	
24	A	Stirling Albion	3-2					5		8^1	6	10	11				7		1	9^2			3		2	12	4			
May 1	A	Morton	2-2					5		8	11	10	14		2	6	7		1	9^2			3				4			
8	A	Hamilton Academical	1-2			12		5	6		8	2	10				11		1	9^1	7		3				4			
15	H	Raith Rovers	4-1					3		6	8	2	10^3				11		1	9^1			5				4			
TOTAL FULL APPEARANCES				2	6	15	2	36	32	32	42	37	16	2	33	14	37	1	42	36	14	3	30	23	5	5	16	1	1	1
TOTAL SUB APPEARANCES					(13)				(1)	(1)	(1)	(8)	(3)	(1)	(14)		(2)	(2)		(7)	(3)			(4)		(5)			
TOTAL GOALS SCORED						1		2	4		12	21	1	1			5			20	3		1						

Small figures denote goalscorers † denotes opponent's own goal

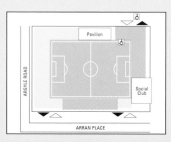

KILBOWIE PARK

Capacity 9,950 (All seated)

Pitch Dimensions 110 yds x 68 yds.

Disabled Facilities Accommodation for about eight wheelchairs by prior arrangement with Club Secretary.

(Stadium plan labels: Pavilion · ARGYLE ROAD · Social Club · ARRAN PLACE)

HOW TO GET THERE

Trains: The electric train service from Glasgow Queen Street and Glasgow Central Low Level both pass through Singer Station, which is a two minute walk from the ground.

Buses: A number of SMT buses pass down Kilbowie Road, which is two minutes walk from the ground. The buses are bound for Faifley, Duntocher and Parkhall and passengers should alight at Singer Station.

Cars: Car Parking is available in side streets adjacent to the park. The private car park in front of Kilbowie is reserved on match days for Directors, Players, Officials, Referee and certain Social Club members.

DUMBARTON

Boghead Park, Miller Street,
Dumbarton, G82 2JA

Chairman
Robert Dawson
Directors
Archibald Hagen
John A. Bell
David Wright
G. James Innes
Player/Manager
Murdo MacLeod
Secretary
Alistair Paton

Telephones
Ground (0389) 62569/67864
Sec. Bus. 041 248 2488
Fax (0389) 62629

Club Shop
Situated in ground - open on
matchdays only

Official Supporters Club
c/o Boghead Park, Miller
Street, Dumbarton

Team Captain
Murdo MacLeod

Club Sponsor
Diadora

LIST OF PLAYERS 1993-94

Name	Date of Birth	Place of Birth	Date of Signing	Height	Weight	Previous Club
Boyd, John Robertson	01/01/69	Greenock	14/11/89	6-0	11.2	Greenock Jnrs
Edgar, David	09/10/71	Paisley	11/02/91	5-8	10.7	Vale of Leven
Fabiani, Roland	24/11/71	Greenock	20/08/93	5-11	10.2	St. Mirren
Foster, Alan	10/3/71	Glasgow	20/02/91	5-8	10.8	Kilsyth Rangers
Gibson, Charles	12/06/61	Dumbarton	09/06/89	5-10	10.10	Stirling Albion
Gow, Stephen	06/12/68	Dumbarton	23/07/87	6-0	11.1	Dumbarton United
MacDonald, John	15/04/61	Glasgow	24/09/93	5-8	9.0	Airdrieonians
MacFarlane, Ian	05/12/68	Bellshill	12/07/91	6-1	12.7	Hamilton Academical
MacLeod, Murdo Davidson	24/09/58	Glasgow	07/07/93	5-9	12.4	Hibernian
Marsland, James	28/08/68	Dumbarton	15/06/90	5-8	10.12	Kilpatrick Juveniles
Martin, Paul John	08/03/65	Bellshill	30/01/91	5-11.5	11.0	Hamilton Academical
McConville, Robert	22/08/64	Bellshill	07/09/91	5-8.5	10.8	Stirling Albion
McGarvey, Martin	16/01/72	Glasgow	20/02/91	5-8	11.0	Irvine Meadow
Meechan, James	14/10/63	Alexandria	05/10/90	5-9	11.7	Irvine Meadow
Melvin, Martin	07/08/69	Glasgow	22/12/90	5-11	11.6	Falkirk
Monaghan, Michael J.	28/06/63	Glasgow	25/08/92	6-0	12.2	Hamilton Academical
Mooney, Martin James	25/09/70	Alexandria	24/09/92	5-7.5	9.11	Falkirk
Nelson, Mark	09/08/69	Bellshill	17/03/92	5-11	11.0	Stenhousemuir
Walker, Thomas	23/12/64	Glasgow	09/10/93	5-7.5	10.10	Ayr United

CLUB FIXTURES 1993-94

Date	Opponent	Venue	Date	Opponent	Venue	Date	Opponent	Venue
Aug 4	League Cup 1		Oct 24	League Cup Final		Feb 12	Dunfermline	
Aug 7	Stirling Albion	A	Oct 30	Clydebank	A		Athletic	A
Aug 11	League Cup 2		Nov 6	**Ayr United**	H	Feb 19	SFA Cup 4	
Aug 14	**Clyde**	H	Nov 10	Hamilton		Feb 26	**Airdrieonians**	H
Aug 21	**Clydebank**	H		Academical	A	Mar 5	**Falkirk**	H
Aug 25	League Cup 3		Nov 13	**Dunfermline**		Mar 12	Greenock Morton	A
Aug 28	Ayr United	A		**Athletic**	H	Mar 19	Brechin City	A
Sept 1	League Cup 4		Nov 20	Airdrieonians	A	Mar 26	**Stirling Albion**	H
Sept 4	**Hamilton**		Nov 27	**Greenock**		Mar 29	Clyde	A
	Academical	H		**Morton**	H	Apr 2	**St. Mirren**	H
Sept 11	St. Mirren	A	Dec 4	Falkirk	A	Apr 9	**Dunfermline**	
Sept 14	**Brechin City**	H	Dec 11	Clyde	A		**Athletic**	H
Sept 18	**Falkirk**	H	Dec 18	**Brechin City**	H	Apr 16	Airdrieonians	A
Sept 22	League Cup S/F		Dec 27	Stirling Albion	A	Apr 23	Falkirk	A
Sept 25	Greenock Morton	A	Jan 1	**Clydebank**	H	Apr 26	**Greenock**	
Sept 28	**Airdrieonians**	H	Jan 8	Ayr United	A		**Morton**	H
Oct 2	Dunfermline		Jan 15	**Hamilton**		Apr 30	Clydebank	A
	Athletic	A		**Academical**	H	May 7	**Ayr United**	H
Oct 9	**Stirling Albion**	H	Jan 22	**Clyde**	H	May 14	Hamilton	
Oct 16	Brechin City	A	Jan 29	SFA Cup 3			Academical	A
Oct 23	**St. Mirren**	H	Feb 5	St. Mirren	A	May 21	SFA Cup Final	

MILESTONES
Year of Formation: 1872
Most Capped Players: J. Lindsay and J. McAulay (8)
Most League Points in a Season:
53 (First Division) - 1986/87
Most League goals scored by a player in a Season: Kenneth Wilson (38) Season 1971/72
Record Attendance: 18,001 v Raith Rovers, 2/3/57
Record Victory: 13-2 v Kirkintilloch, Scottish Cup
Record Defeat: 1–11 v Ayr United and Albion Rovers

SEASON TICKET INFORMATION
Seated

Centre Stand	Adult	£150
	Juvenile/OAP	£125
Stand	Adult	£125
	Juvenile/OAP	£75
Standing	Adult	£75
	Juvenile/OAP	£35

LEAGUE ADMISSION PRICES

Seated	Adult	£7.50
	Juvenile/OAP	£5
Standing	Adult	£5
	Juvenile/OAP	£2.50

Registered Strip:	Shirt - Gold with Black Pattern and Cuffs, Shorts - Black, Stockings - Gold
Change Strip:	Shirt - White with Red and Black Trim, Shorts - Red, Stockings - White

CLUB FACTFILE 1992/93... RESULTS... APPEARANCES... SCORERS

The SONS

Date	Venue	Opponents	Result	MacFarlane I.	Gow S.	Marsland J.	Melvin M.	Martin P.	Dempsey J.	McQuade J.	Meechan J.	Gibson C.	Nelson M.	Gilmour I.	Cowell J.	Willock A.	McConville R.	Boyd J.	Wishart F.	McAnenay M.	Monaghan M.	McDonald D.	Docherty R.	McCarvey M.	Mooney M.	Foster A.	Boag J.	Furphy W.	Young J.	Speirs A.
Aug 1	H	Stirling Albion	4-3	1	2	3	4	5	6	7[2]	8	9	10[1]	11[1]		14														
4	H	Kilmarnock	1-3	1	3	2	4	5	6	7[1]	8	9	10	11	12	14														
8	A	St. Mirren	0-4	1	3	2	4	5		7	10	9	6	11	12		8	14												
15	H	Morton	0-1	1	4	14	6	5			12	8	11				10		3	2		9								
22	A	Clydebank	1-0	1	6	2	4	5	10	7[1]		9	8		12		3		11											
29	H	Raith Rovers	1-2	1	6	2	4	5		7		9[1]	8	11	14		3		10											
Sept 5	A	Cowdenbeath	1-0		6	8		5		7		9[1]	14			12	10		3	2		11			1	4				
12	A	Hamilton Academical	2-3		6	2	4	5		7		9[1]	12		14		10		3[1]			11			1	8				
19	H	Ayr United	0-3		4	2		5		7	12	9					10		3			11			1	6	8	14		
26	A	Dunfermline Athletic	2-3	1	4	2	6	5		7		9	14			12	10		3			8[1]		11[1]						
Oct 3	H	Meadowbank Thistle	3-2	1	2		4	5		7[1]	14	9	12				6		11[1]			8		10	3[1]					
10	A	Stirling Albion	2-1	1	2		4	5		7	8	12[1]	6			14	10		11			9[1]		3						
17	H	St. Mirren	4-2	1	2		4	5		7[1]	6	9[1]	8				10		11[2]			14		12	3					
24	H	Cowdenbeath	1-0	1	4	2	6	5		7[1]	8					12	10		3			11		14	9					
31	A	Raith Rovers	1-4	1	3	2	4	5[1]		7			6		14		10	12				11		8	9					
Nov 7	A	Morton	2-1	1		2	4	5		7[1]	6	9					10		3			12		8	11[1]					
14	H	Clydebank	3-1	1		2	4	5[1]		7[1]	6	9	14				10		3			12		8	11[1]					
21	A	Ayr United	3-5	1		2	4	5		7	6	9[1]					10		3			12		8	11[2]					
28	H	Hamilton Academical	2-2	1		2	4	5		7[1]	8	9							3			12		10	11[1]		6			
Dec 1	H	Meadowbank Thistle	0-1	1	6	2	4	5		7	10	12				14			3			11		8	9					
5	A	Dunfermline Athletic	0-1	1	2		4	5		7		9	14				10		3			12		8	11		6			
12	H	Stirling Albion	0-3	1	3	2	4	5		7	12	9				14	10					8		11			6			
19	A	Kilmarnock	0-1	1	6		4	5		7	8	9				12			3			10		11	14					2
26	H	Morton	3-1	1	6		4	5		7[1]	8[1]	9				14			3[1]			12		10	11					
Jan 2	A	Clydebank	1-3	1	6		4	5		7	8	9				14			3[1]			12	1	10	11					
27	A	Meadowbank Thistle	3-3	1	6[1]	2	4	5		7	8	9							3			14		12	11[1]				10[1]	
30	A	St. Mirren	1-2	1	6	2	4	5			9[1]	14							3	7		8	12	11					10	
Feb 6	H	Raith Rovers	1-2	1		2	4	5			12	9				14	3		7		10	11[1]	8			6				
13	H	Kilmarnock	1-0	1	4	2	6	5			8	9					3		7		11	14	12[1]	10						
20	A	Dunfermline Athletic	2-2	1	4	2	6	5		14	10	9					3		11[1]		7	12	8[1]							
23	A	Cowdenbeath	2-0	1	4	2	6	5		7[1]	14	9					3		11[1]		8	12	10							
27	H	Ayr United	2-0	1	4	2	6	5		7	14	12					3[1]		11		8	9[1]	10							
Mar 6	H	Hamilton Academical	1-1	1	4	2	6	5		7[1]	14	9					3		11		12	10	8							
9	A	Stirling Albion	0-1	1	4		6	5		7	8	9					3		11		10	12	14						2	
13	H	St. Mirren	2-1	1	4	2	6	5		7[1]	8	12					3[1]		9		14	11	10							
20	H	Clydebank	0-2	1		2	4	5		7	8	12					3		9		10	11	6	14						
27	A	Morton	1-2	1	6	2	4			7	8	9					3		11[1]		12	10	5							
Apr 3	H	Cowdenbeath	0-0	1	4	2	6	5		7	8	9					3		11		12	10								
10	A	Raith Rovers	0-2	1	4	2	6	5		14	8	9					3		12	7	11	10								
17	H	Hamilton Academical	2-0	1	5	2	4			7[1]	6[1]	9				10	3		12	8	11	14								
24	A	Ayr United	0-0	1	4	2	6	5		7	10	9					3		14	8	11	12								
May 1	A	Kilmarnock	0-1	1	3	2	4	5		7	6	9				14	10		8	11	12									
8	H	Dunfermline Athletic	0-0	1	5	2	4			7	6	9	14	11			3		10	8	12									
15	A	Meadowbank Thistle	1-2	1	5	2	4				9	14	12				3		8	7[1]	10	6					11			
TOTAL FULL APPEARANCES				40	38	37	42	40	3	38	27	36	9	5	1	17	35	2	27	4	3	26	1	27	15	6	1	3	1	
TOTAL SUB APPEARANCES					(1)					(2)	(7)	(6)	(9)		(7)	(7)	(6)	(2)				(11)		(6)	(3)	(7)		(5)	(1)	
TOTAL GOALS SCORED								1	2	15	2	7	1	1			5		6			1		12	2	1				

Small figures denote goalscorers   † denotes opponent's own goal

BOGHEAD PARK

Capacity 7,503 (Seated 303, Standing 7,200)

Pitch Dimensions 110 yds x 68 yds.

Disabled Facilities Wheelchairs are accommodated on the track.

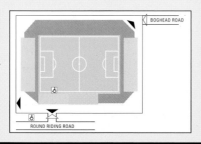

HOW TO GET THERE

Trains: The electric train service from Glasgow Queen Street and Glasgow Central Low Level both pass through Dumbarton East Station and Dumbarton Central Station both of which are situated just under a ten minute walk from the ground.

Buses: There are two main services which pass close to the ground. These are bound for Helensburgh and Balloch from Glasgow.

Cars: Car Parking is available in side streets around the ground. Supporters buses should park on Dumbarton Common.

DUNFERMLINE ATHLETIC

East End Park, Halbeath Road,
Dunfermline, Fife, KY12 7RB

Chairman
C. Roy Woodrow
Vice-Chairman
W. Blair F. Morgan, LL.B., N.P.
Directors
William M. Rennie;
Gavin G. Masterton, F.I.B. (Scot);
Joseph B. Malcolm, B.SC Eng;
James S. Harrison, F.R.I.C.S.
Manager
Bert Paton
**Administration
Manager/Secretary**
Paul A.M. D'Mello
Commercial Manager
Mrs. Audrey M. Kelly
Telephones
Ground/Ticket Office
(0383) 724295
Fax (0383) 723468
Commercial (0383) 721749
Club Shop (0383) 739980
Club Shop
Parker Sports, High Street,
Dunfermline. Open 9.00 a.m.
- 5.00 p.m. Mon. to Sat.
Official Supporters Club
c/o Mrs. J. Malcolm, Secretary,
Dunfermline Athletic
Supporters Club,
15 Downfield, Leuchatsbeath,
Cowdenbeath, KY4 9BF.
Team Captain
Norman McCathie
Club Sponsor
Landmark Home Furnishing

LIST OF PLAYERS 1993-94

Name	Date of Birth	Place of Birth	Date of Signing	Height	Weight	Previous Club
Baillie, William Alexander	06/07/66	Hamilton	10/08/93	6-2	12.0	St. Mirren
Bowes, Mark John	17/02/73	Bangour	26/02/91	5-8	10.8	Gairdoch United
Cooper, Neale James	24/11/63	Darjeeling, India	29/11/91	6-0	13.0	Reading
Cunnington, Edward	12/11/69	Bellshill	10/08/89	5-8	10.7	Chelsea
Davies, William McIntosh	31/05/64	Glasgow	31/10/90	5-6	10.9	Leicester City
Den Bieman, Ivo Johannes	04/02/67	Wamel, Netherlands	05/08/93	6-2	13.0	Dundee
Fraser, Graeme William	07/08/73	Edinburgh	30/06/92	5-11	11.8	Links United
French, Hamish Mackie	07/02/64	Aberdeen	23/10/91	5-10.5	11.4	Dundee United
Hamilton, Lindsay	11/08/62	Bellshill	02/07/92	6-2	13.7	St. Johnstone
Hillcoat, John	16/12/70	East Kilbride	02/08/89	5-11	10.10	St. Mirren
Laing, Derek James	11/11/73	Haddington	17/07/90	5-10	11.4	Salvesen B.C.
McCathie, Norman	23/03/61	Edinburgh	17/08/81	6-0	12.0	Cowdenbeath
McNamara, Jackie	24/10/73	Glasgow	17/09/91	5-8	10.9	Gairdoch United
McWilliams, Derek	16/01/66	Broxburn	10/08/91	5-10	11.7	Falkirk
O'Boyle, George	14/12/67	Belfast	02/08/89	5-7	10.2	Linfield
O'Neill, Hugh	03/01/75	Dunfermline	17/09/91	6-1	11.0	Hill of Beath Swifts
Petrie, Stewart James John	27/02/70	Dundee	27/08/93	5-10	11.11	Forfar Athletic
Preston, Allan	16/08/69	Edinburgh	05/08/93	5-10	11.7	Heart of Midlothian
Robertson, Craig Peter	22/04/63	Dunfermline	30/08/91	5-9	11.2	Aberdeen
Sharp, Raymond	16/11/69	Stirling	18/08/86	5-11	11.0	Gairdoch United
Sinclair, Christopher	11/11/70	Sheffield	10/03/89	5-9	10.10	Sauchie Athletic
Smart, Craig William	23/03/75	Dunfermline	14/07/93	6-0	12.7	Hutchison Vale B.C.
Smith, Paul McKinnon	02/11/62	Edinburgh	06/01/93	5-11	11.4	Falkirk

MILESTONES
Year of Formation: 1885
Most Capped Player: Istvan Kozma (Hungary - 29 - 13 with Dunfermline Athletic)
Most League Points in a Season: 59 (Division 2) - 1925/26
Most League goals scored by a player in a Season: Bobby Skinner (53) Season 1925/26
Record Attendance: 27,816 v Celtic, 30/4/68
Record Victory: 11-2 v Stenhousemuir, Division 2, 27/9/30
Record Defeat: 0-10 v Dundee, Division 2, 22/3/47

CLUB FIXTURES 1993-94

Date	Opponent	Venue
Aug 4	League Cup 1	
Aug 7	Falkirk	A
Aug 11	League Cup 2	
Aug 14	**Clydebank**	H
Aug 21	Brechin City	A
Aug 25	League Cup 3	
Aug 28	**Airdrieonians**	H
Sept 1	League Cup 4	
Sept 4	Clyde	A
Sept 11	Stirling Albion	A
Sept 15	**St. Mirren**	H
Sept 18	**Greenock Morton**	H
Sept 22	League Cup S/F	
Sept 25	Ayr United	A
Sept 29	Hamilton Academical	A
Oct 2	**Dumbarton**	H
Oct 9	**Falkirk**	H
Oct 16	St. Mirren	A
Oct 23	**Stirling Albion**	H
Oct 24	League Cup Final	
Oct 30	**Brechin City**	H
Nov 6	Airdrieonians	A
Nov 10	**Clyde**	H
Nov 13	Dumbarton	A
Nov 20	**Hamilton Academical**	H
Nov 27	**Ayr United**	H
Dec 4	Greenock Morton	A
Dec 11	Clydebank	A
Dec 18	**St. Mirren**	H
Dec 27	Falkirk	A
Jan 1	Brechin City	A
Jan 8	**Airdrieonians**	H
Jan 15	Clyde	A
Jan 22	**Clydebank**	H
Jan 29	SFA Cup 3	
Feb 5	Stirling Albion	A
Feb 12	**Dumbarton**	H
Feb 19	SFA Cup 4	
Feb 26	Hamilton Academical	A
Mar 5	**Greenock Morton**	H
Mar 12	Ayr United	A
Mar 19	St. Mirren	A
Mar 26	**Falkirk**	H
Mar 29	Clydebank	A
Apr 2	**Stirling Albion**	H
Apr 9	Dumbarton	A
Apr 16	**Hamilton Academical**	H
Apr 23	Greenock Morton	A
Apr 27	Ayr Unite	H
Apr 30	**Brechin City**	H
May 7	Airdrieonians	A
May 14	**Clyde**	H
May 21	SFA Cup Final	

SEASON TICKET INFORMATION
Seated

Centre Stand	Adult	£140
	Juvenile/OAP	£75
Exon Enclosure	Adult	£100
	Juvenile/OAP	£50
Family West Wing Stand	Parent and Child	£190
	Extra Parent	£100
	Extra Child	£50
	OAP and Child	£120
Standing	Adult	£100
	Juvenile/OAP	£50

LEAGUE ADMISSION PRICES
Seated

Centre Stand	Adult	£7
	Juvenile/OAP	£4
Wing Stands	Adult	£7
	Juvenile/OAP	£4
Exon Enclosure	Adult	£5
	Juvenile/OAP	£2.50
Standing	Adult	£5
	Juvenile/OAP	£2.50

Registered Strip: Shirt - Black and White Vertical Stripes, Stippled with Red Dots, Shorts - Black with White Side Panel, Stockings - White with Red Chevrons

Change Strip: Shirt - Red with Two Black Stripes on Collar, Shorts - White with Red Side Panel, Stockings - Red with Red and Black Stripe on Top

The PARS

Date	Venue	Opponents	Result	Hamilton L.	Bowes M.	Sharp R.	McCathie N.	Robertson C.	Cooper N.	McWilliams D.	Shannon R.	Grant R.	Leitch S.	Cunnington E.	Davies W.	Kelly N.	O'Boyle G.	Laing D.	Sinclair C.	Chalmers P.	Reilly J.	French H.	Haro M.	Williamson A.	Moyes D.	McAllister P.	McNamara J.	Smith P.	Hillcoat J.
Aug 1	A	Ayr United	†1-1	1	2	3	4	5	6	7	8	9	10	11	12														
5	A	Cowdenbeath	5-2	1		3	4	5^1	6		2	9	10^1		11^2	7	8^1												
8	H	Hamilton Academical	2-1	1		3	4	5	6	14	2	9	10	12	11^2	7	8												
15	A	Kilmarnock	1-0	1		3	4	5	6	7	2	9	10		11			8^1	14										
22	A	Raith Rovers	0-1	1		3	4	5	6	7	2	10	11		8				9	14									
29	H	Clydebank	1-3	1		3	4	5	6	7		9	10^1	12	11	2				8	14								
Sept 5	A	Stirling Albion	5-0	1		3	4^1	5	6	7^1	2	9^1		14	11		10			8^2		12							
12	A	St. Mirren	1-2	1		3	4	5	6	7	2	9		14	11		10			8^1		12							
19	H	Meadowbank Thistle	3-1	1		3			6	7^1	2	9		14	12		10^1			8^1		11		4	5				
26	H	Dumbarton	3-2	1		3			6^1	7	2	9^1		4	14		10			8		11^1		5					
Oct 3	A	Morton	1-0	1		3	4		6	7	2	9^1		14	5		10			8		11							
10	H	Ayr United	1-3	1		3	4		6^1	7	2	9		14	5		10			8		11							
17	A	Hamilton Academical	1-2	1		3	4		6	7^1	2	9			5	14	10			8		11							
24	A	Stirling Albion	1-0	1	2	3			6	7	8	9			12		10			14		11^1			5				
31	A	Clydebank	0-1	1	2	3			6		4		8	11	10			14	9			7			5				
Nov 7	H	Kilmarnock	2-0	1		3	4		6		2	9	12		10			14	8			7^1		11^1	5				
14	A	Raith Rovers	0-1	1		3	4		6		2	9	10	12					8			7		11	5	14			
21	A	Meadowbank Thistle	2-3	1		3	4	6			2		8	11	10^1			9^1		14		7			5				
28	H	St. Mirren	2-0	1		3		4	6	11	2		8^1		10			9^1				7			5		12		
Dec 2	H	Morton	0-0	1		3		4	6	11	2		8		10			9		14		7			5		12		
5	A	Dumbarton	1-0	1		3	4^1	6		11	2		8	12	10			9				7			5				
12	A	Ayr United	0-1	1		3	4	6			2	11	8	12	10			9		14		7			5				
19	H	Cowdenbeath	4-1	1		3	4	6			2	14	8	12	10^1			9		11^1		7^1			5^1				
26	A	Kilmarnock	3-2	1			4	9^1	6		2		8		3	10				11		7^2		12	5				
Jan 2	H	Raith Rovers	0-0	1			4	6		9	2	14	8		3	10				11		7			5				
30	A	Hamilton Academical	2-1	1			6		11	2	8^2			3	10				9		7		5			4		
Feb 2	H	Clydebank	2-0	1			4	6			2	14	8	3	10^1				9^1		7		5			11		
6	A	Morton	1-0	1			4	6			2	14	8	3	10				9^1		7		5			11		
9	A	Stirling Albion	2-1	1			4^1	6	12		2	14	8^1	3	10				9		7		5			11		
13	A	Cowdenbeath	2-1	1			4	6			2	14	8	3	10				9		7		5			11^1		
20	H	Dumbarton	2-2	1		12					2	11^1	8	3	10				9^1		7		5			4		
27	H	Meadowbank Thistle	3-2	1			4	6			2	12	8^1	3	10^1				9^1		14		7			5		11	
Mar 6	A	St. Mirren	1-0	1		12	4	6	11		2		8	3	10^1							7^1		5			9		
10	A	Ayr United	1-1	1			4	6	11		2	14	8	3	10^1							7		5			9		
13	A	Hamilton Academical	2-0	1			4	6			2	14	8	3	10					12		7^2		5			9		
20	A	Raith Rovers	0-2	1			4	6			2	14	8	3	10							7		5			9		
27	H	Kilmarnock	†2-2	1			4	10	6	12	2	14	8^1	3						11		7		5			9		
Apr 3	H	Stirling Albion	0-1	1		3	4	6		11	2	9	12		10				14		7		5			8		
10	A	Clydebank	1-1	1		3	4	8	6		2	14	12		10				9		7^1		5			11		
17	A	St. Mirren	1-2	1			4	10	6		2	12	8	3				14	9		7^1		5		11		1	
24	A	Meadowbank Thistle	1-0	1			4	11	6		2		8	3	10			9	14		7^1		5				1	
May 1	H	Cowdenbeath	0-2	1			4	11	6		2	14	8	3	10			9			7		5				1	
8	A	Dumbarton	0-0	1		3	4	6			2		8		10			9		14		7		5			11	1	
15	H	Morton	1-2	1	2	3	4	6					8		10			12	11	14^1		7		5			9	1	
TOTAL FULL APPEARANCES				39	4	27	30	34	33	22	42	18	34	26	39	4	3	11	1	23		36	2	4	30	1		16	5
TOTAL SUB APPEARANCES						(2)			(3)			(14)	(8)	(8)	(2)		(2)	(5)	(9)	(1)	(2)		(1)			(1)	(2)		
TOTAL GOALS SCORED							2	3	2	3		4	9		10		2	3		9		12		1	1			1	

Small figures denote goalscorers † denotes opponent's own goal

---

EAST END PARK

Capacity 18,328; Seated 4,008, Standing 14,320

Pitch Dimensions 115 yds x 71 yds.

Disabled Facilities Special ramped area in West Enclosure.

HALBEATH ROAD

HOW TO GET THERE

Trains: Dunfermline Station is served by trains from both Glasgow and Edinburgh and the ground is a 15 minute walk from here.

Buses: Buses destined for Kelty, Perth, St. Andrew's and Kirkcaldy all pass close to East End Park.

Cars: Car Parking is available in a large car park adjoining the East End of the ground and there are also facilities in various side streets. Multi-storey car parking approximately 10 minutes walk from ground.

FALKIRK

EST. 1876

Brockville Park,
Hope Street,
Falkirk, FK1 5AX

Chairman
Campbell Christie
Vice-Chairman
George J. Deans
Directors
George Deans;
James Johnston;
Alexander D. Moffat;
Manager
James Jefferies
Secretary
Alexander D. Moffat
Commercial Manager
James Hendry

Telephones
Ground/Ticket Office
(0324) 24121/32487
Fax (0324) 612418;
Commercial (0324) 24121

Club Shop
Brockville Park (behind Main
Stand)

Team Captain
Ian McCall

Club Sponsor
Beazer Homes

LIST OF PLAYERS 1993-94

Name	Date of Birth	Place of Birth	Date of Signing	Height	Weight	Previous Club
Cadette, Richard Ray	21/03/65	Hammersmith	10/01/92	5-8	11.4	Brentford
Drinkell, Kevin	18/06/60	Grimsby	24/07/92	5-11	13.8	Coventry City
Duffy, Cornelius	05/06/67	Glasgow	24/10/90	6-1	11.13	Dundee United
Hamilton, Graeme John	22/01/74	Stirling	19/06/91	5-10	10.10	Gairdoch United
Houston, Peter	19/07/58	Baillieston	04/10/93	5-10	11.0	East Stirlingshire
Hughes, John	09/09/64	Edinburgh	22/08/90	6-0	13.7	Swansea City
Johnston, Forbes D.S.	03/08/71	Aberdeen	08/09/90	5-10	9.12	Musselburgh Athletic
MacKenzie, Scott	07/07/70	Glasgow	08/09/90	5-9	10.5	Musselburgh Athletic
May, Edward	30/08/67	Edinburgh	02/03/91	5-7.5	10.3	Brentford
McCall, Ian Holland	30/09/65	Dumfries	31/07/92	5-9	11.7	Dundee
McDonald, Colin	10/04/74	Edinburgh	08/07/93	5-7	10.8	Hibernian
McLaughlin, Joseph	02/06/60	Greenock	12/09/92	6-1	12.0	Watford
McQueen, Thomas Feeney	01/04/63	Glasgow	06/10/90	5-9	11.7	West Ham United
Oliver, Neil	11/04/67	Berwick-upon-Tweed	07/08/91	5-11	11.10	Blackburn Rovers
Parks, Anthony	28/01/63	Hackney	23/10/92	5-10	13.2	Rotherham United
Rice, Brian	11/10/63	Bellshill	09/08/91	6-1	11.7	Nottingham Forest
Shaw, Gregory	15/02/70	Dumfries	31/12/92	6-0	10.12	Ayr United
Sloan, Scott	14/12/67	Wallsend-on-Sea	08/11/91	5-11	11.3	Newcastle United
Taggart, Craig	17/01/73	Glasgow	03/09/91	5-9	11.0	West Park United
Weir, David Gillespie	10/05/70	Falkirk	01/08/92	6-2	13.7	Celtic B.C.
Westwater, Ian	08/11/63	Loughborough	10/08/91	6-0	13.0	Dunfermline Athletic
Young, Kenneth William	06/05/74	Edinburgh	02/07/92	5-6.5	10.7	Links United

CLUB FIXTURES 1993-94

Date	Opponent	Venue
Aug 4	League Cup 1	
Aug 7	**Dunfermline Athletic**	H
Aug 11	League Cup 2	
Aug 14	Greenock Morton	A
Aug 21	Stirling Albion	H
Aug 25	League Cup 3	
Aug 28	Hamilton Academical	A
Sept 1	League Cup 4	
Sept 4	**Clydebank**	H
Sept 11	**Airdrieonians**	H
Sept 14	Ayr United	A
Sept 18	Dumbarton	A
Sept 22	League Cup S/F	
Sept 25	**St. Mirren**	H
Sept 29	**Clyde**	H
Oct 2	Brechin City	A
Oct 9	Dunfermline Athletic	A
Oct 16	**Ayr United**	H
Oct 23	Airdrieonians	A
Oct 24	League Cup Final	
Oct 30	Stirling Albion	A
Nov 6	**Hamilton Academical**	H
Nov 9	Clydebank	A
Nov 13	**Brechin City**	H
Nov 20	Clyde	A
Nov 27	St. Mirren	A
Dec 4	**Dumbarton**	H
Dec 11	**Greenock Morton**	H
Dec 18	Ayr United	A
Dec 27	**Dunfermline Athletic**	H
Jan 1	**Stirling Albion**	H
Jan 8	Hamilton Academical	A
Jan 15	**Clydebank**	H
Jan 22	Greenock Morton	A
Jan 29	SFA Cup 3	
Feb 5	**Airdrieonians**	H
Feb 12	Brechin City	A
Feb 19	SFA Cup 4	
Feb 26	**Clyde**	H
Mar 5	Dumbarton	A
Mar 12	**St. Mirren**	H
Mar 19	**Ayr United**	H
Mar 26	Dunfermline Athletic	A
Mar 30	**Greenock Morton**	H
Apr 2	Airdrieonians	A
Apr 9	**Brechin City**	H
Apr 16	Clyde	A
Apr 23	**Dumbarton**	H
Apr 27	St. Mirren	A
Apr 30	Stirling Albion	A
May 7	**Hamilton Academical**	H
May 14	Clydebank	A
May 21	SFA Cup Final	

Registered Strip:	Shirt - Dark Blue with Red, White and Black Shoulder Panels, Shorts - White with Navy Blue Piping, Stockings - Red
Change Strip:	Shirt - White with Red, Navy Blue and Black Shoulder Panels, Shorts - Navy Blue with White Piping, Stockings - White

CLUB FACTFILE 1992/93... RESULTS... APPEARANCES... SCORERS

The BAIRNS

Date		Venue	Opponents	Result	Westwater I.	Duffy C.	McQueen T.	Baptie C.	Hughes J.	Rice B.	McAllister K.	May E.	Drinkell K.	Sloan S.	Smith P.	McCall I.	Johnston F.	Taylor A.	Cadette R.	Oliver N.	McGivern S.	McDougall G.	Taggart C.	McLaughlin J.	Lennox G.	Parks A.	Weir D.	Wishart F.	MacKenzie S.	Treanor M.	Shaw G.	Young K.
Aug	1	A	Dundee	2-1	1	2	3	4	5	6	7	8	9^1	10^1	11	14																
	5	A	Heart of Midlothian	0-3	1	2	3		5		7	6	9	10	11		4	8	14													
	8	H	Aberdeen	0-1	1	4	3		5	6	7	8	9	10	11	14				2												
	15	H	Hibernian	2-1	1	4	3^1	10	5	6	7	8^1	9		11	12				2												
	22	A	Airdrieonians	0-2	1	2	3	4	5	6		8	9		11	10	14		12			7										
	29	A	Dundee United	0-2				4	5	6	7	8	9	12	11			3	10	2					1	14						
Sept	5	H	Partick Thistle	0-1				4	5	6	7	8	9	12	11		3	14	10	2						1						
	12	A	St. Johnstone	2-3		4					6	7	14		8	11^1	10	3		2						1	5^1					
	19	H	Celtic	4-5		2	3^1	14			6^1		9	7	11	10^2	4	8								1	5					
	26	H	Motherwell	1-0		2	3				6	9	7^1	11	10		4								8	1	5					
Oct	3	A	Rangers	0-4	1	4	3				12	6	9	7	11	10				2					8		5					
	10	H	Dundee	2-2	1	4	3^1				7	6	9	8	11	10			12	2					5		12					
	17	H	Aberdeen	1-3	1	4	3				7		10^1	9	11	12	6			2					5		8					
	24	H	Dundee United	1-1				5			7	6	9	8^1	4	10	3		12						11	1		2				
	31	A	Partick Thistle	2-1				5			7	6^1	9	8	4	10	3		12^1	14					11	1		2				
Nov	7	H	Airdrieonians	5-1			3	5			7	6^1	9^2	8	4				10^1						11^1	1		2				
	14	H	Hibernian	1-3			3	5			7	6	9	8	4				10						11^1	1		2				
	21	A	Celtic	2-3		14	3	5			7^1	6	9^1	8	4				12	10					11	1		2				
	28	H	St. Johnstone	2-2		4^2	3				7	6	9			10				8					11	1	5	2				
Dec	2	H	Heart of Midlothian	2-1		4	3				7	6	9^1	8		10^1			8^1						11	1	5	2				
	5	A	Motherwell	1-3		4	3				7	6	9	12		10	14		8^1						11	1	5	2				
	12	H	Rangers	1-2	1	4	3				7	6	9	8											11		5	2^1				
	19	A	Dundee	1-2	1	4	3				7	6		12	11	10	14		9^1						8		5	2				
	26	H	Hibernian	3-3	1	4	3				7	6	8^1	12		10^1			9^1						11		5	2				
Jan	2	A	Airdrieonians	1-0		4^1					7	11	8			10	3		9	6					12	1	5	2				
	23	A	Dundee United	1-2		4^1					7	11	8	12		10	3		9	6						1	5	2				
	30	H	Aberdeen	1-4		4	3				7	6	8	11		12^1			9	2						1	5	14	10			
Feb	2	H	Partick Thistle	4-2		4^1				6	14	7^2	11	12		10	3		8^1	9						1	5	2				
	9	A	Rangers	0-5		4				6	7	11	8	14		10	3		9							1	5	2				
	13	A	Heart of Midlothian	1-3		4				6	7	11	8			10	3	14	9^1							1	5	2				
	20	H	Motherwell	1-3		2	3				7	6	8			12^1		14	9					10	5	11	1	4				
	27	H	Celtic	0-3	1	8	3				7	6	12	9		10				2				14	5		4			11		
Mar	10	H	Dundee	1-0	1		3			6	7	11	8			10			9^1	4				14			5	2				
	13	A	Aberdeen	2-2	1	6	3				7	11	8^1			10	12^1		9	4							5	2				
	16	A	St. Johnstone	0-1	1	6	3				7	11	8			10	12		9	4							5	2				
	20	A	Airdrieonians	0-1	1	8	3			6	7	11	9			10			12	4							5	2				
	27	H	Hibernian	1-1	1	8	3				7	9	10^1			12				4							5	2				
Apr	3	H	Dundee United	1-2	1	8		14			7	11	9	10			3			4							5	2		6	12^1	
	10	A	Partick Thistle	1-0	1					6	7	11^1		10			3			4					8		5	2				9
	17	H	St. Johnstone	2-2	1					6	7	11	10^1			12	3	14		4					8		5	2		4	9^1	
	20	A	Celtic	0-1	1	8				6	7	11	10			12	3	14		4							5	2				9
May	1	H	Heart of Midlothian	6-0	1	11	3	8^2	6^1	7			10						9^1	4					5^1			2^1				
	8	A	Motherwell	1-2	1	11	3	8	6^1	7	12		10						9	4							5	2			14	
	15	H	Rangers	1-2	1		3^1	5		6	7			10					9	4		8						2	12		11	14
TOTAL FULL APPEARANCES					24	33	30	8	15	18	40	40	33	21	19	27	17	3	24	24	1	5	3	8	17	15	30	23	2	3	4	
TOTAL SUB APPEARANCES						(1)		(1)		(2)	(1)	(2)	(2)	(8)			(8)	(5)	(5)	(7)	(1)			(2)		(3)		(1)	(1)	(2)	(1)
TOTAL GOALS SCORED						5	4	2		2	3	6	7	6	1	6	1	1	8						1		2	2		2	

Small figures denote goalscorers † denotes opponent's own goal

BROCKVILLE PARK

Capacity 13,840 (Seated 2,661, Standing 11,179)

Pitch Dimensions 110yds x 72 yds

Disabled Facilities Viewing area behind each goal.

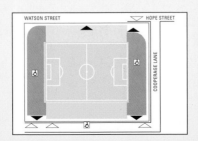

WATSON STREET — HOPE STREET — COOPERAGE LANE

HOW TO GET THERE

Trains: The main Edinburgh–Glasgow railway line passes by the ground and passengers can alight at Grahamston Station. They will then have a walk of 100 yards to the ground.

Buses: All buses departing from the city centre pass by Brockville.

Cars: Car Parking facilities are available in the Meeks Road car park for Coaches and Cars and also in a local shopping car park which can hold 500 cars. Supporters coaches and cars will be directed to the appropriate parking area by the police on duty.

GREENOCK MORTON

Cappielow Park, Sinclair
Street, Greenock, PA15 2TY

Chairman
John Wilson
Directors
Duncan D.F. Rae
Kenneth Woods
Andrew Gemmell
John Kerr
Manager
Allan McGraw
Secretary
Mrs Jane W. Rankin

Telephones
Ground (0475) 23571/26485
Fax (0475) 81084
Ticket Office (0475) 23571

Club Shop
Situated under Main Stand -
Open home matchdays only

Official Supporters Club
Greenock Morton Supporters
Club, Regent Street,
Greenock.

Team Captain
Stephen J. McCahill

Club Sponsor
Buchanans Toffees

LIST OF PLAYERS 1993-94

Name	Date of Birth	Place of Birth	Date of Signing	Height	Weight	Previous Club
Alexander, Rowan Samuel	28/01/61	Ayr	09/08/86	5-7	11.10	Brentford
Beaton, Scott	18/03/72	Greenock	05/07/93	6-0	11.10	Gourock Y.A.C.
Brown, Craig	23/09/71	Greenock	07/06/89	5-11	12.4	Ferguslie United
Collins, Derek J	15/04/69	Glasgow	23/07/87	5-8	10.7	Renfrew Waverley
Doak, Martin	11/05/64	Greenock	07/07/90	6-0	13.6	Adelaide Hellas, Sth Australia
Donaghy, Mark	29/08/72	Glasgow	10/08/93	5-8	9.13	Celtic
Fowler, John James	30/01/65	Glasgow	30/07/93	5-7	11.12	Ashfield Juniors
Gahagan, John	24/08/58	Glasgow	07/09/90	5-9	11.1	Motherwell
Grace, Alexander	20/03/74	Vale of Leven	12/07/93	5-6	10.4	West Bromwich Albion
Graham, Paul Scott	17/05/70	Motherwell	24/07/90	6-2	12.4	Partick Thistle
Hunter, James Addison	20/12/64	Johnstone	18/09/85	5-9	10.10	Glentyan Thistle
Johnstone, Douglas Iain	12/03/69	Irvine	31/08/91	6-2	12.8	Glasgow University
Lilley, Derek Symon	09/02/74	Paisley	13/08/91	5-10.5	12.7	Everton B.C.
Logue, Andrew	09/08/75	Greenock	09/06/93	5-4	9.11	Shamrock B.C.
Mahood, Alan Scott	26/03/73	Kilwinning	23/03/92	5-8	10.10	Nottingham Forest
McArthur, Scott	28/02/68	Johnstone	19/12/90	5-11	11.10	Heart of Midlothian
McCahill, Stephen Joseph	03/09/66	Greenock	02/10/92	6-2	12.0	Celtic
McDonald Ian	28/12/58	Glasgow	18/08/89	5-6	12.0	Partick Thistle
McEwan, Alexander Ian	15/05/70	Glasgow	30/03/92	5-10	12.7	St. Mirren
McGhee, Dennis	01/04/75	Greenock	07/06/93	5-6	10.0	Clyde Thistle
McGoldrick, Kevin	05/08/72	Paisley	06/10/92	6-1	12.6	Arthurlie Juniors
McInnes, Derek John	05/07/71	Paisley	13/08/88	5-7	11.4	Gleniffer Thistle
McClelland, Barry	11/03/75	Glasgow	09/06/93	5-8	10.8	St. Mungo's F.P.
Pickering, Mark Fulton	11/06/65	Glasgow	21/08/88	5-8	11.4	Ardeer Thistle
Rafferty, Stuart	06/03/61	Port Glasgow	21/06/91	5-10	13.8	Dunfermline Athletic
Shearer, Neil John	06/01/75	Paisley	05/07/93	6-1	14.5	St. Mungo's
Thomson, Richard	07/08/71	Lanark	15/06/92	5-9	10.12	Lanark United
Tolmie, James	21/11/60	Glasgow	20/12/91	5-8	10.4	Markaryd, Sweden
Wylie, David	04/04/66	Johnstone	01/08/85	6-0	13.0	Ferguslie United

CLUB FIXTURES 1993-94

Date	Opponent	Venue
Aug 4	League Cup 1	
Aug 7	Clyde	A
Aug 11	League Cup 2	
Aug 14	**Falkirk**	H
Aug 21	St. Mirren	A
Aug 25	League Cup 3	
Aug 28	**Brechin City**	H
Sept 1	League Cup 4	
Sept 4	Airdrieonians	A
Sept 11	Clydebank	A
Sept 14	**Stirling Albion**	H
Sept 18	Dunfermline Athletic	A
Sept 22	League Cup S/F	
Sept 25	**Dumbarton**	H
Sept 28	Ayr United	A
Oct 2	**Hamilton Academical**	H
Oct 9	**Clyde**	H
Oct 16	Stirling Albion	A
Oct 23	**Clydebank**	H

Date	Opponent	Venue
Oct 24	League Cup Final	
Oct 30	**St. Mirren**	H
Nov 6	Brechin City	A
Nov 9	**Airdrieonians**	H
Nov 13	Hamilton Academical	A
Nov 20	**Ayr United**	H
Nov 27	Dumbarton	A
Dec 4	**Dunfermline Athletic**	H
Dec 11	Falkirk	A
Dec 18	**Stirling Albion**	H
Dec 27	Clyde	A
Jan 1	St. Mirren	A
Jan 8	**Brechin City**	H
Jan 15	Airdrieonians	A
Jan 22	**Falkirk**	H
Jan 29	SFA Cup 3	
Feb 5	Clydebank	A
Feb 12	**Hamilton Academical**	H

Date	Opponent	Venue
Feb 19	SFA Cup 4	
Feb 26	Ayr United	A
Mar 5	Dunfermline Athletic	A
Mar 12	**Dumbarton**	H
Mar 19	Stirling Albion	A
Mar 26	**Clyde**	H
Mar 30	Falkirk	A
Apr 2	**Clydebank**	H
Apr 9	Hamilton Academical	A
Apr 16	**Ayr United**	H
Apr 23	**Dunfermline Athletic**	H
Apr 26	Dumbarton	A
Apr 30	**St. Mirren**	H
May 7	Brechin City	A
May 14	**Airdrieonians**	H
May 21	SFA Cup Final	

MILESTONES
Year of Formation: 1874
Most Capped Player: Jimmy Cowan (25)
Most League points in a Season:
69 (Division 2) - 1966/67
Most League goals scored by a player in a Season: Allan McGraw (58) Season 1963/64
Record Attendance: 23,500 v Celtic, 1922
Record Victory: 11-0 v Carfin Shamrock, Scottish Cup, 13/11/1886
Record Defeat: 1-10 v Port Glasgow Athletic, Division 2, 5/5/1884

SEASON TICKET INFORMATION
Seated	Adult	£110
	Juvenile/OAP	£80
Standing	Adult	£95
	Juvenile/OAP	£50

LEAGUE ADMISSION PRICES
Seated	Adult	£7
	Juvenile/OAP	£3.50
Standing	Adult	£5
	Juvenile/OAP	£2.50

Registered Strip: Shirt - Royal Blue Tartan with Royal Blue Collar with White Stripes, Shorts - Royal Blue, Stockings - Royal Blue
Change Strip: Shirt - Jade, Black and White Stripes, Shorts - Black, Stockings - Jade with Two Black Hoops

CLUB FACTFILE 1992/93... RESULTS... APPEARANCES... SCORERS

The TON

Date	Venue	Opponents	Result	Wylie D.	Collins D.	McArthur S.	Rafferty S.	Doak M.	Boag J.	Mathie A.	Mahood A.	Alexander R.	McInnes D.	Hopkin D.	Lilley D.	McDonald I.	MacCabe D.	Johnstone D.	Pickering M.	Fowler J.	Tolmie J.	McCahill S.	Gahagan J.	McChee D.	Thomson R.	Sanders G.	Shearer N.	McEwan A.
Aug 1	H	Kilmarnock	0-2	1	2	3	4	5	6	7	8	9	10	11														
4	H	Clydebank	5-1	1	2	3	4	5	6	7^3	8	9^1	10	11^1	12	14												
8	A	Meadowbank Thistle	3-0	1	2	3	4	5	6	7^1	8^1	9^1	10	11														
15	A	Dumbarton	1-0	1	2	3	4	5	6	7^1	8	9	10	11	12	14												
22	H	St. Mirren	0-1	1	2	3	4	5	6	7	8		10	11		9		12										
29	H	Cowdenbeath	1-0	1	2	3	4	5		7	8	9^1	10	11					6									
Sept 5	A	Ayr United	2-0	1	2	3	4	5		7	8^1	9	10	11					6^1									
12	A	Raith Rovers	1-2	1	2	3	4	5		7	8	9	10	11	12				6	14								
19	H	Hamilton Academical	2-1	1	2	3				7	8^1	9^1	11	10		4		12	6	5	14							
26	A	Stirling Albion	1-1	1	2	3^1	5			7	8	9	10	11					6	4								
Oct 3	H	Dunfermline Athletic	0-1	1	2	3	5			7	8	9	10			11			6	4	14	12						
10	A	Kilmarnock	0-3	1	2		4	5		7	8		10						6		11	9	3					
17	A	Meadowbank Thistle	†4-1	1	2	11	4	5		7^1	8^1					12			6^1	3	10	9						
24	H	Ayr United	2-1	1	2	11	4^1	5		7	8		10			14^1		12	6	3		9						
31	A	Cowdenbeath	3-1	1	2		4	5		7^2	8		10			11^1		12	6	3	14	9						
Nov 7	H	Dumbarton	1-2	1	2					7	8		10			9			6^1	3	14	11	5					
14	A	St. Mirren	3-2	1	2	8^1	14	5		7		9^1				4^1			6	3	12	11						
24	A	Hamilton Academical	1-3	1	2	8	4	5		7		9	10^1			12			6	3		11	14					
28	H	Raith Rovers	3-4	1	2	12		5		7	8^2	9	10			4			6	3		11^1	14					
Dec 2	A	Dunfermline Athletic	0-0	1	2	3	4	5		7		9	10			12			6			8	14	11				
5	H	Stirling Albion	2-2	1	2	10	4	5				9				8	14^1		6^1	3	12	11	7					
19	A	Clydebank	2-2	1	2		4	5		7^2		9	10						6			8	11	3	14			
26	A	Dumbarton	1-3	1	2	3	14			7^1		9	10			4			6			8	12	5	11			
29	H	Kilmarnock	2-0	1	2	3	4			7		9^1	10			14			6^1			8	12	5	11			
Jan 2	H	St. Mirren	1-1	1	2	3	4			7		9	10^1						6			8	12	5	11			
30	A	Meadowbank Thistle	1-1	1	2	11^1	4					14	10			9		12	8	5	3			6	7			
Feb 2	H	Cowdenbeath	3-2	1	2	11	14					9	10			4	8^3	5	3	7	12	6						
6	H	Dunfermline Athletic	0-1	1	2	3	14					9	10			4	8	5	12	7	11	6						
9	A	Ayr United	0-0	1	2	11	4	12				9	10			8		5	3		6	7						
13	H	Clydebank	2-0	1	2	11^1	4	12				9	10			14^1	8	5	3		6	7						
20	A	Stirling Albion	2-0	1	2	11^1	4					9	10			8^1		7	6	3		5						
27	H	Hamilton Academical	1-2	1	2	8	4	5			12	9^1	10	11				7	6	3	14							
Mar 6	A	Raith Rovers	0-2	1	2	10	4			7		9				11		12	6		3	8	5	14				
9	H	Kilmarnock	2-2	1	2	3	12	5^1		7		10	9			4			8	11^1	6	14						
13	H	Meadowbank Thistle	2-0	1	2	3^1	4	5		7^1		10	9			12	14		8	11	6							
20	A	St. Mirren	0-2	1	2	8		5		7		10	9			4		3	12	6	11	14						
27	H	Dumbarton	2-1	1	2	8	12			9^1		10	7			4		6	3	5	11^1	14						
Apr 3	A	Ayr United	1-0	1	2	8	12			9		10	7			4		6^1	3	5	11	14						
10	A	Cowdenbeath	1-0	1	2	8	12^1	6		9		10	7			4		3		5	11							
17	A	Raith Rovers	1-1	1	2	8	4	6		9^1		10	7					3		5	11							
24	A	Hamilton Academical	1-2	1	2	8	4					10	7			9		3	6	5	11^1	14						
May 1	H	Clydebank	2-2	1		3	4			7		10	9^2			5			6	11	8	14	2					
8	H	Stirling Albion	1-3	1		3	4			7^1		10	9			6		2	5	11	8	14						
15	A	Dunfermline Athletic	2-1	1		3	4	6		7		10				2		5	9	11	8	8^2						
TOTAL FULL APPEARANCES				44	41	39	31	27	5	31	17	30	40	9	16	14	10	32	25	13	14	23	16	3	2		1	1
TOTAL SUB APPEARANCES						(7)	(4)			(1)		(1)				(6)	(11)	(3)		(3)	(6)	(7)	(1)	(3)	(6)	(1)	(1)
TOTAL GOALS SCORED						6	2	1		13	6	10	2	1		4	1		6		6	2	2				2

Small figures denote goalscorers † denotes opponent's own goal

CAPPIELOW PARK

Capacity 14,267; Seating 5,257; Standing 9,010

Pitch Dimensions 110 yds x 71 yds.

Disabled Facilities Seating facilities below Grandstand.

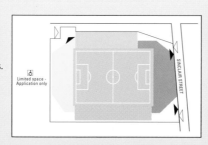

Limited space - Application only
SINCLAIR STREET

HOW TO GET THERE

Buses: Services from Glasgow stop just outside the park. There are also services from Port Glasgow and Gourock.

Trains: The nearest local station is Cartsdyke and it is a five minute walk from here to the ground. There are two to three trains every hour from Glasgow and from Gourock.

Cars: Car Parking is available in James Watt Dock which is on the A8 road just next to the ground.

HAMILTON ACADEMICAL

Douglas Park, Douglas Park Lane, Hamilton, ML3 0DF

Chairman
George J. Fulston
Vice-Chairman
George Whitelaw
Directors
William P. Davidson;
Alistair R. Duguid;
Robert D. Gibb;
James W. Watson
Manager
Iain Munro
Secretary
Scott A. Struthers B.A.
Commercial Manager
George Miller
Telephones
Ground/Commercial
(0698) 286103 (3 lines)
Information Service
0891 666492
Fax (0698) 285422
Club Shop (0698) 284603
Club Shop
"The Acciesshop", c/o
Douglas Park, Douglas Park
Lane, Hamilton, ML3 0DF.
Open 11.30 a.m. - 2.30 p.m.
and 6.30 p.m. - 10.00 p.m.
Mon. to Sat.
Official Supporters Club
The Stand Club,
c/o Douglas Park, Douglas
Park Lane, Hamilton, ML3 0DF
Team Captain
Colin Miller
Club Sponsor
Wilson Homes

LIST OF PLAYERS 1993-94

Name	Date of Birth	Place of Birth	Date of Signing	Height	Weight	Previous Club
Baptie, Crawford Bowie	24/02/59	Glasgow	08/07/93	6-1	11.7	Falkirk
Bonnyman, Philip	06/02/54	Glasgow	03/07/92	5-11.5	12.5	Dunfermline Athletic
Campbell, Duncan M.	11/09/70	Paisley	24/09/93	5-7	10.12	St. Andrew's (Malta)
Chalmers, Paul	31/10/63	Glasgow	07/07/93	5-10	11.0	Dunfermline Athletic
Clark, Gary	13/09/64	Glasgow	25/06/91	5-10	11.3	Clyde
Duffield, Peter	04/02/69	Middlesbrough	24/09/93	5-6	10.7	Sheffield United
Ferguson, Allan Thomas	21/03/69	Lanark	31/12/87	5-10.5	12.3	Netherdale Com A.F.C.
Fitzpatrick, Paul James	05/10/65	Liverpool	10/09/93	6-4	12.12	Birmingham City
Hendry, Craig	30/04/75	East Kilbride	16/08/93	5-8	10.8	East Kilbride Y.C.
Hillcoat, Christopher P.	03/10/69	Glasgow	19/05/87	5-10	10.4	St. Bridget's B.G.
Lorimer, David James	26/01/74	Bellshill	16/09/92	5-9.5	11.0	Hamilton Accies B.C.
McCormick, Steven	10/11/75	Bellshill	14/05/93	5-6	9.10	Mill United
McEntegart, Sean David	01/03/70	Dublin	24/07/92	5-11	12.6	Queen's Park
McGill, Derek	14/10/75	Lanark	28/06/93	5-10.5	11.4	Dunfermline Athletic
McInulty, Stephen James	22/09/71	Bellshill	30/01/93	5-10.5	11.0	Larkhall Thistle
McKenzie, Paul Vincent	22/09/64	Glasgow	30/01/91	5-11	12.4	Dumbarton
McLean, Charles C.N.	08/11/73	Glasgow	08/07/93	5-10	11.0	Celtic
McQuade, John	08/07/70	Glasgow	31/08/93	5-8	10.4	Dumbarton
Miller, Colin Fyfe	04/10/64	Lanark	27/09/88	5-7	12.2	Hamilton Steelers
Napier, Craig Cameron	14/11/65	East Kilbride	19/11/88	5-9	12.0	Clyde
Reid, William Hamilton	18/07/63	Glasgow	25/06/91	5-8	9.12	Clyde
Rennicks, Steven John	28/11/75	Bellshill	12/05/93	5-7	10.2	Hamilton Accies B.C.
Sherry, James	09/09/73	Glasgow	19/05/92	5-7	10.13	Hamilton Accies B.C.
Ward, Kenneth	16/06/63	Blairhall	21/02/92	5-8	11.10	St. Johnstone
Waters, Michael Joseph	28/09/72	Stirling	27/10/92	5-8	12.10	Kilsyth Rangers
Watson, William Copeland	21/09/74	Bellshill	14/07/93	6-0	11.7	Clyde B.C.

CLUB FIXTURES 1993-94

Date	Opponent	Venue
Aug 4	League Cup 1	
Aug 7	Brechin City	A
Aug 11	League Cup 2	
Aug 14	St. Mirren	H
Aug 21	Airdrieonians	A
Aug 25	League Cup 3	
Aug 28	Falkirk	H
Sept 1	League Cup 4	
Sept 4	Dumbarton	A
Sept 11	Clyde	A
Sept 15	Clydebank	H
Sept 18	Ayr United	H
Sept 22	League Cup S/F	
Sept 25	Stirling Albion	A
Sept 29	Dunfermline Athletic	H
Oct 2	Greenock Morton	A
Oct 9	Brechin City	H
Oct 16	Clydebank	A
Oct 23	Clyde	H
Oct 24	League Cup Final	
Oct 30	Airdrieonians	H
Nov 6	Falkirk	A
Nov 10	Dumbarton	H
Nov 13	Greenock Morton	H
Nov 20	Dunfermline Athletic	A
Nov 27	Stirling Albion	H
Dec 4	Ayr United	A
Dec 11	St. Mirren	A
Dec 18	Clydebank	H
Dec 27	Brechin City	A
Jan 1	Airdrieonians	A
Jan 8	Falkirk	H
Jan 15	Dumbarton	A
Jan 22	St. Mirren	H
Jan 29	SFA Cup 3	
Feb 5	Clyde	A
Feb 12	Greenock Morton	A
Feb 19	SFA Cup 4	
Feb 26	Dunfermline Athletic	H
Mar 5	Ayr United	H
Mar 12	Stirling Albion	A
Mar 19	Clydebank	A
Mar 26	Brechin City	H
Mar 30	St. Mirren	A
Apr 2	Clyde	H
Apr 9	Greenock Morton	H
Apr 16	Dunfermline Athletic	A
Apr 23	Ayr United	A
Apr 27	Stirling Albion	H
Apr 30	Airdrieonians	H
May 7	Falkirk	A
May 14	Dumbarton	H
May 21	SFA Cup Final	

MILESTONES

Year of Formation: 1874
Most Capped Player: Colin Miller (Canada) (24)
Most League points in a Season:
57 (First Division) - 1991/92
Most League goals scored by a player in a Season: David Wilson (34) Season 1936/37
Record Attendance: 28,690 v Hearts, Scottish Cup, 3/3/37
Record Victory: 10-2 v Cowdenbeath, Division 1, 15/10/32
Record Defeat: 1–11 v Hibernian, Division 1, 6/11/65

SEASON TICKET INFORMATION

Seated	Adult	£125
	Juvenile/OAP	£65
Standing	Adult	£90
	Juvenile/OAP	£45

LEAGUE ADMISSION PRICES

Seated	Adult	£6
	Juvenile/OAP	£3
Standing	Adult	£5
	Juvenile/OAP	£2.50

	Registered Strip:	Shirt - Red with White Oscilloscope Hoops with Red Collar and Navy Trim, Shorts - White with Red and White Hoop on Leg, Stockings - Red with Navy Blue Turnover
	Change Strip:	Shirt - White with Navy Blue Horizontal Matchsticks with Navy Blue Collar and Red and White Trim, Shorts - Navy Blue with Red and White Hoop on Leg, Stockings - Navy Blue with Red Turnover

The ACCIES

Date	Venue	Opponents	Result	Ferguson A.	Hillcoat C.	Miller C.	Millen A.	Weir J.	Napier J.	Ward K.	McEntegart S.	Clark G.	Reid W.	McDonald P.	Smith T.	McKee K.	Rae G.	Cramb C.	McKenzie P.	Harris C.	McCulloch R.	Waters M.	Lorimer D.	McInulty S.	McLean C.	Doyle P.
Aug 1	H	Meadowbank Thistle	1-3	1	2	3	4	5	6	7	8	9	10	11	11¹	12										
5	H	St. Mirren	0-0	1	3		4		6	7		9	8	11	10	2	5									
8	A	Dunfermline Athletic	†1-2	1		3	4		6	14	7	9	8	11	10	2	5	12								
15	H	Cowdenbeath	3-0	1	2	3			4	6	12	8		14	11	10¹	5	9²		7						
22	A	Stirling Albion	2-0	1	2	3¹	4		6	14	8	12		11	10¹		5	9		7						
29	H	Ayr United	1-1	1	2	3	4		6		8	14¹		11	10		5	9	12	7						
Sept 5	A	Raith Rovers	1-2	1	2	3	4	6			8	14		11¹	10		5	9	12	7						
12	H	Dumbarton	3-2	1		3	4¹	6		10¹		8	11	14		2	5	9¹	12	7						
19	A	Morton	1-2	1	2	3	4			10	14	8¹		11	12		5	9	6	7						
26	A	Clydebank	1-3	1	2	3		6	14	7		8	12	11	10¹		5	9								
Oct 3	H	Kilmarnock	1-1	1	2	3	4	5	6			7	8	11¹	10			9	14							
10	A	Meadowbank Thistle	4-0	1		3		4	5	6		7	8	11	10²	2		9²								
17	A	Dunfermline Athletic	2-1	1		3		4	5	6	12	7	8¹	11	10	2		9¹	14							
24	H	Raith Rovers	2-2	1		3		4	5	6	12	7	8	11¹	10	2		9¹								
31	A	Ayr United	0-0	1		3		4	5	6	10	7	8	11	14	2		9								
Nov 7	A	Cowdenbeath	3-0	1		3		4	5	6	7¹	14	9	8	11¹	10¹	2			12						
14	H	Stirling Albion	1-0		2			4	5	3		8	6	11¹	10			14	7	9	1					
24	H	Morton	3-1	1	2	3²	4	5				8	6	11¹	10			9	7							
28	A	Dumbarton	2-2	1	2	3	4	5		9¹		8	6	11¹	10			12	7	14						
Dec 1	A	Kilmarnock	0-1	1	6	3	4	5				7	8	11	10	2		14	12	9						
8	H	Clydebank	2-0	1	2	3	4	5	6			10	8	11				9¹	7	12¹		14				
19	H	St. Mirren	2-0	1	2	3	4¹	5	6	7		10	8¹	11				9		14						
26	H	Cowdenbeath	4-0	1	2	3	4		6	7¹		10¹	8	11				9¹	12	5		14				
Jan 2	A	Stirling Albion	0-0	1	2	3	4	5	6	7		10	8	11				9		14						
6	H	Meadowbank Thistle	2-0	1	2	3	4	5	6	7²		10	8	11				9		14						
27	H	Kilmarnock	1-2		2	3	4	5	6	7		10	8	11				14	12	9¹	1					
30	A	Dunfermline Athletic	1-2	1	2	3	4	5	6	7		10	8	11	12			9¹	7							
Feb 2	A	Raith Rovers	1-1	1	2	3	4	5	6	12		7	8	11¹	10			9		14						
13	H	St. Mirren	0-0	1	2	3	4	5	6	10			8	11				9	12			7				
20	H	Clydebank	1-0	1	2	3	4	5	6			8	11	10¹				9	12			7				
27	A	Morton	2-1	1	2	3	4	5¹	6	14		7¹	8	11	10			9				12				
Mar 2	H	Ayr United	1-3	1		3	4	5	6	12		7	8	11	10			9	2				14¹			
6	H	Dumbarton	1-1	1		3	4	5		9		7¹	8	11	10	2						12	14	6		
10	A	Meadowbank Thistle	2-1	1		3	4¹	5		9	14	10		11¹	12	2		8					7	6		
13	H	Dunfermline Athletic	0-2	1	6	3	4	5		9		7	8	11	10	2		12	14							
20	A	Stirling Albion	2-0	1	4	3		5		10¹		6¹	8	11		2		9	12				14		7	
27	A	Cowdenbeath	4-0		4			5		10³		6	8	11¹		2		9	12		1	14		7	3	
Apr 3	A	Raith Rovers	2-2		6			4	5			10	7¹	8	11	2¹		9			1	12			3	
10	H	Ayr United	0-1		6			4	5			10	7	8	11	2		9			1	12			3	14
17	A	Dumbarton	0-2					4	5			9	10	7	8	11		2	14		1				3	6
24	H	Morton	2-1					4		3	12	6	8¹		11		2		9	5		1	7		10¹	
May 1	A	St. Mirren	1-2					4		3¹	12	6	8		11		2		9	5		1	7	14	10	
8	H	Clydebank	2-1	1				4		2	10	6	7¹	8	11		12		9¹	5			14		3	
15	A	Kilmarnock	0-0	1				4	6	2	10	7		8	11			9	5			12			3	14
TOTAL FULL APPEARANCES				36	34	29	41	37	27	25	12	34	35	44	22	19	9	25	15	14	8	4	1	8	4	1
TOTAL SUB APPEARANCES								(2)	(9)	(3)	(3)	(2)			(6)	(1)		(8)	(6)	(13)		(7)	(5)	(1)	(2)	
TOTAL GOALS SCORED						3	3	1	1	10		8	3	11	8	1		7	6			1			1	

*Small figures denote goalscorers † denotes opponent's own goal

---

DOUGLAS PARK

Capacity 6,550 (Seated 1,580 Standing 4,970)

Pitch Dimensions 112 yds x 73 yds.

Disabled Facilities A section in front of the Presidents' Stand is reserved for disabled supporters. However, prior arrangement must be made with the secretary.

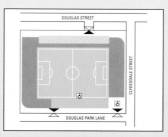

HOW TO GET THERE

Buses: Hamilton Bus Station, which is located in Brandon Street is 10 minutes walk from the ground, and there are numerous services from all over the country which stop there.

Trains: Hamilton West Station is 100 yards from the ground and a frequent service of trains runs from numerous points in the Strathclyde Region. Fans travelling from outside Strathclyde should travel to Glasgow Central Station (Low Level) and board a train from there.

Cars: Car Parking facilities exist for almost 1,000 vehicles just next to the ground (off Douglas Street). There is also a private parking area for Season Ticket holders only. Street parking around the ground is not permitted.

ST. MIRREN

St. Mirren Park, Love Street,
Paisley, PA3 2EJ.
Chairman
Allan W. Marshall, LL.B.
Vice-Chairman
William W. Waters, F.R.I.C.S.,
Directors
Robert Earlie
William Todd, J.P., M.B.E.;
Charles G. Palmer
J. Yule Craig, J.P., C.A.
George P. Campbell
Manager
James Bone
Secretary
A.Robin Craig LL.B.
Chief Executive
Robert Earlie
General Manager
Jack Copland
Commercial Manager
Bill Campbell
Telephones
Ground/Commercial
(041) 889-2558/840 1337
Fax (041) 848 6444
Sec. Bus. (041) 248-6677
Gen. Man. (041) 840-1337
Club Shop (041) 887-0902
Club Shop
St. Mirren Shop, 54 Central
Way, Paisley. Open 9.30 a.m.
- 5.00 p.m. Mon. to Fri. and
9.30 a.m. - 2.00 p.m. on
Saturdays.
Official Supporters Club
St. Mirren Supporters' Club,
11 Knox Street, Paisley.
Team Captain
Norman McWhirter
Club Sponsor
Clanford Motors Ltd.

LIST OF PLAYERS 1993-94

Name	Date of Birth	Place of Birth	Date of Signing	Height	Weight	Previous Club
Baker, Martin	08/06/74	Govan	16/09/92	5-11	10.10	St. Mirren B.C.
Bone, Alexander Syme F.	26/02/71	Stirling	22/10/92	5-9	10.7	Fallin
Combe, Alan	03/04/74	Edinburgh	07/08/93	5-11	10.13	Cowdenbeath
Cummings, Paul Robert	23/03/74	Greenock	16/09/92	5-8	10.5	St. Mirren B.C.
Dawson, Robert M.	01/08/63	Stirling	05/06/87	5-9	10.10	Stirling Albion
Dick, James	21/06/72	Bellshill	06/07/93	5-11	9.3	Airdrieonians
Elliot, David	13/11/69	Glasgow	19/06/91	5-9	11.0	Partick Thistle
Farrell, Stephen Edward	08/03/73	Kilwinning	13/08/92	5-11	11.12	Stoke City
Fullarton, James	20/07/74	Bellshill	13/06/91	5-10	10.6	Motherwell B.C.
Gallagher, Edward Adam	21/11/64	Glasgow	18/12/92	5-9	9.4	Dundee
Gardner, James	27/09/67	Dunfermline	07/09/93	5-10	10.2	Motherwell
Gillies, Kenneth	20/07/74	Glasgow	16/09/92	5-8	11.7	St. Mirren B.C.
Gillies, Richard Charles	24/08/76	Glasgow	12/12/92	5-8	11.7	St. Mirren B.C.
Harvie, Scott Smith	22/11/68	Glasgow	24/09/93	5-7.5	11.8	Partick Thistle
Hewitt, John	09/02/63	Aberdeen	04/09/92	5-8	10.8	Deveronvale
Lavety, Barry	21/08/74	Johnstone	10/08/91	6-0	12.12	Gleniffer Thistle
McDowall, Kenneth	29/07/63	Glasgow	22/09/84	5-10	10.3	Partick Thistle
McIntyre, Paul	18/01/67	Girvan	27/03/91	6-0	12.11	Maybole Juniors
McLaughlin, Barry John	19/04/73	Paisley	01/08/91	5-10	11.2	St. Mirren B.C.
McWhirter, Norman	04/09/69	Johnstone	16/09/85	5-9	9.6	Linwood Rangers B.C.
Money, Israel Campbell	31/08/60	Maybole	08/06/78	5-11	12.3	Dailly Amateurs
Orr, Neil Ian	13/05/59	Greenock	21/07/93	5-10.5	12.2	Hibernian
Paterson, Andrew	05/05/72	Glasgow	10/02/93	5-8	10.7	Bristol City
Peacock, John Scott	17/11/73	Glasgow	19/03/93	6-0	11.4	Queen's Park Rangers
Taylor, Stuart	26/11/74	Glasgow	16/09/92	6-1	10.10	St. Mirren B.C.

MILESTONES
Year of Formation: 1877
Most Capped Player:
Iain Munro and Billy Thomson (7)
Most League Points in a Season:
62 (Division 2) - 1967/68
**Most League goals scored by a player in a
Season:** Dunky Walker (45) Season 1921/22
Record Attendance: 47,438 v Celtic, 7/3/25
Record Victory: 15-0 v Glasgow University, Scottish
Cup, 30/1/60
Record Defeat: 0-9 v Rangers, Division 1,
4/12/1897

CLUB FIXTURES 1993-94

Date	Opponent	Venue	Date	Opponent	Venue	Date	Opponent	Venue
Aug 4	League Cup 1		Oct 23	Dumbarton	A	Feb 5	**Dumbarton**	H
Aug 7	**Airdrieonians**	H	Oct 24	League Cup Final		Feb 12	Clydebank	A
Aug 11	League Cup 2		Oct 30	Greenock Morton A		Feb 19	SFA Cup 4	
Aug 14	Hamilton Academical	A	Nov 6	**Stirling Albion**	H	Feb 26	**Brechin City**	H
			Nov 9	Ayr United	A	Mar 5	**Clyde**	H
Aug 21	**Greenock Morton**	H	Nov 13	**Clydebank**	H	Mar 12	Falkirk	A
			Nov 20	Brechin City	A	Mar 19	**Dunfermline Athletic**	H
Aug 25	League Cup 3		Nov 27	**Falkirk**	H			
Aug 28	Stirling Albion	A	Dec 4	Clyde	A	Mar 26	Airdrieonians	A
Sept 1	League Cup 4		Dec 11	**Hamilton Academical**	H	Mar 30	**Hamilton Academical**	H
Sept 4	**Ayr United**	H						
Sept 11	**Dumbarton**	H	Dec 18	Dunfermline Athletic	A	Apr 2	Dumbarton	A
Sept 15	Dunfermline Athletic	A	Dec 27	**Airdrieonians**	H	Apr 9	**Clydebank**	H
						Apr 16	Brechin City	A
Sept 18	**Clyde**	H	Jan 1	**Greenock Morton**	H	Apr 23	Clyde	A
Sept 22	League Cup S/F		Jan 8	Stirling Albio	A	Apr 27	**Falkirk**	H
Sept 25	Falkirk	A	Jan 15	**Ayr United**	H	Apr 30	Greenock Morton	A
Sept 29	**Brechin City**	H	Jan 22	Hamilton Academical	A	May 7	**Stirling Albion**	H
Oct 2	Clydebank	A				May 14	Ayr United	A
Oct 9	Airdrieonians	A	Jan 29	SFA Cup 3		May 21	SFA Cup Final	
Oct 16	**Dunfermline Athletic**	H						

Registered Strip:	Shirt - Black and White Vertical Stripes Shorts - White, Stockings - White
Change Strip:	Shirt - Black, Red and White Merged Stripes, Shorts - Black with Red and White Trim, Stockings - Red

CLUB FACTFILE 1992/93... RESULTS... APPEARANCES... SCORERS

The BUDDIES

Player columns (left to right): Money C., Dawson R., Reid M., Manley R., Baillie A., Charnley J., Elliot D., Lambert P., Torfason G., McGill D., Broddle J., McIntyre P., Lavety B., McLaughlin B., McDowall K., Fabiani R., McWhirter N., Gillies K., Baker M., Cummings P., McVie G., Farrell S., Hewitt J., Fullarton J., Gillies R., Taylor S., Gallagher E., Fridge L., Beattie J., Bone A., Peacock J., McGrotty G., Watson D., Paterson A., Hetherston B.

Date	Venue	Opponents	Result
Aug 1	A	Raith Rovers	0-7
5	A	Hamilton Academical	0-0
8	H	Dumbarton	4-0
15	H	Clydebank	0-0
22	A	Morton	1-0
29	H	Stirling Albion	0-0
Sept 5	A	Meadowbank Thistle	2-0
12	H	Dunfermline Athletic	2-1
19	A	Kilmarnock	2-1
26	H	Ayr United	2-0
Oct 3	A	Cowdenbeath	†2-1
10	A	Raith Rovers	†1-1
17	A	Dumbarton	2-4
24	H	Meadowbank Thistle	1-1
31	A	Stirling Albion	1-0
Nov 7	A	Clydebank	2-1
14	H	Morton	2-3
21	H	Kilmarnock	0-1
28	A	Dunfermline Athletic	0-2
Dec 2	H	Cowdenbeath	5-0
5	A	Ayr United	0-2
12	H	Raith Rovers	1-3
19	H	Hamilton Academical	0-2
26	H	Clydebank	3-2
Jan 2	A	Morton	1-1
16	H	Stirling Albion	1-0
27	A	Cowdenbeath	3-0
30	H	Dumbarton	2-1
Feb 3	H	Meadowbank Thistle	2-1
13	A	Hamilton Academical	0-0
20	H	Ayr United	1-0
27	A	Kilmarnock	0-1
Mar 6	A	Dunfermline Athletic	0-1
10	H	Raith Rovers	1-1
13	A	Dumbarton	1-2
20	H	Morton	2-0
27	H	Clydebank	3-0
Apr 3	A	Meadowbank Thistle	1-2
10	A	Stirling Albion	1-2
17	H	Dunfermline Athletic	2-1
24	H	Kilmarnock	2-1
May 1	H	Hamilton Academical	2-1
8	A	Ayr United	3-3
15	H	Cowdenbeath	1-2

TOTAL FULL APPEARANCES: 25 34 5 20 38 14 38 38 1 6 13 14 32 2 12 34 8 29 1 3 15 25 24 2 2 18 18 2 2 7 1 1

TOTAL SUB APPEARANCES: (2) (1) (3) (1) (6)(10) (1) (6) (11) (3) (3) (4) (3) (1) (6) (1) (7) (1) (2) (1)

TOTAL GOALS SCORED: 2 4 1 5 1 2 1 18 3 1 1 1 2 5 1 12

Small figures denote goalscorers † denotes opponent's own goal

---

T. MIRREN PARK

Capacity 12,395 (Seated 6,380, Standing 6,015)

Pitch Dimensions 112 yds x 73 yds.

Disabled Facilities For certain matches special arrangements can be made if prior notice is given.

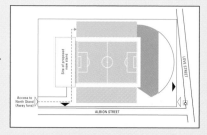

HOW TO GET THERE

Trains: There is a frequent train service from Glasgow Central Station and all coastal routes pass through Gilmour Street. The ground is about 400 yards from the station.

Buses: All SMT coastal services, plus buses to Johnstone and Kilbarchan, pass within 300 yards of the ground.

Cars: The only facilities for car parking are in the streets surrounding the ground.

STIRLING ALBION

Forthbank Stadium,
Springkerse, Stirling, FK7 7UJ

Chairman
Peter McKenzie

Vice-Chairman
Peter Gardiner, C.A.

Directors
Duncan B. MacGregor
John L. Smith

Manager
John Brogan

Office Secretary
Mrs Marlyn Hallam

Telephones
Ground (0786) 450399
Sec. Home (0786) 461581
Sec. Bus (0786) 462166 Ext. 221
Ticket Office (0786) 450399
Fax (0786) 448592

Club Shop
At Forthbank Stadium

Official Supporters Club
Forthbank Stadium,
Springkerse, Stirling, FK7 7UJ

Team Captain
Douglas Lawrie

Club Sponsor
McKenzie Trailers

LIST OF PLAYERS 1993-94

Name	Date of Birth	Place of Birth	Date of Signing	Height	Weight	Previous Club
Armstrong, Paul	27/10/65	Glasgow	25/07/91	5-11	11.0	Cork City
Brogan, John Gerald	09/03/54	Hamilton	23/07/91	5-8	11.6	Unattached
Callaghan, Thomas	28/08/69	Glasgow	04/09/92	5-10	11.4	East Fife
Conway, Vincent M.	25/02/75	Bellshill	05/07/93	5-11	12.6	Milngavie Wanderers
Docherty, Anthony Joseph	24/01/71	East Kilbride	01/10/91	5-8	10.8	Dunfermline Athletic
Flynn, David Graeme P.	16/08/67	Stirling	05/07/93	5-10	12.3	Bannockburn A.F.C.
Kerr, James	17/01/59	Hamilton	15/08/90	5-11	11.7	Partick Thistle
Kinross, Scott Joseph	05/11/72	Stirling	06/08/93	5-10	10.7	Motherwell
Lawrie, Douglas Gibb	11/06/66	Falkirk	15/12/89	5-10	11.1	Airdrieonians
McAneny, Paul James	11/11/73	Glasgow	11/09/93	5-10	11.5	Saltcoats Victoria
McCallum, Mungo	28/10/65	Bellshill	21/08/92	5-10	11.7	Stenhousemuir
McCormack, John Thomas	22/07/65	Stirling	10/08/91	5-9	10.0	Meadowbank Thistle
McGeown, Mark	10/05/70	Paisley	13/10/88	5-10	11.0	Blantyre Victoria
McInnes, Ian	22/03/67	Hamilton	09/08/90	5-8	9.13	Stranraer
McKenna, Adrian Paul	31/03/71	Glasgow	20/10/92	6-2	10.9	Airdrieonians
Mitchell, Colin	25/05/65	Bellshill	28/07/88	5-9	11.8	Airdrieonians
Pew, David John	28/08/71	Glasgow	23/07/91	5-10	10.5	Greenhills
Reilly, Robert Piper	23/09/59	Kilmarnock	04/10/91	5-10	11.1	Kilmarnock
Sinclair, James Arthur	31/07/57	Glasgow	23/07/91	5-9	11.4	Unattached
Tait, Thomas	08/09/67	Ayr	12/09/92	5-10	11.7	Kilmarnock
Watson, Paul	16/07/68	Bellshill	08/12/90	5-11	11.7	Thorniewood United
Watters, William Devlin	05/06/64	Bellshill	23/08/91	5-9.5	11.1	Queen of the South

CLUB FIXTURES 1993-94

Date	Opponent	Venue	Date	Opponent	Venue	Date	Opponent	Venue
Aug 4	League Cup 1		Oct 23	Dunfermline		Feb 12	Clyde	A
Aug 7	**Dumbarton**	H		Athletic	A	Feb 19	SFA Cup 4	
Aug 11	League Cup 2		Oct 24	League Cup Final		Feb 26	**Clydebank**	H
Aug 14	Ayr United	A	Oct 30	**Falkirk**	H	Mar 5	Airdrieonians	A
Aug 21	Falkirk	A	Nov 6	St. Mirren	A	Mar 12	**Hamilton**	
Aug 25	League Cup 3		Nov 9	**Brechin City**	H		**Academical**	H
Aug 28	**St. Mirren**	H	Nov 13	**Clyde**	H	Mar 19	**Greenock**	
Sept 1	League Cup 4		Nov 20	Clydebank	A		**Morton**	H
Sept 4	Brechin City	A	Nov 27	Hamilton		Mar 26	Dumbarton	A
Sept 11	**Dunfermline**			Academical	A	Mar 29	**Ayr United**	H
	Athletic	H	Dec 4	**Airdrieonians**	H	Apr 2	Dunfermline	
Sept 14	Greenock Morton	A	Dec 11	**Ayr United**	H		Athletic	A
Sept 18	Airdrieonians	A	Dec 18	Greenock Morton	A	Apr 9	**Clyde**	H
Sept 22	League Cup S/F		Dec 27	**Dumbarton**	H	Apr 16	Clydebank	A
Sept 25	**Hamilton**		Jan 1	Falkirk	A	Apr 23	**Airdrieonians**	H
	Academical	H	Jan 8	**St. Mirren**	H	Apr 27	Hamilton	
Sept 28	**Clydebank**	H	Jan 15	Brechin City	A		Academical	A
Oct 2	Clyde	A	Jan 22	Ayr United	A	Apr 30	**Falkirk**	H
Oct 9	Dumbarton	A	Jan 29	SFA Cup 3		May 7	St. Mirren	A
Oct 16	**Greenock**		Feb 5	**Dunfermline**		May 14	**Brechin City**	H
	Morton	H		**Athletic**	H	May 21	SFA Cup Final	

MILESTONES
Year of Formation: 1945
Most League points in a Season:
59 (Division 2) - 1964/65
Most League goals scored by a player in a Season: Joe Hughes (26) Season 1969/70
Record Attendance: 26,400 v Celtic, Scottish Cup, 11/3/59
Record Victory: 20-0 v Selkirk, Scottish Cup, 8/12/84
Record Defeat: 0-9 v Dundee United, League, 30/12/67

SEASON TICKET INFORMATION
Seated   Adult £120
        Juvenile £60

LEAGUE ADMISSION PRICES
Seated   Adult £6
        Juvenile £3

Registered Strip: Shirt - Red with White Sleeves with Two Red Bands and White Collar with Navy Band, Shorts - White with Red, Navy, Red Leg Band, Stockings - Red, White Turnover with Red, White, Navy Band

Change Strip: Shirt - Royal Blue with White Sleeves with Royal Blue and Red Print, Red Collar, Shorts - Royal Blue with White, Red, White Leg Band, Stockings - Royal Blue, Royal Blue Turnover with White, Red, White Touching Bands

CLUB FACTFILE 1992/93... RESULTS... APPEARANCES... SCORERS

The ALBION

Date	Venue	Opponents	Result	McGeown M.	Mitchell C.	Watson P.	Shanks D.	Lawrie D.	Clark R.	Reilly R.	Moore V.	Watters W.	McInnes I.	Armstrong P.	Docherty R.	Docherty A.	Taylor G.	Robertson S.	Kerr J.	McCallum M.	Brown I.	McCormack J.	Tait T.	Ross B.	Dempsey J.	Callaghan T.	Pew D.	McKenna A.	Brogan J.
Aug 1	A	Dumbarton	3-4	1	2	3	4	5	6	7²	8	9	10¹	11	12	14													
4	A	Raith Rovers	0-0	1	2		4		6	7	8	9	14	3	12	11	5	10											
8	H	Cowdenbeath	2-1	1	2		4		5	7	8¹	9¹	14	3	12	11		10	6										
15	H	Meadowbank Thistle	1-0	1	2		4		5		8	9	7¹	3	11	12		10	6										
22	A	Hamilton Academical	0-2	1	2		4		5		8	9	7	3	11			10	6	12	14								
29	A	St. Mirren	0-0	1	2	3	4		5		8	9	10	11	12	14			6	7									
Sept 5	H	Dunfermline Athletic	0-5	1	2	3			5	7	8	9	10	11	4	14			6	12									
12	H	Kilmarnock	0-1	1		3	4			7		9	12	11			14	5	6			2	8	10					
19	A	Clydebank	1-4	1			4			7		9	10	11					6	14¹			8	2	5	12			
26	H	Morton	1-1	1	2¹	3		5			8	9	14						10	6	11				4	7			
Oct 3	A	Ayr United	1-2	1	2	3	14	5		7	8	9¹	4						10	6					11	12			
10	H	Dumbarton	1-2	1	2		14	5¹			8	9	4	3					10	6		12			11	7			
17	A	Cowdenbeath	1-1	1	2	3	4	5			14	9¹	8	11					10	6		7							
24	A	Dunfermline Athletic	0-1	1	6	3	2	5			8	9	4	11					10		14				12		7		
31	H	St. Mirren	0-1	1	2	3	4	5		9	8	12		11		10			6						14		7		
Nov 7	H	Meadowbank Thistle	4-1	1	2	3	4¹			12¹	5	14	7¹	11		10			6						8¹		9		
14	A	Hamilton Academical	0-1	1	2	3		5		12	8	14	7	11		10			6						4		9		
21	A	Clydebank	0-1	1	6	3	2			7	8	9	10	11		14	5					4			12				
28	A	Kilmarnock	0-1	1	2	3		5		7	8		10	11		14					6	4				12	9		
Dec 1	H	Ayr United	0-0	1	2	3		5		7	8		10	11		12					6	4				9	14		
5	A	Morton	2-2	1	2	3		5		12		7	11	14	8		6				4			10¹		9¹			
12	A	Dumbarton	3-0	1	2²	3		5¹		12		8	11						7		6	4			10		9		
29	H	Raith Rovers	0-3	1	2	3		5		12		8	11	14					7		6	4			10		9		
Jan 2	H	Hamilton Academical	0-0	1	6	3		5		7		8	11	14					12		2	4			10		9		
16	A	St. Mirren	0-1	1	2	3		5		14		9	7	10		8			6			4			14	11			
26	A	Ayr United	2-2	1	2	3		5		14		9¹	7	10		8			6			4			12	11¹			
Feb 6	A	Meadowbank Thistle	†1-1	1		3	14	5				9	7	10					6		2	4			8	11	12		
9	H	Dunfermline Athletic	1-2	1		3	4	5		12			7	10					6		2	8			14	11¹	9		
13	A	Raith Rovers	0-2	1		3	4			12	14		7	10					6		2			5	8	11	9		
16	A	Cowdenbeath	2-1	1	2	3	4			8		14¹	7	10					6					5	12	11¹	9		
20	H	Morton	0-2	1	2	3	4	5		8			14	7	10				6	9		12				11			
27	A	Clydebank	1-1	1	2			5		10	8	9¹	14	3					6	12		4			7	11			
Mar 6	H	Kilmarnock	2-0	1	2			5		10	8	9²	12	3					6	14		4			7	11			
9	H	Dumbarton	1-0	1	2			5		10	8	9	12	3						14¹		6	4		7	11			
13	H	Cowdenbeath	1-1	1	2			5		10	8	9¹	12	3						14		6	4		7	11			
20	A	Hamilton Academical	0-2	1	2		6	5		10	8	9	12	3						14			4		7	11			
27	H	Meadowbank Thistle	2-2	1	2	3		5		10	8	9¹	7	6						11			4¹						
Apr 3	A	Dunfermline Athletic	1-0	1	2	3				10	8¹		12	7	11				14			6	4					9	5
10	H	St. Mirren	2-1	1	2	3				10	8²	12	7	11				14				6	4					9	5
17	H	Kilmarnock	0-3	1	2	3				10	8	12	7	11				14				6	4					9	5
24	H	Clydebank	2-3	1	2					10	8	9	7	3¹				14		6	12	11	4¹						5
May 1	A	Raith Rovers	2-1	1	6	3¹	8	5					7	11¹					12			9	2		4		10		14
8	H	Morton	3-1	1	6		2	8	5			12	7¹	11					6	9²			3	4			10	14	
15	H	Ayr United	1-1	1	6		2	5				8	14¹	7	11				12			9	3	4			10		
TOTAL FULL APPEARANCES				44	39	31	21	28	7	24	28	25	34	42	3	7	4	9	26	9	1	18	26	2	4	18	17	17	
TOTAL SUB APPEARANCES						(3)				(9)	(3)	(9)	(9)		(4)	(17)				(10)	(3)		(1)		(8)	(3)	(2)	(1)
TOTAL GOALS SCORED				3	1	1	2			3	4	11	4	2					4				2			2	3	1	

*Small figures denote goalscorers † denotes opponent's own goal

‌ORTHBANK STADIUM

‌apacity 3,808; Seated 2,508; ‌tanding 1,300

‌itch Dimensions 110 yds x 74 yds

‌isabled Facilities Disabled access, ‌oilets and spaces for 36

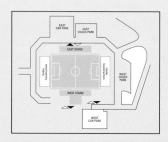

HOW TO GET THERE

Trains: The nearest station is Stirling Railway Station, which is approx. 2 miles from the ground. A bus service from Goosecroft Road travels to the stadium (buses run every 25 mins from 1.50pm - 2.40pm and return to town at 4.50pm).

Buses: To Goosecroft Bus Station, Stirling, and bus to stadium from Goosecroft Road (outside Bus Station) every 25 mins from 1.50pm - 2.40pm and return to town at 4.50pm.

Cars: Follow signs for A91 St Andrew's/Alloa. Car parking is available in the club car park. Home support in West Car Park and visiting support in East Car Park.

CLYDE AND BRECHIN GO UP AFTER NAIL-BITING FINISH

THE promotion issue in the Second Division was not settled until the final seconds of a long and nerve-wracking season.... and even then it was some considerable time after the final whistle had been blown at two of the venues before clubs knew their true fate.

Champions Clyde and Brechin, whom fate and the Scottish League computer had decreed should face each other on that final day, ultimately celebrated, for both were promoted.

However, that left Stranraer distraught, for their officials, players and supporters had been celebrating for some minutes after their emphatic last-day 5-2 win over Stenhousemuir at Ochilview in the belief that, for the first time in their history, they would be playing the next season in the First Division by virtue of taking second place.

That assumption, however, was made on an incorrect scoreline concerning Brechin which had been relayed to them. When finally informed of the true outcome, their

Manager Alex McAnespie admitted, "This is the worst moment of my career in football. I am so sorry for everyone connected with the club - players, officials, and most of all, the supporters, for so much endeavour has been put into our campaign throughout this season."

For Clyde and Brechin, the outcome of their work over the season was the expectation that they would be testing their skills at a higher level next time around.

Clyde, guided by the experienced Manager Alex Smith, had been considered favourites from the start of the campaign, and that imposed its own pressure, particularly as they were still the 'nomads' of Scottish football, playing all their "home" games at Douglas Park, Hamilton.

With the longer-term prospect of a move in the future to Cumbernauld and a custom-built 10,000 seated stadium, there was a desire within the club for success. But there were to be a number of hurdles to overcome before eventual success and Manager Smith is quick to point out that during the season,

Champions Clyd

there were a number of important turning points in their campaign

He remembers, "We had a spell around October when we stuttered after losing to Brechin, but then took 12 points from six games which stood us in good stead at the turn of the year.

Then we had a very important game on the last Saturday of February when we defeated East Fife and during that game our experienced striker Frank McGarvey scored a very good goal. Another very important score was that of Gordon Wylde later in the season when we were trailing by one goal a Stranraer. With seven minutes to go he equalised to give us a share of the points and that was a big point for us at that time."

Smith, looking back over the season, spots a lesson not only for himself but for all Managers. He concludes, "There was a stage when we were faced with a lot of disappointment, but we did not panic. We did not change things, but kept working very hard and with the help of my backroom team, we all came through it."

During the season, Clyde saw rookie goalkeeper Scott Howie prosper to become a Scotland Under-21 International, and the much travelled striker Frank McGarvey completed the season in glory by scoring the third goal in the win over Queen of the South which saw the club become Champions of the division.

While Clyde's future was assured before that final day of the season, their opponents Brechin, were on a knife edge vieing with Stranraer for that second promotion place.

Their Manager John Ritchie and his backroom staff had met in an Edinburgh restaurant the previous evening to plot the winning of the two necessary points against Clyde which would gain them promotion, but could not have envisaged the frantic last stages of a dramatic match, when early disappointment turned to success and joy with a late late goal from Mark Miller to secure the two points required for promotion.

Manager Ritchie, however, will not be in charge this campaign, having moved to a full-time position based in Edinburgh as one of the S.F.A.'s Community Development Officers.

Forfar, under their Manager Tommy Campbell, were also in close contact with the promotion issue until the final stages and at one time threatened along with Brechin to make it a one-two for the North-East.

Alloa Manager Hugh McCann enjoyed another relatively successful season at the helm at Recreation Park. After missing promotion on the final day of the previous season, all those attached to the club knew that it would take a major effort to continue that very high standard.

McCann, who assisted the club financially by selling one of his top players, Paul Sheerin to Southampton, succeeded in motivating his players once more, and it was not until late in the campaign that they dropped out of the promotion scene. However, his talents did not go unnoticed and he received reward for his efforts, for Premier Division Heart of Midlothian

spotted his potential and during the summer months appointed him as their Assistant Manager.

Last season was notable also, for the number of managerial changes, as high profile candidates were attracted into the division. The call for success was strong throughout the long campaign and lack of success led to the waygoing of a number of Managers who had opened the season full of hope and optimism.

This led to Alex Totten, who had taken St. Johnstone to the Premier Division from the depths of the Second Division, yet again taking over the managerial reins after a short spell outside the game, when he was appointed Manager of East Fife.

Two former Celtic favourites, Tommy Gemmell and Danny McGrain, also returned to football with Gemmell coming back for a second stint with Albion Rovers, while McGrain took up his first managerial position, being appointed boss of Arbroath.

By contrast, another former Celt, Dom Sullivan, decided that he had spent enough time trying to revive the fortunes of East Stirling and moved aside for his assistant Bobby McCulley to take over.

Terry Christie, a seemingly permanent fixture at Meadowbank, until his resignation during the course of last season, made a comeback with Stenhousemuir and

brought much needed stability by lifting the club from the basement area of the table to a respectable mid-table position.

The ebullient Jim Leishman had a difficult season at Montrose and eventually left to be replaced by John Holt, who played for so much of his career in nearby Dundee, learning his trade under Jim McLean at Tannadice.

Queen of the South, who had experimented without a Manager, finally succumbed to the necessities of the modern-day game and brought back Billy McLaren for a second spell, appointing him after he had been in charge of Albion Rovers for only a few weeks.

By contrast, Jimmy Crease at Berwick, continued his efforts to quietly re-shape the playing staff, while similar efforts are being made off the field by the Directors to resurrect the financial side of the club.

And of course, the popular Eddie Hunter continued to labour long and hard with Queen's Park as he faced up to the onerous task in these highly professional times of attracting young talented players to play only for the pleasure of playing, knowing that each year, he will lose the best of his youngsters to the professional ranks.

BILL MARWICK
(Freelance)

Brechin City celebrate promotion to the First Division

ALBION ROVERS

Cliftonhill Stadium,
Main Street, Coatbridge,
ML5 3RB.

Chairman
Jack McGoogan, LL.B., D.M.S., N.P.
Vice-Chairman
Robin W. Marwick, J.P., R.I.B.A.
Directors
David Lyttle;
David Forrester, C.A.
Manager
Thomas Gemmell
Secretary
David Forrester, C.A.
Commercial Manager
Laurie Cameron

Telephones
Ground (0236) 432350
Sec. Home (0236) 421892
Sec. Bus. (0236) 433438
Commercial (041) 771-4585

Club Shop
Cliftonhill Stadium, Main
Street, Coatbridge, ML5 3RB.
Open one hour prior to
kick-off at first team home
matches.

Team Captain
Thomas Spence

Club Sponsor
John C. Dalziel (Airdrie)
Limited

LIST OF PLAYERS 1993-94

Name	Date of Birth	Place of Birth	Date of Signing	Height	Weight	Previous Club
Burns, Robert	26/02/63	Paisley	24/09/93	5-10	11.10	Largs Thistle
Cadden, Stephen Joseph	26/11/68	Calderpark	10/02/88	6-0	11.6	Motherwell
Conn, Samuel Craig	26/10/61	Lanark	01/10/93	5-11	12.0	Airdrieonians
Fraser, Alasdair	29/01/68	Coatbridge	02/08/93	5-10	11.0	East Fife
Gallagher, John	02/06/69	Glasgow	29/11/91	5-9	10.10	Arbroath
Horne, John	23/05/72	Glasgow	19/08/93	5-8	11.0	Pollok
Kelly, James	04/09/71	Stirling	19/12/91	5-10	11.0	Airdrieonians
Kerrigan, Steven John	09/10/72	Bellshill	22/07/92	6-0	11.8	Newmains Juveniles
McBride, Martin Joseph	22/03/71	Glasgow	22/07/92	5-9	10.7	Campsie Black Watch
McCaffrey, John Brendan	17/10/72	Glasgow	29/08/92	6-1	12.0	Heart of Midlothian
McConnachie, Ronald A.	01/11/72	Greenock	06/11/91	6-4	11.2	Greenock Morton
McKeown, Desmond M.	18/01/70	Glasgow	05/01/90	5-11	11.0	Airdrieonians
McQuade, Alan	13/01/75	Glasgow	04/06/93	5-6	9.8	Motherwell B.C.
Mirner, Eamonn	10/06/66	Glasgow	26/06/92	6-0	11.6	Queen's Park
Riley, Darren Stephen	02/10/71	Glasgow	22/07/92	5-10	12.7	Campsie Black Watch
Scott, Martin	27/04/71	Bellshill	31/07/92	5-10	10.0	Clyde
Seggie, David	13/11/74	Bellshill	13/07/92	5-7	9.7	Monklands Juveniles
Spence, Thomas Agnew	04/01/60	Airdrie	23/07/93	6-0	13.4	East Fife
Taylor, Gordon	28/11/70	Falkirk	03/08/93	6-0	11.6	Stirling Albion

CLUB FIXTURES 1993-94

Date	Opponent	Venue	Date	Opponent	Venue	Date	Opponent	Venue
Aug 4	League Cup 1		Oct 30	Montrose	A	Feb 19	**East**	
Aug 7	**Alloa**	H	Nov 6	**Forfar Athletic**	H		**Stirlingshire**	H
Aug 11	League Cup 2		Nov 13	**Cowdenbeath**	H	Feb 26	Stranraer	A
Aug 14	Forfar Athletic	A	Nov 20	Queen of the		Mar 5	**Montrose**	H
Aug 21	**Queen's Park**	H		South	A	Mar 12	Queen of the	
Aug 25	League Cup 3		Nov 27	Arbroath	A		South	A
Aug 28	Stranraer	A	Dec 4	**East**		Mar 19	**Queen's Park**	H
Sept 1	League Cup 4			**Stirlingshire**	H	Mar 26	Stenhousemuir	A
Sept 4	Berwick Rangers	A	Dec 11	SFA Cup 1		Apr 2	East Fife	A
Sept 11	**Stenhousemuir**	H	Dec 18	Alloa	A	Apr 9	**Cowdenbeath**	H
Sept 18	Cowdenbeath	A	Dec 27	**Montrose**	H	Apr 16	Berwick Rangers	A
Sept 22	League Cup S/F		Jan 1	Queen's Park	A	Apr 23	**Forfar Athletic**	H
Sept 25	**Queen of the**		Jan 8	SFA Cup 2		Apr 30	**Alloa**	H
	South	H	Jan 15	**Stranraer**	H	May 7	Arbroath	A
Oct 2	East Stirlingshire	A	Jan 22	Meadowbank		May 14	**Meadowbank**	
Oct 9	**Arbroath**	H		Thistle	A		**Thistle**	H
Oct 16	**Meadowbank**		Jan 29	**East Fife**	H	May 21	SFA Cup Final	
	Thistle	H	Feb 5	Stenhousemuir	A			
Oct 23	East Fife	A	Feb 12	**Berwick**				
Oct 24	League Cup Final			**Rangers**	H			

MILESTONES
Year of Formation: 1882
Most Capped Player: John White (1)
Most League Points in a Season:
54 (Division 2) - 1929/30
Most League goals scored by a player in a Season: John Renwick (41) - Season 1932/33
Record Attendance: 27,381 v Rangers, 8/2/36
Record Victory: 12-0 v Airdriehill, Scottish Cup, 3/9/1887
Record Defeat: 1–11 v Partick Thistle, League Cup, 11/8/93

SEASON TICKET INFORMATION
Seated   Adult £60
             Juvenile/OAP £40
Standing Adult £50
             Juvenile/OAP £35

LEAGUE ADMISSION PRICES
Seated   Adult £5
             Juvenile/OAP £3.50
Standing Adult £4
             Juvenile/OAP £2.50

Registered Strip: Shirt - Yellow with Red Trim, Shorts - Yellow, Stockings - Yellow

Change Strip: Shirt - White with Black Trim, Shorts - White, Stockings - White

CLUB FACTFILE 1992/93... RESULTS... APPEARANCES... SCORERS

The WEE ROVERS

Player columns, left to right: Guidi M., Walsh R., McKeown D., Kelly J., Armour N., Riley D., McBride M., Cadden S., Ferguson W., McCoy G., Scott M., Archer S., Hendry A., Moore S., Kerrigan S., McCaffrey J., Brown R., Kiernan D., Millar G., Conway M., Gaughan M., McDonald D., Seggie D., McGuigan R., Fraser A., McConnachie R., Pryde A., Gallagher J., Gray W., MacAulay I., Andrews G., Pathak J., Jackson S., Houston J., McQuade A., Mirner E.

Date	Venue	Opponents	Result	Guidi	Walsh	McKeown	Kelly	Armour	Riley	McBride	Cadden	Ferguson	McCoy	Scott	Archer	Hendry	Moore	Kerrigan	McCaffrey	Brown	Kiernan	Millar	Conway	Gaughan	McDonald	Seggie	McGuigan	Fraser	McConnachie	Pryde	Gallagher	Gray	MacAulay	Andrews	Pathak	Jackson	Houston	McQuade	Mirner
Aug 8	A	Clyde	0-2	1	2	3	4	5	6	7	8	9	10	11	12	14																							
15	H	Queen's Park	3-2	1	2	3	4	5	14^{1}	7	6	9	10^{2}	11	12	8																							
22	A	Queen of the South	3-0	1	2	3^{1}	4	5	8	7	6	9^{1}	10^{1}	11	12						14																		
29	A	Brechin City	0-2	1	2	3	4	5		7	6	9		10	11	12					14	8																	
Sept 5	H	Berwick Rangers	1-1	1	2	3	4	5		7	6	9^{1}		10		11				8	12	14																	
12	H	Montrose	2-2	1		3	4	5		7	6			10		11		9^{2}	8								2	12											
19	H	Stranraer	1-1	1		3		5		7		9	12	10^{1}		11		4	8		6						2	14											
26	A	East Stirlingshire	1-1	1		3	5			12	7	9^{1}	14	10		11		4	8		6						2												
Oct 3	H	Alloa	0-1	1		3	5			6	7	9	14	10		11		4	8	12		2																	
10	A	Arbroath	0-2	1		3	4	14		7	6	12		10	11			9	5								2	8											
17	H	Forfar Athletic	2-1	1	2	3		4		7	6	9		10^{1}	11^{1}			8	5								12	14											
24	A	Stenhousemuir	0-2	1	2	3		4		7	6			10	11	14		9	5								8	12											
31	A	East Fife	0-5	1		3				7	6			10		11		14	5		4		2				12	8	9										
Nov 7	H	Brechin City	1-4			3	2	6		7		9		10^{1}				8	5	4			11					1	14										
14	A	Berwick Rangers	1-1		2	3	6^{1}	4		12	7	9		14				10	5	8			11					1											
21	H	Stranraer	1-1			3	6			7		10		12^{1}	4	11		9	14	5		2	8					1											
28	A	Montrose	1-2	1		5				7		9	12	10^{1}	4	11		8			2		6						3										
Dec 12	H	Clyde	1-2			3	2		5	6	8	10	9^{1}		11	7		4			12							1	14										
26	A	Alloa	0-4			3			7			10	9	6		8		4			2	5	14					1	12	11									
Jan 2	A	Queen's Park	0-1		14	6			4	7		12	10	9		8		5			2							1	3	11									
9	H	Queen of the South	2-1		14	4			8	7		10	11^{1}	12		6^{1}		5			2							1	3	9									
16	A	East Fife	0-5		12	3	4			6	7			10	9			11			2	14						1	8	5									
30	A	East Stirlingshire	2-2	1						10	7	8		9^{1}		11		4			2	5						14	6^{1}	3									
Feb 6	A	Forfar Athletic	2-3	1		12				5	6			10	9^{2}			11	14	4		2	3												7	8			
13	H	Arbroath	0-1	1	12	3				8	6			11				9			2	5						7	10	4						14			
16	H	Stenhousemuir	0-0		8	4				6	10			11				9			2							5	3	7			12	1					
20	A	Alloa	0-1		4	2				5	7	6		9				8	11									10	3				12	1	14				
27	H	Stranraer	1-2			3				10	12	4^{1}		11				8	9	5		2						6						1	7				
Mar 6	A	Montrose	1-1			4	3^{1}			5	7	6		9				11	2									10		12			8	1	14				
13	H	Berwick Rangers	0-2			4	3			8	10			11				9	2						6			14		12			5	1	7				
20	H	Queen's Park	1-1			3				7	5			11				12^{1}	9^{1}	2					6			10					8	1	14	4			
27	A	Queen of the South	1-3			3				8	12	5		11^{1}				10	9						6					14			2	1	7	4			
Apr 3	H	East Fife	4-2			3				11	7	8		10				6	9^{4}	5								14					2	1		4			
10	A	Forfar Athletic	2-5			3	4			11	7	8		10				6	9^{1}	5^{1}							14			12			2	1					
17	A	Clyde	0-4	1		3	4			12	8			10				7	9	5										6			2						11
24	H	Stenhousemuir	0-2			3	4			2	14	10		8				7	9	5										11			1						6
May 1	H	Arbroath	1-2			3	2			4		8		10^{1}				7	9	11							14			6			1						5
8	A	Brechin City	0-2			3	2				8	11		9				7	10	5								1	6				12						4
15	A	East Stirlingshire	1-0			3	6			2		7		10^{1}				9							8			1	11								14		4
TOTAL FULL APPEARANCES				18	10	37	22	11	17	31	30	13	7	37	9	19	24	29	2	3	13	3	10	1	5	1	10	4	11	7	3	2	1	7	11	3	8		
TOTAL SUB APPEARANCES					(4)	(1)		(1)	(1)	(6)		(2)	(4)	(2)	(2)	(5)	(2)	(5)			(1)	(2)	(1)				(4)		(6)					(3)	(2)	(5)	(3)	(1)	(4)
TOTAL GOALS SCORED					1	2	1			1		3		16	1			1	8	1										1									

Small figures denote goalscorers † denotes opponent's own goal

---

CLIFTONHILL STADIUM

Capacity 1,238 (Seated 538; Standing 700)

Pitch Dimensions 100 yds x 70 yds.

Disabled Facilities Access from East Stewart Street with toilet facilities and space for wheelchairs, cars etc. Advanced contact with club advised - this area is uncovered.

HOW TO GET THERE

Buses: The ground is conveniently situated on the main Glasgow–Airdrie bus route and there is a stop near the ground. Local buses serving most areas of Coatbridge and Airdrie pass by the stadium every few minutes.

Trains: The nearest railway station is Coatdyke on the Glasgow–Airdrie line and the ground is a ten minute walk from there. The frequency of service is about 15 minutes.

Cars: A large car park is situated behind the ground with access off Albion Street, and vehicles may also be parked in Hillcrest Avenue, Albion Street and East Stewart Street, which are all adjacent to the ground.

ALLOA

Recreation Park, Clackmannan Road, Alloa, FK10 1RR.

Chairman
Robert F. Hopkins
Vice-Chairman
George Ormiston
Directors
Patrick Lawlor
Ronald J. Todd
Manager
William Lamont
Secretary
Ewen G. Cameron.
Commercial Manager
William McKie

Telephones
Ground/Commercial
(0259) 722695
Sec. Bus. (0324) 612472
Sec. Home (0259) 750899
Com.Manager's Home
(0259) 30572

Official Supporters Club
c/o Recreation Park,
Clackmannan Road, Alloa,
FK10 1RR

Team Captain
John McNiven

Club Sponsor
Campbell Homes

LIST OF PLAYERS 1993-94

Name	Date of Birth	Place of Birth	Date of Signing	Height	Weight	Previous Club
Bennett, John Neil	22/08/71	Falkirk	09/08/91	5-7	10.0	St. Johnstone
Binnie, Neil	25/12/67	Stirling	28/03/91	6-2	12.4	Bonnybridge Jnrs
Butter, James Ross	14/12/66	Dundee	27/08/90	6-1	12.2	St. Johnstone
Campbell, Colin	05/01/70	Edinburgh	15/05/91	5-11	12.0	Armadale Thistle
Crombie, Lawrence	27/05/71	Edinburgh	12/12/92	5-11	12.0	Lochend United
Gibson, John	20/04/67	Blantyre	31/10/92	5-10	10.10	Hastings Town
Hendry, Michael	20/12/65	Bishopton	03/10/91	5-11	10.12	Stirling Albion
Herd, William Beaton	02/10/59	Edinburgh	31/03/93	5-8	11.7	Morwell Fallons
Lamont, Peter Mitchell	24/11/66	Glasgow	08/10/93	6-1	12.2	Shettleston Juniors
Lee, Robert	19/05/66	Broxburn	04/08/88	5-10	11.0	Fauldhouse United
Mackay, John Alexander	15/10/70	Johannesburg	01/09/92	5-10	10.7	Bonnybridge Jnrs
McAnenay, Michael S.P.	16/09/66	Glasgow	09/10/93	5-10	10.7	Dumbarton
McAvoy, Neil	29/07/72	Stirling	09/08/91	6-2	11.7	Sauchie Jnrs
McCormick, Stephen	19/03/65	Seafield	21/03/92	5-10	11.4	Stenhousemuir
McCulloch, Keith George	27/05/67	Edinburgh	28/08/87	5-10	12.0	Cowdenbeath
McNiven, John Martin	23/12/62	Glasgow	01/08/92	5-11	10.7	Stranraer
Moffat, Barrie	27/12/72	Bangour	09/10/90	5-8	10.4	Gairdoch Colts U'18s
Newbigging, William M.	07/09/68	Blairhall	18/08/90	5-10	13.0	Hill of Beath Jnrs
Ramsay, Steven	13/04/67	Germiston	05/08/88	5-9	11.0	Easthouses B.C.
Russell, Greig	11/01/73	Stirling	26/08/91	5-4	9.12	Sauchie Jnrs
Smillie, Steven	14/02/74	Broxburn	12/12/92	5-7	9.10	Bonnybridge Jnrs
Tait, Gavin James	28/07/61	Edinburgh	01/09/92	6-0	12.0	Berwick Rangers
Willock, Andrew	13/01/64	Southend-on-Sea	09/10/93	5-6	9.12	Dumbarton

CLUB FIXTURES 1993-94

Date	Opponent	Venue
Aug 4	League Cup 1	
Aug 7	Albion Rovers	A
Aug 11	League Cup 2	
Aug 14	**Cowdenbeath**	H
Aug 21	**East Stirlingshire**	H
Aug 25	League Cup 3	
Aug 28	East Fife	A
Sept 1	League Cup 4	
Sept 4	Stenhousemuir	A
Sept 11	**Stranraer**	H
Sept 18	Queen of the South	A
Sept 22	League Cup S/F	
Sept 25	**Montrose**	H
Oct 2	**Meadowbank Thistle**	H
Oct 9	Forfar Athletic	A
Oct 16	Arbroath	A
Oct 23	**Berwick Rangers**	H

Date	Opponent	Venue
Oct 24	League Cup Final	
Oct 30	**Queen's Park**	H
Nov 6	Cowdenbeath	A
Nov 13	**Queen of the South**	H
Nov 20	Montrose	A
Nov 27	**Forfar Athletic**	H
Dec 4	Meadowbank Thistle	A
Dec 11	SFA Cup 1	
Dec 18	**Albion Rovers**	H
Dec 27	Queen's Park	A
Jan 1	East Stirlingshire	A
Jan 8	SFA Cup 2	
Jan 15	**East Fife**	H
Jan 22	**Arbroath**	H
Jan 29	Berwick Rangers	A
Feb 5	Stranraer	A
Feb 12	**Stenhousemuir**	H

Date	Opponent	Venue
Feb 19	Meadowbank Thistle	A
Feb 26	**Queen of the South**	H
Mar 5	**East Stirlingshire**	H
Mar 12	Arbroath	A
Mar 19	Berwick Rangers	A
Mar 26	**Stranraer**	H
Apr 2	Stenhousemuir	A
Apr 9	**Queen's Park**	H
Apr 16	**Cowdenbeath**	H
Apr 23	Montrose	A
Apr 30	Albion Rovers	A
May 7	**Forfar Athletic**	H
May 14	**East Fife**	H
May 21	SFA Cup Final	

MILESTONES
Year of Formation: 1883
Most Capped Player: Jock Hepburn (1)
Most League goals scored by a player in a Season: William Crilley (49) Season 1921/22
Record Attendance: 13,000 v Dunfermline Athletic, 26/2/39
Record Victory: 9-2 v Forfar Athletic, Division 2, 18/3/33
Record Defeat: 0-10 v Dundee, Division 2 and Third Lanark, League Cup

SEASON TICKET INFORMATION
Seated	Adult	£75
	Juvenile/OAP	£45
Standing	Adult	£60
	Juvenile/OAP	£30

LEAGUE ADMISSION PRICES
Seated	Adult	£5
	Juvenile/OAP	£3
Standing	Adult	£4
	Juvenile/OAP	£2

Registered Strip: Shirt - Gold with Two Black Hoops on Sleeves, Shorts - Black with Gold Inserts on Sides, Stockings - Gold with Two Black Hoops at Tops

Change Strip: Shirt - White with Two Black Hoops on Sleeves, Shorts - White with Black Inserts, Stockings - White with Two Black Hoops at Tops

CLUB FACTFILE 1992/93... RESULTS... APPEARANCES... SCORERS

The WASPS

Date	Venue	Opponents	Result	Butter J.	Newbigging W.	McAvoy N.	Romaines S.	McCulloch K.	Campbell C.	Moffat B.	McNiven J.	Smith S.	Hendry M.	Sheerin P.	Bennett N.	Conroy J.	Lee R.	Wilcox D.	McCormick S.	Ramsay S.	Tait G.	Russell G.	Thomson J.	Campbell K.	Gibson J.	Crombie L.	Herd W.	Binnie N.
Aug 8	H	Berwick Rangers	2-0	1	2	3	4	5	6	7^1	8^1	9	10	11	12	14												
15	A	East Fife	0-2	1	2	11			6	7	8	9	10	4			3	5	12	14								
22	H	Stenhousemuir	2-1	1	2^2	3			6	7	8	9		4	14	12		5	10	11								
29	H	Clyde	1-5	1	2	3		5	6		8	9^1	12	4		7		14	10	11								
Sept 5	A	Forfar Athletic	1-1	1	2	3		5	6	12	8	9	7^1	14				10	11	4								
12	H	Arbroath	0-2	1	2			5	6	12	8	9	7	14		3		10	11	4								
19	A	East Stirlingshire	2-4	1	2	14^1	4	5	6	7		9^1	10			3		12	11	8								
26	H	Brechin City	3-2	1	2	14	7	5		10		9^1	12	8	3		4		6^1	11^1								
Oct 3	A	Albion Rovers	1-0	1	2^1		5		10	6	9		7	3		4		8	11									
10	H	Stranraer	1-4	1	2	14		5		10	6	9	12^1	7	3		4		8	11								
17	A	Queen of the South	2-1	1	2^1	5		14	6	10^1		7	9		11		4		8	12	3							
24	H	Queen's Park	0-0	1	2	5		6	10	14	7	9		11		4		8	12	3								
31	A	Montrose	4-1	1	2	5		6	10^3	8	7^1	9		3		4		11	12	14								
Nov 7	H	Clyde	1-1	1	2	5		6	10	8	7^1	9		3		4		11	14	12								
14	A	Forfar Athletic	1-1	1	2	5		6	10	8	7	9		3		4		11^1	12									
21	H	East Stirlingshire	1-0	1	2	5		6	10	8	7	9		3		4		11^1	12	14								
28	A	Arbroath	0-0	1	2	5		6	10	8	7	9		3		4		11	12	14								
Dec 12	A	Berwick Rangers	2-2	1	2	5		6	10^1	8	7		3		4	9^1		11		12								
26	H	Albion Rovers	†4-0	1	2	11		5	6	10^1	8^1	9^1		3		4	12		14	7								
Jan 2	A	East Fife	0-2	1		11		5	6	10	8		3		4	9		14	12	7	2							
26	H	Montrose	3-0	1	2	5^1		6	10^1	8	7		3		4	9		11	12^1	14								
30	A	Brechin City	2-4	1	2	5		6	10	8	9		3		4^1	14^1		7	12	11								
Feb 2	A	Stenhousemuir	1-0	1		5^1		2	6	10	8	14	3		4	9		12	11	7								
6	H	Queen of the South	2-2	1	14	5		2	6		8	10	3^1		4	9^1		12	11	7								
9	A	Queen's Park	3-0	1	14	5		2	6	7^1	9^2	10	3		4	12		11	8									
13	A	Stranraer	2-1	1	14	5^1		2	6	7^1	8	9	10	3		4		12	11									
20	A	Albion Rovers	1-0	1	2	6		5		7^1	8	9	10	3		4		14	12	11								
27	A	East Stirlingshire	2-0	1	2	11		5		7^1	8	9	10	3		4		14	12	6^1								
Mar 6	A	East Fife	2-2	1	2	11		5		7^2	8	9	10	3		4		14	6									
13	H	Montrose	3-1	1	2	11^1		6	7^1	8	9^1	10	3		4		14	12	5									
20	H	Berwick Rangers	0-2	1	2	11	14	6	7	8	9	10	3		4		12	5										
27	A	Brechin City	0-1	1		10		5	6	7	8	9	12	3		4		11	2									
Apr 3	H	Arbroath	0-3	1		11		·5	6	10	8	9		3	2		14	7	12	4								
10	A	Queen's Park	2-2	1		11	8	2	6	10		14	9^1	3		4^1	12	7	5									
17	A	Stranraer	3-3	1		11		5	6	9^2	8		10^1	3		4	12	14	7	2								
24	H	Clyde	1-1	1		11		5	6	10		9^1	3		4	12	8	14	7	2								
May 1	H	Stenhousemuir	0-2	1		11		5	6	10	8	12	9	3		4		14	2	7								
8	A	Forfar Athletic	1-1		2	11		5	6	9		10	3		8^1	14		4	7	1								
15	A	Queen of the South	7-0			11^1		5	6	10^2	4	9	14	3^1		12^2		8^1	2	7	1								
TOTAL FULL APPEARANCES				37	27	34	4	25	33	35	31	32	24	7	30	1	6	31	9	6	18	5	2	9	18	3	2	
TOTAL SUB APPEARANCES					(3)		(4)	(1)	(1)	(2)	(1)	(2)	(5)		(2)	(3)	(2)		(1)	(9)	(3)	(2)	(19)		(2)	(9)	(1)	
TOTAL GOALS SCORED					·	4	6			19	2	9	5		1		1	2	5			5	2				1	

Small figures denote goalscorers † denotes opponent's own goal

---

RECREATION PARK

Capacity 4,111 (Seated 424, Standing 3,687)

Pitch Dimensions 110 yds x 75 yds.

Disabled Facilities Accommodation for wheelchairs and invalid carriages in front of Stand. Disabled toilets are also available.

HOW TO GET THERE

Trains: The nearest railway station is Stirling, which is seven miles away. Fans would have to connect with an inter-linking bus service to reach the ground from here.

Buses: There are three main services which stop outside the ground. These are the Dunfermline–Stirling, Stirling–Clackmannan and Falkirk–Alloa buses.

Cars: Car Parking is available in the car park adjacent to the ground and this can hold 175 vehicles.

ARBROATH

Gayfield Park, Arbroath,
DD11 1QB.
President
John D. Christison
Vice-President
Charles Kinnear
Committee
R. Alan Ripley (Treasurer);
David Kean;
Duncan Ferguson;
Andrew J. Warrington;
Ian S.C. Wyllie;
Alexander C. Watt.
Manager
Daniel F. McGrain M.B.E.
Secretary
Andrew J. Warrington
Commercial Manager
David Kean

Telephones
Ground/Ticket Office/Club
Shop (0241) 72157
Sec. Home (0241) 52194
Sec. Bus (0382) 303483
Commercial (0382) 77783

Club Shop
Gayfield Park, Arbroath, DD11
1QB. Open on match days
and weekday mornings

Official Supporters Club
Brothock Bridge, Arbroath

Team Captain
Jim Hamilton

Club Sponsor
Tayblast

LIST OF PLAYERS 1993-94

Name	Date of Birth	Place of Birth	Date of Signing	Height	Weight	Previous Club
Adam, Charles	05/04/62	Dundee	22/11/91	6-0	13.0	Forfar Athletic
Buckley, Graham	31/10/63	Edinburgh	29/12/92	5-7	10.0	Cowdenbeath
Buick, Garry Robert	12/01/75	Arbroath	27/08/93	5-5.5	10.4	Arbroath Sporting Club
Carling, John	18/03/75	Dundee	08/08/92	5-7	10.0	Dundee Violet
Clouston, Bruce	01/12/66	Broxburn	27/08/93	5-10	11.2	Stenhousemuir
Diver, Daniel	15/11/66	Paisley	10/09/93	6-0	12.7	Stranraer
Easton, Scott Milne	20/11/75	Dundee	31/03/93	6-0	12.0	Arbroath Sporting Club
Elliot, David Euan	23/12/74	Dundee	10/08/93	5-9.5	10.3	Tayside B.C.
Farnan, Craig	07/04/71	Dundee	20/05/88	5-10	12.3	Forfar West End
Ferguson, Wayne Ross	06/08/74	Forfar	03/03/93	5-8	10.7	Forfar West End
Florence, Steven	28/10/71	Dundee	20/05/88	5-6	10.5	Arbroath Lads Club
Hamilton, James Michael	09/12/66	Duntocher	25/01/89	5-9	11.0	Yoker Athletic
Jackson, Derek	29/08/65	Alloa	02/08/93	5-8	10.2	Sauchie
King, Thomas David	23/01/70	Dumbarton	02/06/93	5-8	9.8	Clydebank
Martin, Craig Richard Smith	16/04/71	Haddington	30/08/91	6-0	11.10	Heart of Midlothian
Martin, Michael David	27/08/75	Arbroath	04/08/93	6-1	10.7	Arbroath Victoria
McKillop, Alan Robert	30/11/63	Perth	27/08/93	6-1	12.0	Brechin City
McKinnon, Colin	29/08/69	Glasgow	01/09/93	6-0	11.7	East Stirlingshire
Mitchell, Brian Charles	29/02/68	Arbroath	27/07/84	5-8	13.0	Arbroath Lads Club
Sorbie, Stuart Graham	07/09/63	Glasgow	10/07/90	5-9.5	10.5	Raith Rovers
Strachan, Jeffrey Malcolm	09/08/69	Arbroath	19/11/92	5-10.5	10.0	Arbroath Sporting Club
Tindal, Kevin Douglas	11/04/71	Arbroath	16/01/91	5-9	12.7	Forfar West End
Will, Barry James	09/09/72	Dundee	28/08/92	5-11	11.0	Lochee United

CLUB FIXTURES 1993-94

Date	Opponent	Venue
Aug 4	League Cup 1	
Aug 7	**Queen of the South**	H
Aug 11	League Cup 2	
Aug 14	Montrose	A
Aug 21	**Forfar Athletic**	H
Aug 25	League Cup 3	
Aug 28	Berwick Rangers	A
Sept 1	League Cup 4	
Sept 4	Stranraer	A
Sept 11	**Queen's Park**	H
Sept 18	**Stenhousemuir**	H
Sept 22	League Cup S/F	
Sept 25	Meadowbank Thistle	A
Oct 2	**Cowdenbeath**	H
Oct 9	Albion Rovers	A
Oct 16	**Alloa**	H
Oct 23	East Stirlingshire	A
Oct 24	League Cup Final	
Oct 30	East Fife	A

Date	Opponent	Venue
Nov 6	**Montrose**	H
Nov 13	Stenhousemuir	A
Nov 20	**Meadowbank Thistle**	H
Nov 27	**Albion Rovers**	H
Dec 4	Cowdenbeath	A
Dec 11	SFA Cup 1	
Dec 18	Queen of the South	A
Dec 27	**East Fife**	H
Jan 1	Forfar Athletic	A
Jan 8	SFA Cup 2	
Jan 15	**Berwick Rangers**	H
Jan 22	Alloa	A
Jan 29	**East Stirlingshire**	H
Feb 5	Queen's Park	A
Feb 12	**Stranraer**	H
Feb 19	Stenhousemuir	A
Feb 26	**Montrose**	H

Date	Opponent	Venue
Mar 5	Forfar Athletic	A
Mar 12	**Alloa**	H
Mar 19	East Stirlingshire	A
Mar 26	**Meadowbank Thistle**	H
Apr 2	Cowdenbeath	A
Apr 9	**Queen of the South**	H
Apr 16	Stranraer	A
Apr 23	**Queen's Park**	H
Apr 30	East Fife	A
May 7	**Albion Rovers**	H
May 14	Berwick Rangers	A
May 21	SFA Cup Final	

MILESTONES
Year of Formation: 1878
Most Capped Player: Ned Doig (2)
Most League Points in a Season:
57 (Division 2) - 1966/67
Most League goals scored by a player in a Season: David Easson (45) Season 1958/59
Record Attendance: 13,510 v Rangers, Scottish Cup, 23/2/52
Record Victory: 36-0 v Bon Accord, Scottish Cup, 12/9/1885
Record Defeat: 1-9 v Celtic, League Cup, 25/8/93

SEASON TICKET INFORMATION
Seated	Adult	£80
	OAP	£45
Standing	Adult	£70
	Juvenile/OAP	£45

LEAGUE ADMISSION PRICES
Seated	Adult	£5
	Juvenile/OAP	£3.50
Standing	Adult	£4
	Juvenile/OAP/Unemployed(with UB40)	£2.50

Registered Strip: Shirt - Maroon with White and Sky Blue Shoulder Flashes, Shorts - White with Maroon and Sky Blue Flashes on Thighs, Stockings - Maroon with White and Sky Blue Hooped Tops
Change Strip: Shirt - White with Maroon and Sky Blue Shoulder Flashes, Shorts - Maroon with White and Sky Blue Flashes on Thighs, Stockings - White with Maroon and Sky Blue Hooped Tops

CLUB FACTFILE 1992/93... RESULTS... APPEARANCES... SCORERS

The RED LICHTIES

Date	Venue	Opponents	Result	Balfour D.	Hamilton J.	Martin C.	Mitchell B.	Farnan C.	Boyd W.	Tindal K.	Adam C.	Macdonald K.	McNaughton B.	Sorbie S.	Tosh P.	Holmes W.	Godfrey P.	Sneddon H.	Harkness C.	Florence S.	Will B.	Buckley G.	Strachan J.
Aug 8	H	Brechin City	0-0	1	2	3	4	5	6	7	8	9	10	11	12	14							
15	A	Forfar Athletic	1-1	1		3	4	7	6	12	8	9	2^{1}	11	10		5						
22	H	East Stirlingshire	4-5	1		3	4	7	6	12^{1}	8	9^{1}	2	11^{2}	10	14	5						
29	H	Queen's Park	2-1	1		3		7	6	4	8	9	2	11^{2}	10		5		12				
Sept 5	A	Clyde	0-2	1		3	2	7	6	4	8	9	10	11	12		5		14				
12	A	Alloa	2-0			3	2	7	6	4	8	9	14	11^{1}	10	12	5^{1}		1				
19	H	East Fife	1-3			3	2	7	6	4	8^{1}	9		11	10	12	5		1				
26	H	Montrose	3-4	12		3	2	7	6	4	8	9^{1}		11	10^{2}	14	5		1				
Oct 3	A	Berwick Rangers	1-5	12		3^{1}	2	7	6	4	8	9	14	11	10		5		1				
10	H	Albion Rovers	2-0			3	2	7	6	4^{1}		9	14	11^{1}	8		5		1	10			
17	A	Stenhousemuir	3-1	12		3	2	7	6	4	8	9		11^{2}		14	5^{1}		1	10			
24	H	Queen of the South	0-0			3	2	7	6	4	12	9		11	8		5		1	10			
31	A	Stranraer	0-1	12		3	2	7	6	4	5	9		11	8	14			1	10			
Nov 7	A	Queen's Park	1-0	10		3	2	7		4	5	9	8	11^{1}			14		1	6			
14	H	Clyde	1-1	7		3	4	6	12	2	5	9		10	11	14^{1}			1	8			
21	A	East Fife	3-1	7		3	4	6		2	5^{1}	9		11	10^{2}				1	8			
28	H	Alloa	0-0	7		3	4	6		2	5	9		11	10				1	8			
Dec 12	A	Brechin City	0-2			3	4	6		2	5	9		11	10				1	8	7		
Jan 2	A	Forfar Athletic	2-3			3	4	6		5	2		10	9	11^{2}	12			1		7	8	
5	H	Berwick Rangers	0-1			3	4	6		5	2		10	11	9				1		7	8	
20	H	Stranraer	2-1	7		3	4	6		5	2^{1}	9		10	11^{1}				1	8			
30	A	Montrose	1-1	7		3	4	6		5	2			11^{1}	12				1	8	9	10	
Feb 2	A	Queen of the South	1-0	7		3	4	6		5		8	14^{1}	11	12				1	10	2	9	
10	H	Stenhousemuir	3-2	7		3	5	6	4	2		9		11^{2}	12				1	8		10^{1}	
13	A	Albion Rovers	1-0	7		3	4	6		5	2	9^{1}		11	12				1	8	14	10	
20	H	Brechin City	2-0				4			5	2	6	9	10^{1}	11^{1}				1	8	7		3
23	A	East Stirlingshire	2-1			3	4			5	2^{1}	6	9	12	11^{1}	10			1	8	7		
27	A	Queen's Park	1-2			3	4			5	2	6^{1}	9	12	11	10			1	8	7		14
Mar 9	A	Clyde	0-2	7			4	6		5	14	10	12	11	9				1	8	2	3	
16	H	East Stirlingshire	0-0	7		4		6		5	2	10	9	11					1	8		3	
20	A	Queen of the South	†3-2	7		4		6		5	12	10	9	11	2^{1}				1	8		3^{1}	
27	A	Stenhousemuir	2-1	7		4	9	6		5		10		11	2^{1}				1	8	14	3^{1}	
Apr 3	A	Alloa	3-0	7		14	4	6		5			9	11^{1}	2^{2}				1	8		10	3
10	H	Berwick Rangers	6-0	7		14	4	6		5			9^{1}	11^{1}	2^{1}				1	8	12	10^{3}	3
17	A	Montrose	0-2	7			4	6		5			9	11	2				1	8	12	10	3
24	H	Stranraer	1-4	7		3^{1}	4	6		5			9	11	2				1	8	12	10	
May 1	A	Albion Rovers	2-1	7		3	4	6		5	10			11	2^{2}				1	8			9
8	H	East Fife	3-0	7			4	6		5	3^{1}	9^{1}		11	2				1	8		10^{1}	
15	H	Forfar Athletic	0-0	7			4	6		5	3	9		11	2				1	8		10	
TOTAL FULL APPEARANCES				5	21	32	36	36	34	29	28	28	12	39	26		11		34	28	9	14	7
TOTAL SUB APPEARANCES					(4)	(2)				(1)	(4)	(1)	(1)	(6)		(8)	(8)		(2)		(5)		(1)
TOTAL GOALS SCORED						2				5	4	4	3	19	12		2					6	1

Small figures denote goalscorers † denotes opponent's own goal

GAYFIELD PARK

Capacity 6,488 (Seated 715, Standing 5,773)

Pitch Dimensions 115 yds x 71 yds.

Disabled Facilities Enclosure at each end of Stand with wide steps to take a wheelchair. Toilet facilities are also available.

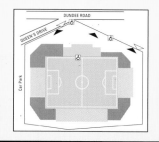

HOW TO GET THERE

Buses: Arbroath is on the main route from both Glasgow and Edinburgh to Aberdeen. Buses from these three cities, plus Stirling, Dundee and Perth all stop at Arbroath Bus Station at hourly intervals. There is also a local service between Dundee–Arbroath and Aberdeen and this service is half hourly until 7.00 p.m. Between 7.00 p.m. and 10.45 p.m. the service is hourly. The bus station is 10 minutes walk from the ground.

Trains: Arbroath is on the Inter-City 125 route from London to Aberdeen and there are frequent local services between Arbroath, Dundee and Edinburgh. Trains also travel north from Glasgow, Stirling and Perth. The station is a 15 minute walk from the ground.

Cars: There is free parking for 500 cars just next to the ground in Queen's Drive.

BERWICK RANGERS

Shielfield Park, Shielfield
Terrace, Tweedmouth, Berwick
Upon Tweed, TD15 2EF
Chairman
Robert W. McDowell
Vice-Chairman
Thomas Davidson
Directors
John H. Hush, Peter McAskill,
James M.S. Rose, Kenneth A.
Rutherford , James G. Bell,
Colin Walker F.C.C.A.,
William M. McLaren
Manager
James Crease
Club Secretary
Dennis J. McCleary
Company Secretary
Colin Walker F.C.C.A.
Commercial Manager
Conrad I. Turner

Telephones
Ground/Ticket Office
(0289) 307424
Sec. Home (0289) 307623
24hr Information Service
0891 800697
Com.Manager's Home
(0289) 307969

Club Shop
Supporters Shop situated
within the ground. Open
during first team match days

Official Supporters Club
c/o Shielfield Park,
Tweedmouth, Berwick Upon
Tweed, TD15 2EF

Team Captain
Steve Richardson

Club Sponsor
Polychrome

LIST OF REGISTERED PLAYERS 1993-94

Name	Date of Birth	Place of Birth	Date of Signing	Height	Weight	Previous Club
Banks, Alan	25/02/70	Edinburgh	27/07/93	5-11	11.0	Meadowbank Thistle
Coughlin, John Joseph	11/04/63	New York	27/07/93	5-11	14.0	Meadowbank Thistle
Cowan, Mark	16/01/71	Edinburgh	15/07/93	6-0	12.7	Armadale Thistle
Cunningham, Craig	30/07/69	Edinburgh	03/08/92	6-0	11.10	Newtongrange Star
Gallacher, Stuart	25/02/72	Bangour	14/09/93	5-7	10.7	Dunfermline Athletic
Gibson, Kevin James	08/12/63	Aberdeen	31/03/93	5-11	12.0	Linlithgow Rose
Graham, Thomas N.	25/08/65	Edinburgh	03/07/87	5-8	11.7	Edina Hibs
Hall, Anthony	17/01/69	Hartlepool	05/08/92	6-1	12.4	East Fife
Irvine, William	28/12/63	Stirling	09/10/92	5-10	11.3	Meadowbank Thistle
Kane, Kevin	30/12/69	Edinburgh	01/03/93	5-10	12.4	Meadowbank Thistle
Malone, Leslie Andrew	08/08/74	Edinburgh	28/10/92	5-8	9.6	Strathbrock Juveniles
Muir, Steven	22/12/69	Livingston	12/03/93	6-1	11.7	Armadale Thistle
Neil, Martin	16/04/70	Ashington	31/03/93	5-8	11.7	Dundee United
O'Connor, Gary	07/04/74	Newtongrange	19/02/93	6-2	12.0	Heart of Midlothian
Richardson, Stephen	12/05/61	Edinburgh	04/12/92	6-0	13.0	Newtongrange Star
Scott, David	18/04/63	Edinburgh	17/09/92	5-8	12.0	Edinburgh United
Sokoluk, John Anthony	22/05/65	Edinburgh	21/09/93	5-10	11.0	Whitley Bay
Valentine, Craig	16/07/70	Edinburgh	03/08/92	5-8	11.0	Easthouses B.C.
Watson, John Martin	13/02/59	Edinburgh	20/07/93	6-0	12.6	Airdrieonians
Wilson, Mark	31/07/74	Dechmont	17/02/93	5-11	10.8	Fauldhouse Utd B.C.

CLUB FIXTURES 1993-94

Date	Opponent	Venue
Aug 4	League Cup 1	
Aug 7	**East Fife**	H
Aug 11	League Cup 2	
Aug 14	East Stirlingshire	A
Aug 21	Meadowbank Thistle	A
Aug 25	League Cup 3	
Aug 28	**Arbroath**	H
Sept 1	League Cup 4	
Sept 4	**Albion Rovers**	H
Sept 11	Cowdenbeath	A
Sept 18	**Stranraer**	H
Sept 22	League Cup S/F	
Sept 25	Forfar Athletic	A
Oct 2	Stenhousemuir	A
Oct 9	**Queen's Park**	H
Oct 16	**Montrose**	H
Oct 23	Alloa	A
Oct 24	League Cup Final	
Oct 30	Queen of the South	A

Date	Opponent	Venue
Nov 6	**East Stirlingshire**	H
Nov 13	Stranraer	A
Nov 20	**Forfar Athletic**	H
Nov 27	Queen's Park	A
Dec 4	**Stenhousemuir**	H
Dec 11	SFA Cup 1	
Dec 18	East Fife	A
Dec 27	**Queen of the South**	H
Jan 1	**Meadowbank Thistle**	H
Jan 8	SFA Cup 2	
Jan 15	Arbroath	A
Jan 22	Montrose	A
Jan 29	**Alloa**	H
Feb 5	**Cowdenbeath**	H
Feb 12	Albion Rovers	A
Feb 19	**Stranraer**	H
Feb 26	Queen's Park	A
Mar 5	**East Fife**	H

Date	Opponent	Venue
Mar 12	Montrose	A
Mar 19	**Alloa**	H
Mar 26	Cowdenbeath	A
Apr 2	Queen of the South	A
Apr 9	**Forfar Athletic**	H
Apr 16	**Albion Rovers**	H
Apr 23	Meadowbank Thistle	A
Apr 30	**Stenhousemuir**	H
May 7	East Stirlingshire	A
May 14	**Arbroath**	H
May 21	SFA Cup Final	

MILESTONES
Year of Formation: 1881
Most League points in a Season:
54 (Second Division) - 1978/79
Most League goals scored by a player in a Season: Ken Bowron (38) Season 1963/64
Record Attendance: 13,365 v Rangers, 28/1/67
Record Victory: 8-1 v Forfar Athletic, Division 2, 25/12/65
Record Defeat: 1–9 v Hamilton Academical, First Division, 9/8/80

SEASON TICKET INFORMATION
Seated	President's Box	£200
	Adult	£80
	Youth/OAP	£40
(For Family tickets add £20 per child under-14)		
Standing	Adult	£60
	Youth/OAP	£40

LEAGUE ADMISSION PRICES
Seated	Adult	£5
	Youth/Unemployed (with UB40)	£2.50
	Under 14	£1
Standing	Adult	£4
	Youth/Unemployed (with UB40)	£2.50
	Under 14	£1

Registered Strip: Shirt - Gold with Black Vertical Stripes, Shorts - Black with Gold Flash, Stockings - Gold with Two Black Hoops

Change Strip: Shirt - Sky Blue with Maroon Diagonal Stripes, Shorts - Maroon with Sky Blue Flash, Stockings - Sky Blue with Two Maroon Hoops

CLUB FACTFILE 1992/93... RESULTS... APPEARANCES... SCORERS

The BORDERERS

Date	Venue	Opponents	Result	Egen J.	Davidson G.	O'Donnell J.	Brownlee P.	Hall A.	Thorpe B.	Hendrie T.	Valentine C.	Cunningham C.	Bickmore S.	Graham T.	Waldie I.	Cass M.	Fisher W.	Thomson G.	Scott D.	Robertson J.	Neilson D.	Hutchinson I.	Irvine W.	Kerr D.	Malone L.	Massie K.	Richardson S.	Shell K.	Anderson P.	Wilson M.	Murray P.	McGovern P.	O'Connor G.	Kane K.	Muir S.	Neil M.	Gibson K.
Aug 8	A	Alloa	0-2	1	2	3	4	5	6	7	8	9	10	11	12																							
15	A	Stenhousemuir	3-1	1	6¹	3		4		2	8	9	12	10¹	14	5¹		7	11																			
22	A	Brechin City	1-5	1	2	3		5	10	4	8	9		11¹	12	6	7																					
29	A	Montrose	3-1	1	7²	3		5	14	2	8	11		10	6	4			9¹	12																		
Sept 5	A	Albion Rovers	1-1		4¹	3		5	12	2	8	11		10		6	7		9	14			1															
12	A	Queen of the South	0-1		4			5	10	2	8	11		12		6	7		9	3			1															
19	H	Queen's Park	1-0		4			5	10	2	8	11				6	7¹		9	3			1															
26	A	East Fife	2-4		4			5	10	2	8	11				6	7¹		9	3¹			1	14														
Oct 3	H	Arbroath	5-1		4			5		2	10²	11		12¹		6	7		9²	8			1			3												
10	A	Forfar Athletic	3-5		4			5		2	7	10		11¹	12	6			9	8			1			3¹	14¹											
17	H	East Stirlingshire	2-5					5		4	10	11¹		12		6	14		9¹	2			1			3	7		8									
24	H	Stranraer	1-2					5		2	10	9		11¹	14	6	8		4				1			3	7		12									
31	A	Clyde	0-2		4			5		2	8	10		11		6			9	12			1			3	7		14									
Nov 7	H	Montrose	3-0		4			5		2	10	14		11					9²	8	3	7¹	1			6												
14	H	Albion Rovers	1-1		4			5		2	10			11					9	8	3	7¹	1			6												
21	A	Queen's Park	0-4					5		2	10			11		6	14		9	8	3	7	1				12		4									
28	H	Queen of the South	1-4					5		2	3	4		11			8		9¹	14	10	7	1			6	12											
Dec 12	H	Alloa	2-2		4					8	2	3		10					9²			7	1			6	5											
Jan 2	H	Stenhousemuir	1-1		4			6		2	3	8		11					9		10	7¹	1				5		12									
5	A	Arbroath	1-0					8		2	3	10		11					12¹	14		7	1		9	6	5		4									
16	A	Clyde	0-3		4			8		2	3	10		11	14				9			7	1			6	5		12									
23	A	Stranraer	3-1		4			5		2	3	10¹		11					9			7¹	1			6¹			8									
30	H	East Fife	3-0		2			8			3	10¹		11	14				9¹		12	7¹	1			6	5		4									
Feb 6	H	Brechin City	0-2		4			8		2	3			11	10				9		12	7	1			6	5											
10	A	East Stirlingshire	0-2		4			8		14	3	10		11					9		12	7	1			6	5				2							
13	H	Forfar Athletic	2-1		2		4			12	3	11¹		9¹						14	8		1				5							7		6	10	
20	A	Queen of the South	3-0					5		2	3	10¹		11¹	14						7					6			8	4	9¹		1					
27	H	Stenhousemuir	0-0		4					2	3	9					8		7							5			6	10	1							
Mar 6	H	Clyde	0-1		2			8		14	3	9		11							6	7				5			12	4				1	10			
13	A	Albion Rovers	2-0		2		4				3	10¹		6						12	9¹						5		7					1	11	8		
20	A	Alloa	2-0		4					2	3	9		11				14		12	10						5		7¹					1	6¹	8		
27	H	Montrose	2-0		4			5		2	3	9		11²					12		10								7					1	6	8		
Apr 3	H	Brechin City	2-1		2		4¹				3	9		11				14			10						5		7				12	1	6	8¹		
10	A	Arbroath	0-6		2		4				3			11					9		10						5		7	14			12	1	6	8		
17	A	Forfar Athletic	2-0		4			8			3	9¹		11							10¹						5		14					1	6		7	2
24	H	Queen's Park	1-1		4			8			3	9		11							12						10¹	14	5		7			1	6			2
May 1	H	East Stirlingshire	0-0		4			8			3	9		11							10						5		12	14				1	6		7	2
8	A	Stranraer	1-3		4			8			3	9		11							10						5¹		12	14				1	6		7	2
15	A	East Fife	2-1		4			8		12	3	9		11							10						14		5	10¹				1	6		7	2
TOTAL FULL APPEARANCES				4	31	5	1	37	5	26	38	28	2	38	3	13	10	1	22	10	9	12	28	1	1	13	22	1	8	12	8	2	13	11	3	6	5
TOTAL SUB APPEARANCES						(2)	(4)			(1)	(1)			(11)		(2)			(5)	(4)		(8)	(1)		(3)	(4)				(4)	(4)			(2)		
TOTAL GOALS SCORED					4			1			9	9	1	1		2			11	1			1			9	2						2	1		1	1

*Small figures denote goalscorers † denotes opponent's own goal

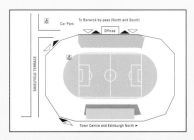

Ground plan labels: To Berwick by-pass (North and South) · Car Park · Offices · SHIELFIELD TERRACE · Town Centre and Edinburgh North

SHIELFIELD PARK
Capacity 1,100 (Seated 500, Standing 600)
Pitch Dimensions 112 yds x 76 yds.
Disabled Facilities Supporters should enter via gate adjacent to ground turnstiles (see ground plan).
The ground is approximately 1.5 miles from the town centre (South) and is situated in Shielfield Terrace, Tweedmouth.

HOW TO GET THERE
Buses: The local bus route from the railway station is the Spittal/Highcliffe service and the nearest stop to the ground is Mountroad. The park is about a mile from this stop and is signposted. Buses bound for Prior Park also pass the ground (The latter service is from the town centre).
Trains: The only railway station is Berwick, which is situated on the East Coast line and a frequent service operates at various stages during the day. From just outside the station, fans can board the Spittal bus service which will then take them near the ground (see above).
Cars: There is a large car park at the rear of the ground. (Nominal charge).

COWDENBEATH

Central Park, High Street,
Cowdenbeath, KY4 9QQ

Chairman
Gordon McDougall
Vice-Chairman
Eric Mitchell
Directors
Ian Fraser;
Albert Tait;
Paul McGlinchey
Manager

Secretary
Thomas Ogilvie
Commercial Director
Ian Fraser

Telephones
Ground/Ticket Office/
Information Service
(0383) 511205/610166
Sec. Home (0383) 513013
Fax (0383) 512132
Commercial (0383) 610166

Club Shop
Situated at Stadium

Official Supporters Club
Central Park,
Cowdenbeath, KY4 9QQ

Team Captain
David Watt

Club Sponsor
GMP Scotland Ltd. (Racewall)

LIST OF PLAYERS 1993-94

Name	Date of Birth	Place of Birth	Date of Signing	Height	Weight	Previous Club
Archibald, Eric	25/03/65	Dunfermline	13/10/89	5-11	13.0	Hill of Beath
Barclay, Alexander Bruce	28/11/74	Edinburgh	07/08/93	5-7	10.0	Whitehill Welfare
Bennett, William Alister	05/07/55	Newburgh	12/08/92	5-8	11.0	Arbroath
Bowmaker, Kevin	03/04/75	Edinburgh	05/07/93	5-7	11.13	Links United
Callaghan, William T.	23/03/67	Dunfermline	17/09/92	5-10.5	12.7	Montrose
Carr, Roger	13/09/74	Edinburgh	28/07/93	5-6	10.4	Links United
Davidson, Ian	15/08/69	Edinburgh	05/07/93	5-8	9.8	Musselburgh Athletic
Douglas, Hugh Jarvie	20/03/64	Haddington	10/11/88	5-11	13.1	Berwick Rangers
Durkin, Paul Joseph	27/08/74	Dechmont	10/09/93	5-6	10.0	Livingston United
Filshill, Stewart	04/10/74	Kirkcaldy	07/08/93	6-1	12.9	Raith Rovers
Harris, Colin	22/02/61	Sanquhar	31/03/93	6-0	12.2	Hamilton Academical
Henderson, Nicholas S.	08/02/69	Edinburgh	18/09/92	5-10	11.1	Raith Rovers
Herd, William David	03/09/65	Buckhaven	30/07/92	5-11	12.7	East Fife
Hunter, Paul	30/08/68	Kirkcaldy	15/07/93	5-9	10.7	Hull City
Knowles, Alan Francis	22/01/75	Falkirk	02/09/93	5-6	10.9	Musselburgh Athletic
Lee, Iain Caird Cameron	07/07/67	Hamilton	28/08/92	5-9	10.7	St. Johnstone
Maloney, James John	03/10/74	Edinburgh	09/08/93	5-11	15.10	Lothian United
Maratea, Domenico	10/04/74	Edinburgh	22/09/92	5-9	12.4	Kelty Hearts
McMahon, Barry	08/04/71	Edinburgh	23/11/92	6-1	12.2	Kelty Hearts
Petrie, Edward	15/06/73	Bathgate	13/07/92	5-10	12.7	Bathgate United U'21
Russell, Robert	11/02/57	Glasgow	18/10/93	5-8.5	10.3	Cumbernauld United
Scott, Colin Andrew	30/11/66	Edinburgh	22/03/89	5-8	13.0	East Fife
Stout, Donald McLaughlin	14/04/72	Johannesburg	07/11/92	5-5.5	10.12	Lochend United
Thomson, James	31/07/69	Edinburgh	22/07/93	5-6	10.0	Alloa
Watt, David	05/03/67	Edinburgh	15/06/88	5-7	11.6	Easthouses B.C.
Young, Allan John	06/08/74	Edinburgh	24/09/93	5-11	10.13	Dunbar United

CLUB FIXTURES 1993-94

Date	Opponent	Venue
Aug 4	League Cup 1	
Aug 7	**Meadowbank Thistle**	H
Aug 11	League Cup 2	
Aug 14	Alloa	A
Aug 21	**East Fife**	H
Aug 25	League Cup 3	
Aug 28	Stenhousemuir	A
Sept 1	League Cup 4	
Sept 4	Queen's Park	A
Sept 11	**Berwick Rangers**	H
Sept 18	**Albion Rovers**	H
Sept 22	League Cup S/F	
Sept 25	Stranraer	A
Oct 2	Arbroath	A
Oct 9	**East Stirlingshire**	H
Oct 16	**Queen of the South**	H
Oct 23	Montrose	A

Date	Opponent	Venue
Oct 24	League Cup Final	
Oct 30	Forfar Athletic	A
Nov 6	Alloa	H
Nov 13	Albion Rovers	A
Nov 20	**Stranraer**	H
Nov 27	East Stirlingshire	A
Dec 4	**Arbroath**	H
Dec 11	SFA Cup 1	
Dec 18	Meadowbank Thistle	A
Dec 27	**Forfar Athletic**	H
Jan 1	East Fife	A
Jan 8	SFA Cup 2	
Jan 15	**Stenhousemuir**	H
Jan 22	Queen of the South	A
Jan 29	**Montrose**	H
Feb 5	Berwick Rangers	A
Feb 12	**Queen's Park**	H
Feb 19	Forfar Athletic	A
Feb 26	**Stenhousemuir**	H

Date	Opponent	Venue
Mar 5	**Meadowbank Thistle**	H
Mar 12	East Stirlingshire	A
Mar 19	Montrose	A
Mar 26	**Berwick Rangers**	H
Apr 2	**Arbroath**	H
Apr 9	Albion Rovers	A
Apr 16	Alloa	A
Apr 23	**East Fife**	H
Apr 30	**Queen's Park**	H
May 7	Stranraer	A
May 14	**Queen of the South**	H
May 21	SFA Cup Final	

MILESTONES
Year of Formation: 1881
Most Capped Player: Jim Paterson (3)
Most League Points in a Season:
60 (Division 2) - 1938/39
Most League goals scored by a player in a Season: Willie Devlin (40) Season 1925/26
Record Attendance: 25,586 v Rangers, 21/9/49
Record Victory: 12-0 v St. Johnstone, Scottish Cup, 21/1/28
Record Defeat: 1–11 v Clyde, Division 2, 6/10/51

SEASON TICKET INFORMATION
Seated	Adult	£90
	Juvenile/OAP	£45
Standing	Adult	£80
	Juvenile/OAP	£40

LEAGUE ADMISSION PRICES
Seated	Adult	£5
	Juvenile/OAP	£3
Standing	Adult	£4
	Juvenile/OAP	£2.50

Registered Strip: Shirt - Royal Blue with White Collar, 3 White Flashes with Red Trim on Right Shoulder, Shorts - Royal Blue with White Flash on Sides and Red Piping Around Legs, Stockings - Royal Blue with White Vertical Stripe on Tops

Change Strip: Shirt - Red with White Collar, 3 White Flashes with Blue Trim on Right Shoulder, Shorts - Red with White Flashes on Sides and Blue Piping Around Legs, Stockings - Red with White Vertical Stripe on Tops

The COWDEN

Date	Venue	Opponents	Result	Lamont W.	Watt D.	Robertson A.	McGovern D.	Archibald E.	Irvine N.	Wright J.	Malone G.	Condie T.	Buckley G.	Johnston P.	Syme W.	Scott C.	Herd W.	Lamont P.	Combe A.	Petrie E.	Ferguson S.	Bennett W.	Lee I.	Douglas H.	Dixon A.	Callaghan W.	Henderson N.	O'Hanlon S.	Archibald A.	Maratea D.	Kelso M.	McMahon B.	Stout D.	Bowmaker K.	Harris C.
Aug 1	H	Clydebank	3-3	1	2	3^3	4	5	6	7	8	9	10	11	12	14																			
5	H	Dunfermline Athletic	2-5	1	2	3	4	5	6	7^1	8^1	9	10	11		12	14																		
8	A	Stirling Albion	1-2				4	5	6	7	8	9^1		12	11				3	10	1	2	14												
15	A	Hamilton Academical	0-3				4	5	6	7	8	9	10	14	12		3			1	2	11													
22	H	Meadowbank Thistle	1-5				4		6	7	8	9	14		10^1	12	3		1	2	11	5													
29	A	Morton	0-1	1			4	5	6	7	8	9	12		11	14	3		2			10													
Sept 5	H	Dumbarton	0-1	1	2		4	5	6		8	9	7		11	12				10	3	14													
12	A	Ayr United	1-0	1	2	3	4	5		7	8	9^1	12		11		14			10	6														
19	H	Raith Rovers	0-3	1	2	3		5		7	8	9			11		4			10	6		12												
26	H	Kilmarnock	0-3	1	2	3		5		7	8	9	14				4			10	6		11												
Oct 3	H	St. Mirren	1-2	1	2	3		5		7^1	8	9					4	12		10			11	6											
10	A	Clydebank	1-4	1	2	3		5		7			8	4	12					10	14		11^1	6											
17	A	Stirling Albion	1-1		2	3		5		7	8	14			4	9				10	12		11^1	6	1										
24	A	Dumbarton	0-1			3	4	5			8	9				6		1	2	10			11	7		14									
31	H	Morton	1-3			3	4	5	14	8^1	9	11				6		1	2	10				7											
Nov 7	H	Hamilton Academical	0-3	12	3	4	5			7		9	11			6		1	2	10		14		8											
14	A	Meadowbank Thistle	0-2			3	4	5		7		9	11			6		1	2	10	14			8											
21	A	Raith Rovers	0-3	1	14	3	4	5		7	8	9	12			10			2	6				11											
Dec 2	H	St. Mirren	0-5	1		3	4	5	14	8	9	12				10			2	6		11	7												
5	H	Kilmarnock	2-3		8		4	5	14			11						1	2	6		9^2	7	10	3										
8	H	Ayr United	2-2		8	6	4			12			11^1			3		1	2	5	14	9^1	7	10											
12	H	Clydebank	1-3		8		4	5				11				3		1	2	6	14	9^1	7	10											
19	A	Dunfermline Athletic	1-4		8							11				3		1	2	12	5^1	14	9	7		10	6								
26	A	Hamilton Academical	0-4	1	2		4				12	14	11			3			8				9	7		10	6								
Jan 20	A	Meadowbank Thistle	2-2	2	3	4	5				12	11^1				10		1	8				6	9^2	7^1										
27	H	St. Mirren	0-3	2	3	4	5				12	11				14	10	1	8				6	9	7										
Feb 2	A	Morton	2-3	1	2	3^1	4	5		11^1						10			8				6	14	9	7									
13	H	Dunfermline Athletic	1-2	1	2	3	4			11		14				10	8		5				6		9^1	7^1			12						
16	A	Stirling Albion	1-2	1	2^1	3	4			11		10				10	8						6		9	7	5		12						
20	A	Kilmarnock	1-1	1	2	3	4			11		9				10	8						6	12		7^1			14	5					
23	A	Dumbarton	0-2	1	2		4	5		11						10	8		3				7	9					12	6					
27	H	Raith Rovers	0-2	1	2			5		12		11				10			8				6	14	9	7			3	4					
Mar 6	A	Ayr United	1-3	1	2	3^1	4	5		11		14				10							6	12	9	7				8					
9	A	Clydebank	0-5	1	2	3		5				11											12	9	7				4	14				
13	A	Stirling Albion	1-1		2	3		5				14				10	6^1	1	8				11	9	7				4						
20	A	Meadowbank Thistle	1-3	1	2	3		5				11				10	8						6	9^{12^1}					4	7					
27	H	Hamilton Academical	0-4			3		5		12						8		1	2				6	14	9^{11}				4	7	10				
Apr 3	A	Dumbarton	0-0			3		5		7						8		1	2				10	6	9				4						11
10	H	Morton	0-1		2	3		5		7							1	8					10	6	14	9	12		4						11
17	H	Ayr United	0-1	1	2	3		5		7							8						10	6	9	11			4						11
24	A	Raith Rovers	1-4	1	2	3^1				7						10	5		8				6	11	9		12		4						14
May 1	A	Dunfermline Athletic	2-0	1	2					7						10	3		5		4	6	9^2	8		14									11
8	H	Kilmarnock	0-3	1	2					7						10	3		5		4	6	12	9	8										11
15	A	St. Mirren	2-1		2					7						10	3		1	5		4	6	12	9^1	8^1			14						11
TOTAL FULL APPEARANCES				25	32	30	27	33		7	28	16	25	12	3	5	14	33	2	18	32	2	1	18	28	3	29	30	1	6	4		12	2	1	5
TOTAL SUB APPEARANCES				(2)					(9)		(5)	(7)	(1)	(2)	(5)	(2)	(3)			(1)	(1)		(1)	(3)	(14)	(1)	(2)		(1)	(6)	(1)		(1)	(1)	
TOTAL GOALS SCORED					1	6				3	2	3	1			1				1				1		9	5								

*Small figures denote goalscorers † denotes opponent's own goal

CENTRAL PARK

Capacity 4,706 (Seated 1,000, Standing 3,706)

Pitch Dimensions 107 yds x 66 yds.

Disabled Facilities Direct access from car park into designated area within ground. Toilet and catering facilities also provided.

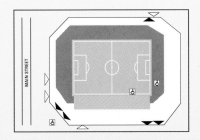

HOW TO GET THERE

Trains: There is a regular service of trains from Edinburgh and Glasgow (via Edinburgh) which call at Cowdenbeath and the station is only 400 yards from the ground.

Buses: A limited Edinburgh–Cowdenbeath service stops just outside the ground on matchdays and a frequent service of Dunfermline–Ballingry buses also stop outside the ground, as does the Edinburgh–Glenrothes service.

Cars: Car parking facilities are available in the club car park for 300 cars. There are also another 300 spaces at the Stenhouse Street car park, which is 200 yards from the ground.

EAST FIFE
SCOTLAND
FOOTBALL CLUB

EAST FIFE

Bayview Park, Wellesley Road,
Methil, Fife, KY8 3AG.

Chairman
James W. Baxter
Vice-Chairman
Stephen Baxter
Directors
John Fleming;
James Stevenson;
Robert Young
Manager
Alexander Totten
Secretary
William McPhee
Commercial Manager
James Bonthrone

Telephones
Ground/Commercial
(0333) 426323
Fax (0333) 426376

Club Shop
A Supporters' Club Shop is
situated within the Ground.

Team Captain
Stuart Beedie

Club Sponsor
Andrew Forrester, Leven

LIST OF PLAYERS 1993-94

Name	Date of Birth	Place of Birth	Date of Signing	Height	Weight	Previous Club
Allan, Gilbert Chapman	21/02/73	St. Andrews	05/12/90	6-0	9.7	Anstruther Colts
Andrew, Benjamin	05/02/73	Perth	20/08/90	5-8	9.6	Lochore Welfare Jnrs
Barron, Douglas	25/10/61	Edinburgh	31/03/93	5-11	10.0	Clydebank
Beaton, David Robert	08/08/67	Bridge of Allan	24/11/90	5-11	11.4	Falkirk
Beedie, Stuart	16/08/60	Aberdeen	22/07/93	5-10.5	11.0	Dundee
Bell, Graham	29/03/71	St. Andrews	12/08/87	5-10	11.0	St. Andrews Juveniles
Burgess, Stuart Robert	22/10/62	Broxburn	25/06/92	6-3	13.0	Kilmarnock
Burns, William	10/12/69	Motherwell	07/08/91	5-10	11.7	Rochdale
Charles, Raymond	17/06/61	Leicester	21/03/87	6-0	11.7	Montrose
Gibb, Richard	22/04/65	Bangour	17/09/93	5-7	11.0	Armadale Thistle
Gowrie, Raleigh Neill	14/04/71	Edinburgh	07/04/93	5-7	11.4	Bonnyrigg-Poltonhall
Hildersley, Ronald	06/04/65	Kirkcaldy	17/09/93	5-5	10.7	Halifax Town
Hope, Douglas	14/06/71	Edinburgh	15/08/88	5-8	11.0	Hutchison Vale B.C.
Irvine, Alan James	29/11/62	Broxburn	12/08/93	6-2	14.5	Portadown
Long, Derek	20/08/74	Broxburn	29/05/92	5-10	12.0	Newburgh Juniors
McBride, Joseph	17/08/60	Glasgow	06/07/91	5-8.5	11.2	Dundee
Reilly, John	21/03/62	Dundee	02/08/93	5-7.5	10.10	Dunfermline Athletic
Scott, Robert	13/01/64	Bathgate	19/07/90	5-9	11.2	Colchester United
Sneddon, Alan	12/03/58	Baillieston	27/07/93	5-11	12.3	Motherwell
Taylor, Paul Henry	02/12/70	Falkirk	19/10/89	5-10	11.7	Sauchie Jnrs
Williamson, Andrew	04/09/69	Kirkcaldy	10/07/93	6-0	11.0	Dunfermline Athletic
Wilson, Ewan	01/10/68	Dunfermline	15/04/93	6-2	12.0	Strathmilgo United

CLUB FIXTURES 1993-94

Date	Opponent	Venue
Aug 4	League Cup 1	
Aug 7	Berwick Rangers	A
Aug 11	League Cup 2	
Aug 14	**Stenhousemuir**	H
Aug 21	Cowdenbeath	A
Aug 25	League Cup 3	
Aug 28	**Alloa**	H
Sept 1	League Cup 4	
Sept 4	**Queen of the South**	H
Sept 11	Meadowbank Thistle	A
Sept 18	Queen's Park	A
Sept 22	League Cup S/F	
Sept 25	**East Stirlingshire**	H
Oct 2	**Forfar Athletic**	H
Oct 9	Montrose	A
Oct 16	Stranraer	A
Oct 23	**Albion Rovers**	H
Oct 24	League Cup Final	

Date	Opponent	Venue
Oct 30	**Arbroath**	H
Nov 6	Stenhousemuir	A
Nov 13	**Queen's Park**	H
Nov 20	East Stirlingshire	A
Nov 27	**Montrose**	H
Dec 4	Forfar Athletic	A
Dec 11	SFA Cup 1	
Dec 18	**Berwick Rangers**	H
Dec 27	Arbroath	A
Jan 1	**Cowdenbeath**	H
Jan 8	SFA Cup 2	
Jan 15	Alloa	A
Jan 22	**Stranraer**	H
Jan 29	Albion Rovers	A
Feb 5	**Meadowbank Thistle**	H
Feb 12	Queen of the South	A
Feb 19	Montrose	A
Feb 26	**Forfar Athletic**	H

Date	Opponent	Venue
Mar 5	Berwick Rangers	A
Mar 12	**Queen's Park**	H
Mar 19	Stranraer	A
Mar 26	**East Stirlingshire**	H
Apr 2	**Albion Rovers**	H
Apr 9	Meadowbank Thistle	A
Apr 16	**Queen of the South**	H
Apr 23	Cowdenbeath	A
Apr 30	**Arbroath**	H
May 7	Stenhousemuir	A
May 14	Alloa	A
May 21	SFA Cup Final	

MILESTONES
Year of Formation: 1903
Most Capped Player: George Aitken (5)
Most League Points in a Season:
57 (Division 2) - 1929/30
Most League goals scored by a player in a Season: Henry Morris (41) Season 1947/48
Record Attendance: 22,515 v Raith Rovers, 2/1/50
Record Victory: 13-2 v Edinburgh City, Division 2, 11/12/37
Record Defeat: 0-9, v Hearts, Division 1, 5/10/57

SEASON TICKET INFORMATION
Seated	Adult	£72.50
	Juvenile/OAP	£46
Standing	Adult	£62.50
	Juvenile/OAP	£41

LEAGUE ADMISSION PRICES
Seated	Adult	£4.50
	Juvenile/OAP	£3
Standing	Adult	£4
	Juvenile/OAP	£2.50

Registered Strip:	Shirt - Amber with Black Vertical Stripe with White Pin Stripe, Shorts - Amber with Black and White Stripe Side Panel, Stockings - Amber with 3 Black Stripes on Top
Change Strip:	Shirt - White with Black Vertical Stripe with Amber Pin Stripe, Shorts - Black with White Side Panel with Black/Amber Stripe, Stockings - Black with Amber Turnover

CLUB FACTFILE 1992/93... RESULTS... APPEARANCES... SCORERS

The FIFERS

Best-effort reconstruction of the appearances grid. Small figures denote goalscorers.

Date	Venue	Opponents	Result	Moffat J.	Bell G.	Spence T.	Burns W.	Beaton D.	McCracken D.	Elliott D.	Brown W.	Scott R.	Sludden J.	McBride J.	Hope D.	Skelligan R.	Burgess S.	Taylor P.	Allan G.	Charles R.	Blyth A.	Andrew B.	Speirs A.	Lennox S.	Fraser A.	Wilson E.	Gibson J.	Barron D.	Long D.
Aug 8	H	Stenhousemuir	1-1	1	2	3	4	5	6	7¹	8	9	10	11	12	14													
15	H	Alloa	2-0	1			6	3	4	7	8	9¹	10	11¹			14	2	5										
22	A	Clyde	2-2	1	12		6	5	4	7	8	9¹	10¹	11			14	2		3									
29	H	Forfar Athletic	0-3	1	14		6	5	4	7	8	9	10	11				2		3	12								
Sept 5	A	Queen's Park	3-1		2	3¹			6	14	8	9¹	10	11¹			4	5	7	1									
12	H	East Stirlingshire	2-2				6	3	2	7	8	9	10²	11			4	5	12	1									
19	A	Arbroath	3-1			3	7	2		14	8¹	9²	10	11			4	5	6	1									
26	H	Berwick Rangers	4-2			3	14	7	6	12¹	8	9¹	10¹	11¹			4	5	2	1									
Oct 3	A	Stranraer	1-2			3	12	7	6		8	9¹	10	11			4	5	2	14									
10	H	Queen of the South	2-5			3	6	5		12	8	9	10²	11	7		4	2	14	1									
17	A	Brechin City	0-1		2	3	11	5		12	8	9	10			7	4	6	14	1									
24	H	Montrose	2-3		2	3	4		6		8	9	10	11²	12		5	14		1	7								
31	A	Albion Rovers	5-0		2	3	7	6		14	8	9²	10²	11			4¹		5	1	12								
Nov 7	A	Forfar Athletic	2-2		2		7	6		12	8	9²	10	11			4	5	3	1									
14	H	Queen's Park	2-1		2		7	6		12	8	9	10¹	11¹		4	5	14	3	1									
21	H	Arbroath	1-3		2		7¹	6		12	8	9	10	11			4	5	3	1		14							
28	A	East Stirlingshire	6-1		2		7	3		12	8²		10	11¹		4²	5	6	9¹	1									
Dec 12	A	Stenhousemuir	1-3		2			3			8		10	11	7	4	5	6	9			12¹	14						
26	H	Stranraer	0-1		2		4	3			8	9	10	11			4	5	6	1		12	7						
Jan 2	H	Alloa	2-0		2		7	3		14	8	9¹	10	11¹			5		6	1		12	4						
16	H	Albion Rovers	5-0			3		5		12	8		10	11²		7	4²	2	6	1		9¹	14						
23	A	Montrose	3-1		2			5		12¹	8		10²	11		7	4	3	6	1		9	14						
26	H	Clyde	1-1		2	3	7¹			12	8	9	10	11			4	5	6	1		14							
30	A	Berwick Rangers	0-3		2	3	4	5		12	8		10	11		7			6	1		9	14						
Feb 9	H	Brechin City	1-0		2	3	7	11		14	8	9¹	10				4	5	6	1		12							
13	A	Queen of the South	1-1		2	3	7	4			8	9¹	10				4	5	6	1		12							
20	A	Forfar Athletic	2-1			3	14	6¹		12	8¹		10	11			4	5	2	1		9		7					
27	H	Clyde	2-3		12		7¹	4			8		10	11¹			5	2	6	1		9	14			3			
Mar 6	H	Alloa	2-2		14	3	6	4¹		12	8	9¹	10	11			5	2		1				7					
13	A	Queen's Park	2-2		12	3	6¹	5			8	9	10¹	11			4	2		1		14		7					
20	A	East Stirlingshire	3-1			3	4	5		14	8	9¹	10¹	11¹				2	6	1				7					
27	H	Stranraer	1-1			3	4	5			8¹	9	10	11		7		2	6	1		14		12					
Apr 3	A	Albion Rovers	2-4		2	3	7	5			8	9¹	10	11¹					6	1		12	14					4	
10	H	Stenhousemuir	2-1			3	6	5¹			8	9	10	11		7		2		1		12¹	14					4	
17	A	Queen of the South	0-2			3	6	5			8	9	10	11		7		2		1		12	14					4	
24	H	Montrose	0-0			3	6	5			8	9	10	11		7		2		1								4	
May 1	H	Brechin City	1-2		12	3	6	5¹			8	9	10	11		7		2		1		14						4	
8	A	Arbroath	0-3		2	3	6	5			8	9	10	11		7	4			1		14		12					
15	H	Berwick Rangers	1-2		2	3	6	5		7	8	9¹	10	11		7				1		14							4
TOTAL FULL APPEARANCES				4	19	24	34	35	10	9	32	26	31	33	33	14	21	24	18	32		9		8	3	3	1	5	1
TOTAL SUB APPEARANCES					(6)		(3)		(2)	(13)	(2)	(2)	(1)	(1)		(4)	(6)		(2)	(8)		(1)	(12)	(2)	(1)	(3)			(1)
TOTAL GOALS SCORED							4	5			3	4	16	13	9	7	5		2			2						

*Small figures denote goalscorers † denotes opponent's own goal

---

BAYVIEW PARK

Capacity 5,385 (Seated 600, Standing 4,785)

Pitch Dimensions 110 yds x 71 yds.

Disabled Facilities Area available at ...st End of Stand.

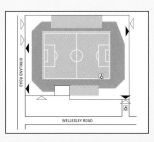

KIRKLAND ROAD · WELLESLEY ROAD

HOW TO GET THERE

Trains: The nearest railway station is Kirkcaldy (8 miles away), and fans will have to catch an inter-linking service from here to the ground.

Buses: A regular service from Kirkcaldy to Leven passes outside the ground, as does the Leven to Dunfermline service.

Cars: There is a car park behind the ground, with entry through Kirkland Road.

EAST STIRLINGSHIRE

Firs Park, Firs Street, Falkirk,
FK2 7AY.

Chairman
William Laird
Vice-Chairman
G. Marshall Paterson;
Directors
William W.H. Lawless;
Alexander S.H. Forsyth
Alexander C. Mitchell
Angus Williamson
Manager
Billy Little
Secretary
G. Marshall Paterson
Commercial Manager
Thomas Kirk

Telephones
Ground (0324) 23583
Sec. Home (0324) 562752
Commercial (Business)
0786 443434

Club Shop
At ground. Open Mon-Fri
10am-2pm (except Thursday)
and on all home matchdays

Team Captain
Brian Ross

Club Sponsor
Greenaway Roofing
Contractors

LIST OF PLAYERS 1993-94

Name	Date of Birth	Place of Birth	Date of Signing	Height	Weight	Previous Club
Conroy, John James	03/11/70	Glasgow	04/08/93	5-7	10.2	Alloa
Craig, David William	11/06/69	Glasgow	06/09/91	6-1	11.7	Partick Thistle
Crews, Barry	29/10/73	Stirling	28/08/93	5-5	10.0	Ayr United
Fitzpatrick, James	17/12/75	Glasgow	09/08/93	5-8	10.0	Motherwell B.C.
Geraghty, Michael John	30/10/70	Glasgow	15/09/92	5-10	9.1	Stranraer
Imrie, Paul	30/06/67	Stirling	30/07/92	5-11	12.0	Plean Amateurs
Kemp, Brian	30/11/64	Falkirk	28/08/92	5-7	10.8	Stenhousemuir
Loney, James	29/08/75	Stirling	28/08/93	5-9	10.0	Denny Hertbertshire
Macdonald, Kenneth S.	09/03/61	Dundee	10/09/93	5-9	11.12	Stirling Albion
McAulay, Ian	06/06/74	Glasgow	05/03/93	5-4	10.0	Tower Hearts
McDougall, Gordon	17/02/71	Bellshill	16/07/93	6-2	12.3	Falkirk
McInally, Michael A.	21/05/76	Stirling	09/08/93	5-8.5	10.7	Stenhousemuir
Millar, Glen Archibald	02/09/66	Falkirk	28/08/93	6-1	13.0	Queen's Park
Roberts, Paul	24/03/70	Glasgow	20/05/92	6-0	12.0	Arbroath
Robertson, Stuart	29/09/59	Glasgow	11/06/93	5-6	9.12	Ayr United
Ross, Brian	15/08/67	Stirling	31/03/91	5-11	10.7	Ayr United
Russell, Gordon Alan	03/03/68	Falkirk	04/08/86	5-9.5	10.0	Gairdoch United
Speirs, Anthony	01/05/68	Paisley	04/08/93	5-9	11.1	Dumbarton
Thomson, Steven	19/04/73	Glasgow	02/09/91	6-0	10.12	Airdrieonians
Tierney, Scott	06/02/69	Falkirk	20/08/92	6-1	13.0	B.P. Amateurs
Yates, Derek Alexander	26/12/72	Falkirk	04/12/92	6-0	11.7	Stenhousemuir

CLUB FIXTURES 1993-94

Date	Opponent	Venue
Aug 4	League Cup 1	
Aug 7	Stenhousemuir	A
Aug 11	League Cup 2	
Aug 14	**Berwick Rangers**	**H**
Aug 21	Alloa	A
Aug 25	League Cup 3	
Aug 28	**Meadowbank Thistle**	**H**
Sept 1	League Cup 4	
Sept 4	**Montrose**	**H**
Sept 11	Queen of the South	A
Sept 18	**Forfar Athletic**	**H**
Sept 22	League Cup S/F	
Sept 25	East Fife	A
Oct 2	**Albion Rovers**	**H**
Oct 9	Cowdenbeath	A
Oct 16	Queen's Park	A
Oct 23	**Arbroath**	**H**
Oct 24	League Cup Final	
Oct 30	**Stranraer**	**H**
Nov 6	Berwick Rangers	A
Nov 13	Forfar Athletic	A
Nov 20	**East Fife**	**H**
Nov 27	**Cowdenbeath**	**H**
Dec 4	Albion Rovers	A
Dec 11	SFA Cup 1	
Dec 18	**Stenhousemuir**	**H**
Dec 27	Stranraer	A
Jan 1	**Alloa**	**H**
Jan 8	SFA Cup 2	
Jan 15	Meadowbank Thistle	A
Jan 22	**Queen's Park**	**H**
Jan 29	Arbroath	A
Feb 5	**Queen of the South**	**H**
Feb 12	Montrose	A
Feb 19	Albion Rovers	A
Feb 26	**Meadowbank Thistle**	**H**
Mar 5	Alloa	A
Mar 12	**Cowdenbeath**	**H**
Mar 19	**Arbroath**	**H**
Mar 26	East Fife	A
Apr 2	Montrose	A
Apr 9	**Stenhousemuir**	**H**
Apr 16	Forfar Athletic	A
Apr 23	**Stranraer**	**H**
Apr 30	Queen of the South	A
May 7	**Berwick Rangers**	**H**
May 14	Queen's Park	A
May 21	SFA Cup Final	

MILESTONES
Year of Formation: 1881
Most Capped Player: Humphrey Jones (5) (Wales)
Most League Points in a Season:
55 (Division 2) - 1931/32
Most League goals scored by a player in a Season: Malcolm Morrison (36) Season 1938/39
Record Attendance: 12,000 v Partick Thistle, Scottish Cup, 19/2/21
Record Victory: 11-2 v Vale of Bannock, Scottish Cup, 22/9/1888
Record Defeat: 1-12 v Dundee United, Division 2, 13/4/36

SEASON TICKET INFORMATION
Seated	Adult	£50
	Juvenile/OAP	£30
	Family Ticket	£50
Standing	Adult	£35
	Juvenile/OAP	£20
	Family Ticket	£35

LEAGUE ADMISSION PRICES
Seated	Adult	£3.50
	Juvenile/OAP	£2.50
Standing	Adult	£3
	Juvenile/OAP	£2

Registered Strip: Shirt - White with Black Horizontal Stripes on Right Side, with White Sleeve and Black Sleeve, Shorts - White with Black Horizontal Stripes on Right Leg, Stockings - Black with White Bands
Change Strip: Shirt - Royal Blue with White Triangles on Right Sleeve, Shorts - Black, Stockings - Royal Blue with White Bands

CLUB FACTFILE 1992/93... RESULTS... APPEARANCES... SCORERS

The SHIRE

Date	Venue	Opponents	Result	Imrie P.	Russell G.	Friar P.	Ross B.	Craig D.	Houston P.	McKinnon C.	Thomson S.	Roberts P.	Walker D.	Auld A.	Barclay S.	McMillan C.	Tierney S.	Mackie S.	Lawson O.	Kemp B.	McCarter S.	Geraghty M.	Woods T.	Watson G.	O'Sullivan D.	MacFadyen I.	Yates D.	Clark R.	McAulay I.
Aug 8	H	Montrose	0-2	1	2	3	4	5	6	7	8	9	10	11	12	14													
15	H	Clyde	1-2	1	2	3	4	5		6	7	8	10	11						9^1	12								
22	A	Arbroath	5-4	1	5	6	4	3		7	8	11^3	10^1	14	12^1	2	9												
29	H	Queen of the South	1-2		2	5	4	3	12	7^1	8	10	11				14			9	1	6							
Sept 5	A	Stranraer	1-4		5	7	4	3	9	2	11	10					12			8	1	6^1	14						
12	A	East Fife	2-2	1	2	8	4	5	9	7	6	12	10						3^1	11^1									
19	H	Alloa	4-2	1	8^1		4	5	9^1	6	7	12	10^1						3	11^1	2								
26	H	Albion Rovers	1-1	1	8		4	5	9	6	7		10^1						3	11	2								
Oct 3	A	Brechin City	1-2	12	8^1		4	5	9	6	7	14	10						3	11	1	2							
10	H	Stenhousemuir	3-7	2^1	6	4	3	9		7^1	12		10						8	11^1	1				5				
17	A	Berwick Rangers	5-2	2	8^1	6^1		9		7^1	12^1	10^1							3	11	1	4			5				
24	A	Forfar Athletic	1-0	2	8	6		9		7		10^1							3	11	1	4			5				
31	H	Queen's Park	2-4	2	8	6		9^2		7	12	10							3	11	1	4			5				
Nov 7	A	Queen of the South	2-1	3			5	9		7	8	10	12				14		8	11	1	6^2			4	2			
14	H	Stranraer	1-2	2	6			9		7	8		10		12^1				3	11	1				5				
21	A	Alloa	0-1		6		14	9		7	8	12	10	11					3	9	1	4			5	2			
28	H	East Fife	1-6	2	6			9		7	8	14	10		12^1				3	11	1	4			5				
Dec 12	A	Montrose	1-4		11	6		7^1		8	2		10		4				3	9	1				5				
26	A	Brechin City	0-0		2			8		7	6		10		9				3	11	1	4			5				
Jan 2	H	Clyde	1-5		14	4		2^1		7	12	8	10		9				3	11	1	6			4				
23	A	Forfar Athletic	1-5		7			9		8		10^1			5	14	12		3	11	1	2			4	6			
30	A	Albion Rovers	2-2		7	4		9		8	11^2	10			5	14	12		3		1	2			6				
Feb 2	H	Queen's Park	2-2		7^1	4		9		8		10			6	11^1			3		1	5	2						
10	H	Berwick Rangers	2-0		7	4		9			2	10	14		6	12	8		3^1	11^1	1				5				
13	A	Stenhousemuir	2-1		7	4		9^1		2		10			6		8		3	11^1	1				5				
20	A	Stranraer	0-0		7	4		12		9	2	10			6		8		3	11	1				5				
23	A	Arbroath	1-2		7	4		9		2		10			6		8		3	11^1	1				5				
27	A	Alloa	0-2	14	7	4		9		2	12	10			6		8		3	11	1				5				
Mar 13	H	Forfar Athletic	0-2	11	7	4		8		2	10				14		9		3			12		1	5	6			
16	A	Arbroath	0-0		2	11	4			8	7	9					10		3			12		1	5	6			
20	H	East Fife	1-3	1	2	11	4			8	7	9^1		10					3			12			5	6			
27	A	Clyde	1-2	1	2	11	4			8	7	12				9			3	10^1	6				5				
Apr 3	H	Queen's Park	4-1	1	2	7	10^2			8	4^1	9^1							3	11	6				5			14	
10	H	Brechin City	0-5	1	2	7	4	6		8	10	9				12			3	11					5			14	
17	A	Stenhousemuir	0-2	1	2	6	4			8	7	12			14	9			3	11					5			10	
24	H	Queen of the South	1-2		2		4	6		8	7	9^1			14	10			3	11	12	1			5				
May 1	H	Berwick Rangers	0-0	1	2			10		8	7	9			6				3	11	4				5				
8	H	Montrose	0-0	1	4			10		8		9			14	7			3	11	2				5			6	
15	A	Albion Rovers	0-1	1	4			6		8		10			9	2			3	11	12			14	5			7	
TOTAL FULL APPEARANCES				14	22	30	34	16	16	36	32	20	25	2	13	6	15	2	36	29	19	23	10	2	21	3	3		
TOTAL SUB APPEARANCES				(2)	(1)			(3)		(2)	(10)	(1)	(2)		(6)	(7)	(5)	(1)			(1)		(5)		(1)				(2)
TOTAL GOALS SCORED				1	4	1	2	3		5	2	9	6		1				4	3		7			2				

*Small figures denote goalscorers † denotes opponent's own goal

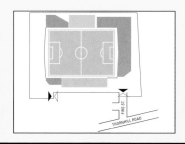

HOW TO GET THERE

Trains: Passengers should alight at Grahamston station and the ground is then a ten minute walk.
Buses: All buses running from the city centre pass close by the ground. The Grangemouth via Burnbank Road and the Tamfourhill via Kennard Street services both stop almost outside the ground.
Cars: Car parking is available in the adjacent side streets and in the car park adjacent to the Social Club. This can take 100 cars and there are also spaces available in the car park adjacent to the major stores around the ground.

FORFAR ATHLETIC

Station Park, Carseview Road,
Forfar, DD8 3BT.

Chairman
George A. Enston
Vice-Chairman
David McGregor
Directors
James Robertson; Ralph J.
Stirton; William C. Taylor; Ian
Stewart; Donald R. Cameron
Manager
Tom Campbell
Secretary
David McGregor

Telephones
Ground
(0307) 463576/462259
Sec. Home (0307) 464924
Sec. Bus. (0307) 462255
Fax (0307) 466956
Club Shop (0307) 65959

Club Shop
45 East High Street, Forfar.
Open 9.00 a.m. - 5.00 p.m.
Mon, Tue, Thur and Fri.

Official Supporters Club
c/o Mrs. Yvonne Nicoll,
24 Turfbeg Drive, Forfar.

Team Captain
Ian Heddle

Club Sponsor
Ramsay Ladders

LIST OF PLAYERS 1993-94

Name	Date of Birth	Place of Birth	Date of Signing	Height	Weight	Previous Club
Arthur, Gordon	30/05/58	Kirkcaldy	08/09/93	5-11	12.0	Raith Rovers
Bingham, David Thomas	03/09/70	Dunfermline	08/12/92	5-10	10.7	St. Johnstone
Cameron, Darren James	29/08/73	Edinburgh	16/09/92	5-8	10.2	Links S.C. Under 21's
Donaldson, Greig William	01/04/71	Dunfermline	03/07/92	5-10	12.0	Heart of Midlothian
Downie, Ian	16/11/72	Dunfermline	07/09/93	5-6.5	9.0	Dunfermline Athletic
Glass, Scott	04/02/72	South Africa	02/10/92	5-8	10.4	Blairgowrie Jnrs
Glennie, Stuart Philip	07/10/75	Torphins	14/09/93	5-10	11.2	Banchory St. Ternan
Gray, Barrie James	04/10/73	Dundee	02/09/93	6-1	11.7	Arbroath
Hall, Andrew	16/08/69	Perth	16/03/93	6-0	12.9	Jeanfield Swifts
Hamill, Alexander	30/10/61	Coatbridge	24/10/86	5-8	11.4	Hamilton Academical
Heddle, Ian Alexander	21/03/63	Dunfermline	07/08/92	5-10	11.0	St. Johnstone
Kopel, Scott Andrew	25/02/70	Blackburn	11/10/93	5-8	11.5	Brechin City
Leddie, Paul	11/10/74	Dundee	21/05/93	5-11	11.8	St. Johnstone
Mann, Robert Alexander	11/01/74	Dundee	21/07/92	6-2	13.3	St. Johnstone
McCafferty, Andrew	22/12/73	St. Andrew's	03/12/92	5-4.5	9.5	Brechin City
McIntyre, Scott	10/05/73	Perth	08/07/92	5-6	10.7	Newburgh Juniors
McPhee, Ian	31/01/61	Perth	27/09/91	5-8	9.13	Airdrieonians
Mearns, Gary	16/12/71	Dundee	11/08/90	5-8	10.0	Dundee United
Moffat, James	27/01/60	Dunfermline	15/07/93	6-0	12.0	Montrose
Morris, Robert Martin	07/03/57	St. Andrews	13/11/80	5-11	10.12	Halbeath Jnrs
Philliben, Robert Devine	19/03/68	Stirling	02/08/93	5-8	10.12	Stenhousemuir
Russell, Neil	29/05/71	Kirkcaldy	13/10/92	6-3	14.3	Tay Thistle
Sheridan, John	16/01/75	Dundee	25/09/92	5-9.5	10.0	Lochee United
Smith, Raymond	01/04/72	Airdrie	13/10/92	5-8	11.3	A.S.C. Perth
Winter, Gordon	20/07/62	Dundee	29/03/89	6-0	12.0	Downfield Jnrs

CLUB FIXTURES 1993-94

Date	Opponent	Venue
Aug 4	League Cup 1	
Aug 7	Queen's Park	A
Aug 11	League Cup 2	
Aug 14	**Albion Rovers**	**H**
Aug 21	Arbroath	A
Aug 25	League Cup 3	
Aug 28	**Queen of the South**	**H**
Sept 1	League Cup 4	
Sept 4	**Meadowbank Thistle**	**H**
Sept 11	**Montrose**	**H**
Sept 18	East Stirlingshire	A
Sept 22	League Cup S/F	
Sept 25	**Berwick Rangers**	**H**
Oct 2	East Fife	A
Oct 9	**Alloa**	**H**
Oct 16	Stenhousemuir	A
Oct 23	**Stranraer**	**H**
Oct 24	League Cup Final	
Oct 30	**Cowdenbeath**	**H**
Nov 6	Albion Rovers	A
Nov 13	**East Stirlingshire**	**H**
Nov 20	Berwick Rangers	A
Nov 27	Alloa	A
Dec 4	**East Fife**	**H**
Dec 11	SFA Cup 1	
Dec 18	**Queen's Park**	**H**
Dec 27	Cowdenbeath	A
Jan 1	**Arbroath**	**H**
Jan 8	SFA Cup 2	
Jan 15	Queen of the South	A
Jan 22	**Stenhousemuir**	**H**
Jan 29	Stranraer	A
Feb 5	Montrose	A
Feb 12	Meadowbank Thistle	A
Feb 19	**Cowdenbeath**	**H**
Feb 26	East Fife	A
Mar 5	**Arbroath**	**H**
Mar 12	Stenhousemuir	A
Mar 19	**Queen of the South**	**H**
Mar 26	Queen's Park	A
Apr 2	**Meadowbank Thistle**	**H**
Apr 9	Berwick Rangers	A
Apr 16	**East Stirlingshire**	**H**
Apr 23	Albion Rovers	A
Apr 30	**Stranraer**	**H**
May 7	Alloa	A
May 14	**Montrose**	**H**
May 21	SFA Cup Final	

SEASON TICKET INFORMATION
Seated	Adult	£75
	Juvenile/OAP	£37.50
Standing	Adult	£65
	Juvenile/OAP	£32.50

LEAGUE ADMISSION PRICES
Seated	Adult	£4.50
	Juvenile/OAP	£2.50
Standing	Adult	£4
	Juvenile/OAP	£2

Registered Strip: Shirt - Royal Blue, Sky Blue and White Geometric Patterns, Shorts - White, Stockings - Royal Blue with White Turnover

Change Strip: Shirt - White with Navy/Sky Blue Collar, Shorts - Navy Blue, Stockings - Navy Blue with White Turnover

CLUB FACTFILE 1992/93... RESULTS... APPEARANCES... SCORERS

The SKY BLUES

Small figures denote goalscorers. Superscript numbers indicate goals scored.

Date	Venue	Opponents	Result	Thomson S.	McIntyre S.	Hamill A.	Morris R.	Mann R.	Winter G.	McKenna I.	McPhee I.	Petrie S.	Donaldson G.	Pryde I.	Heddle I.	Perry J.	McAulay A.	Mearns G.	Price G.	Sheridan J.	Smith R.	Glass S.	Byrne J.	Bingham D.	McCafferty A.	Cameron D.	Hall A.
Aug 8	H	Queen of the South	5-1	1	2	3	4	5	6^1	7^1	8	9^2	10^1		11	12	14										
15	H	Arbroath	1-1	1	2	3	4	5	6	7	8	9^1	10		11		14										
22	A	Queen's Park	2-1	1	7	3^1	4	5	6	12	8	9^1	10		11		14	2									
29	A	East Fife	3-0	1		3	4	5	6	12^1	8^1	9	10^1		11		7	2			14						
Sept 5	H	Alloa	1-1	1		3	4	5	6	7	8	9	10^1		11	12		2									
12	H	Stenhousemuir	3-1	1		3	4	5	6^1	7	8	9^2	10		11	12		2									
19	A	Clyde	0-0	1		3	4	5	6	7	8		10		11			2									
26	H	Stranraer	4-1	1		3	4	5	6^1	7	8^1	9^1	10		11^1	14	12	2									
Oct 3	A	Montrose	0-0	1		3	4	5	6	7	8	9			11	12		2		10							
10	H	Berwick Rangers	5-3	1		3	4	5	6	7	8^1	9^3	10^1		11			2		14	12						
17	A	Albion Rovers	1-2	1	8	3	4	5	6	7		9	10		11			2^1		14							
24	A	East Stirlingshire	0-1	1	12	8	4	5	6	7		9	10		11			2		14		3					
31	H	Brechin City	0-1	1	7	3	4	5	6	12	8	9			11			2		14	10						
Nov 7	H	East Fife	2-2	1	2	3	4	5	6^1	7		9^1			11	12	8			10	14						
14	H	Alloa	1-1	1	7	3	4	5	6	10	8	9^1			11			2									
21	H	Clyde	2-4	1	7	3	4	5	6	10^1	8	9			11			2		12^1							
28	A	Stenhousemuir	0-2	1	2	3	4	5	10	7	8	9	6		11	12											
Dec 12	A	Queen of the South	1-1	1	12	8	4	5		7	3				11			2			9			6	10^1	14	
Jan 2	A	Arbroath	3-2	1	12	10	4	5	6		3	9^1			11^1			2		8^1				7		14	
19	H	Montrose	4-3	1	4	10			5^1	6^1	12	3			11^1			2		8				7^1			
23	A	East Stirlingshire	5-1	1	2	10			5	6	4^3	3			11^1			12		8^1				7		14	
26	H	Queen's Park	2-0	1	2	10			5	6^1	4	3			11			12		8				7^1		14	
30	A	Stranraer	0-2	1	2	10			5	6	4	3			11			12		8				7		14	
Feb 2	A	Brechin City	2-1	1		10			5	6	4	3	9^2		11			2		8				7	12	14	
6	H	Albion Rovers	†3-2	1	2	10			5	6^1	4	3	9		11			8^1		14				7	12		
13	A	Berwick Rangers	1-2	1	2	10			6	4	3	9			11			8	14^1					7	12	5	
20	A	East Fife	1-2	1	2	10			6	4	3	9^1			11			12	8					7		5	
27	A	Queen of the South	4-2	1		3			5	6	9^1	8	10^1		11^1			2						7^1		4	
Mar 6	H	Stenhousemuir	1-0	1	2	3			5	6^1	9	8	10		11		4				12			7		14	
13	A	East Stirlingshire	2-0	1	2	3			5	6	14^1	8	10		11			12		9				7	4^1		
20	A	Montrose	3-1	1	4	3			5	6		8	10^1		11^1			9		14				7^1			2
27	H	Queen's Park	2-2	1	4^1	3	2			6	12^1	8	9		11					14				7	10		5
Apr 3	A	Stranraer	1-3	1	2	3			6	12	8	10			11		4			14				7^1	9	5	
10	H	Albion Rovers	5-2	1	2	3			5	6	14	8	9^3		11		4			10^2				7	12		
17	H	Berwick Rangers	0-2	1	2	3			5	6		8	9		11		4		14	10				7	12		
24	A	Brechin City	1-0	1	2	3			5	6	14^1	8	10		11		4			9				7			
May 1	A	Clyde	2-3	1	2	3	6^1	5			14	8	10		11		4			12	9^1					7	
8	H	Alloa	1-1	1	2	3	4	5		6	14	8	10		11		7				9^1						
15	A	Arbroath	0-0	1	2	3	4	5		6	12	8	9		11		10							7	14		
TOTAL FULL APPEARANCES				39	27	39	23	35	37	24	36	37	11	1	37		1	28		7	15	1	1	20	6	2	2
TOTAL SUB APPEARANCES					(3)					(12)				(1)		(3)	(6)	(3)	(2)	(7)	(10)				(12)	(1)	
TOTAL GOALS SCORED					1	1	1	1	8	10	3	21	4		6			1		1				8	6	1	

Small figures denote goalscorers † denotes opponent's own goal

STATION PARK

Capacity 8,732 (Seated 800, Standing 7,932)

Pitch Dimensions 115 yds x 69 yds.

Disabled Facilities Ramp entrance to Main Stand.

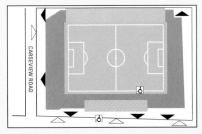

CARSEVIEW ROAD

HOW TO GET THERE

Buses: There is a regular service of buses departing from Dundee City Centre into Forfar. The bus station in the town is about half a mile from the ground. There is also a local service.

Trains: The nearest railway station is Dundee (14 miles away) and fans who travel to here should then board a bus for Forfar from the city centre. Arbroath station is also about 14 miles away.

Cars: There are car parking facilities in adjacent streets to the ground and also in the Market Muir car park.

MEADOWBANK THISTLE

Meadowbank Stadium,
Edinburgh, EH7 6AE

Hon President
John P. Blacklaw, C.ENG., M.I.E.E.
Chairman
William L. Mill
Vice-Chairman
Hugh Cowan
Directors
William P. Hunter (Treasurer)
John L. Bain B.E.M.
Walter Hay
Robert Clark
Manager
Donald Park
Secretary
William P. Hunter
Commercial Manager
Gordon Graham

Telephones
Ground (031) 661-5351
Sec. Bus./Ticket Office/
Information Service
(0875) 812383
Sec. Home (0875) 811876
Fax (0875) 811130
Commercial (031) 661 2902

Official Supporters Club
Mr. Keith Brown, 100h
Saughton Road North,
Edinburgh EH12 7JN.
Eastern: Colin Penman, 198
South Seton Park, Port Seton
EH32 0BS

Team Captain
Gordon McLeod

Club Sponsor
PAR Scaffolding Ltd.

LIST OF PLAYERS 1993-94

Name	Date of Birth	Place of Birth	Date of Signing	Height	Weight	Previous Club
Bailey, Lee	10/07/72	Edinburgh	04/08/92	6-0	10.0	Hibernian
Brock, John Paul	16/04/71	Edinburgh	14/09/93	6-3	12.0	Civil Service Strollers
Coulston, Douglas	12/08/71	Glasgow	28/07/92	5-10	11.0	Moray House College
Coyle, Malcolm Arthur	19/03/74	Musselburgh	18/07/92	6-2	11.0	Hutchison Vale B.C.
Davidson, Graeme	18/01/68	Edinburgh	23/07/93	5-10	11.0	Berwick Rangers
Duthie, Mark	19/08/72	Edinburgh	25/08/90	5-8	10.0	Edina Hibs
Elder, Stuart Richard	25/07/66	Rinteln	25/09/92	6-1	13.0	Lochore Welfare
Ellison, Steven	03/03/70	Edinburgh	25/08/90	6-1	12.3	Lochend B.C.
Fleming, Derek	05/12/73	Falkirk	30/03/93	5-7	10.2	Broxburn Athletic
Graham, Thomas	12/05/68	Edinburgh	18/06/90	6-0	13.0	Cavalry Park B.C.
Hutchison, Mark	13/07/73	Edinburgh	22/06/91	5-10	10.7	Links United
Little, Ian James	10/12/73	Edinburgh	25/08/90	5-6	8.12	Tynecastle B.C.
McCartney, Craig	18/11/71	Edinburgh	30/07/93	5-9	11.0	Links United B.C.
McLeod, Gordon Thomas	02/09/67	Edinburgh	25/09/92	5-9	11.2	Dundee
Murray, Malcolm	26/07/64	Buckie	04/09/92	5-11	11.4	Clydebank
Nicol, Andrew	03/12/60	Falkirk	31/07/91	5-9	11.5	Falkirk
Price, Gavin Gilbert	29/10/74	Perth	29/07/93	5-11	12.0	Kinnoull
Rutherford, Paul	23/02/67	Sunderland	10/10/92	5-9	11.0	Falkirk
Ryrie, Bryan	24/07/71	Edinburgh	13/09/91	5-6	10.0	Penicuik Athletic
Scott, Symon Robert	15/12/70	Edinburgh	18/06/90	5-10	10.1	Campsie Black Watch
Williamson, Robert	12/01/75	Edinburgh	23/07/93	5-8	10.11	Hutchison Vale B.C.
Williamson, Stewart	10/12/61	Lasswade	02/08/88	6-0	11.7	Cowdenbeath
Wilson, Stuart	21/09/65	Edinburgh	01/06/92	5-10	12.0	Bo'ness United

CLUB FIXTURES 1993-94

Date	Opponent	Venue	Date	Opponent	Venue	Date	Opponent	Venue
Aug 4	League Cup 1		Nov 6	Stranraer	A	Mar 19	**Stenhousemuir**	**H**
Aug 7	Cowdenbeath	A	Nov 13	**Montrose**	**H**	Mar 26	Arbroath	A
Aug 11	League Cup 2		Nov 20	Arbroath	A	Apr 2	Forfar Athletic	A
Aug 14	**Stranraer**	**H**	Nov 27	Queen of the		Apr 9	**East Fife**	**H**
Aug 21	**Berwick**			South	A	Apr 16	Queen's Park	A
	Rangers	**H**	Dec 4	**Alloa**	**H**	Apr 23	**Berwick**	
Aug 25	League Cup 3		Dec 11	SFA Cup 1			**Rangers**	**H**
Aug 28	East Stirlingshire	A	Dec 18	**Cowdenbeath**	**H**	Apr 30	Montrose	A
Sept 1	League Cup 4		Dec 27	Stenhousemuir	A	May 7	**Queen of the**	
Sept 4	Forfar Athletic	A	Jan 1	Berwick Rangers	A		**South**	**H**
Sept 11	**East Fife**	**H**	Jan 8	SFA Cup 2		May 14	Albion Rovers	A
Sept 18	Montrose	A	Jan 15	**East**		May 21	SFA Cup Final	
Sept 22	League Cup S/F			**Stirlingshire**	**H**			
Sept 25	**Arbroath**	**H**	Jan 22	**Albion Rovers**	**H**			
Oct 2	Alloa	A	Jan 29	Queen's Park	A			
Oct 9	**Queen of the**		Feb 5	East Fife	A			
	South	**H**	Feb 12	**Forfar Athletic**	**H**			
Oct 16	Albion Rovers	A	Feb 19	Alloa	A			
Oct 23	**Queen's Park**	**H**	Feb 26	East Stirlingshire	A			
Oct 24	League Cup Final		Mar 5	Cowdenbeath	A			
Oct 30	**Stenhousemuir**	**H**	Mar 12	**Stranraer**	**H**			

MILESTONES
Year of Formation: 1974
Most League Points in a Season:
55 (Second Division) - 1986/87
Most League goals scored by a player in a Season: John McGachie (21) Season 1986/87
Record Attendance: 4,000 v Albion Rovers, 9/9/74
Record Victory: 6-0 v Raith Rovers, Second Division, 9/11/85
Record Defeat: 0-8 v Hamilton Academical, Division 2, 14/12/74

SEASON TICKET INFORMATION
Seated		
	Adult	£65
	Juvenile/OAP	£32
	Parent and Juvenile	£85

LEAGUE ADMISSION PRICES
Seated		
	Adult	£4
	Juvenile/OAP	£2.50
	Parent and Juvenile	£5.50

	Registered Strip:	Shirt - Amber with Black Trim, Shorts - Black, Stockings - Amber
	Change Strip:	Shirt - White with Black Trim, Shorts - Black, Stockings - White

The THISTLE

Date	Venue	Opponents	Result	McQueen J.	Coughlin J.	Armstrong G.	Williamson S.	Grant D.	Banks A.	Wilson S.	Ryrie B.	Irvine W.	Roseburgh D.	Bailey L.	Little I.	Duthie M.	Kane K.	Young J.	Murray M.	Coyle M.	Ellison S.	Nicol A.	Elder S.	McLeod G.	Rutherford P.	Logan S.	McNeill W.	Graham T.	Neil C.	Scott S.	Rae G.	Hutchison M.	Fleming D.
Aug 1	A	Hamilton Academical	3-1	1	2	3	4	5	6[1]	7	8	9[1]	10	11	12[1]	14																	
4	A	Ayr United	2-1	1	2	3	4	5	6	8	7	9[1]	10	11	12[1]	14																	
8	H	Morton	0-3	1	2	3	4	5	6	8	7	9	10	11	12	14																	
15	H	Stirling Albion	0-1	1	2	3	4	5	6	8	7	9	10	11	12																		
22	H	Cowdenbeath	5-1	1	2[1]	3	4	5	6	8	7	12[2]	10[1]	9[1]	11	14																	
29	A	Kilmarnock	0-1	1	2	3	4	5	6	8	7	9	11	10	14																		
Sept 5	A	St. Mirren	0-2	1	2	3	4	5	6			9	10	11	12	14		7	8														
12	H	Clydebank	1-0	1	2	3	4		6	8		12	14	10[1]	11			7	5	9													
19	A	Dunfermline Athletic	1-3	1	2	3	4		6	8		12	10[1]	11				14	7	5	9												
26	A	Raith Rovers	0-2		2	3	4		6	8			10			7		12	11		9	1		5	14								
Oct 3	A	Dumbarton	2-3		2[1]	3	4		6				10		11		12	7		9	1		5	14	8[1]								
10	H	Hamilton Academical	0-4		2	3	4		6	8			10		12			7			1	5	11			9	14						
17	A	Morton	1-4			3	4		6	8			10	14	7					11		1	2		5	9[1]	12						
24	A	St. Mirren	1-1	1	2		4		6	7			10			11			12		3			5		8	9[1]	14					
31	H	Kilmarnock	1-1	1	2		4		6	8[1]			10		12	11			3				5	14	7			9					
Nov 7	A	Stirling Albion	1-4		2				6	8			10	12[1]		11			3			1	4	14	7			9	5				
14	H	Cowdenbeath	2-0		2		4		6	8			11[1]	7					3			1	5	12	10	9[1]							
21	H	Dunfermline Athletic	3-2		2		4		6	8[2]			11	7	12				3			1	5	10[1]	9				14				
28	A	Clydebank	0-0				4			8			11	7	14				3			1	6	5	10	9			2				
Dec 1	A	Dumbarton	1-0				4		6	8[1]			11	7	14				3			1	2	5	10	9							
5	A	Raith Rovers	0-5		12		4		6				11	7	14				3			1	2	5	10	9				8			
19	H	Ayr United	1-0				4		6	8			11	7					2	14[1]	1			3	10	9						5	
Jan 6	A	Hamilton Academical	0-2	1			4		3	8			12	11	7				2	14				6	10	9						5	
16	A	Kilmarnock	0-5				4		6	8			12	11	7			14	2					3	10	9						5	
20	A	Cowdenbeath	2-2	1						14			6	11[2]	8	7		9	10					3								5	12
27	A	Dumbarton	3-3	10			4			7	11		6	8		14		2						3		9[2]						5[1]	
30	H	Morton	1-1	10			4			6	7[1]		14	12		9	2		2		1			3								5	11
Feb 3	A	St. Mirren	1-2		6		4			8			3[1]	7	12	10		9	2	14	1											5	11
6	H	Stirling Albion	†1-1		10		4			11			3	7					2		1			6	8	9						5	
13	A	Ayr United	0-1		3		4			8			6	7	12				2		1			10	9							5	11
20	A	Raith Rovers	1-1		2					8			6	7[1]	10		9				1			3	4							5	11
27	A	Dunfermline Athletic	2-3		2					8			6	7	10[1]	14					1			3	4	9						5[1]	11
Mar 10	A	Hamilton Academical	1-2		4					8	14		6	7[1]	12				2					3	10	9			5				11
13	A	Morton	0-2		6		4			8	14		3	7	10				2		1			5	9								11
20	A	Cowdenbeath	3-1		3		4			14	8		6[1]	7					2		1			10	9[1]							5	11[1]
27	A	Stirling Albion	2-2		3		4			8			6[1]	7	12				2		1			10[1]	9							5	11
31	H	Clydebank	0-1		3		4			8			6	7	12				2		1			14	10	9						5	11
Apr 3	A	St. Mirren	2-1		4					14	8		6	7	11[2]				2		1			3	10	9						5	12
14	A	Kilmarnock	1-1	1	4					12	8		6	7					2					3	10	9[1]						5	11
17	A	Clydebank	1-3	1	4					12	8		6	7	11				2					3	10	9[1]						5	14
24	A	Dunfermline Athletic	0-1	1	4					11	8		6	7	12				2					3	10	9						5	14
May 1	H	Ayr United	1-2	1	8		4						6	7[1]	12				2					3	10	9						5	11
8	A	Raith Rovers	2-3	1	14		4						6[1]	7	12				2					10	9[1]							5	11 3
15	H	Dumbarton	2-1	1					2				6[1]	7	8[1]			4						10	9							5	11 3
TOTAL FULL APPEARANCES				18	35	13	35	7	24	39	7	6	35	29	26	5	3	10	32	4	26	11	21	28	27			2	2	1	1	21	13	3
TOTAL SUB APPEARANCES				(2)				(4)			(4)	(3)	(2)	(1)	(14)	(13)	(7)	(1)		(3)					(6)		(3)		(1)			(3)	(1)
TOTAL GOALS SCORED					2				1	4			4	8	7	7	1				1			3	9							2	1

*Small figures denote goalscorers † denotes opponent's own goal

---

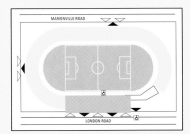

MEADOWBANK STADIUM

Capacity 16,000 (All Seated) (Only 7,500 Capacity Main Stand Used)

Pitch Dimensions 105 yds x 72 yds.

Disabled Facilities By prior arrangement with Secretary.

HOW TO GET THERE

Buses: A frequent service of buses all pass close to the ground and any of the following can be boarded in Princes Street, St. Andrew Square or Leith Street: Eastern Scottish - C1, C5, C6, 34/35, 42/46, 104, 106, 107, 108, 112, 113, 124, 125, 129, 130 and 137. Ian Glass - 7, 8 and 12. Lothian Region Transport - 4, 5, 15, 26, 34/35, 42/46, 43, 44, 44A, 45, 51, 85 and 86. Lowland Scottish - 104, 106, 124 and 125.

Trains: Trains from all over the country can be taken into Edinburgh Waverley Station and from there supporters can take any of the above buses to the Stadium. Please note that although a Station was opened at Meadowbank for the Commonwealth Games, it is no longer in use for public transport.

Cars: Meadowbank Stadium is located in London Road just 1 mile to the East of Princes Street and approximately 1/2 mile away from Easter Road. Car parking facilities are good, with accommodation for 600 cars at Meadowbank Sports Centre. Visiting supporters' coaches are advised to park in Lower London Road to the immediate South West of the Stadium.

MONTROSE

Links Park Stadium,
Wellington Street, Montrose,
DD10 8QD.

Chairman
Bryan D. Keith
Directors
Malcolm J. Watters
Michael G. Craig
Ronald Clark
Honorary President
William Johnston, M.B.E., J.P.
Player/Manager
John W. Holt
Secretary
Malcolm J. Watters

Telephones
Ground/Commercial/Club
Shop (0674) 73200
Sec. Home (0674) 83354
Sec. Bus. (0674) 74941
Fax (0674) 77311

Club Shop
At Stadium. Open 9.00 a.m. -
5.00 p.m. Mon to Fri. and on
matchdays.

Official Supporters Club
c/o Links Park Stadium,
Wellington Street, Montrose,
DD10 8QD

Team Captain
Neil Irvine

Club Sponsor
Bon Accord Glass

LIST OF PLAYERS 1993-94

Name	Date of Birth	Place of Birth	Date of Signing	Height	Weight	Previous Club
Breen, Philip	10/09/74	Aberdeen	30/03/93	5-10.5	10.10	Bon Accord Juniors
Burnett, Clark	02/08/73	Aberdeen	23/01/93	5-9	10.3	Albion Rangers U'18s
Christie, Gary Thomas	06/07/70	Dundee	27/11/91	5-9	10.8	East Craigie
Cooper, Craig	17/01/73	Arbroath	19/06/93	5-10	10.13	Portcullis
Craib, Mark	08/02/70	St. Andrew's	17/07/92	5-10	11.12	Dundee
Craib, Stephen Thomas	14/01/72	Dundee	16/03/91	5-10	10.7	Elmwood J.F.C.
Dornan, Andrew	19/08/61	Aberdeen	29/01/90	5-8.5	10.13	Worcester City
Fleming, John Munro	23/11/63	Edinburgh	07/09/90	5-9	11.8	Arbroath
Garden, Mark	07/08/75	Aberdeen	02/08/93	5-11	11.8	Middlefield United
Grant, Derek	19/05/66	Edinburgh	12/09/92	6-2	12.8	Meadowbank Thistle
Haro, Mark	21/10/71	Irvine	12/07/93	6-2	11.7	Dunfermline Athletic
Holt, John William	21/11/56	Dundee	12/05/93	5-9.5	12.4	Deveronvale
Houghton, Grant Paul	04/04/74	Dundee	17/07/92	5-10	10.0	Unattached
Irvine, Neil Donald	13/10/65	Edinburgh	12/09/92	5-10	11.1	Cowdenbeath
Kennedy, Allan	11/03/64	Arbroath	02/08/93	5-9	10.0	Forfar West End
Larter, David	18/03/60	Edinburgh	27/07/87	5-10.5	11.4	Dalkeith
Lavelle, Mark	26/04/74	Hitchin, Herts	20/03/93	5-11	11.5	Bon Accord Juniors
Massie, Ronald Wilson	04/10/75	Montrose	28/08/93	5-11	11.5	Montrose Roselea
McKenna, Ian Scott	09/10/68	Glasgow	13/07/93	5-10	11.3	Forfar Athletic
Mitchell, Craig	30/11/75	Aberdeen	28/08/93	5-11	11.7	Aberdeen Lads Club
Ritchie, Murray	18/09/73	Aberdeen	24/09/92	5-10	11.0	Burnley
Robertson, Ian William	14/10/66	Motherwell	26/07/91	5-9	10.10	Aberdeen
Smith, James	14/05/61	Elderslie	07/02/92	6-1	11.4	Airdrieonians
Smith, Levi	19/03/74	Hastings	06/08/93	5-8	11.0	Clydebank
Tosh, James David	12/09/74	Arbroath	19/06/93	6-0	10.11	Arbroath Lads Club
Wolecki, Edward	13/03/66	Dundee	05/08/93	5-10	10.7	Deveronvale
Yeats, Craig	28/09/69	Aberdeen	11/09/92	5-9	10.7	Keith

CLUB FIXTURES 1993-94

Date	Opponent	Venue	Date	Opponent	Venue	Date	Opponent	Venue
Aug 4	League Cup 1		Nov 6	Arbroath	A	Mar 5	Albion Rovers	A
Aug 7	Stranraer	A	Nov 13	Meadowbank Thistle	A	Mar 12	**Berwick Rangers**	**H**
Aug 11	League Cup 2		Nov 20	**Alloa**	**H**	Mar 19	**Cowdenbeath**	**H**
Aug 14	**Arbroath**	**H**	Nov 27	East Fife	A	Mar 26	Queen of the South	A
Aug 21	**Stenhousemuir**	**H**	Dec 4	**Queen of the South**	**H**	Apr 2	**East Stirlingshire**	**H**
Aug 25	League Cup 3		Dec 11	SFA Cup 1		Apr 9	Stranraer	A
Aug 28	Queen's Park	A	Dec 18	**Stranraer**	**H**	Apr 16	Stenhousemuir	A
Sept 1	League Cup 4		Dec 27	Albion Rovers	A	Apr 23	**Alloa**	**H**
Sept 4	East Stirlingshire	A	Jan 1	Stenhousemuir	A	Apr 30	**Meadowbank Thistle**	**H**
Sept 11	Forfar Athletic	A	Jan 8	SFA Cup 2		May 7	Queen's Park	A
Sept 18	**Meadowbank Thistle**	**H**	Jan 15	**Queen's Park**	**H**	May 14	Forfar Athletic	A
Sept 22	League Cup S/F		Jan 22	**Berwick Rangers**	**H**	May 21	SFA Cup Final	
Sept 25	Alloa	A	Jan 29	Cowdenbeath	A			
Oct 2	Queen of the South	A	Feb 5	**Forfar Athletic**	**H**			
Oct 9	**East Fife**	**H**	Feb 12	**East Stirlingshire**	**H**			
Oct 16	Berwick Rangers	A	Feb 19	**East Fife**	**H**			
Oct 23	**Cowdenbeath**	**H**	Feb 26	Arbroath	A			
Oct 24	League Cup Final							
Oct 30	**Albion Rovers**	**H**						

MILESTONES
Year of Formation: 1879
Most Capped Player: Sandy Keiller (2)
Most League Points in a Season: 53 (Division 2) -
1974/75 and (Second Division) - 1984/85
**Most League goals scored by a player in a
Season:** Brian Third (28) Season 1972/73
Record Attendance: 8,983 v Dundee, 17/3/73
Record Victory: 12-0 v Vale of Leithen, Scottish
Cup, 4/1/75
Record Defeat: 0-13 v Aberdeen, 17/3/51

SEASON TICKET INFORMATION
Seated or Standing
Adult £70
Juvenile/OAP £45
Family (1 Adult and 1 Juvenile) £80

LEAGUE ADMISSION PRICES
Seated or Standing
Adult £4
Juvenile/OAP £2.50

Registered Strip: Shirt - White with 4 Navy Blue and 1 Red Diagonal Stripe with Navy Blue Collar and Cuffs, Shorts - Navy Blue, Stockings - Navy Blue with Red Tops

Change Strip: Shirt - Tangerine with Royal Blue, White and Tangerine Sleeves, Shorts - Royal Blue with Tangerine and White Stripes, Stockings - Royal Blue with Tangerine and White Bands

CLUB FACTFILE 1992/93... RESULTS... APPEARANCES... SCORERS

The GABLE ENDIES

Date	Venue	Opponents	Result	Larter D.	Morrison B.	Fleming J.	Fraser C.	Forbes G.	Forsyth S.	Craib M.	Robertson I.	Logan A.	Craib S.	Dolan A.	Maver C.	Callaghan W.	Houghton G.	Smith J.	Fotheringham J.	Garden M.	Kelly M.	Irvine N.	Grant D.	Yeats C.	McGovern P.	Allan M.	Smith L.	Furphy W.	Christie G.	Kasule V.	Moffat J.	Nelson M.	Masson P.	Burnett C.	Davidson G.	Lavelle M.	Ritchie M.	Jack R.
Aug 8	A	East Stirlingshire	2-0	1	2	3	4	5	6	7¹	8	9	10¹	11																								
15	A	Brechin City	1-3	1	2	3		5	6	4	8	10	11			7	9¹	14																				
22	H	Stranraer	0-2	1	12	3			6	4	2	11	9			7	10	8	5	14																		
29	H	Berwick Rangers	1-3	1		3	7¹	6	10	4	2	8	11	12		9		5																				
Sept 5	H	Stenhousemuir	0-1	1			10	6	7	4	3	8	11			9	12	5		2	14																	
12	A	Albion Rovers	2-2	1			7	6	2	4	3	14				5				10	8	9²	11															
19	A	Queen of the South	5-1	1			7²	6	2¹	4	3	14¹	10			5				8	9¹	11																
26	H	Arbroath	4-3	1		3¹		7	4	2	10¹					6	5			12¹	8	9	11¹															
Oct 3	H	Forfar Athletic	0-0	1		3	7		2	6	4	9	11			5				14	8		10															
10	A	Clyde	2-1	1		3	7²		2	6	4	9				5				14	8		10	11														
17	H	Queen's Park	0-2	1		3	7		4	11	2	9	14			5				6			8	10	12													
24	A	East Fife	†3-2	1		3	7	5	2	4		10			8	6				11	9²	14		12														
31	H	Alloa	1-4	1		3	7	5	2	4					8	6				11	9¹		10															
Nov 7	A	Berwick Rangers	0-3	1	12	3	7	4		6	2				11					8	9	14	10															
14	A	Stenhousemuir	0-2	1	2			4	6	3					7					8	9	11		10	14													
21	A	Queen of the South	1-0	1	2		11		5	3					7¹					8	9	6		10		4	12											
28	H	Albion Rovers	2-1	1	2		6		5	3	14				7					8	9	4	10¹			12¹	11											
Dec 12	A	East Stirlingshire	4-1		2		5		4	3¹	11¹	14			7					8	9¹		10				1	6¹										
Jan 2	H	Brechin City	0-2		2		5	6	4	3	10									8	9	12				7	1	11										
9	A	Stranraer	1-3		2	3	5		4	8		14			6					9¹	10	11		7		1												
19	A	Forfar Athletic	3-4		2	3	4	5		8¹	10				6					9	7¹	11¹		12		1		14										
23	H	East Fife	1-3			3		4	6	10	12				5					9¹	8	11		7		1		2										
26	A	Alloa	0-3			3		4	10	12	7				5					9	8	11		6		1		2										
30	H	Arbroath	1-1			3		5	4	2					7¹					10	9	6	11	8		1												
Feb 6	H	Queen's Park	1-3			3	5		4	2					7					9	8¹	11	10		1	6	12											
13	H	Clyde	1-2			3		4	6	8									9		5	10¹		14	1	11	7	2										
20	H	Stenhousemuir	†1-4			3		4	6	8									9	7	5	10		12	1	11	14	2										
27	H	Brechin City	0-0			3		6	7	9	12				11	5				8	10			4	1		2											
Mar 6	H	Albion Rovers	1-1			3		6	7	9	14¹					5				4	10	12		8		1		2	11									
13	A	Alloa	1-3	1		3		6	7	9					12					4	5¹	14		10			8		2	11								
20	H	Forfar Athletic	1-3	1				6	3	9¹	11				14				5	7	4		8	10					2	12								
27	A	Berwick Rangers	0-2	1				4	3	12					2	5					8	10	11			7							6	9				
Apr 3	A	Queen of the South	0-1	1				4	3						12	2	5				11		8	10		7							6	9				
10	A	Clyde	1-2	1				4	3	8	7¹				2	5				11	10			9		12							14	6				
17	H	Arbroath	2-0	1				4	3	8¹	7¹				2	5					10			12		11							6	9				
24	A	East Fife	0-0	1				4	3	8	7				2	5				10	14			12		11							6	9				
May 1	H	Stranraer	0-2	1				4	3	8	7				2	5				12	10	6		2									11					
8	A	East Stirlingshire	0-0	1					3	8	7				2	5				11	10	6											4	9				
15	H	Queen's Park	3-1	1	2			3		11	7				2	5				6	14¹			10		12							8	4	9²			
TOTAL FULL APPEARANCES				27	10	22	18	12	14	38	36	17	16	1	18	4	10	28	2	3	25	28	20	2	20	1	13	1	12	5	8	1	6	5	6			
TOTAL SUB APPEARANCES					(2)					(4)	(5)	(1)	(5)		(2)		(1)		(5)		(7)		(5)	(1)	(7)				(3)		(2)						
TOTAL GOALS SCORED					1	5		1	2	1	4	3				4	1			1	10	4		3		1		1									2

Small figures denote goalscorers † denotes opponent's own goal

INKS PARK STADIUM

Capacity 4,338 (Seated 1,358; Standing 2,980)

Pitch Dimensions 113 yds x 70 yds.

Disabled Facilities Area set aside for wheelchairs and designated area in stand.

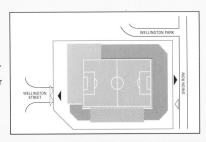

HOW TO GET THERE

Trains: Montrose is on the Inter-City 125 route from London to Aberdeen and also on the Glasgow-Aberdeen route. There is a regular service and the station is about 15 minutes walk from the ground.

Buses: An hourly service of buses from Aberdeen and Dundee stop in the town centre and it is a 15 minute walk from here to the ground.

Cars: Car parking is available in the small car park at the ground and there are numerous side streets all round the park which can be used if necessary.

QUEEN OF THE SOUTH

Palmerston Park, Terregles Street, Dumfries, DG2 9BA

Chairman
William R.K. Jardine
Vice-Chairman
William Houliston
Directors
William J. Harkness, C.B.E.
William Murray
Manager
William McLaren
Secretary
Mrs. Doreen Alcorn
Commercial Manager
John Paterson

Telephones
Ground/Ticket
Office/Information Service
(0387) 54853
Commercial (0387) 54853
Club Shop (0387) 54853.

Club Shop
Palmerston Park, Terregles Street, Dumfries.
Open 1.30 p.m. - 3.00 p.m. on home match days

Official Supporters Club
c/o Palmerston Park, Terregles Street, Dumfries, DG2 9BA.

Team Captain
George Rowe

Club Sponsor
Galloway Frozen Foods

LIST OF PLAYERS 1993-94

Name	Date of Birth	Place of Birth	Date of Signing	Height	Weight	Previous Club
Bell, Archie McCallum	12/04/66	Kilmarnock	01/05/91	6-0	12.4	Annbank
Bryce, Thomas	27/01/60	Johnstone	03/08/93	5-8	11.10	Clydebank
Cook, Andrew	06/11/75	Dumfries	29/09/93	5-11	9.8	Kello Rovers
Davidson, Alan	17/04/60	Airdrie	06/12/89	5-10	11.0	Floreat Athena
Gillespie, Alan	01/08/70	Bellshill	21/11/91	6-1	11.7	Ayr United
Jackson, David	06/12/68	Motherwell	15/06/93	5-7	10.6	Queen's Park
Kelly, Patrick	04/02/68	Paisley	20/07/93	5-7	10.0	Stranraer
Mallan, Stephen Patrick	30/08/67	Glasgow	03/08/93	5-11	12.7	Clyde
McColm, Robert James	25/08/74	Dumfries	03/08/93	5-10	12.0	Annan Athletic
McFarlane, Andrew	22/02/70	Glasgow	30/10/90	5-7	10.7	Arthurlie
McGhie, William	13/11/61	Glasgow	26/07/89	5-10	10.7	Partick Thistle
McGuire, Douglas John	06/09/67	Bathgate	12/06/91	5-8	11.4	Cumnock Juniors
McGuire, James	27/09/62	Irvine	15/12/88	5-8	10.7	Kilmarnock
McKeown, Brian	31/10/56	Motherwell	09/11/90	5-7	11.7	Airdrieonians
McLaren, John Stuart	20/04/75	Glasgow	05/10/93	6-0	10.8	Airdrieonians Y.T.S.
Mills, Douglas	06/01/66	Rutherglen	27/03/86	6-2	13.0	Albion Rovers
Parker, James Waterson	12/09/65	Dumfries	24/08/93	5-6	11.7	Gretna
Proudfoot, Kevin David	20/01/76	Dumfries	24/08/93	5-6	11.7	Dumfries HFP
Rowe, John George	23/08/68	Glasgow	26/08/92	6-0	11.7	Clydebank
Sermanni, Peter Hugh	09/07/71	Glasgow	27/08/92	5-9	10.0	Clydebank
Shanks, David Thow	18/04/62	Bellshill	28/07/93	6-0	11.7	Stirling Albion
Sim, William	13/08/63	Dumfries	07/03/85	5-7	11.6	Kello Rovers
Thomson, Andrew	01/04/71	Motherwell	28/07/89	5-10	9.7	Jerviston B.C.

CLUB FIXTURES 1993-94

Date	Opponent	Venue
Aug 4	League Cup 1	
Aug 7	Arbroath	A
Aug 11	League Cup 2	
Aug 14	**Queen's Park**	H
Aug 21	**Stranraer**	H
Aug 25	League Cup 3	
Aug 28	Forfar Athletic	A
Sept 1	League Cup 4	
Sept 4	East Fife	A
Sept 11	**East Stirlingshire**	H
Sept 18	**Alloa**	H
Sept 22	League Cup S/F	
Sept 25	Albion Rovers	A
Oct 2	**Montrose**	H
Oct 9	Meadowbank Thistle	A
Oct 16	Cowdenbeath	A
Oct 23	**Stenhousemuir**	H
Oct 24	League Cup Final	

Date	Opponent	Venue
Oct 30	**Berwick Rangers**	H
Nov 6	Queen's Park	A
Nov 13	Alloa	A
Nov 20	**Albion Rovers**	H
Nov 27	**Meadowbank Thistle**	H
Dec 4	Montrose	A
Dec 11	SFA Cup 1	
Dec 18	**Arbroath**	H
Dec 27	Berwick Rangers	A
Jan 1	Stranraer	A
Jan 8	SFA Cup 2	
Jan 15	**Forfar Athletic**	H
Jan 22	**Cowdenbeath**	H
Jan 29	Stenhousemuir	A
Feb 5	East Stirlingshire	A
Feb 12	**East Fife**	H
Feb 19	**Queen's Park**	H
Feb 26	Alloa	A
Mar 5	Stranraer	A

Date	Opponent	Venue
Mar 12	**Albion Rovers**	H
Mar 19	Forfar Athletic	A
Mar 26	**Montrose**	H
Apr 2	**Berwick Rangers**	H
Apr 9	Arbroath	A
Apr 16	East Fife	A
Apr 23	**Stenhousemuir**	H
Apr 30	**East Stirlingshire**	H
May 7	Meadowbank Thistle	A
May 14	Cowdenbeath	A
May 21	SFA Cup Final	

MILESTONES
Year of Formation: 1919
Most Capped Player: William Houliston (3)
Most League Points in a Season:
55 (Second Division) - 1985/86
Most League goals scored by a player in a Season: J. Gray (33) Season 1927/28
Record Attendance: 24,500 v Hearts, Scottish Cup, 23/2/52
Record Victory: 11-1 v Stranraer, Scottish Cup, 16/1/32
Record Defeat: 2-10 v Dundee, Division 1, 1/12/62

SEASON TICKET INFORMATION
Seated	Adult	£73
	Juvenile/OAP	£55
Standing	Adult	£57
	Juvenile/OAP	£40

LEAGUE ADMISSION PRICES
Seated	Adult	£4.50
	Juvenile/OAP	£3.50
Standing	Adult	£4
	Juvenile/OAP	£3

Registered Strip:	Shirt - Royal Blue with White Collar, Shorts - White with Royal Blue Side Panel, Stockings - Royal Blue with White and Yellow Stripe on Top
Change Strip:	Shirt - Yellow with Royal Blue Collar, Shorts - Royal Blue with Yellow Side Panel, Stockings - Yellow with White and Royal Blue Stripe on Top

The DOONHAMERS

Date	Venue	Opponents	Result	Davidson A.	Dickson J.	McFarlane A.	Mills D.	Hetherington K.	Gordon S.	Wright B.	Bell A.	Thomson A.	Robertson J.	McGuire J.	Templeton H.	McGhie W.	Fraser G.	Sim W.	Rowe G.	Sermanni P.	McGuire D.	Hoy D.	McKeown B.	Henderson D.	Hair P.	Frye D.	Sharp K.	McCulloch D.	Gillespie A.
Aug 8	A	Forfar Athletic	1-5	1	2	3	4	5	6	7	8	9	10[1]	11	12	14													
15	A	Stranraer	2-2	1	2	3	4			7	10	9	11[1]	8	12[1]	5	6												
22	H	Albion Rovers	0-3	1	2	8	5		14	7		9	11	10	12	4	6	3											
29	A	East Stirlingshire	2-1	1	2		5		6	7		9[1]	11			10	3	4	8[1]										
Sept 5	H	Brechin City	0-0	1		3	5		6	7		9	11	10		2	12	4	8										
12	H	Berwick Rangers	1-0	1		3	5			7		9[1]	10	11		2		4	6	8									
19	A	Montrose	1-5	1	14	3	5			7	12	9[1]	11	10		2	6	4	8										
26	A	Queen's Park	2-1	1	12	3	5			7	8	9	11			2[1]		4	6	10[1]									
Oct 3	A	Clyde	3-1		2	3	5		14		8	9[2]	11			6		4	7	10[1]		1							
10	A	East Fife	5-2			5	3		2		8	9[3]	11			12	6	14	4	7	10[2]	1							
17	H	Alloa	1-2		6	3			2		8	9	11[1]			14	5		4	7	10	1	12						
24	A	Arbroath	0-0			5	3		2	11	8	9				14			4	7	10	1	6						
31	H	Stenhousemuir	0-1			5	3		2		8	9	11			14			4	7	10	1	6	12					
Nov 7	A	East Stirlingshire	†1-2			5	3				8	9			12	2			4	7	11	1	6	10					
14	A	Brechin City	0-3		2	3	5				8	9	11	10		14			4		12	1	6	7					
21	H	Montrose	0-1		2	3	5			7	8	9				12		10			14	1	4	11					
28	H	Berwick Rangers	4-1		2	11[1]	5		14			9[1]		10		3			4	12	7[1]	1	6	8[1]					
Dec 12	H	Forfar Athletic	1-1		6	10[1]			2			9	12					8	3	5	7	1	4	11					
Jan 2	A	Stranraer	2-0		2	8			12			11	9[1]	14	5	6	3		4	7		1		10[1]					
9	A	Albion Rovers	1-2		2	6			12	8		11	14	9[1]	5				3	4	7	1		10					
26	A	Stenhousemuir	1-1		2	11			7			9	10[1]		6				3	5		1	4	8					
30	H	Queen's Park	5-2		2	11			7			9[2]	10	6[2]	3	5			12		4	8[1]	1						
Feb 2	H	Arbroath	0-1		2	10	5		7			9		11	6	14	3	4			1	8							
6	A	Alloa	2-2		2	3	6		11			9[1]	10		5	7[1]	12	1	4	8		14							
13	H	East Fife	1-1		6[1]				2			9	11	5	3	4	7	10	1	8		14							
16	A	Clyde	1-2		10				2	4	12	9		5	3	6	7	11	1	8[1]		14							
20	A	Berwick Rangers	0-3		10	5			4	8		9		2	3	6	11		1			7							
27	H	Forfar Athletic	2-4		2	6			14	7	8	9[1]			5[1]	3	4		10	1		11							
Mar 6	H	Brechin City	1-2		2	6			10	7	8	9	12		5	3	4[1]		14	1		11							
13	A	Stenhousemuir	1-2		2	6			8	7	14	9[1]			5	3	4		11	12	1	10							
20	A	Arbroath	2-3		2	8			7	6		9[2]			5	3	4		10	1		11							
27	H	Albion Rovers	3-1		7	6[1]			5			9	12[1]		2	3	4		8[1]	11	1	10							
Apr 3	A	Montrose	1-0		8	6			4			9	12		2	3	5		10	7	1	11[1]							
10	A	Stranraer	3-3		8				4	6		9[1]	12		2	3	5[1]		10	7	1	11[1]							
17	H	East Fife	2-0		10	6			4	3		9[1]			2	5	8		7	1	11[1]								
24	A	East Stirlingshire	2-1		10	5			6	8		9[2]	12		2	3	7		1	4	11								
May 1	A	Queen's Park	1-1		10	5			8	3		9			2	4	7	14	1	6	11[1]								
8	H	Clyde	2-3		10				5	4	6	9[1]	12		2	14	3	8	7	11[1]	1								
15	H	Alloa	0-7		10				5	12	9	11			2	4	7	6	1									3	
TOTAL FULL APPEARANCES				8	27	37	19	1	16	25	20	38	15	15	1	31	6	18	36	27	19	28	12	25	3			1	1
TOTAL SUB APPEARANCES					(2)				(6)		(4)			(8)	(1)	(7)	(3)	(4)	(2)		(1)	(7)		(1)	(1)		(1)	(2)	
TOTAL GOALS SCORED						4						21	4	3	1	4			2	3	5			9				

Small figures denote goalscorers   † denotes opponent's own goal

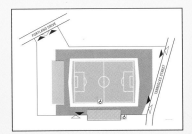

PALMERSTON PARK

Capacity 6,750 (Seated 1,300, Standing 5,450)

Pitch Dimensions 112 yds x 73 yds.

Disabled Facilities On application to Club Secretary.

HOW TO GET THERE

Trains: There is a reasonable service to Dumfries Station from Glasgow on Saturdays, but the service is more limited in midweek. The station is about 3/4 mile from the ground.

Buses: Buses from Glasgow, Edinburgh, Ayr and Stranraer all pass within a short distance of the park.

Cars: The car park may be reached from Portland Drive or King Street and has a capacity for approximately 174 cars.

QUEEN'S PARK

Hampden Park, Letherby Drive, Mount Florida, Glasgow, G42 9BA.

President
Malcolm Mackay

Committee
W. Lindsay Ross, M.A., LL.B. (Treasurer); Martin B. Smith, LL.B., N.P.; Peter G. Buchanan; William S. Burgess; Robert L. Cromar F.I.B.S.; Ian G. Harnett B.SC.; William Omand; Austin Reilly B.SC.; James Nicholson, H. Gordon Wilson.

Coach
Edward Hunter

Secretary
James C. Rutherford

Telephones
Ground 041-632-1275
Fax 041-636-1612

Official Supporters Club
c/o Secretary,
Keith McAllister, 58 Brunton Street, Glasgow, G44 3NQ.

Club Shop
Home matches only -
Hampden Park (Police Building at end of West Stand) 2.15 p.m. - 3.00 p.m. and 4.45 p.m. - 5.00 p.m. on home match days.

Team Captain
Graeme Elder

Club Sponsor
British Engine Insurance Ltd.

LIST OF PLAYERS 1993-94

Name	Date of Birth	Place of Birth	Date of Signing	Height	Weight	Previous Club
Black, Simon	07/01/76	Paisley	12/06/93	5-9	10.7	Unattached
Bradley, Robert	04/11/71	Bellshill	07/08/92	5-10	10.0	Queen's Park Youth
Brodie, David	04/01/71	Hardgate	22/09/93	5-9.5	11.8	Glenwood Amateurs
Brodie, Gordon	04/07/72	Vale of Leven	25/09/93	6-0	11.5	Glenwood
Callan, Dominic	20/09/66	Glasgow	14/08/90	5-10	10.7	Vale of Leven
Campbell, Stephen	24/07/71	Glasgow	11/10/93	6-1	12.7	Yoker Athletic U/21
Cassidy, Martin	22/12/71	Glasgow	24/07/93	5-9	11.2	Campsie Black Watch
Caven, Ross	04/08/65	Glasgow	12/08/82	6-0	12.0	Possil Y.M.C.A.
Chalmers, James	03/02/70	Glasgow	25/07/91	6-0	11.4	Yoker Athletic
Crooks, George Campbell	04/05/65	Glasgow	10/07/92	5-7	10.7	Bishopbriggs B.C.
Elder, Graeme	21/11/61	Glasgow	08/07/86	6-1	13.0	Drumchapel Y.M.C.A.
Fitzpatrick, Stephen	04/12/71	Greenock	03/08/93	6-2	11.10	Port Glasgow H.S.
Graham, David	27/01/71	Bellshill	25/07/91	5-10	10.8	Queen's Park Youth
Henrici, Gordon	14/10/73	Glasgow	11/10/93	5-11	11.3	Clydebank B.C.
Kavanagh, James	12/09/70	East Kilbride	12/06/93	6-1	11.0	Muirend Amateurs
Kelly, Kevin	24/09/71	Glasgow	24/07/93	5-11	12.7	Broadholm
Kerr, Gary	24/02/74	Paisley	12/06/93	5-11	11.0	Hamilton Academical
Mackenzie, Keith M.	06/04/61	Saltburn	08/07/86	6-0	12.10	Muirend A.F.C.
Maxwell, Ian	02/05/75	Glasgow	24/07/93	6-3	12.5	Unattached
McConnell, Gerald	12/08/74	Motherwell	24/07/93	5-11	10.0	Unattached
McCormick, Stephen	14/08/69	Dumbarton	25/07/91	6-4	11.4	Yoker Athletic
McPhee, Brian	23/10/70	Glasgow	26/08/93	5-10	11.4	Rutherglen Amateurs
Moir, Alexander	20/03/68	Glasgow	03/08/93	6-3	13.0	Barr & Stroud A.F.C.
Moonie, David	09/10/72	Durban, S.A.	24/07/93	5-11	11.1	Dunfermline Athletic
O'Brien, John	16/08/67	Glasgow	29/07/89	5-10	11.7	Campsie Black Watch
O'Neill, John	03/01/74	Glasgow	25/07/91	5-10	10.4	Unattached
Orr, Garry	27/11/73	Glasgow	14/02/92	5-4	10.10	Dundee Utd
Orr, James P.	01/02/72	Blantyre	25/07/91	5-9	11.2	Queen's Park Youth
Rodden, James	13/08/65	Glasgow	17/09/87	5-9	11.0	Pollok
Sneddon, Scott	07/12/71	Dechmont	10/07/92	6-2	11.4	Unattached
Stevenson, Colin	28/02/72	Glasgow	25/07/91	5-9	10.7	Unattached

CLUB FIXTURES 1993-94

Date	Opponent	Venue	Date	Opponent	Venue	Date	Opponent	Venue
Aug 4	League Cup 1		Oct 30	Alloa	A	Feb 26	Berwick Rangers	H
Aug 7	Forfar Athletic	H	Nov 6	Queen of the South	H	Mar 5	Stenhousemuir	H
Aug 11	League Cup 2		Nov 13	East Fife	A	Mar 12	East Fife	A
Aug 14	Queen of the South	A	Nov 20	Stenhousemuir	H	Mar 19	Albion Rovers	A
Aug 21	Albion Rovers	A	Nov 27	Berwick Rangers	A	Mar 26	Forfar Athletic	H
Aug 25	League Cup 3		Dec 4	Stranraer	A	Apr 2	Stranraer	H
Aug 28	Montrose	H	Dec 11	SFA Cup 1		Apr 9	Alloa	A
Sept 1	League Cup 4		Dec 18	Forfar Athletic	A	Apr 16	Meadowbank Thistle	H
Sept 4	Cowdenbeath	H	Dec 27	Alloa	H	Apr 23	Arbroath	A
Sept 11	Arbroath	A	Jan 1	Albion Rovers	H	Apr 30	Cowdenbeath	A
Sept 18	East Fife	H	Jan 8	SFA Cup 2		May 7	Montrose	H
Sept 22	League Cup S/F		Jan 15	Montrose	A	May 14	East Stirlingshire	H
Sept 25	Stenhousemuir	A	Jan 22	East Stirlingshire	A	May 21	SFA Cup Final	
Oct 2	Stranraer	H	Jan 29	Meadowbank Thistle	H			
Oct 9	Berwick Rangers	A	Feb 5	Arbroath	H			
Oct 16	East Stirlingshire	H	Feb 12	Cowdenbeath	H			
Oct 23	Meadowbank Thistle	A	Feb 19	Queen of the South	A			
Oct 24	League Cup Final							

MILESTONES

Year of Formation: 1867
Most Capped Player: Walter Arnott (14)
Most League Points in a Season:
57 (Division 2) - 1922/23
Most League goals scored by a player in a Season: William Martin (30) Season 1937/38
Record Attendance: 149,547, Scotland v England, 17/4/37
Record Victory: 16-0 v St. Peters, Scottish Cup, 29/8/1885
Record Defeat: 0-9 v Motherwell, Division 1, 29/4/30

SEASON TICKET INFORMATION

Seated (Centre/West Stand) Adult £50
Juvenile/OAP £25

LEAGUE ADMISSION PRICES

All seated areas Adult £3.50
Juvenile/OAP £2

Registered Strip: Shirt - 1" White and Black Hoops, Shorts - White, Stockings - White with 2 Black Hoops

Change Strip: Shirt - Red, Shorts - Red, Stockings - Red

CLUB FACTFILE 1992/93... RESULTS... APPEARANCES... SCORERS

The SPIDERS

Small figures denote goalscorers. Best-effort reconstruction of the appearance/scorers grid follows; goalscorer counts shown as superscripts (e.g. 10^1).

Date	Venue	Opponents	Result	Moonie D.	Callan D.	Morris S.	Elder G.	Mackay M.	Jackson D.	Caven R.	Graham D.	Orr G.	McCormick S.	O'Neil J.	Greig D.	Bradley R.	O'Brien J.	Chalmers J.	Ferguson P.	Crooks G.	Orr J.	Devlin W.	Mackenzie K.	Millar G.	Sneddon S.	Rodden J.	Stevenson C.	Kerr G.	Henrici G.	Black S.	Kavanagh J.	McIntyre D.	Bryers C.
Aug 8	H	Stranraer	1-1	1	2	3	4	5	6	7	8	9	10^1	11	12	14																	
15	A	Albion Rovers	2-3	1	2	3	4	5	6	7^1	8	14	10	12	11^1	9																	
22	H	Forfar Athletic	1-2	1	2	3	4	5	6	7	8	9	10	12	11		14																
29	A	Arbroath	1-2		2		4	5		8	10		7	6		9		1	3	14^1													
Sept 5	H	East Fife	1-3		6	3	4	5^1		9	11	8	7	10		14		1		12	2												
12	H	Clyde	1-6		2	12		5		9	7^1	8	6	10				1		4	3	11											
19	A	Berwick Rangers	0-1	1	7		4	5		9	8	2		10	11			3		6													
26	H	Queen of the South	†1-2	1	2		4	5	8	7	3	9			12					11			10	6									
Oct 3	A	Stenhousemuir	0-2		6		4	5		8	7	3		10	11		1			9			14	2	12								
10	H	Brechin City	1-2		6		4	5		8	7	3		9	11		1			12			2	10^1									
17	A	Montrose	2-0		7			5		8^1	3	6	10	14			1			9			11^1	2	4								
24	A	Alloa	0-0				4	5		7	3	6	10				1		14	9			12	11	8	2						
31	H	East Stirlingshire	4-2		7^1			5	8	10^1	3	6	9^2				1			12			11	2	4								
Nov 7	H	Arbroath	0-1		7			5	8	10	3	6	14	9			1			12			11	2	4								
14	A	East Fife	1-2		4			5	9	7	8	6	10^1	11			1		3	12	2								14				
21	H	Berwick Rangers	4-0		7			5	9^1	10^2	14	6	11				1		3	4	12	2^1								8			
28	A	Clyde	1-4		7^1			5	9	10	8	14	11				1		3	4	12	6	2										
Dec 12	A	Stranraer	1-1		4			6	8	9	7	11					1		12		5	10^1	3	2									
26	H	Stenhousemuir	2-2		4			8	7^1	3	6	11^1	12				1		9			10	2	5	14								
Jan 2	H	Albion Rovers	1-0		4			5	8	7^1	14	6	11	12			1			10	3	2	9										
26	A	Forfar Athletic	0-2					5	8	7		6	10	9			1		2			14	11	3	4								
30	A	Queen of the South	2-5					4	5	8	10^1	7	14	9			1		2			11^1	3	7									
Feb 2	H	East Stirlingshire	2-2					4	5	7^1	9		$8 6^1$	10			1			2			11	3	2								
6	H	Montrose	3-1					5	9	7	8	6	10				1		2			14	11^2	3^1	4	12						
9	H	Alloa	0-3					5	9	7		6	10	14			1		2			8	11	3	4								
13	A	Brechin City	0-1	1				5	7		8	6	9	14	11				2			12	10	3	4								
20	A	Clyde	†3-2	1				5	9	7	3	6	10^1	14	8					12			11^1	2	4								
27	H	Arbroath	2-1	1				5	8	7	3^1	6	11	9						10^1	2	4	12										
Mar 6	A	Stranraer	2-4	1				5	8	7	3	6	11	9					2	14^1	10	4	12^1										
13	H	East Fife	2-2	1				5^1	9	7	8	6	11	12					4	14	3	10^1	2										
20	A	Albion Rovers	1-1					5^1	9	7		6	10				1		4	12	3	8	11	2	14								
27	A	Forfar Athletic	2-2					5	8		6		10^1				1		4	11^1	3	7	9	2									
Apr 3	A	East Stirlingshire	1-4				4	5	9		8	6	10				1		14	11	3	7^1	12	2									
10	A	Alloa	2-2	1			7		9		3	6	10^1				8	5	11	4	14^1	2											
17	H	Brechin City	1-0			14		5	9	7		6	11^1				1		2	3	4	10	8	12									
24	A	Berwick Rangers	1-1			6		5	9	7		8	11	10^1			1		12	2	3	4											
May 1	H	Queen of the South	1-1					5^1	3	9	7	6	10	11			1		12	8	4	2											
8	A	Stenhousemuir	0-0					5	2	7	14	6	11	9			1		3	10	12	4	8										
15	A	Montrose	1-3					5	8	11	6	7^1	9				1		12	2	10	14	4	3									
TOTAL FULL APPEARANCES				11	12	4	27	33	35	34	29	33	30	19	5	3	28	1	3	11	6	2	5	11	22	24	26	2	4	9			
TOTAL SUB APPEARANCES					(1)	(1)				(3)	(2)	(2)	(8)	(3)	(2)	(1)				(5)				(15)	(4)	(2)		(2)	(5)		(1)	(1)
TOTAL GOALS SCORED								3	3	1	11	1	1	5	6				1				1		9	2	1		3			

*Small figures denote goalscorers † denotes opponent's own goal

---

HAMPDEN PARK

Capacity 37,960 (All seated)

Pitch Dimensions 115 yds x 75 yds.

Disabled Facilities Capacity 222 - Wheelchair 54, Ambulant Seated 48, Ambulant Standing 120.

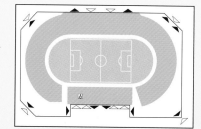

HOW TO GET THERE

Trains: There are two stations within five minutes walk of the ground. Mount Florida Station, on the Cathcart Circle and King's Park Station. A 15 minute service runs from Glasgow Central.

Buses: Services more suitable for the Mount Florida end are Nos. 5, 5A, 5B, M5, M14, 31, 34, 37, 66, 66A, 66B, 89, 90, 96 and 97. For the King's Park end, Nos. 12, 12A, 22, 74, 89 and 90 are more suitable. These leave from Glasgow City Centre.

Cars: Car parking facilities are available in the car park at the front of the Stadium, which is capable of holding 1,200 vehicles. Side streets can also be used on major occasions.

STENHOUSEMUIR

Ochilview Park,
Gladstone Road,
Stenhousemuir, FK5 4QL.
Chairman
Greig H.C. Thomson
Vice-Chairman
A. Terry Bulloch
Directors
David O. Reid; Sidney S.
Collumbine; Gordon Cook
(Treasurer); James S.B.
Gillespie; Alistair Jack; John G.
Sharp; Alan J. McNeill
Manager
Terry Christie
Secretary
A. Terry Bulloch
Commercial Manager
Greig H.C. Thomson
Telephones
Ground/Club Shop
(0324) 562992
Sec. Home (0324) 20763
Sec. Bus. (0786) 474605
Commercial Bus.
(0324) 472611
Commercial Home
(0324) 553195
Information 0891 884414
Club Shop
Ochilview Park, Gladstone
Road, Stenhousemuir, FK5
4QL. Open during first team
home match days between
2.00 p.m. until 5.00 p.m.
Official Supporters Club
Ochilview Park, Gladstone
Road, Stenhousemuir,
FK5 4QL.
Team Captain
Eddie Hallford
Club Sponsor
G&J Sports

LIST OF PLAYERS 1993-94

Name	Date of Birth	Place of Birth	Date of Signing	Height	Weight	Previous Club
Aitchison, James	10/10/76	Edinburgh	05/08/93	5-10	10.7	Whitehill Welfare
Aitken, Neil	27/04/71	Edinburgh	26/01/90	6-1	11.7	Penicuik Athletic
Armstrong, Graeme John	23/06/56	Edinburgh	31/10/92	5-9	10.12	Meadowbank Thistle
Bell, David	22/10/61	Falkirk	27/07/92	5-7	10.5	Dunipace Jnrs
Buchanan, Gordon	20/10/61	Glasgow	09/09/93	6-0	11.12	Unattached
Clarke, John	23/11/70	Glasgow	04/05/92	5-11	11.10	Milngavie Wanderers
Dickov, Stephen	30/05/69	Glasgow	29/09/92	5-4	10.4	West Calder
Donaldson, Euan Gordon	20/08/75	Falkirk	18/05/93	5-10	10.7	"S" Form
Farmer, Alan	15/05/76	Falkirk	16/10/93	5-10.5	10.7	ICI Juveniles
Fisher, James	14/10/67	Bridge of Allan	18/01/92	5-10	10.11	Bo'ness United
Godfrey, Peter James	22/10/57	Falkirk	18/11/92	6-0	11.7	Arbroath
Haddow, Lloyd Simon	21/01/71	Lanark	13/02/92	6-1	11.6	Fauldhouse United
Hallford, Edward	04/10/67	Shotts	11/06/90	5-8	11.2	Shotts Bon Accord
Harkness, Michael	24/08/68	Edinburgh	26/08/93	6-1.5	12.6	Arbroath
Irvine, John George	22/07/63	Musselburgh	21/03/92	6-0	12.13	Alloa
Logan, Stephen	02/09/61	Glasgow	26/11/92	5-9	10.12	Meadowbank Thistle
Mathieson, Miller Stewart	19/12/64	Surrey	14/11/91	5-11	11.12	Edinburgh United
O'Neill, Peter	30/05/72	Glasgow	24/04/93	5-8	9.7	Larkhall Thistle
Roseburgh, David	30/06/59	Loanhead	26/08/93	5-10.5	9.9	Meadowbank Thistle
Sprott, Adrian	23/03/62	Edinburgh	05/08/93	5-8	10.0	Meadowbank Thistle
Steel, Thomas Wright	28/02/68	Kilmarnock	29/05/92	6-0	11.9	Hurlford United
Swanson, Darren	12/02/76	Stirling	25/06/93	5-10	11.7	"S" Form
Wilson, Christopher C.	21/06/72	Paisley	25/06/93	6-3	13.12	Campsie Black Watch

CLUB FIXTURES 1993-94

Date	Opponent	Venue
Aug 4	League Cup 1	
Aug 7	East Stirlingshire	H
Aug 11	League Cup 2	
Aug 14	East Fife	A
Aug 21	Montrose	A
Aug 25	League Cup 3	
Aug 28	Cowdenbeath	H
Sept 1	League Cup 4	
Sept 4	Alloa	H
Sept 11	Albion Rovers	A
Sept 18	Arbroath	A
Sept 22	League Cup S/F	
Sept 25	Queen's Park	H
Oct 2	Berwick Rangers	H
Oct 9	Stranraer	A
Oct 16	Forfar Athletic	H
Oct 23	Queen of the South	A
Oct 24	League Cup Final	

Date	Opponent	Venue
Oct 30	Meadowbank Thistle	A
Nov 6	East Fife	H
Nov 13	Arbroath	H
Nov 20	Queen's Park	A
Nov 27	Stranraer	H
Dec 4	Berwick Rangers	A
Dec 11	SFA Cup 1	
Dec 18	East Stirlingshire	A
Dec 27	Meadowbank Thistle	H
Jan 1	Montrose	H
Jan 8	SFA Cup 2	
Jan 15	Cowdenbeath	A
Jan 22	Forfar Athletic	A
Jan 29	Queen of the South	H
Feb 5	Albion Rovers	H
Feb 12	Alloa	A
Feb 19	Arbroath	H
Feb 26	Cowdenbeath	A

Date	Opponent	Venue
Mar 5	Queen's Park	A
Mar 12	Forfar Athletic	H
Mar 19	Meadowbank Thistle	A
Mar 26	Albion Rovers	H
Apr 2	Alloa	H
Apr 9	East Stirlingshire	A
Apr 16	Montrose	H
Apr 23	Queen of the South	A
Apr 30	Berwick Rangers	A
May 7	East Fife	H
May 14	Stranraer	A
May 21	SFA Cup Final	

Registered Strip: Shirt - Maroon with Sky Blue Stripe, Shorts - White, Stockings - Maroon with Sky Blue Hoops on Top

Change Strip: Shirt - Sky Blue with White and Navy Blue Shoulder Flash, Shorts - Navy Blue, Stockings - Navy Blue

CLUB FACTFILE 1992/93... RESULTS... APPEARANCES... SCORERS

The WARRIORS

Date	Venue	Opponents	Result	Kelly C.	Clarke J.	Kemp B.	Barr R.	Prior S.	Fisher J.	Aitken N.	Bell D.	Mathieson M.	Steel T.	Irvine J.	Hallford E.	Clouston B.	Haddow L.	Anderson P.	Barnstaple K.	Tracey K.	Reid J.	Lytwyn C.	Mackie P.	Dickov S.	Armstrong G.	Godfrey P.	McLafferty W.	Logan S.	Black K.
Aug 8	A	East Fife	1-1	1	2	3¹	4	5	6	7	8	9	10	11	12														
15	H	Berwick Rangers	1-3	1	6	8	4	5	10			7¹	12	11	3	2	9	14											
22	A	Alloa	1-2		2			12	11		8	10¹		6	3	7	4	1	5	9									
29	H	Stranraer	1-2		2			12	5	11	8¹	10	6		3	7	4	1	14	9									
Sept 5	A	Montrose	1-0		2			8	14	11	7	10¹	6		3	12	4	1	5	9									
12	A	Forfar Athletic	1-3		2		4	8	7¹	10	11				3	14	12	6	1	5	9								
19	A	Brechin City	2-4				12	4	11¹	2	7	9			3	8	10¹	6	1	5		14							
26	A	Clyde	0-0		5		4	7	12	8	9	10			3	2	6	1				11							
Oct 3	H	Queen's Park	2-0		4			5	11	2	6	9¹	14		3	8		1				7	10¹						
10	A	East Stirlingshire	7-3		4			12	11	2¹	6	9⁴			3	8	14	5	1			7¹	10¹						
17	H	Arbroath	1-3		4			12	11	2	6¹	9			3	8	14	5	1			7	10						
24	H	Albion Rovers	2-0						11	2¹	6	9			3	8	7	5	1			14¹	12	10	4				
31	A	Queen of the South	1-0						6	2		9¹			3	8	11		1			10	7		4	5			
Nov 7	A	Stranraer	0-0						6	2		9			3	8	11		1			10	12		4	5		7	
14	H	Montrose	2-0						6	2		9²			3	8	11		1			10	7		4	5			
21	A	Brechin City	2-2						6	2		9¹			3	8	11		1			10¹			4	5		7	
28	H	Forfar Athletic	2-0						6	2	14	9¹			3	8	11		1			10			4	5	12¹	7	
Dec 12	H	East Fife	3-1		2				6			9²			3	8	11		1			10¹			4	5	12	7	
26	A	Queen's Park	2-2						6	2	14¹	9¹			3	8	11		1			10			4	5	12	7	
Jan 2	A	Berwick Rangers	1-1						6	2	14	9	8		3		11¹		1			10	12		4	5		7	
26	A	Queen of the South	1-1						6	2		9		11	3	8			1			10	14		4	5	12¹	7	
30	H	Clyde	0-2						6	2		9			3	8	11		1			12	14		4	5	10	7	
Feb 2	H	Alloa	0-1		14					2		9			3	8	11		1			12	6		4	5	10	7	
10	A	Arbroath	2-3		14				6	2		9²			3		11		1			12	8	10	4	5		7	
13	H	East Stirlingshire	1-2		2				6		8	9¹			3	14	11		1			10	7		4	5			12
16	A	Albion Rovers	0-0	1	5				6	2		9		11	3	8						10	12		4			7	
20	A	Montrose	4-1	1	5				6¹			9¹		11¹	3	8						10¹			4			7	2
27	H	Berwick Rangers	0-0	1	5				6		14	9		11	3	8						10¹	12		4			7	2
Mar 6	A	Forfar Athletic	0-1	1	5				6	2	14	9		11	3	8						10	12		4			7	
13	H	Queen of the South	2-1	1	2				6			9¹	12	11¹	3	8						10			4	5		7	
20	H	Brechin City	3-0	1	5				6	2	8	9²		11	3							10	4¹					7	
27	A	Arbroath	1-2	1	5				6	2	8	9	12	11¹	3							10			4			7	
Apr 3	H	Clyde	†3-0	1	5				6	2		9	12	11	3¹							10	8¹		4			7	
10	A	East Fife	1-2	1	5				6	2	14	9¹	12	11	3	8						10			4			7	
17	H	East Stirlingshire	†2-0	1	8				6	2		9¹	12	11	3							10			4	5		7	
24	A	Albion Rovers	2-0	1	8				6	2	14	9¹	12¹	11	3							10			4	5		7	
May 1	A	Alloa	2-0	1	8				6	2		9	12	11¹	3							10¹			4	5		7	
8	H	Queen's Park	0-0	1	8				6	2	14	9	12	11	3							10			4	5		7	
15	A	Stranraer	2-5	1	8				6	2		9		11¹	3							10¹	12		4	5		7	
TOTAL FULL APPEARANCES				16	26	2	4	6	36	23	15	39	22	8	38	27	24	9	23	4	1	13	8	10	28	19	4	22	2
TOTAL SUB APPEARANCES					(2)			(5)	(1)	(1)	(10)		(2)	(5)	(1)	(2)	(4)	(1)		(1)		(4)	(5)	(7)			(4)	(1)	
TOTAL GOALS SCORED						1			2	2	3	26	6	3	1					3		3	1	3		1	2		

Small figures denote goalscorers † denotes opponent's own goal

---

OCHILVIEW PARK

Capacity 3,520 (Seated 340, Standing 3,180)

Pitch Dimensions 113 yds x 74 yds.

Disabled Facilities Accommodation for disabled in front of Stand. Toilet facilities also provided.

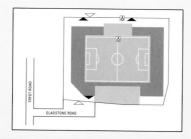

GLADSTONE ROAD

TRYST ROAD

HOW TO GET THERE

Trains: The nearest station is Larbert, which is about a mile away from the ground.

Buses: Buses from Glasgow to Dunfermline, Leven, Dundee and Kirkcaldy pass through Stenhousemuir town centre and this is only a short distance from the park. There is also a regular bus service from Falkirk.

Cars: There is a large car park on the north side of the ground.

STRANRAER

Stair Park, London Road,
Stranraer, DG9 8BS.

Chairman
George F. Compton
Vice-Chairman
R.A. Graham Rodgers
Committee
Alex Clanachan; Andrew
Hannah (Treasurer); James
Robertson; James Hannah;
Robert J. Clanachan;
Thomas Rice; James Bark;
Leo R. Sprott; Alexander
McKie; Nigel Redhead.
Manager
Alex McAnespie
Secretary
R.A. Graham Rodgers

Telephones
Ground (0776) 3271
Sec. Home/Ticket
Office/Information Service
(0776) 2194

Club Shop
Rear of old stand.
2.30-3.00pm and half-time on
matchdays.

Team Captain
Kenny Brannigan

Club Sponsor
Sealink

LIST OF PLAYERS 1993-94

Name	Date of Birth	Place of Birth	Date of Signing	Height	Weight	Previous Club
Brannigan, Kenneth	08/06/65	Glasgow	22/11/91	6-0	12.4	East Stirlingshire
Brown, James William	29/01/72	Dumfries	29/07/93	5-10	10.0	Motherwell
Cody, Stephen	01/06/69	Calderbank	22/07/92	5-9	11.6	Falkirk
Duffy, Bernard John	28/07/61	Kilmarnock	22/06/88	5-10.5	11.7	Annbank United
Duncan, Graham	02/02/69	Glasgow	30/06/89	5-11	11.6	Dumbarton
Ferguson, William	30/08/67	Glasgow	15/01/93	5-11	11.0	Albion Rovers
Gallagher, Anthony	16/03/63	Bellshill	31/03/88	6-1	12.3	Albion Rovers
Grant, Alexander	27/02/62	Glasgow	20/07/90	6-1	12.12	Partick Thistle
Henderson, Darren	12/10/66	Kilmarnock	15/07/93	5-11	11.0	Queen of the South
Hughes, James Francis	07/05/65	Kilwinning	29/03/91	5-10	11.5	Ayr United
McCann, James	03/09/62	Greenock	23/03/91	5-10	11.7	Ayr United
McIntyre, Stephen	15/05/66	Ayr	04/08/92	6-0	11.6	Hereford United
McLean, Paul	25/07/64	Johnstone	24/10/92	5-10	12.0	Ayr United
Millar, Graham	12/03/65	Bellshill	25/03/93	5-8	11.0	Albion Rovers
Ross, Stephen	27/01/65	Glasgow	22/09/92	5-9	10.10	Clyde
Sloan, Thomas	24/08/64	Irvine	19/07/91	5-9.5	10.10	Kilmarnock
Spittal, John Ian	14/02/65	Glasgow	10/03/89	6-1	12.0	Partick Thistle
Walker, Derek John	03/07/66	Bellshill	29/07/93	5-5	9.1	East Stirlingshire

CLUB FIXTURES 1993-94

Date	Opponent	Venue	Date	Opponent	Venue	Date	Opponent	Venue
Aug 4	League Cup 1		Nov 6	**Meadowbank Thistle**	**H**	Mar 5	**Queen of the South**	**H**
Aug 7	**Montrose**	**H**	Nov 13	**Berwick Rangers**	**H**	Mar 12	Meadowbank Thistle	A
Aug 11	League Cup 2		Nov 20	Cowdenbeath	A	Mar 19	**East Fife**	**H**
Aug 14	Meadowbank Thistle	A	Nov 27	Stenhousemuir	A	Mar 26	Alloa	A
Aug 21	Queen of the South	A	Dec 4	**Queen's Park**	**H**	Apr 2	Queen's Park	A
Aug 25	League Cup 3		Dec 11	SFA Cup 1		Apr 9	**Montrose**	**H**
Aug 28	**Albion Rovers**	**H**	Dec 18	Montrose	A	Apr 16	**Arbroath**	**H**
Sept 1	League Cup 4		Dec 27	**East Stirlingshire**	**H**	Apr 23	East Stirlingshire	A
Sept 4	**Arbroath**	**H**	Jan 1	**Queen of the South**	**H**	Apr 30	Forfar Athletic	A
Sept 11	Alloa	A	Jan 8	SFA Cup 2		May 7	**Cowdenbeath**	**H**
Sept 18	Berwick Rangers	A	Jan 15	Albion Rovers	A	May 14	**Stenhousemuir**	**H**
Sept 22	League Cup S/F		Jan 22	East Fife	A	May 21	SFA Cup Final	
Sept 25	**Cowdenbeath**	**H**	Jan 29	**Forfar Athletic**	**H**			
Oct 2	Queen's Park	A	Feb 5	**Alloa**	**H**			
Oct 9	**Stenhousemuir**	**H**	Feb 12	Arbroath	A			
Oct 16	**East Fife**	**H**	Feb 19	Berwick Rangers	A			
Oct 23	Forfar Athletic	A	Feb 26	**Albion Rovers**	**H**			
Oct 24	League Cup Final							
Oct 30	East Stirlingshire	A						

MILESTONES
Year of Formation: 1870
Most League points in a Season:
53 (Second Division) - 1992/93
Most League goals scored by a player in a Season: D. Frye (27) Season 1977/78
Record Attendance: 6,500 v Rangers, 24/1/48
Record Victory: 7-0 v Brechin City, Division 2, 6/2/65
Record Defeat: 1–11 v Queen of the South, Scottish Cup, 16/1/32

SEASON TICKET INFORMATION
Seated	Adult	£60
	Juvenile	£35
	OAP	£28
Standing	Adult	£50
	Juvenile	£28
	OAP	£23

LEAGUE ADMISSION PRICES
Seated	Adult	£5
	Juvenile/OAP	£3.50
Standing	Adult	£4
	Juvenile/OAP	£2.50

Registered Strip: Shirt - Royal Blue with White Trimmings, Shorts - White with Royal Blue Triangle Stockings - Royal Blue

Change Strip: Shirt - White with Royal Blue Trimmings, Shorts - White with Blue Diamonds on Sides Stockings - White

The BLUES

Date	Venue	Opponents	Result	Duffy B.	McIntyre S.	Hughes J.	Spittal I.	Duncan G.	Butler J.	Kelly P.	Sloan T.	Diver D.	Cody S.	Love J.	Grant A.	Geraghty M.	Brannigan K.	McCann J.	Evans S.	Gallagher A.	Ross S.	McLean P.	Smith A.	Fraser A.	Ferguson W.	Millar G.
Aug 8	A	Queen's Park	1-1	1	2	3	4	5¹	6	7	8	9	10	11	12	14										
15	H	Queen of the South	2-2	1	2	3	4	11		8	7¹	9¹	10		14		5	6			12					
22	A	Montrose	2-0	1	2	3	4	12		14	7¹	9¹			8		5	6			11	10				
29	A	Stenhousemuir	2-1	1	2¹	3	4	14		12	7	9¹			10		5	6			11	8				
Sept 5	H	East Stirlingshire	4-1	1	2	3¹	4	12			7²	9¹		14	8		5	6			11	10				
12	A	Brechin City	1-1	1	2¹	3	4	12			7	9			8		5	6			11	10				
19	H	Albion Rovers	1-1	1	2	3		10			7¹	9		14	8		5	6			11	4				
26	H	Forfar Athletic	1-4	1	2	3	4	10			7	9¹		14	8		5	6			11	12				
Oct 3	H	East Fife	2-1	1	2	3	4	10		14	7¹	9		11	8		5	6¹								
10	A	Alloa	4-1	1	2	3	4	11		14	7	9³			8		5	6			12	10¹				
17	H	Clyde	1-1	1	2	3	4				7	9		11	8¹		5	6			12	10				
24	A	Berwick Rangers	2-1		2	3		6¹		14	7	9	10		8		5	4		1	11¹					
31	H	Arbroath	1-0		2	3		6			7	9	12	11	8¹		5	4		1	10	14				
Nov 7	H	Stenhousemuir	0-0		2	3		6			7	9	12	11	8		5	4		1	10					
14	A	East Stirlingshire	2-1		2	3¹	4				7	9		11¹	8		5	6		1	10	14				
21	A	Albion Rovers	1-1		2	3	4	14			7¹	9		11	8		5	6		1	10	12				
28	H	Brechin City	0-0		2	3	4				7	9	10	11	8		5	6		1		14				
Dec 12	H	Queen's Park	1-1		2	3	4				7¹	9	12	11	8		5	6		1	10	14				
26	A	East Fife	1-0		2	3	4				7	9	14	11¹	8		5	6		1	12	10				
Jan 2	A	Queen of the South	0-2		2	3	4				7	9	12	11	8		5	6		1	10	14				
9	H	Montrose	3-1		2	3	4				7	9¹	14¹	11	8		5	6		1	10¹	12				
20	A	Arbroath	1-2		2	3	4				7	9¹		11	8		5	6		1	10	12				
23	H	Berwick Rangers	1-3		2	3		6			7	9	12	11	8		5	4		1	10	14¹				
30	H	Forfar Athletic	2-0		2	3					7	9		11	8	12	5	4		1	6	10¹				14¹
Feb 6	A	Clyde	0-0		2	3					7	9	10	11	8	12	5	4		1	6	14				
13	H	Alloa	1-2		2	3					7	9	10¹	11	8	12	5	4		1	6	14				
20	H	East Stirlingshire	0-0		2	3					7	9	10	11	8		5	4		1	6	14			12	
27	A	Albion Rovers	2-1		2	3		12			7	9¹			8		5	4		1	6	11¹			10	
Mar 6	H	Queen's Park	4-2		2	3		12			7¹	9		11	8¹		5	4	14	1	6²				10	
13	A	Brechin City	†1-0		2	3		12			7	9		11	8		5	4		1	6	10			14	
20	H	Clyde	1-1		2	3		12			7	9		11	8¹		5	4		1	6	10			14	
27	A	East Fife	1-1			3					7¹	9		11	8		5	4		1	6	10				2
Apr 3	H	Forfar Athletic	3-1		2			12			7	9		11	8²		5	4		1	6	14			10	3¹
10	A	Queen of the South	3-3		2			12			7²	9		11	8		5	4		1	6	14			10¹	3
17	H	Alloa	3-3		2	3		12			7¹	9	10¹	11	8		5			1	6	14		9¹		4
24	A	Arbroath	4-1	1	2	3		14			7²	9		11	8¹		5	4		12	6¹				10	
May 1	A	Montrose	2-0	1	2	3					7	9		11	8¹		5	4			6¹				10	
8	H	Berwick Rangers	3-1	1	2	3¹					7	9¹		11	8¹		5	4			6				10	
15	A	Stenhousemuir	5-2	1	2	3					7¹	9¹		11	8¹		5¹	4		14	6				10	12¹
TOTAL FULL APPEARANCES				15	26	37	15	35	2	9	38	21	20	11	36		38	35	6	23	24	22		1	4	11
TOTAL SUB APPEARANCES					(1)			(4)		(14)		(4)	(9)	(9)	(2)	(1)			(4)	(2)		(1)	(2)	(2)	(7)
TOTAL GOALS SCORED					2	2		8			19	11	1		11	1					5	5			2	1

*Small figures denote goalscorers † denotes opponent's own goal

---

STAIR PARK

Capacity 5,000 (Seated 700, Standing 4,300)

Pitch Dimensions 110 yds x 70 yds.

Disabled Facilities By prior arrangement with Club Secretary.

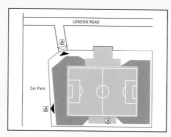

HOW TO GET THERE

Trains: There is a regular service of trains from Ayr and the station is only 1 mile from the ground.
Buses: Two services pass the park. These are the buses from Glenluce to Portrodie and the Dumfries–Stranraer service.
Cars: Car parking is available in the club car park at the ground, where there is space for approximately 50 vehicles and also in the side streets around the park.

SCOTTISH FOOTBALL LEAGUE - FINAL TABLES 1992-93

PREMIER DIVISION CHAMPIONSHIP

	P	W	L	D	F	A	Pts
Rangers	44	33	4	7	97	35	73
Aberdeen	44	27	7	10	87	36	64
Celtic	44	24	8	12	68	41	60
Dundee United	44	19	16	9	56	49	47
Heart of Midlothian	44	15	15	14	46	51	44
St. Johnstone	44	10	14	20	52	66	40
Hibernian	44	12	19	13	54	64	37
Partick Thistle	44	12	20	12	50	71	36
Motherwell	44	11	20	13	46	62	35
Dundee	44	11	21	12	48	68	34
Falkirk	44	11	26	7	60	86	29
Airdrieonians	44	6	21	17	35	70	29

PREMIER RESERVE LEAGUE

	P	W	L	D	F	A	Pts
Heart of Midlothian	33	20	6	7	66	32	47
Dundee United	33	20	7	6	70	42	46
Rangers	33	16	8	9	75	41	41
Motherwell	33	16	11	6	69	50	38
Hibernian	33	14	11	8	63	53	36
Celtic	33	15	13	5	70	55	35
Aberdeen	33	9	14	10	42	50	28
Airdrieonians	33	13	18	2	53	71	28
Partick Thistle	33	10	16	7	59	71	27
Dundee	33	9	17	7	44	66	25
Falkirk	33	8	16	9	50	76	25
St. Johnstone	33	6	19	8	49	103	20

FIRST DIVISION CHAMPIONSHIP

	P	W	L	D	F	A	Pts
Raith Rovers	44	25	4	15	85	41	65
Kilmarnock	44	21	11	12	67	40	54
Dunfermline Athletic	44	22	14	8	64	47	52
St. Mirren	44	21	14	9	62	52	51
Hamilton Academical	44	19	13	12	65	45	50
Morton	44	19	15	10	65	56	48
Ayr United	44	14	12	18	49	44	46
Clydebank	44	16	15	13	71	66	45
Dumbarton	44	15	22	7	56	71	37
Stirling Albion	44	11	20	13	44	61	35
Meadowbank Thistle	44	11	23	10	51	80	32
Cowdenbeath	44	3	34	7	33	109	13

RESERVE LEAGUE (EAST)

	P	W	L	D	F	A	Pts
Dunfermline Athletic	24	20	3	1	96	33	41
Dundee United	24	19	3	2	69	19	40
Aberdeen	24	14	5	5	39	20	33
Raith Rovers	24	14	7	3	52	23	31
East Fife	24	12	8	4	49	52	28
Hibernian	24	11	8	5	32	30	27
Alloa	24	9	9	6	24	34	24
Meadowbank Thistle	24	9	12	3	42	42	21
Forfar Athletic	24	6	13	5	40	67	17
Cowdenbeath	24	6	15	3	40	61	15
Montrose	24	4	13	7	30	52	15
Arbroath	24	4	17	3	29	70	11
Brechin City	24	3	18	3	25	64	9

SECOND DIVISION CHAMPIONSHIP

	P	W	L	D	F	A	Pts
Clyde	39	22	7	10	77	42	54
Brechin City	39	23	9	7	62	32	53
Stranraer	39	19	5	15	69	44	53
Forfar Athletic	39	18	11	10	74	54	46
Alloa	39	16	11	12	63	54	44
Arbroath	39	18	13	8	59	50	44
Stenhousemuir	39	15	14	10	59	48	40
Berwick Rangers	39	16	16	7	56	64	39
East Fife	39	14	15	10	70	64	38
Queen of the South	39	12	18	9	57	72	33
Queen's Park	39	8	19	12	51	73	28
Montrose	39	10	22	7	46	71	27
East Stirlingshire	39	8	22	9	50	85	25
Albion Rovers	39	6	23	10	36	76	22

RESERVE LEAGUE (WEST)

	P	W	L	D	F	A	Pts
Rangers	28	20	4	4	70	32	44
Ayr United	28	15	5	8	63	37	38
Kilmarnock	28	14	8	6	75	50	34
Stirling Albion	28	15	9	4	72	62	34
Hamilton Academical	28	12	8	8	55	41	32
Clyde	28	12	9	7	51	34	31
St. Mirren	28	12	9	7	53	43	31
Morton	28	13	10	5	49	43	31
Clydebank	28	13	11	4	48	41	30
Partick Thistle	28	9	9	10	55	58	28
Albion Rovers	28	10	11	7	51	49	27
Dumbarton	28	8	15	5	57	71	21
Stenhousemuir	28	4	17	7	35	70	15
Queen's Park	28	3	18	7	30	79	13
East Stirlingshire	28	4	21	3	31	85	11

PRELIMINARY ROUND

17th August, 1992
Raith Rovers 4, Arbroath 1
Dumbarton 0, Hamilton A. 1

1st September, 1992
Albion Rovers 0, Alloa 1

21st September, 1992
Cowdenbeath 0, Montrose 5

24th September, 1992
Stirling Albion 2, Clyde 5

1st October, 1992
Queen's Park 0, Kilmarnock 4
East Stirlingshire 2, East Fife 3
(A.E.T. - 1-1 after 90 minutes)

ROUND 1

15th October, 1992
Clydebank 1, Kilmarnock 3

22nd October, 1992
Dunfermline Athletic 3,
Meadowbank Thistle 1

26th October, 1992
Brechin City 5, Clyde 4
(A.E.T. - 2-2 after 90 minutes)
Forfar Athletic 1, Alloa 1
(A.E.T. - 0-0 after 90 minutes. Forfar Athletic won
4-2 on Kicks from the Penalty Mark)

29th October, 1992
Stenhousemuir 0, Hamilton A. 3

2nd November, 1992
Raith Rovers 7, Morton 2

11th November, 1992
East Fife 3, St Mirren 1

15th November, 1992
Montrose 5, Ayr United 1

ROUND 2

9th December, 1992
Kilmarnock 4, Brechin City 1

13th December, 1992
Montrose 1, East Fife 3

14th December 1992
Raith Rovers 1, Dunfermline Ath. 1
(A.E.T. - 1-1 after 90 minutes. Raith Rovers won
5-1 on Kicks from the Penalty Mark)

5th January, 1993
Forfar Athletic 2, Hamilton A. 3

ROUND 3

19th January, 1993
Dundee 3, Rangers 5

20th January, 1993
Hibernian 1, Falkirk 1
(A.E.T. - 1-1 after 90 minutes. Hibernian won 4-2
on Kicks from the Penalty Mark)

1st February, 1993
Dundee United 1, Kilmarnock 1
(A.E.T. - 1-1 after 90 minutes. Dundee United
won 4-1 on Kicks from the Penalty Mark)

9th February, 1993
Airdrieonians 3, Celtic 2
(A.E.T. - 2-2 after 90 minutes)

10th February, 1993
Heart of Midlothian 2, Motherwell 0
Aberdeen 2, Hamilton Academical 3

16th February, 1993
St Johnstone 4, Raith Rovers 0

24th February, 1993
Partick Thistle 6, East Fife 0

ROUND 4

25th February, 1993
Hamilton A. 3, Airdrieonians 2
(A.E.T. - 2-2 after 90 minutes)

8th March, 1993
Heart of Mid. 0, Dundee United 1

10th March, 1993
Partick Thistle 2, Rangers 5

23rd March, 1993
St Johnstone 2, Hibernian 3
(A.E.T. - 2-2 after 90 minutes)

SEMI-FINALS

29th March, 1993
Dundee United 0,
Hamilton Academical 1

1st May, 1993
Rangers 1, Hibernian 0

FINAL

13th May, 1993
Hamilton Academical 1,
Rangers 3
(A.E.T. - 1-1 after 90 minutes)

HAMILTON ACADEMICAL:
R McCulloch, K McKee, T Augaitis,
(R McBrearty), J Sherry, P McKenzie,
S McInulty, G Clark, S McEntegart,
C Cramb, C McLean, (M Dunn),
D Lorimer

RANGERS: C Scott, N Caldwell,
S Watson, B Reid, J McGregor,
D Dodds, G Shields, (D Chisholm),
I Nicolson, (M Fraser),D Hagen,
C Miller, P Patterson

Scorers:
Hamilton Academical: D Lorimer
Rangers: J McGregor, D Chisholm,
and 1 own goal.

Referee: J. Rowbotham (Kirkcaldy).
Attendance: 1,418.

SCOTTISH FOOTBALL LEAGUE CHAMPIONS

Year	Division One	Points	Division Two	Points
1890/91	Dumbarton/Rangers	29	-	-
1891/92	Dumbarton	37	-	-
1892/93	Celtic	29	-	-
1893/94	Celtic	29	Hibernian	29
1894/95	Heart of Midlothian	31	Hibernian	30
1895/96	Celtic	30	Abercorn	27
1896/97	Heart of Midlothian	28	Partick Thistle	31
1897/98	Celtic	33	Kilmarnock	29
1898/99	Rangers	36	Kilmarnock	32
1899/1900	Rangers	32	Partick Thistle	29
1900/01	Rangers	35	St Bernards	25
1901/02	Rangers	28	Port Glasgow	32
1902/03	Hibernian	37	Airdrieonians	35
1903/04	Third Lanark	43	Hamilton Academical	37
1904/05	Celtic (after play-off)	41	Clyde	32
1905/06	Celtic	49	Leith Athletic	34
1906/07	Celtic	55	St Bernards	32
1907/08	Celtic	55	Raith Rovers	30
1908/09	Celtic	51	Abercorn	31
1909/10	Celtic	54	Leith Athletic	33
1910/11	Rangers	52	Dumbarton	31
1911/12	Rangers	51	Ayr United	35
1912/13	Rangers	53	Ayr United	34
1913/14	Celtic	65	Cowdenbeath	31
1914/15	Celtic	65	Cowdenbeath	37
1915/16	Celtic	67	(No Competition)	
1916/17	Celtic	64	(No Competition)	
1917/18	Rangers	56	(No Competition)	
1918/19	Celtic	58	(No Competition)	
1919/20	Rangers	71	(No Competition)	
1920/21	Rangers	76	(No Competition)	
1921/22	Celtic	67	Alloa	60
1922/23	Rangers	55	Queen's Park	57
1923/24	Rangers	59	St Johnstone	56
1924/25	Rangers	60	Dundee United	50
1925/26	Celtic	58	Dunfermline Athletic	59
1926/27	Rangers	56	Bo'ness	56
1927/28	Rangers	60	Ayr United	54
1928/29	Rangers	67	Dundee United	51
1929/30	Rangers	60	Leith Athletic*	57
1930/31	Rangers	60	Third Lanark	61
1931/32	Motherwell	66	East Stirlingshire*	55
1932/33	Rangers	62	Hibernian	54
1933/34	Rangers	66	Albion Rovers	45
1934/35	Rangers	55	Third Lanark	52
1935/36	Celtic	66	Falkirk	59
1936/37	Rangers	61	Ayr United	54
1937/38	Celtic	61	Raith Rovers	59
1938/39	Rangers	59	Cowdenbeath	60
1939/40	(No Competition)		(No Competition)	
1940/41	(No Competition)		(No Competition)	
1941/42	(No Competition)		(No Competition)	
1942/43	(No Competition)		(No Competition)	
1943/44	(No Competition)		(No Competition)	
1944/45	(No Competition)		(No Competition)	
1945/46	(No Competition)		(No Competition)	
1946/47	Rangers	46	Dundee	45
1947/48	Hibernian	48	East Fife	53
1948/49	Rangers	46	Raith Rovers*	42
1949/50	Rangers	50	Morton	47
1950/51	Hibernian	48	Queen of the South*	45
1951/52	Hibernian	45	Clyde	44
1952/53	Rangers*	43	Stirling Albion	44
1953/54	Celtic	43	Motherwell	45
1954/55	Aberdeen	49	Airdrieonians	46
1955/56	Rangers	52	Queen's Park	54
1956/57	Rangers	55	Clyde	64
1957/58	Heart of Midlothian	62	Stirling Albion	55
1958/59	Rangers	50	Ayr United	60
1959/60	Heart of Midlothian	54	St Johnstone	53
1960/61	Rangers	51	Stirling Albion	55
1961/62	Dundee	54	Clyde	54
1962/63	Rangers	57	St Johnstone	55
1963/64	Rangers	55	Morton	67
1964/65	Kilmarnock*	50	Stirling Albion	59
1965/66	Celtic	57	Ayr United	53
1966/67	Celtic	58	Morton	69
1967/68	Celtic	63	St Mirren	62
1968/69	Celtic	54	Motherwell	64
1969/70	Celtic	57	Falkirk	56
1970/71	Celtic	56	Partick Thistle	56
1971/72	Celtic	60	Dumbarton¥	52
1972/73	Celtic	57	Clyde	56
1973/74	Celtic	53	Airdrieonians	60
1974/75	Rangers	56	Falkirk	5

Champions on goal average
¥ Champions on goal difference

First Division Champions Raith Rovers celebrate their first League title in 44 years.

Year	Premier Division	Points	First Division	Points	Second Division	Points
1975/76	Rangers	54	Partick Thistle	41	Clydebank¥	40
1976/77	Celtic	55	St Mirren	62	Stirling Albion	55
1977/78	Rangers	55	Morton¥	58	Clyde¥	53
1978/79	Celtic	48	Dundee	55	Berwick Rangers	54
1979/80	Aberdeen	48	Heart of Midlothian	53	Falkirk	50
1980/81	Celtic	56	Hibernian	57	Queen's Park	50
1981/82	Celtic	55	Motherwell	61	Clyde	59
1982/83	Dundee United	56	St Johnstone	55	Brechin City	55
1983/84	Aberdeen	57	Morton	54	Forfar Athletic	63
1984/85	Aberdeen	59	Motherwell	50	Montrose	53
1985/86 ●	Celtic¥	50	Hamilton Academical	56	Dunfermline Athletic	57
1986/87 ●	Rangers	69	Morton	57	Meadowbank Thistle	55
1987/88 ●	Celtic	72	Hamilton Academical	56	Ayr United	61
1988/89 ▲	Rangers	56	Dunfermline Athletic	54	Albion Rovers	50
1989/90 ▲	Rangers	51	St Johnstone	58	Brechin City	49
1990/91 ▲	Rangers	55	Falkirk	54	Stirling Albion	54
1991/92 ▲	Rangers	72	Dundee	58	Dumbarton	52
1992/93	Rangers	73	Raith Rovers	65	Clyde	54

¥ Champions on goal difference.

● Competition known as Fine Fare League. ▲Competition known as B & Q League.

1975/76

Premier Division

24	K Dalglish (Celtic)
22	W Pettigrew (Motherwell)
16	J Graham (Ayr United)
15	J Deans (Celtic)
	D Johnstone (Rangers)
14	J Scott (Aberdeen)
13	A Duncan (Hibernian)
12	G Wallace (Dundee)
	T McAdam (Dundee United)
10	R Lennox (Celtic)
	M Henderson (Rangers)

First Division

17	J Bourke (Dumbarton)
	J Whiteford (Falkirk)
16	D Somner (Partick Thistle)
14	N Hood (Clyde)
	W Thomas (Hamilton Academical)
	Joe Craig (Partick Thistle)
13	J Bone (Arbroath)
12	R Livingstone (Montrose)
	D McDowell (St Mirren)
11	P Dickson (Queen of the South)
	I Reid (Queen of the South)

Second Division

18	M Lawson (Stirling Albion)
15	W Morrison (Alloa)
14	J Wight (Stenhousemuir)
13	D Cooper (Clydebank)
12	J McCallan (Clydebank)
	J Traynor (Stranraer)
11	J McCabe (Stranraer)
10	I R Smith (Berwick Rangers)
	J Murphy (Cowdenbeath)
	A White (Forfar Athletic)

1976/77

Premier Division

21	W Pettigrew (Motherwell)
19	R Glavin (Celtic)
18	J Harper (Aberdeen)
16	W McCall (Ayr United)
	J Craig (Celtic)
	D Parlane (Rangers)
15	P Sturrock (Dundee United)
	W Gibson (Heart of Midlothian)
	D Johnstone (Rangers)
14	K Dalglish (Celtic)

First Division

36	W Pirie (Dundee)
27	J McCallan (Clydebank)
25	M Larnach (Clydebank)
22	A Ritchie (Morton)
20	M McGhee (Morton)
19	J Bourke (Dumbarton)
17	D Hyslop (St Mirren)
15	D Whiteford (Airdrieonians)
	J Bone (Arbroath)
	W McColl (Clydebank)
	P Dickson (Queen of the South)

Second Division

24	J F Frye (Stranraer)
20	D McLean (Albion Rovers)
19	G Forrest (Alloa)
17	G Hunter (Cowdenbeath)
	J McCabe (Stranraer)
16	R Robb (Brechin City)
	N Hood (Clyde)
15	B Donnelly (Queen's Park)
13	W Semple (Albion Rovers)
	A Evans (Dunfermline Athletic)
	R Gray (Stirling Albion)

1977/78

Premier Division

25	D Johnstone (Rangers)
20	G Smith (Rangers)
17	J Harper (Aberdeen)
	F McGarvey (St Mirren)
16	A MacLeod (Hibernian)
15	D Somner (Partick Thistle)
12	A Jarvie (Aberdeen)
	W McCall (Ayr United)
10	J Edvaldsson (Celtic)
	A O'Hara (Partick Thistle)

First Division

35	W Pirie (Dundee)
22	J Cairney (Airdrieonians)
20	W Gibson (Heart of Midlothian)
	J Goldthorp (Morton)
	A Ritchie (Morton)
19	D O'Connor (St Johnstone)
17	W Williamson (Dundee)
16	J McGrogan (Hamilton Academical)
	A Busby (Heart of Midlothian)
	M McGhee (Morton)

Second Division

27	J F Frye (Stranraer)
23	D McLean (Albion Rovers)
21	N Hood (Clyde)
20	R Franchetti (Albion Rovers)
	W Steele (Cowdenbeath)
15	J Ward (Clyde)
	J Harley (Cowdenbeath)
14	W Laing (Berwick Rangers)
	E Tait (Berwick Rangers)
	T Docherty (East Stirlingshire)
	F Wilson (Stenhousemuir)

1978/79

Premier Division

22	A Ritchie (Morton)
19	J Harper (Aberdeen)
13	S Archibald (Aberdeen)
	F McGarvey (St Mirren)
11	R Thomson (Morton)
	D Somner (Partick Thistle)
	G Smith (Rangers)
10	D Dodds (Dundee United)
	J Melrose (Partick Thistle)
9	W Kirkwood (Dundee United)
	R Callachan (Hibernian)
	D Johnstone (Rangers)
	W Stark (St Mirren)

First Division

28	B Millar (Clydebank)
23	A Clark (Airdrieonians)
21	J Bourke (Kilmarnock)
19	B McLaughlin (Ayr United)
18	R Graham (Hamilton Academical)
16	W Pirie (Dundee)
	J Goldthorp (Airdrieonians)
15	I Redford (Dundee)
14	G Phillips (Ayr United)
	G G Wallace (Raith Rovers)
	J Brogan (St Johnstone)

Second Division

24	B Cleland (Albion Rovers)
20	J Morton (Berwick Rangers)
	W Steele (Cowdenbeath)
	M Leonard (Dunfermline Athletic)
17	K Mackie (East Fife)
16	I M Campbell (Brechin City)
	A McNaughton (Stenhousemuir)
14	T Docherty (East Stirlingshire)
13	W Irvine (Alloa)
	I Ballantyne (Queen's Park)

1979/80

Premier Division

25	D Somner (St Mirren)
19	A Ritchie (Morton)
17	C McAdam (Partick Thistle)
14	W Pettigrew (Dundee United)
	D Johnstone (Rangers)
12	S Archibald (Aberdeen)
	A Jarvie (Aberdeen)
11	R Thomson (Morton)
10	G McCluskey (Celtic)
	G Strachan (Aberdeen)

First Division

22	A Clark (Airdrieonians)
	J Brogan (St Johnstone)
17	B Millar (Clydebank)
	A McNaughton (Dunfermline Athletic)
	W Gibson (Heart of Midlothian)
16	J F Frye (Ayr United)
	G Sharp (Dumbarton)
13	E Tait (Berwick Rangers)
	W Irvine (Morton)
	I Ballantyne (Raith Rovers)

Second Division

25	I M Campbell (Brechin City)
21	R Alexander (Queen of the South)
	J Gillespie (Queen's Park)
20	J Clark (Forfar Athletic)
18	P Houston (Albion Rovers)
17	J Jobson (Meadowbank Thistle)
15	G Murray (Montrose)
	I Gibb (Stranraer)
14	C McIntosh (Alloa)
	I Paterson (Brechin City)
	A Grant (East Stirlingshire)

1980/81

Premier Division	First Division	Second Division
23 F McGarvey (Celtic)	22 A McCoist (St Johnstone)	20 S Hancock (Stenhousemuir)
16 C Nicholas (Celtic)	20 A McNaughton (Dunfermline Athletic)	19 D Masterston (Clyde)
14 D Dodds (Dundee United)	19 E Sinclair (Dundee)	J Robertson (Queen of the South)
13 M McGhee (Aberdeen)	18 B Millar (Clydebank)	18 J Liddle (Cowdenbeath)
P Sturrock (Dundee United)	15 A MacLeod (Hibernian)	17 G McCoy (Queen's Park)
D Somner (St Mirren)	14 B Gallagher (Dumbarton)	15 J Harley (Arbroath)
12 C McAdam (Rangers)	13 J Fairlie (Hamilton Academical)	14 A Holt (Alloa)
11 J MacDonald (Rangers)	G Rae (Hibernian)	R Alexander (Queen of the South)
10 W McCall (Aberdeen)	A Kidd (Motherwell)	13 N J Watt (Forfar Athletic)
A Clark (Airdrieonians)	12 W Jamieson (Hibernian)	J McGregor (Queen's Park)
G McCluskey (Celtic)	W Irvine (Motherwell)	
W Kirkwood (Dundee United)	I Ballantyne (Raith Rovers)	
F McDougall (St Mirren)		

1981/82

Premier Division	First Division	Second Division
21 G McCluskey (Celtic)	20 B Millar (Clydebank)	23 D Masterton (Clyde)
15 A Clark (Airdrieonians)	W Irvine (Motherwell)	21 D Robb (Arbroath)
P Sturrock (Dundee United)	19 B McLaughlin (Motherwell)	16 S Evans (Albion Rovers)
14 D Dodds (Dundee United)	17 J Morton (St Johnstone)	M Lawson (Berwick Rangers)
J MacDonald (Rangers)	16 W Pettigrew (Heart of Midlothian)	I M Campbell (Brechin City)
13 F McAvennie (St Mirren)	J Brogan (St Johnstone)	G Forrest (Cowdenbeath)
12 I Ferguson (Dundee)	15 B Cleland (Motherwell)	G Scott (East Fife)
E Bannon (Dundee United)	14 J Bourke (Kilmarnock)	15 J Jobson (Meadowbank Thistle)
11 J Hewitt (Aberdeen)	13 J F Frye (Ayr United)	14 S Murray (Alloa)
G Rae (Hibernian)	A McNaughton (Dunfermline Athletic)	13 L McComb (Alloa)
J Bett (Rangers)		M Caithness (East Fife)
		J Colquhoun (Stirling Albion)

1982/83

Premier Division	First Division	Second Division
29 C Nicholas (Celtic)	26 J Brogan (St Johnstone)	23 I M Campbell (Brechin City)
22 D Dodds (Dundee United)	22 M Johnston (Partick Thistle)	22 R Alexander (Queen of the South)
17 F McGarvey (Celtic)	21 R Williamson (Clydebank)	21 J Colquhoun (Stirling Albion)
16 M McGhee (Aberdeen)	J Robertson (Heart of Midlothian)	16 K Macdonald (Forfar Athletic)
R Milne (Dundee United)	19 T Coyne (Clydebank)	15 W Gavine (Arbroath)
12 E Black (Aberdeen)	18 C Harris (Raith Rovers)	W Steele (Arbroath)
G Strachan (Aberdeen)	16 D O'Connor (Heart of Midlothian)	G Murray (Stenhousemuir)
11 M MacLeod (Celtic)	15 J Fairlie (Hamilton Academical)	14 R Thomson (East Fife)
B McClair (Motherwell)	14 D Masterton (Clyde)	R Torrance (Stirling Albion)
10 E Bannon (Dundee United)	13 R Russell (Raith Rovers)	13 S Evans (Albion Rovers)
J MacDonald (Rangers)		W Gibson (Cowdenbeath)
		C McIntosh (Cowdenbeath)
		T Hendrie (Meadowbank Thistle)

1983/84

Premier Division	First Division	Second Division
23 B McClair (Celtic)	19 I M Campbell (Brechin City)	22 J Liddle (Forfar Athletic)
18 W Irvine (Hibernian)	17 J F Frye (Clyde)	18 J Harley (Arbroath)
15 D Dodds (Dundee United)	J McNeil (Morton)	17 A Grant (Queen's Park)
J Robertson (Heart of Midlothian)	16 D Robertson (Morton)	16 G Durie (East Fife)
13 M McGhee (Aberdeen)	J Kerr (Raith Rovers)	14 G Forrest (Stenhousemuir)
G Strachan (Aberdeen)	15 A McInally (Ayr United)	13 G Gibson (East Stirlingshire)
W McCall (Dundee)	J Coyle (Dumbarton)	K Macdonald (Forfar Athletic)
F McDougall (St Mirren)	13 K Ashwood (Dumbarton)	G Murray (Stenhousemuir)
12 J Hewitt (Aberdeen)	J Bourke (Dumbarton)	12 J Clark (Forfar Athletic)
I Ferguson (Dundee)	K McDowall (Partick Thistle)	W Irvine (Stirling Albion)
F McAvennie (St Mirren)		
J Scanlon (St Mirren)		

1984/85

Premier Division	First Division	Second Division
22 F McDougall (Aberdeen)	22 G McCoy (Falkirk)	27 B Slaven (Albion Rovers)
19 B McClair (Celtic)	21 D MacCabe (Airdrieonians)	22 K Wright (Raith Rovers)
17 E Black (Aberdeen)	19 J F Frye (Clyde)	21 W Irvine (Stirling Albion)
16 F McAvennie (St Mirren)	17 J Flood (Airdrieonians)	19 P Smith (Raith Rovers)
15 W Stark (Aberdeen)	K Eadie (Brechin City)	18 J Nicholson (Queen's Park)
F McGarvey (Celtic)	14 K Macdonald (Forfar Athletic)	16 D Lloyd (Alloa)
14 P Sturrock (Dundee United)	A Sprott (Meadowbank Thistle)	K Ward (Cowdenbeath)
M Johnston (Celtic)	12 G Murray (East Fife)	15 J Watson (Dunfermline Athletic)
12 A McCoist (Rangers)	B Millar (Kilmarnock)	12 I Paterson (Cowdenbeath)
10 E Bannon (Dundee United)	A Logan (Partick Thistle)	S Maskrey (East Stirlingshire)
		D Somner (Montrose)

1985/86

Premier Division	First Division	Second Division
24 A McCoist (Rangers)	23 J Brogan (Hamilton Academical)	24 J Watson (Dunfermline Athletic)
22 B McClair (Celtic)	22 K Eadie (Brechin City)	21 P Smith (Raith Rovers)
20 J Robertson (Heart of Midlothian)	15 J Gilmour (Falkirk)	K Wright (Raith Rovers)
19 S Cowan (Hibernian)	14 S Kirk (East Fife)	17 D Jackson (Meadowbank Thistle)
15 M Johnston (Celtic)	I Bryson (Kilmarnock)	A Lawrence (Meadowbank Thistle)
14 F McDougall (Aberdeen)	J McNeil (Morton)	W Irvine (Stirling Albion)
R Stephen (Dundee)	13 G McCoy (Dumbarton)	15 C McGlashan (Cowdenbeath)
12 D Dodds (Dundee United)	12 J F Frye (Clyde)	I Campbell (Dunfermline Athletic)
A Clark (Heart of Midlothian)	11 J Flood (Airdrieonians)	T Bryce (Queen of the South)
11 E Bannon (Dundee United)	M Jamieson (Alloa)	S Cochrane (Queen of the South)
J Brown (Dundee)	S Sorbie (Alloa)	
	J McNaught (Hamilton Academical)	
	S McGivern (Kilmarnock)	
	G Smith (Partick Thistle)	

1986/87

Premier Division	First Division	Second Division
35 B McClair (Celtic)	23 R Alexander (Morton)	26 J Sludden (Ayr United)
33 A McCoist (Rangers)	21 G McCoy (Dumbarton)	25 W Brown (St Johnstone)
23 M Johnston (Celtic)	20 T Bryce (Queen of the South)	22 C Harris (Raith Rovers)
19 R Fleck (Rangers)	18 D Robertson (Morton)	21 J McGachie (Meadowbank Thistle)
16 J Robertson (Heart of Midlothian)	17 O Coyle (Dumbarton)	14 S Sorbie (Alloa)
I Ferguson (Dundee United)	K Macdonald (Forfar Athletic)	J Fotheringham (Arboath)
15 A McInally (Celtic)	15 B McNaughton (East Fife)	W Blackie (Cowdenbeath)
13 J Colquhoun (Heart of Midlothian)	13 D MacCabe (Airdrieonians)	R Grant (Cowdenbeath)
12 G Harvey (Dundee)	J Watson (Dunfermline Athletic)	13 R Caven (Queen's Park)
W Stark (Aberdeen)	12 C Adam (Brechin City)	K Wright (Raith Rovers)
	J Murphy (Clyde)	B Cleland (Stranraer)
	S Burgess (East Fife)	

1987/88

Premier Division	First Division	Second Division
33 T Coyne (Dundee)	25 G Dalziel (Raith Rovers)	31 J Sludden (Ayr United)
31 A McCoist (Rangers)	20 D MacCabe (Airdrieonians)	23 J Brogan (Stirling Albion)
26 J Robertson (Heart of Midlothian)	K Macdonald (Forfar Athletic)	H Templeton (Ayr United)
A Walker (Celtic)	17 J Hughes (Queen of the South)	19 T Walker (Ayr United)
15 J Colquhoun (Heart of Midlothian)	P Hunter (East Fife)	17 P O'Brien (Queen's Park)
F McAvennie (Celtic)	16 C Harkness (Kilmarnock)	16 W Watters (St Johnstone)
K Wright (Dundee)	C McGlashan (Clyde)	15 G Buckley (Brechin City)
13 C Robertson (Dunfermline Athletic)	D Walker (Clyde)	14 P Rutherford (Alloa)
11 I Ferguson (Dundee United)	15 C Campbell (Airdrieonians)	13 T Coyle (St Johnstone)
10 J Bett (Aberdeen)	14 O Coyle (Dumbarton)	C Gibson (Stirling Albion)
P Chalmers (St Mirren)	C Harris (Raith Rovers)	
I Durrant (Rangers)	J McGachie (Meadowbank Thistle)	
P Kane (Hibernian)		

1988/89

Premier Division	First Division	Second Division
16 M McGhee (Celtic)	22 K Macdonald (Airdrieonians)	23 C Lytwyn (Alloa)
C Nicholas (Aberdeen)	21 K Eadie (Clydebank)	21 G Murray (Montrose)
14 S Kirk (Motherwell)	19 G McCoy (Partick Thistle)	18 C Gibson (Stirling Albion)
13 S Archibald (Hibernian)	18 R Jack (Dunfermline Athletic)	16 W McNeill (East Stirlingshire)
12 K Drinkell (Rangers)	17 H Templeton (Ayr United)	15 C Adam (Brechin City)
F McAvennie (Celtic)	16 T Bryce (Clydebank)	J Brogan (Stirling Albion)
11 P Chalmers (St Mirren)	O Coyle (Clydebank)	J Chapman (Albion Rovers)
10 M Paatelainen (Dundee United)	C McGlashan (Clyde)	A Graham (Albion Rovers)
9 T Coyne (Dundee/Celtic)	15 J Sludden (Ayr United)	13 S MacIver (Dumbarton)
K Gallacher (Dundee United)	14 C Campbell (Airdrieonians)	11 J Fotheringham (Arbroath)
A McCoist (Rangers)	J Watson (Dunfermline Athletic)	D Lloyd (Stranraer)
W Stark (Celtic)		P Teeven (Albion Rovers)

1989/90

Premier Division	First Division	Second Division
17 J Robertson (Heart of Midlothian)	27 O Coyle (Airdrieonians/Clydebank)	23 W Watters (Kilmarnock)
16 R Jack (Dunfermline Athletic)	21 K Eadie (Clydebank)	20 C Gibson (Dumbarton)
15 M Johnston (Rangers)	20 G Dalziel (Raith Rovers)	19 S MacIver (Dumbarton)
14 A McCoist (Rangers)	19 R Grant (St Johnstone)	16 J Reid (Stirling Albion)
13 W Dodds (Dundee)	18 C Campbell (Partick Thistle)	A Ross (Cowdenbeath)
12 S Crabbe (Heart of Midlothian)	17 D McWilliams (Falkirk)	S Sloan (Berwick Rangers)
G Torfason (St Mirren)	15 K Macdonald (Raith Rovers/Airdrieonians)	15 D Lloyd (Stirling Albion)
11 N Cusack (Motherwell)	13 A Moore (St Johnstone)	S McCormick (Stenhousemuir)
C Nicholas (Aberdeen)	12 S Maskrey (St Johnstone)	14 P Hunter (East Fife)
K Wright (Dundee)	11 R Alexander (Morton)	V Moore (Stirling Albion)
	J Charnley (Partick Thistle)	
	C McGlashan (Clyde)	

1990/91

Premier Division	First Division	Second Division
18 T Coyne (Celtic)	29 K Eadie (Clydebank)	17 M Hendry (Queen's Park)
14 D Arnott (Motherwell)	25 G Dalziel (Raith Rovers)	A Speirs (Stenhousemuir)
H Gillhaus (Aberdeen)	21 D MacCabe (Morton)	16 A Ross (Cowdenbeath/Berwick Rangers)
13 E Jess (Aberdeen)	20 O Coyle (Airdrieonians)	15 A MacKenzie (Cowdenbeath)
12 D Jackson (Dundee United)	18 K Wright (Dundee)	14 C Harkness (Stranraer)
J Robertson (Heart of Midlothian)	16 S Stainrod (Falkirk)	D Lloyd (Stirling Albion)
M Walters (Rangers)	W Dodds (Dundee)	J McQuade (Dumbarton)
11 M Johnston (Rangers)	S McGivern (Falkirk)	K Todd (Berwick Rangers)
A McCoist (Rangers)	D Roseburgh (Meadowbank Thistle)	13 S McCormick (Stenhousemuir)
10 M Hateley (Rangers)	14 G McCluskey (Hamilton Academical)	V Moore (Stirling Albion)
	P Ritchie (Brechin City)	
	R Williamson (Kilmarnock)	

1991/92

Premier Division	First Division	Second Division
34 A McCoist (Rangers)	26 G Dalziel (Raith Rovers)	26 A Thomson (Queen of the South)
21 M Hateley (Rangers)	22 K Eadie (Clydebank)	21 G Buckley (Cowdenbeath)
C Nicholas (Celtic)	19 W Dodds (Dundee)	J Sludden (East Fife)
18 P Wright (St Johnstone)	18 A Mathie (Morton)	19 J Gilmour (Dumbarton)
15 T Coyne (Celtic)	C McGlashan (Partick Thistle)	18 D Diver (East Stirlingshire)
S Crabbe (Heart of Midlothian)	17 W Watters (Stirling Albion)	P Lamont (Cowdenbeath)
D Ferguson (Dundee United)	14 G Clark (Hamilton Academical)	17 S McCormick (Queen's Park)
14 G Creaney (Celtic)	A Graham (Ayr United)	16 R Scott (East Fife)
J Robertson (Heart of Midlothian)	13 T Smith (Hamilton Academical)	D Thompson (Clyde)
12 E Jess (Aberdeen)	12 C Brewster (Raith Rovers)	14 T Sloan (Stranraer)
	G McCluskey (Hamilton Academical)	

1992/93

Premier Division	First Division	Second Division
34 A McCoist (Rangers)	32 G Dalziel (Raith Rovers)	26 M Mathieson (Stenhousemuir)
22 D Shearer (Aberdeen)	22 C Brewster (Raith Rovers)	23 A Ross (Brechin City)
19 M Hateley (Rangers)	21 C Flannigan (Clydebank)	21 S Petrie (Forfar Athletic)
16 P Connolly (Dundee United)	20 K Eadie (Clydebank)	A Thomson (Queen of the South)
W Dodds (Dundee)	18 B Lavety (St Mirren)	19 B Moffat (Alloa)
M-M Paatelainen (Aberdeen)	15 J McQuade (Dumbarton)	T Sloan (Stranraer)
14 P Wright (St Johnstone)	13 A Mathie (Morton)	S Sorbie (Arbroath)
13 S Booth (Aberdeen)	12 H French (Dunfermline Athletic)	16 F McGarvey (Clyde)
D Jackson (Hibernian)	E Gallagher (St Mirren)	M Scott (Albion Rovers)
A Payton (Celtic)	J Henry (Clydebank)	R Scott (East Fife)
	M Mooney (Dumbarton)	

LEADING GOALSCORERS - CLUB BY CLUB SINCE 1975/76

ABERDEEN

Season	Div	No. of Goals	Player
1975–76	P	14	J. Scott
1976–77	P	18	J. Harper
1977–78	P	17	J. Harper
1978–79	P	19	J. Harper
1979–80	P	12	S. Archibald
			A. Jarvie
1980–81	P	13	M. McGhee
1981–82	P	11	J. Hewitt
1982–83	P	16	M. McGhee
1983–84	P	13	M. McGhee
			G. Strachan
1984–85	P	22	F. McDougall
1985–86	P	14	F. McDougall
1986–87	P	12	W. Stark
1987–88	P	10	J. Bett
1988–89	P	16	C. Nicholas
1989–90	P	11	C. Nicholas
1990–91	P	14	H. Gillhaus
1991–92	P	12	E. Jess
1992–93	P	22	D. Shearer

AIRDRIEONIANS

Season	Div	Goals	Player
1975–76	F	8	D. Whiteford
1976–77	F	15	D. Whiteford
1977–78	F	22	J. Cairney
1978–79	F	23	A. Clark
1979–80	F	22	A. Clark
1980–81	P	10	A. Clark
1981–82	P	15	A. Clark
1982–83	F	12	B. Millar
1983–84	F	11	J. Flood
1984–84	F	21	D. MacCabe
1985–86	F	11	J. Flood
1986–87	F	13	D. MacCabe

1987–88	F	20	D. MacCabe
1988–89	F	22	K. Macdonald
1989–90	F	10	O. Coyle
1990–91	F	20	O. Coyle
1991–92	P	11	O. Coyle
1992-93	P	9	O. Coyle

ALBION ROVERS

1975–76	S	7	J. Brogan
1976–77	S	20	D. McLean
1977–78	S	23	D. McLean
1978–79	S	24	B. Cleland
1979–80	S	18	P. Houston
1980–81	S	12	I. Campbell
1981–82	S	16	S. Evans
1982–83	S	13	S. Evans
1983–84	S	11	T. McGorm
1984–85	S	27	B. Slaven
1985–86	S	6	S. Conn
			V. Kasule
			A. Rodgers
1986–87	S	11	C. Wilson
1987–88	S	10	A. Graham
1988–89	S	15	J. Chapman
			A. Graham
1989–90	F	10	M. McAnenay
1990–91	S	12	M. McAnenay
1991–92	S	11	G. McCoy
1992-93	S	16	M. Scott

ALLOA

1975–76	S	15	W. Morrison
1976–77	S	19	G. Forrest
1977–78	F	7	D. Wilson
1978–79	S	13	W. Irvine
1979–80	S	14	C. McIntosh
1980–81	S	14	A. Holt

1981–82	S	14	S. Murray
1982–83	F	12	L. McComb
1983–84	F	10	D. Lloyd
1984–85	S	16	D. Lloyd
1985–86	F	11	M. Jamieson
			S. Sorbie
1986–87	S	14	S. Sorbie
1987–88	S	14	P. Rutherford
1988–89	S	23	C. Lytwyn
1989–90	F	9	P. Lamont
1990–91	S	11	J. Irvine
1991–92	S	12	M. Hendry
1992–93	S	19	B. Moffat

ARBROATH

1975–76	F	13	J. Bone
1976–77	F	15	J. Bone
1977–78	F	9	J. Fletcher
1978–79	F	9	S. Mylles
			T. Yule
1979–80	F	10	T. Yule
1980–81	S	15	J. Harley
1981–82	S	21	D. Robb
1982–83	S	15	W. Gavine
			W. Steele
1983–84	S	18	J. Harley
1984–85	S	6	R. Brown
1985–86	S	14	M. McWalter
1986–87	S	14	J. Fotheringham
1987–88	S	13	A. McKenna
1988–89	S	11	J. Fotheringham
1989–90	S	12	J. Marshall
1990–91	S	10	M. Bennett
			S. Sorbie
1991–92	S	12	S. Sorbie
1992–93	S	19	S. Sorbie

AYR UNITED

1975–76	P	16	J. Graham
1976–77	P	16	W. McCall
1977–78	P	12	W. McCall
1978–79	P	19	B. McLaughlin
1979–80	F	16	J.F. Frye
1980–81	F	10	J.F. Frye
			E. Morris
1981–82	F	13	J.F. Frye
1982–83	F	7	J.F. Frye
			M. Larnach
			A. McInally
1983–84	F	15	A. McInally
1984–85	F	8	G. Collins
			J. McNiven
1985–86	F	6	D. Irons
1986–87	S	26	J. Sludden
1987–88	S	31	J. Sludden
1988–89	F	17	H. Templeton
1989–90	F	10	T. Bryce
1990–91	F	11	T. Bryce
1991–92	F	14	A. Graham
1992–93	F	9	A. Graham

BERWICK RANGERS

1975–76	S	10	I.R. Smith
1976–77	S	8	W. Laing
1977–78	S	8	W. Laing
			E. Tait
1978–79	S	20	J. Morton
1979–80	F	13	E. Tait
1980–81	F	8	E. Tait
1981–82	S	16	M. Lawson
1982–83	S	8	I. Cashmore
			S. Romaines
1983–84	S	9	P. Davidson
			A. O'Hara

1984–85 S 9 P. Davidson
1985–86 S 12 J. Sokoluk
1986–87 S 8 E. Tait
1987–88 S 3 M. Cameron
H. Douglas
T. Graham
G. Leitch
C. Lytwyn
M. Thompson
1988–89 S 10 J. Hughes
1989–90 S 16 S. Sloan
1990–91 S 14 K. Todd
1991–92 S 12 S. Bickmore
1992-93 S 11 D. Scott

BRECHIN CITY

1975–76 S 7 A. Rice
1976–77 S 16 R. Robb
1977–78 S 10 J. Morton
1978–79 S 16 I.M. Campbell
1979–80 S 25 I.M. Campbell
1980–81 S 11 I.M. Campbell
1981–82 S 16 I.M. Campbell
1982–83 S 23 I.M. Campbell
1983–84 S 19 I.M. Campbell
1984–85 F 17 K. Eadie
1985–86 F 22 K. Eadie
1986–87 F 12 C. Adam
1987–88 S 15 G. Buckley
1988–89 S 15 C. Adam
1989–90 S 12 G. Lees
1990–91 F 14 P. Ritchie
1991–92 S 12 P. Ritchie
1992-93 S 23 A. Ross

CELTIC

1975–76 P 24 K. Dalglish
1976–77 P 19 R. Glavin
1977–78 P 10 J. Edvaldsson
1978–79 P 7 A. Lynch
T. McAdam
1979–80 P 10 G. McCluskey
1980–81 P 23 F. McGarvey
1981–82 P 21 G. McCluskey
1982–83 P 29 C. Nicholas
1983–84 P 23 B. McClair
1984–85 P 19 B. McClair
1985–86 P 22 B. McClair
1986–87 P 35 B. McClair
1987–88 P 26 A. Walker
1988–89 P 16 M. McGhee
1989–90 P 8 D. Dziekanowski
1990–91 P 18 T. Coyne
1991–92 P 21 C. Nicholas
1992-93 P 13 A. Payton

CLYDE

1975–76 F 14 N. Hood
1976–77 S 16 N. Hood
1977–78 S 21 N. Hood
1978–79 F 10 J Ward
1979–80 F 11 N. Hood
1980–81 S 19 D. Masterton
1981–82 S 23 D. Masterton
1982–83 F 14 D. Masterton
1983–84 F 17 J.F. Frye
1984–85 F 19 J.F. Frye
1985–86 F 12 J.F.Frye
1986–87 F 12 J. Murphy
1987–88 F 16 C. McGlashan
D. Walker
1988–89 F 16 C. McGlashan
1989–90 F 11 C. McGlashan
1990–91 F 8 S. Mallan
1991–92 S 16 D. Thompson
1992-93 S 16 F. McGarvey

CLYDEBANK

1975–76 S 13 D. Cooper
1977–77 F 27 J. McCallan
1977–78 P 5 J. McCormack
1978–79 F 28 B. Millar
1979–80 F 17 B. Millar
1980–81 F 18 B. Millar
1981–82 F 20 B. Millar
1982–83 F 21 R. Williamson
1983–84 F 10 T. Coyne

1984–85 F 11 M. Conroy
1985–86 P 7 M. Conroy
D. Lloyd
1986–87 P 9 M. Conroy
S. Gordon
1987–88 F 11 M. Conroy
1988–89 F 21 K. Eadie
1989–90 F 21 K. Eadie
1990–91 F 29 K. Eadie
1991–92 F 22 K. Eadie
1992-93 F 21 C. Flannigan

COWDENBEATH

1975–76 S 10 J. Murphy
1976–77 S 17 G. Hunter
1977–78 S 20 W. Steele
1978–79 S 20 W. Steele
1979–80 S 13 W. Steele
1980–81 S 18 J. Liddle
1981–82 S 16 G. Forrest
1982–83 S 13 W. Gibson
C. McIntosh
1983–84 S 7 I. Paterson
1984–85 S 16 K. Ward
1985–86 S 15 C. McGlashan
1986–87 S 14 W. Blackie
R. Grant
1987–88 S 11 R. Grant
1988–89 S 8 A. McGonigal
1989–90 S 16 A. Ross
1990–91 S 15 A. MacKenzie
1991–92 S 26 G. Buckley
1992-93 F 9 W. Callaghan

DUMBARTON

1975–76 F 17 J. Bourke
1976–77 F 19 J. Bourke
1977–78 F 15 D. Whiteford
J. Whiteford
1978–79 F 9 R. Blair
1979–80 F 16 G. Sharp
1980–81 F 14 B. Gallagher
1981–82 F 9 R. Blair
1982–83 F 10 R. Blair
1983–84 F 15 J. Coyle
1984–85 F 7 J. Coyle
1985–86 F 13 G. McCoy
1986–87 F 21 G. McCoy
1987–88 F 14 O. Coyle
1988–89 S 13 S. MacIver
1989–90 S 20 C. Gibson
1990–91 S 14 J. McQuade
1991–92 S 19 J. Gilmour
1992-93 F 15 J. McQuade

DUNDEE

1975–76 P 12 G. Wallace
1976–77 F 36 W. Pirie
1977–78 F 35 W. Pirie
1978–79 F 16 W. Pirie
1979–80 P 9 I. Redford
1980–81 P 19 E. Sinclair
1981–82 P 12 I. Ferguson
1982–83 P 9 I. Ferguson
1983–84 P 13 W. McCall
1984–85 P 8 R. Stephen
1985–86 P 14 R. Stephen
1986–87 P 12 G. Harvey
1987–88 P 33 T. Coyne
1988–89 P 9 T. Coyne
1989–90 P 13 W. Dodds
1990–91 F 18 K. Wright
1991–92 P 19 W. Dodds
1992-93 P 16 W. Dodds

DUNDEE UNITED

1975–76 P 12 T. McAdam
1976–77 P 15 P. Sturrock
1977–78 P 9 G. Fleming
1978–79 P 10 D. Dodds
1979–80 P 14 W. Pettigrew
1980–81 P 14 D. Dodds
1981–82 P 15 P. Sturrock
1982–83 P 22 D. Dodds
1983–84 P 15 D. Dodds
1984–85 P 14 P. Sturrock
1985–86 P 12 D. Dodds

1986–87 P 16 I. Ferguson
1987–88 P 11 I. Ferguson
1988–89 P 10 M. Paatelainen
1989–90 P 7 D. Jackson
M. Paatelainen
1990–91 P 12 D. Jackson
1991–92 P 17 D. Ferguson
1992-93 P 16 P. Connolly

DUNFERMLINE ATHLETIC

1975–76 F 10 K. Mackie
1976–77 S 13 A. Evans
1977–78 S 11 R. Morrison
1978–79 S 20 M. Leonard
1979–80 F 17 A. McNaughton
1980–81 F 20 A. McNaughton
1981–82 F 13 A. McNaughton
1982–83 F 8 R. Forrest
S. Morrison
1983–84 S 9 S. Morrison
1984–85 S 15 J. Watson
1985–86 S 24 J. Watson
1986–87 F 13 J. Watson
1987–88 P 13 C. Robertson
1988–89 F 18 R. Jack
1989–90 P 16 R. Jack
1990–91 P 8 R. Jack
1991–92 P 6 D. Moyes
1992-93 F 12 H. French

EAST FIFE

1975–76 F 8 K. Hegarty
A. Rutherford
1976–77 F 9 W. Gillies
K. Hegarty
1977–78 F 11 K. Mackie
1978–79 S 17 K. Mackie
1979–80 S 7 J. Lumsden
K. Mackie
1980–81 S 10 R. Thomson
1981–82 S 16 G. Scott
1982–83 S 14 R. Thomson
1983–84 S 16 G. Durie
1984–85 F 12 G. Murray
1985–86 F 14 S. Kirk
1986–87 F 15 B. McNaughton
1987–88 F 17 P. Hunter
1988–89 S 9 P. Hunter
1989–90 S 14 P. Hunter
1990–91 S 10 W. Brown
R. Scott
1991–92 S 21 J. Sludden
1992-93 S 16 R. Scott

EAST STIRLINGSHIRE

1975–76 S 8 J. Mullin
1976–77 S 11 I. Cochrane
1977–78 S 14 T. Docherty
1978–79 S 14 T. Docherty
1979–80 S 14 A. Grant
1980–81 F 7 P. Lamont
D. McCaig
1981–82 F 4 J. Blair
R. Edgar
P. Lamont
1982–83 S 6 C. Gibson
1983–84 S 13 C. Gibson
1984–85 S 12 S. Maskrey
1985–86 S 12 S. Maskrey
1986–87 S 5 A. McGonigal
J. Paisley
D. Strange
1987–88 S 9 G. Murray
1988–89 S 16 W. McNeill
1989–90 S 4 W. McNeill
D. Wilcox
C. Wilson
1990–91 S 10 C. Lytwyn
Dk. Walker
1991–92 S 18 D. Diver
1992-93 S 9 P. Roberts

FALKIRK

1975–76 F 17 J. Whiteford
1976–77 F 5 D. Ford
1977–78 S 13 A. McRoberts
1978–79 S 11 A. McRoberts

1979–80 S 13 P. Leetion
1980–81 F 5 C. Spence
1981–82 F 10 W. Herd
1982–83 F 8 P. Houston
1983–84 F 11 K. McAllister
1984–85 F 22 G. McCoy
1985–86 F 15 J. Gilmour
1986–87 P 6 K. Eadie
1987–88 P 9 C. Baptie
1988–89 F 12 A. Rae
1989–90 F 17 D. McWilliams
1990–91 F 16 S. Stainrod
1991–92 P 9 K. McAllister
E. May
1992-93 P 8 R. Cadette

FORFAR ATHLETIC

1975–76 S 10 A. White
1976–77 S 10 A. White
1977–78 S 11 A. Rae
1978–79 S 11 A. Rae
1979–80 S 20 J. Clark
1980–81 S 13 N.J. Watt
1981–82 S 9 J. Clark
S. Hancock
1982–83 S 16 K. Macdonald
1983–84 S 22 J. Liddle
1984–85 F 14 K. Macdonald
1985–86 F 10 J. Clark
1986–87 F 17 K. Macdonald
1987–88 F 20 K. Macdonald
1988–89 F 12 K. Ward
1989–90 F 8 C. Brewster
1990–91 F 12 G. Whyte
1991–92 F 8 G. Winter
1992-93 S 21 S. Petrie

HAMILTON ACADEMICAL

1975–76 F 14 W. Thomas
1976–77 F 7 J. McGrogan
1977–78 F 16 J. McGrogan
1978–79 F 18 R. Graham
1979–80 F 11 J. Fairlie
R. Graham
1980–81 F 13 J. Fairlie
1981–82 F 10 J. Fairlie
1982–83 F 15 J. Fairlie
1983–84 F 9 D. Somner
1984–85 F 8 J. Brogan
J. McGachie
1985–86 F 23 J. Brogan
1986–87 P 6 J. Brogan
1987–88 F 10 M. Caughey
1988–89 P 5 S. Gordon
C. Harris
1989–90 F 9 C. Harris
1990–91 F 14 G. McCluskey
1991–92 F 14 G. Clark
1992-93 F 11 P. McDonald

HEART OF MIDLOTHIAN

1975–76 P 8 A. Busby
W. Gibson
1976–77 P 15 W. Gibson
1977–78 F 20 W. Gibson
1978–79 P 8 D. O'Connor
1979–80 P 17 W. Gibson
D. O'Connor
1981–82 F 16 W. Pettigrew
1982–83 F 21 J. Robertson
1983–84 P 14 J. Robertson
1984–85 P 8 A. Clark
J. Robertson
1985–86 P 20 J. Robertson
1986–87 P 16 J. Robertson
1987–88 P 26 J. Robertson
1988–89 P 5 J. Colquhoun
I. Ferguson
1989–90 P 17 J. Robertson
1990–91 P 12 J. Robertson
1991–92 P 15 S. Crabbe
1992-93 P 11 J. Robertson

HIBERNIAN

1975–76 P 13 A. Duncan
1976–77 P 8 R. Smith
1977–78 P 16 A. MacLeod

Season			
1978–79	P	9	R. Callachan
1979–80	P	8	A. MacLeod
1980–81	F	15	A. MacLeod
1981–82	P	11	G. Rae
1982–83	P	6	G. Murray
			G. Rae
			R. Thomson
1983–84	P	18	W. Irvine
1984–85	P	8	G. Durie
			P. Kane
1985–86	P	19	S. Cowan
1986–87	P	9	G. McCluskey
1987–88	P	10	P. Kane
1988–89	P	13	S. Archibald
1989–90	P	8	K. Houchen
1990–91	P	6	P. Wright
1991–92	P	11	M. Weir
1992-93	P	13	D. Jackson

KILMARNOCK

Season			
1975–76	F	10	I. Fallis
1976–77	F	10	I. Fallis
1977–78	F	13	D. McDowell
1978–79	F	21	J. Bourke
1979–80	P	9	R. Street
1980–81	P	5	J. Bourke
1981–82	F	14	J. Bourke
1982–83	P	9	B. Gallagher
1983–84	F	11	R. Clark
			B. Gallagher
1984–85	F	12	B. Millar
1985–86	F	14	I. Bryson
1986–87	F	10	I. Bryson
1987–88	F	16	C. Harkness
1988–89	F	12	W. Watters
1989–90	S	23	W. Watters
1990–91	F	14	R. Williamson
1991–92	F	10	C. Campbell
1992-93	F	11	G. McCluskey

MEADOWBANK THISTLE

Season			
1975–76	S	7	K. Davidson
1976–77	S	8	K. Davidson
			J. Hancock
1977–78	S	6	K. Davidson
			T. Downie
			J. Hancock
1978–79	S	7	G. Adair
1979–80	S	17	J. Jobson
1980–81	S	12	J. Jobson
1981–82	S	15	J. Jobson
1982–83	S	13	T. Hendrie
1983–84	F	10	C. Robertson
1984–85	F	14	A. Sprott
1985–86	S	17	D. Jackson
			A. Lawrence
1986–87	S	21	J. McGachie
1987–88	F	14	J. McGachie
1988–89	F	6	D. Roseburgh
1989–90	F	8	B. McNaughton
1990–91	F	15	D. Roseburgh
1991–92	F	8	D. Roseburgh
1992-93	F	9	P. Rutherford

MONTROSE

Season			
1975–76	F	12	R. Livingstone
1976–77	F	13	D. Robb
1977–78	F	10	R. Livingstone
1978–79	F	12	G. Murray
1979–80	S	15	G. Murray
1980–81	S	12	G. Murray
			D. Robb
1981–82	S	9	I. Campbell
1982–83	S	12	E. Copeland
1983–84	F	7	N. Burke
1984–85	S	12	D. Somner
1985–86	F	6	M. Allan
1986–87	F	10	I. Paterson
1987–88	S	11	H. Mackay
1988–89	S	21	G.S. Murray
1989–90	P	10	D. Powell
1990–91	S	11	G. Murray
1991–92	F	9	J. McGachie
1992-93	S	10	D. Grant

MORTON

Season			
1975–76	F	5	J. Goldthorp
			J. Harley
			R. Sharp
1976–77	F	22	A. Ritchie
1977–78	F	20	J. Goldthorp
			A. Ritchie
1978–79	P	22	A. Ritchie
1979–80	P	19	A. Ritchie
1980–81	P	8	A. Ritchie
1981–82	P	6	A. Ritchie
1982–83	P	7	J. Rooney
1983–84	F	17	J. McNeil
1984–85	P	5	J. Gillespie
1985–86	F	14	J. McNeil
1986–87	F	23	R. Alexander
1987–88	P	8	Jim Boag
1988–89	F	11	R. Alexander
1989–90	F	11	R. Alexander
1990–91	F	21	D. MacCabe
1991–92	F	18	A. Mathie
1992-93	F	13	A. Mathie

MOTHERWELL

Season			
1975–76	P	22	W. Pettigrew
1976–77	P	21	W. Pettigrew
1977–78	P	8	V. Davidson
1978–79	P	9	W. Pettigrew
			G. Stevens
1979–80	F	13	W. Irvine
1980–81	F	13	A. Kidd
1981–82	F	20	W. Irvine
1982–83	P	11	B. McClair
1983–84	P	7	J. Gahagan
1984–85	F	9	A. Harrow
			R. Stewart
1985–86	P	9	J. Reilly
1986–87	P	10	S. Kirk
			A. Walker
1987–88	P	9	S. Cowan
1988–89	P	14	S. Kirk
1989–90	P	11	N. Cusack
1990–91	P	14	D. Arnott
1991–92	P	8	D. Arnott
1992-93	P	10	S. Kirk

PARTICK THISTLE

Season			
1975–76	F	16	D. Somner
1976–77	P	11	D. Somner
1977–78	P	15	D. Somner
1978–79	P	11	D. Somner
1979–80	P	17	C. McAdam
1980–81	P	7	A. Higgins
			A. O'Hara
1981–82	P	9	M. Johnston
1982–83	P	22	M. Johnston
1983–84	F	13	K. McDowall
1984–85	F	12	A. Logan
1985–86	F	11	G. Smith
1986–87	F	10	C. West
1987–88	F	13	E. Gallagher
1988–89	F	19	G. McCoy
1989–90	F	18	C. Campbell
1990–91	F	13	D. Elliot
1991–92	F	18	C. McGlashan
1992-93	P	12	G. Britton

QUEEN OF THE SOUTH

Season			
1975–76	F	11	P. Dickson
			I. Reid
1976–77	F	15	P. Dickson
1977–78	F	8	T. Bryce
1978–79	F	12	T. Bryce
1979–80	S	21	R. Alexander
1980–81	S	19	J. Robertson
1981–82	F	12	G. Phillips
1982–83	S	8	R. Alexander
1983–84	S	9	J. Robertson
1984–85	S	9	G. Cloy
1985–86	S	15	T. Bryce
			S. Cochrane
1986–87	F	20	T. Bryce
1987–88	F	17	J. Hughes
1988–89	F	7	G. Fraser
1989–90	S	8	S. Gordon
1990–91	S	11	A. Thomson
1991–92	S	26	A. Thomson
1992-93	S	21	A. Thomson

QUEEN'S PARK

Season			
1975–76	S	8	H. McGill
			A. McNaughton
1976–77	S	15	B. Donnelly
1977–78	S	8	B. Donnelly
1978–79	S	13	I. Ballantyne
1979–80	S	21	J. Gillespie
1980–81	S	17	G. McCoy
1981–82	F	10	G. Crawley
1982–83	F	10	J. Gilmour
1983–84	S	17	A. Grant
1984–85	S	18	J. Nicholson
1985–86	S	11	G. Fraser
1986–87	S	13	R. Caven
1987–88	S	17	P. O'Brien
1988–89	S	9	M. Hendry
1989–90	S	10	M. Hendry
1990–91	S	17	M. Hendry
1991–92	S	17	S. McCormick
1992-93	S	11	R. Caven

RAITH ROVERS

Season			
1975–76	S	9	M. Robertson
			G. Wallace
1976–77	F	8	G. Wallace
1977–78	S	11	R. Duncan
1978–79	S	14	G.G. Wallace
1979–80	F	13	I. Ballantyne
1980–81	F	12	I. Ballantyne
1981–82	F	12	I. Ballantyne
1982–83	F	18	C. Harris
1983–84	F	16	J. Kerr
1984–85	S	22	K. Wright
1985–86	S	21	P. Smith
			K. Wright
1986–87	F	22	C. Harris
1987–88	F	25	G. Dalziel
1988–89	F	11	G. Dalziel
1989–90	F	20	G. Dalziel
1990–91	F	25	G. Dalziel
1991–92	F	26	G. Dalziel
1992-93	F	32	G. Dalziel

RANGERS

Season			
1975–76	P	15	D. Johnstone
1976–77	P	16	D. Parlane
1977–78	P	25	D. Johnstone
1978–79	P	11	G. Smith
1979–80	P	14	D. Johnstone
1980–81	P	12	C. McAdam
1981–82	P	14	J. MacDonald
1982–83	P	10	J. MacDonald
1983–84	P	9	A. Clark
			A. McCoist
1984–85	P	12	A. McCoist
1985–86	P	24	A. McCoist
1986–87	P	33	A. McCoist
1987–88	P	31	A. McCoist
1988–89	P	12	K. Drinkell
1989–90	P	15	M. Johnston
1990–91	P	12	M. Walters
1991–92	P	34	A. McCoist
1992-93	P	34	A. McCoist

ST. JOHNSTONE

Season			
1975–76	P	8	J. O'Rourke
1976–77	F	8	I. Anderson
1977–78	F	19	D. O'Connor
1978–79	F	14	J. Brogan
1979–80	F	22	J. Brogan
1980–81	F	22	A. McCoist
1981–82	F	17	J. Morton
1982–83	F	26	J. Brogan
1983–84	P	9	J. Brogan
1984–85	F	9	J. Reid
1985–86	S	11	W. Brown
1986–87	S	25	W. Brown
1987–88	S	16	W. Watters
1988–89	S	25	S. Maskrey
1989–90	F	19	R. Grant
1990–91	P	9	H. Curran
1991–92	P	18	P. Wright
1992-93	P	14	P. Wright

ST. MIRREN

Season			
1975–76	F	12	D. McDowell
1976–77	F	17	D. Hyslop
1977–78	P	17	F. McGarvey
1978–79	P	13	F. McGarvey
1979–80	P	25	D. Somner
1980–81	P	13	D. Somner
1981–82	P	13	F. McAvennie
1982–83	P	9	F. McAvennie
1983–84	P	13	F. McDougall
1984–85	P	16	F. McAvennie
1985–86	P	7	G. Speirs
1986–87	P	10	F. McGarvey
1987–88	P	10	P. Chalmers
1988–89	P	11	P. Chalmers
1989–90	P	12	G. Torfason
1990–91	P	4	P. Kinnaird
			K. McDowall
			G. Torfason
1991–92	P	8	G. Torfason
1992-93	F	18	B. Lavety

STENHOUSEMUIR

Season			
1975–76	S	14	J. Wight
1976–77	S	7	F. Coulston
1977–78	S	14	F. Wilson
1978–79	S	16	A. McNaughton
1979–80	S	12	D. Jack
1980–81	S	20	S. Hancock
1981–82	S	8	B. Jenkins
1982–83	S	15	G. Murray
1983–84	S	14	G. Forrest
1984–85	S	6	H. Erwin
			A. McNaughton
1985–86	S	11	J. Sinnet
1986–87	S	5	A. Bateman
			P. Russell
1987–88	S	10	T. Condie
1988–89	S	9	C. Walker
1989–90	S	15	S. McCormick
1990–91	S	14	A. Speirs
1991–92	S	6	M. Mathieson
1992-93	S	26	M. Mathieson

STIRLING ALBION

Season			
1975–76	S	18	M. Lawson
1976–77	S	13	R. Gray
1977–78	F	13	W.B. Steele
1978–79	F	7	W.B. Steele
1979–80	F	11	A. Kennedy
1980–81	F	4	G. Armstrong
			W.B. Steele
1981–82	S	13	J. Colquhoun
1982–83	S	21	J. Colquhoun
1983–84	S	12	W. Irvine
1984–85	S	21	W. Irvine
1985–86	S	17	W. Irvine
1986–87	S	7	S. Gavin
			C. Gibson
1987–88	S	23	J. Brogan
1988–89	S	18	C. Gibson
1989–90	S	16	J. Reid
1990–91	S	14	D. Lloyd
1991–92	F	17	W. Watters
1992-93	F	11	W. Watters

STRANRAER

Season			
1975–76	S	12	J. Traynor
1976–77	S	24	J.F. Frye
1977–78	S	27	J.F. Frye
1978–79	S	11	A. Harvey
1979–80	S	15	I. Gibb
1980–81	S	7	H. Hay
1981–82	S	11	S. Sweeney
1982–83	S	12	S. Sweeney
1983–84	S	11	J. McGuire
1984–85	S	10	J. Sweeney
1985–86	S	8	J. McGuire
			S. Mauchlen
1986–87	S	13	B. Cleland
1987–88	S	8	B. Cleland
1988–89	S	11	D. Lloyd
1989–90	S	13	C. Harkness
1990–91	S	14	C. Harkness
1991–92	S	14	T. Sloan
1992-93	S	19	T. Sloan

THE SKOL CUP is the most eye-catching of tournaments. With its Final played in October, it stands directly in every side's line of sight as the season begins. This sparkling tournament is viewed in different ways by various teams.

Everyone has extravagant dreams, but some hope, above all, for a crowd-pulling tie, excitement and a crisp cheque to keep the Bank Manager at bay. For a club such as Stranraer, Rangers are the ideal opponents. The Third Round draw paired them at Stair Park.

Stranraer deserved their moment. The Second Division side's key result had come in the previous round. There are few clubs in Scotland who can claim to have outfought and outlasted Airdrie at Broomfield. Stranraer did just that, falling behind twice and still winning through substitute Lex Grant's extra-time goal.

Rangers' progress had been lacking in such drama. Their Second Round was composed of a 5-0 victory over Dumbarton, with the match relocated from Boghead to Hampden. Although Ally McCoist scored one there were rash suggestions that the Golden Boot striker had lost form.

McCoist corrected the misunderstanding with a hat trick in the 5-0 victory at Stair Park. That looked like business-as-usual but it was all new to one member of the Rangers team.

Neil Murray, at 19, made his debut. He already had a university degree and by the end of the season he would graduate with honours in football as well, scoring in the Scottish Cup Final.

Most of Rangers' rivals were still successfully shadowing Walter Smith's team. The forlorn exception were the Skol Cup holders, Hibs. Kilmarnock's 3-2 triumph, in extra-time, at Rugby Park hinted at the staying power which would take Tommy Burns' veterans into the Premier Division nine months' later.

There were ordeals elsewhere, as well, but they served to underline

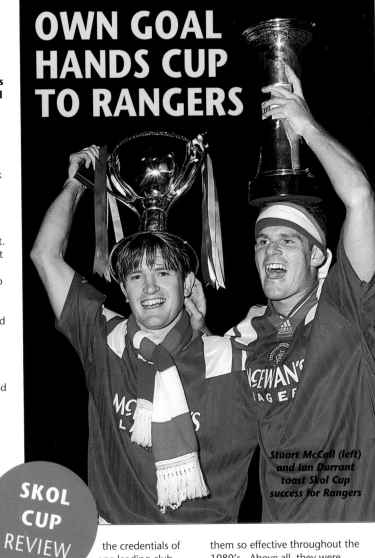

OWN GOAL HANDS CUP TO RANGERS

Stuart McCall (left) and Ian Durrant toast Skol Cup success for Rangers

SKOL CUP REVIEW

the credentials of one leading club.

The Pittodrie support may have growled at the sight of Aberdeen toiling to a 1-0 extra-time victory over 1991 finalists Dunfermline but the fact that they had survived a sticky contest was significant.

Willie Miller, in his first full season as Aberdeen Manager, was imposing himself. Personnel had been adjusted. Striker Duncan Shearer had been signed from Blackburn and Lee Richardson would soon join from the same club.

Aberdeen, though, were really reinforced by the return of an old ally. There were glimpses of the steely character which had made

them so effective throughout the 1980's. Above all, they were learning even from their bad days. Miller's team lost a League match at Ibrox in August after leading but never looked so vulnerable again.

They retained their poise even when an unhelpful Fourth Round draw sent them to Brockville. Falkirk were developing a powerful reputation as an attacking side but Aberdeen swamped them. Shearer scored a hat-trick in the 4-1 win.

St. Johnstone too made themselves at home on someone else's ground. They beat Kilmarnock 3-1 at Rugby Park. The remaining Fourth Round ties, though, had far more convoluted plots. Celtic had an exhausting nervous match in dinburgh before defeating Hearts 2-1.

The sense of jeopardy was even more intense at Tannadice. Richard Gough and McCoist twice put Rangers ahead but it was more difficult to put the match beyond a resilient Dundee United side. Victor Ferreyra and Paddy Connolly came up with equalisers on each occasion.

Jim McLean's team had proved adept at clawing their way back into the game and it took an extra-time strike from Pieter Huistra before Rangers could shake themselves free. Rangers domination of Scottish football has not meant that they can drift easily through the season.

The hardiness which was to take them to the verge of the European Cup Final may have its origins in this country's approach to football. There are understandable complaints about the crowded programme and the injuries or losses of form it produces, but the Scottish game does also produce highly competitive players.

A bunch of them were waiting for Rangers in the Semi-Finals. St. Johnstone came to Hampden still peeved with themselves over a sloppy 3-0 defeat by Rangers in the Scottish Cup the previous season. The Perth side would not be so tame again.

Their then Manager Alex Totten had taken the club from the Second Division and firmly established them at the top level. He accepted, though, that expectations had risen as the club climbed. Totten recognised that St. Johnstone needed to show more conviction in the major games.

They began brightly at Hampden and Vinnie Arkins might have scored but mishit his volley. Andy Goram then made an excellent save, even if it did come from a misplaced header by a team-mate, Richard Gough.

St. Johnstone had their chances but Rangers specialised in goals, not might-have-beens. Incisive attacking gave Ally McCoist his second hat-

trick of the 1992 Skol Cup and produced comely figures of 16 goals in 14 games for the striker. Rangers won 3-1.

Some might have described McCoist's second as a Kevin McGowne own goal, but the greedy forward insisted on awarding it to himself. McGowne, in any case, was scarcely about to claim it.

The hat-trick was to make McCoist the Skol Cup's top scorer with eight goals. For the fourth time he collected the prize which accompanies that honour, a holiday. There will be a terrible shock in store for McCoist when he one day has to give a travel agent some of his own money.

There was to be no abundance of goals in the other Semi-Final. Aberdeen's tense tie with Celtic on a foul night contained little relaxed play. The Glasgow side had reason for their trepidation. It had been ten years since Celtic last beat Aberdeen at Hampden.

Their record didn't improve. Eoin Jess snapped up the only goal just before the interval after Paul McStay had blocked a Mixu Paatelainen header on the line. Celtic threatened in the last few minutes but Gerry Creaney's shot came back out from the underside of the bar.

Aberdeen and Rangers would meet in the Final for the fourth time in six years. It was as if this national competition had become a private contest. Their matches, though, are always engrossing even for neutrals.

Both sides faced challenges even before they emerged before the

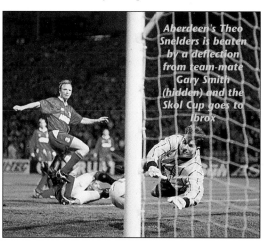

Aberdeen's Theo Snelders is beaten by a deflection from team-mate Gary Smith (hidden) and the Skol Cup goes to Ibrox

45,298 crowd. Rangers had been emotionally and physically drained by their European Cup clash with Leeds United at Ibrox in the previous midweek. Miller was required to make difficult decisions about team selection.

Both Scott Booth and Jim Bett were only just available after injury. The forward was placed on the bench but Bett started the Final after playing just 45 minutes in the previous nine matches.

It was to be Rangers who found the more measured form initially and Ian Ferguson crashed a drive against the post. Their goal, in 14 minutes, had a curious element, however. Goalkeeper Theo Snelders, worried by the new pass-back law, decided not to catch the ball as it broke from team-mate David Winnie and chested it down instead.

In the process, he gave possession to Man-of-the-Match Stuart McCall who scored easily. Aberdeen looked tormented at this stage, especially when the influential Roy Aitken was forced to depart with a thigh strain after 26 minutes.

They showed maturity in regrouping and scored a majestic equaliser 18 minutes into the second half as Shearer whirled to send a fine drive past Goram. Aberdeen, though, had not altered the whole nature of the match. Rangers continued to show more menace even though their captain, Richard Gough, had to go off with a groin strain.

Seven minutes from the end of extra-time, Aberdeen's fine defender, Gary Smith, strained to reach David Robertson's cross and succeeded only in glancing the ball past Snelders. It was a cruel conclusion but Rangers merited their victory.

The tenth and last Final under the sponsorship of Skol Lager though, should have been a cause of celebration far beyond Govan. The game reminded you of how bright and brisk the tournament had grown over those years.

KEVIN McCARRA
(Scotland on Sunday)

FIRST ROUND

Saturday, 1st August, 1992

Stenhousemuir 2, Arbroath 3

Stenhousemuir: C Kelly, B Clouston, E Hallford, P Anderson, S Prior, J Fisher, B Kemp, T Steel, (D Bell), M McCallum, (L Haddow), M Mathieson, J Irvine
Scorers: T Steel, J Irvine
Arbroath: D Balfour, J Hamilton, C Martin, B Mitchell, C Farnan, W Boyd, K Tindal, (W Holmes), C Adam, K Macdonald, (P Tosh), B McNaughton, S Sorbie
Scorers: K Tindal, C Adam, K Macdonald

East Stirlingshire 0, Alloa 1

East Stirlingshire: P Imrie, C McMillan, G Russell, B Ross, D Craig, P Houston, C McKinnon, S Ferguson, (S Thomson), P Roberts, (S Barclay), D Walker, A Auld
Alloa: J Butter, W Newbigging, R Lee, P Sheerin, K McCulloch, C Campbell, B Moffat, J McNiven, S Smith, (J Conroy), M Hendry, N McAvoy. Sub: S Ramsay
Scorer: B Moffat

Stranraer 0, East Fife 0

(A.E.T.) Stranraer won 5-4 on Kicks from the Penalty Mark

Stranraer: B Duffy, J McCann, J Hughes, I Spittal, A Gallagher, S Evans, P Kelly, (G Duncan), T Sloan, D Diver, S Cody, (A Grant), J Love
East Fife: R Charles, P H Taylor, T Spence, W Burns, G Bell, D McCracken, D Elliott, W Brown, R Scott, J Sludden, J McBride, (D Hope). Sub: R Skelligan

Tuesday, 4th August, 1992

Brechin City 2, Albion Rovers 1

Brechin City: R Allan, P McLaren, H Cairney, R Brown, A McKillop, I Paterson, G Lees, G Hutt, A Heggie, M Miller, P O'Brien.
Subs: A Smart, R Baillie
Scorers: R Brown, M Miller
Albion Rovers: M Guidi, R Walsh, D McKeown, J Kelly, N Armour, D Riley, M McBride, S Cadden, W Ferguson, G McCoy, M Scott, (S Moore). Sub: S Archer
Scorer: W Ferguson

Queen's Park 1, Clyde 3

Queen's Park: D Moonie, D Callan, S Morris, G Elder, M Mackay, D Jackson, (J Orr), D Graham, R Caven, G Orr, S McCormick, J O'Neill. Sub: D Greig
Scorer: S McCormick
Clyde: S Howie, R McFarlane, S Tennant, G Wylde, K Knox, J Thomson, D Thompson, G McCheyne, (K Quinn), F McGarvey, S Clarke, S Morrison, (P Ronald)
Scorers: D Thompson, S Clarke (2)

Wednesday, 5th August, 1993

Queen of the South 3, Berwick Rangers 0

Queen of the South: A Davidson, J Dickson, W Sim, H Templeton, K Hetherington, D Mills, B Wright, S Gordon, A Thomson, A Bell, J Robertson. Subs: A McFarlane, G Fraser
Scorer: H Templeton (3)
Berwick Rangers: K Massie, G Davidson, J O'Donnell, P Brownlee, A Hall, B Thorpe, M Cass, C Valentine, C Cunningham, (W Fisher), S Bickmore, T Graham.
Sub: J McGovern

SECOND ROUND

Tuesday, 11th August, 1992

Dumbarton 0, Rangers 5

(Played at Hampden Park)

Dumbarton: I MacFarlane, J Marsland, J Boyd, S Gow, P Martin, M Melvin, J McQuade, M Nelson, (J Meechan), C Gibson, R McConville, J Cowell, (A Willock)
Rangers: A Maxwell, S Nisbet, D Robertson, R Gough, D McPherson, I Durrant, D Gordon, S McCall, (J Brown), A McCoist, (P Rideout), M Hateley, A Mikhailitchenko
Scorers: I Durrant, D Gordon, A McCoist, M Hateley, A Mikhailitchenko

Partick Thistle 2, Ayr United 0

Partick Thistle: C Nelson, R Law, D McVicar, G Peebles, (P Kinnaird), P G Tierney, M Clark, G Britton, (G Shaw), R Farningham, C McGlashan, D Irons, I Cameron
Scorers: R Farningham, P Kinnaird
Ayr United: C Duncan, D Kennedy, G Agnew, W Furphy, G McVie, G Robertson, J Traynor, A McTurk, T Walker, P McLean, (A Fraser), G Mair. Sub: G Hood

Morton 2, Kilmarnock 3

(A.E.T.) 1-1 after 90 minutes

Morton: D Wylie, D Collins, S McArthur, S Rafferty, (I McDonald), M Doak, J Boag, A Mathie, (D Lilley), A Mahood, R Alexander, D McInnes, D Hopkin
Scorers: A Mathie, R Alexander
Kilmarnock: R Geddes, H Burns, T Black, R Montgomerie, C Paterson, (C Campbell), T Burns, I Porteous, (R Williamson), M Skilling, R Jack, T Tait, A Mitchell
Scorers: T Burns (2), R Jack

Airdrieonians 2, Stranraer 3

(A.E.T.) 2-2 after 90 minutes

Airdrieonians: J Martin, P Jack, (W Reid), A Stewart, J Sandison, G Caesar, (J Watson), K Black, J Boyle, E Balfour, S Conn, O Coyle, D Kirkwood
Scorers: S Conn, D Kirkwood
Stranraer: B Duffy, S McIntyre, (A Gallagher), J Hughes, I Spittal, K Brannigan, J McCann, T Sloan, S Cody, D Diver, (A Grant), S Evans, G Duncan
Scorers: T Sloan, S Cody, A Grant

Meadowbank Thistle 0, Dundee 3

Meadowbank Thistle: J McQueen, J Coughlin, (M Hutchison), G Armstrong, S Williamson, D Grant, M Duthie, B Ryrie, S Wilson, W Irvine, D Roseburgh, I Little, (W McNeill)
Dundee: J Leighton, A Dinnie, S Beedie, J Duffy, J McGowan, (K Bain), G McKeown, I Den Bieman, D Vrto, I Gilzean, (D Campbell), W Dodds, G Rix
Scorers: J McGowan, W Dodds, D Campbell

Brechin City 4, Hamilton Academical 2

Brechin City: R Allan, P McLaren, H Cairney, R Brown, A McKillop, G Hutt, G Lees, D Scott, A Heggie, (A Ross), M Miller, P O'Brien, (R Lorimer)
Scorers: G Hutt, G Lees, M Miller, A Ross
Hamilton Academical: A Ferguson, C Harris, C Miller, A Millen, G Rae, (C Hillcoat), J Weir, K Ward, W Reid, G Clark, (S McEntegart), T Smith, P McDonald
Scorers: G Clark, T Smith

Dundee United 6, Queen of the South 1

Dundee United: A Main, J Clark, M Malpas, W McKinlay, (J McInally), F Van Der Hoorn, D Narey, J O'Neil, I G Johnson, A Cleland, D Ferguson, P Connolly, (V Ferreyra)
Scorers: W McKinlay, I G Johnson (2), P Connolly (2) V Ferreyra
Queen of the South: A Davidson, J Dickson, A McFarlane, D Mills, W McGhie, S Gordon, (G Fraser), B Wright, A Bell, A Thomson, H Templeton: J Robertson. Sub: W Sim

Motherwell 4, Clyde 2

Motherwell: W Thomson, A Sneddon, R McKinnon, N Simpson, B Martin, L Nijholt, (I Ferguson), S Kirk, J McLeod, (P Shepstone), D Arnott, I Angus, D Cooper
Scorers: I Angus, I Ferguson (3)
Clyde: S Howie, R McFarlane, S Tennant, G Wylde, C Speirs, J Thomson, (S Morrison), D Thompson, K Knox, F McGarvey, (K Quinn), S Clarke, P Ronald
Scorers: C Speirs, D Thompson

Alloa 1, St Johnstone 3

Alloa: J Butter, W Newbigging, R Lee, P Sheerin, D Wilcox, C Campbell, B Moffat, J McNiven, (S Ramsay), S Smith, M Hendry, N McAvoy, (N Bennett)
Scorer: N McAvoy
St Johnstone: A Rhodes, S Baltacha, S McAuley, G McGinnis, J Inglis, J Davies, (P Cherry), A Moore, (S Maskrey), T Turner, P Wright, G Torfason, H Curran
Scorers: P Wright (2), H Curran

Wednesday, 12th August, 1992

Heart of Midlothian 1, Clydebank 0

Heart of Midlothian: H Smith, A McLaren, McKinlay, C Levein, G Hogg, G Mackay, W Foster), J Robertson, D Ferguson, I Baird, Wright, S Crabbe. Sub: G Snodin
Scorer: A McLaren
Clydebank: S Woods, M Murray, M McIntosh, Goldie, S Sweeney, S Jack, J Henry, Flannigan), P Harvey, K Eadie, T Bryce, Wilson, (D Henderson)

Hibernian 4, Raith Rovers 1

Hibernian: C Reid, W Miller, G Mitchell, N Orr, Beaumont, M MacLeod, M Weir, Tortolano), B Hamilton, K Wright, G Evans, McGinlay. Sub: M McGraw
Scorers: B Hamilton, G Evans (2), P McGinlay
Raith Rovers: G Arthur, J McStay, I MacLeod, Coyle, (C Cameron), R Raeside, J Nicholl, Thomson, (A Mackenzie), G Dalziel, Hetherston, C Brewster, J Dair
Scorer: J McStay

Stirling Albion 0, Celtic 3
(Played at Hampden Park)

Stirling Albion: M McGeown, C Mitchell, Armstrong, D Shanks, R Clark, J Kerr, McInnes, (I Brown), V Moore, W Watters, Robertson, (A Docherty), R Docherty
Celtic: G Marshall, M McNally, T Boyd, Galloway, A Mowbray, D Wdowczyk, O'Neil, S Fulton, (P Grant), G Creaney, Nicholas, (T Coyne), J Collins
Scorers: G Creaney (2), T Coyne

Falkirk 4, Forfar Athletic 1

Falkirk: I Westwater, F Johnston, T McQueen, Duffy, J Hughes, B Rice, (E May), McAllister, I McCall, K Drinkell, S Sloan, Baptie), P Smith.

Scorers: K McAllister, K Drinkell, P Smith, E May
Forfar Athletic: S Thomson, S McIntyre, (I Pryde), A Hamill, R Morris, R Mann, G Winter, I McKenna, (J Perry), I McPhee, S Petrie, G Donaldson, I Heddle
Scorer: I Heddle

Arbroath 0, Aberdeen 4

Arbroath: D Balfour, J Hamilton, (W Holmes), C Martin, B Mitchell, P Godfrey, W Boyd, C Farnan, C Adam, K Macdonald, P Tosh, (B McNaughton), S Sorbie
Aberdeen: T Snelders, S McKimmie, D Winnie, R Aitken, (S Thomson), B Irvine, G Smith, P Mason, J Bett, (S Wright), E Jess, D Shearer, M-M Paatelainen
Scorers: E Jess, D Shearer, M-M Paatelainen (2)

St Mirren 1, Cowdenbeath 0

St Mirren: C Money, R Dawson, (A McDonald), M Reid, R Manley, W A Baillie, J Beattie, D Elliot, P Lambert, D McGill, (B McLaughlin), B Lavety, J Broddle
Scorer: B Lavety
Cowdenbeath: A Combe, E Petrie, W Herd, W Bennett, E Archibald, S Ferguson, J Wright, G Malone, T Condie, P Lamont, (G Buckley), P Johnston, (W Syme)

Montrose 0, Dunfermline Athletic 6

Montrose: D Larter, S Forsyth, J Fleming, M Craib, J Smith, G Forbes, C Fraser, (C Maver), I Robertson, A Logan, W Callaghan, S Craib. Sub: B Morrison
Dunfermline Athletic: L Hamilton, R Shannon, (E Cunnington), R Sharp, N McCathie, C Robertson, N Cooper, (D Laing), D McWilliams, G O'Boyle, R Grant, S Leitch, W Davies
Scorers: D McWilliams, G O'Boyle (2), R Grant, S Leitch, W Davies

THIRD ROUND

Tuesday, 18th August, 1992

Dundee United 3, St Mirren 0

Dundee United: A Main, J Clark, M Malpas, J McInally, F Van Der Hoorn, M Krivokapic, J O'Neil, I G Johnson, A Cleland, D Ferguson, P Connolly. Subs: V Ferreyra, A Preston
Scorers: J O'Neil, D Ferguson (2)
St Mirren: C Money, R Dawson, M Reid, R Manley, W A Baillie, R Fabiani, (D McGill), D Elliot, P Lambert, K McDowall, J Beattie, (B Lavety), J Broddle

Kilmarnock 3, Hibernian 1
(A.E.T.) 1-1 after 90 minutes

Kilmarnock: R Geddes, H Burns, T Black, R Montgomerie, T Tait, T Burns, R Williamson, (G McCluskey), M Skilling, R Jack, S McSkimming,, (C Campbell), A Mitchell
Scorers: R Jack, S McSkimming, G McCluskey
Hibernian: C Reid, W Miller, G Mitchell, N Orr, D Beaumont, C Milne, (G Evans), M Weir, B Hamilton, (T McIntyre), K Wright, D Jackson, P McGinlay
Scorer: K Wright

Wednesday, 19th August, 1992

St Johnstone 2, Partick Thistle 2
(A.E.T.) 2-2 after 90 minutes. St Johnstone won 4-3 on Kicks from the Penalty Mark

St Johnstone: A Rhodes, S Baltacha, S McAuley, G McGinnis, J Inglis, J McClelland, A Moore, T Turner, (J Davies), P Wright, G Torfason, (S Maskrey), H Curran
Scorers: S McAuley, P Wright
Partick Thistle: C Nelson, R Law, D McVicar, M Clark, (P Kinnaird), P G Tierney, P McLaughlin, (M McWalter), G Shaw, R Farningham, G Britton, D Irons, I Cameron
Scorers: G Shaw, G Britton

Rangers' Stuart McCall (No. 2) beats Aberdeen 'keeper Theo Snelders to put Rangers one-up in the Skol Cup Final.

Stranraer 0, Rangers 5

Stranraer: B Duffy, S McIntyre, J Hughes, I Spittal, K Brannigan, J McCann, T Sloan, A Gallagher, D Diver, S Evans, G Duncan, (A Grant). Sub: S Cody
Rangers: A Goram, N Murray, D Robertson, R Gough, D McPherson, I Ferguson, I Durrant, S McCall, (J Brown), A McCoist, M Hateley, P Huistra. Sub: A Mikhailitchenko
Scorers: A McCoist (3), M Hateley (2)

Celtic 1, Dundee 0

Celtic: G Marshall, B O'Neil, T Boyd, P Grant, A Mowbray, (S Slater), M McNally, J Miller, P McStay, A Payton, G Creaney, (S Fulton), J Collins
Scorer: A Payton
Dundee: J Leighton, A Dinnie, S Beedie, J Duffy, J McGowan, K Ratcliffe, I Den Bieman, D Vrto, I Gilzean, W Dodds, G Rix. Sub: K Bain, D Campbell

Brechin City 1, Heart of Midlothian 2
(A.E.T.) 1-1 after 90 minutes

Brechin City: R Allan, P McLaren, H Cairney, R Brown, A McKillop, G Hutt, G Lees, W D Scott, (R Lorimer), A Heggie, (P O'Brien), M Miller, A Ross
Scorer: R Brown
Heart of Midlothian: H Smith, A McLaren, T McKinlay, C Levein, G Hogg, G Mackay, J Robertson, D Ferguson, (G Snodin), I Baird, (S Crabbe), A Mauchlen, W Foster
Scorers: T McKinlay, J Robertson

Aberdeen 1, Dunfermline Athletic 0 (A.E.T.)

Aberdeen: T Snelders, S McKimmie, S Wright, R Aitken, (S Thomson), B Irvine, G Smith, P Mason, (P Kane), J Bett, E Jess, D Shearer, M-M Paatelainen
Scorer: M-M Paatelainen
Dunfermline Athletic: L Hamilton, R Shannon, (D Laing), R Sharp, N McCathie, C Robertson, N Cooper, D McWilliams, G O'Boyle, (E Cunnington), R Grant, S Leitch, W Davies

Motherwell 0 Falkirk 1

Motherwell: W Thomson, L Nijholt, R McKinnon, N Simpson, (I Angus),

E Kromheer, B Martin, D Arnott, S Kirk, P Baker, (I Ferguson), P O'Donnell, D Cooper
Falkirk: I Westwater, N Oliver, T McQueen, C Baptie, J Hughes, B Rice, K McAllister, E May, K Drinkell, I McCall, P Smith. Subs: F Johnston, R Cadette
Scorer: K Drinkell

FOURTH ROUND

Tuesday, 25th August, 1992

Kilmarnock 1, St Johnstone 3

Kilmarnock: R Geddes, H Burns, (C Campbell), T Black, R Montgomerie, C Paterson, T Burns, A Mitchell, T Tait, R Jack, G McCluskey, (R Williamson), S McSkimming
Scorer: C Campbell
St Johnstone: A Rhodes, S Baltacha, S McAuley, G McGinnis, (P Cherry), J Inglis, J McClelland, S Maskrey, T Turner, P Wright, G Torfason, (I Redford), H Curran
Scorers: S Maskrey, P Wright, G Torfason

Wednesday, 26th August, 1992

Dundee United 2, Rangers 3
(A.E.T.) 2-2 after 90 minutes

Dundee United: A Main, J Clark, M Malpas, J McInally, F Van Der Hoorn, D Narey, J O'Neil, I G Johnson, A Cleland, (B Welsh), V Ferreyra, (A Preston), P Connolly
Scorers: V Ferreyra, P Connolly
Rangers: A Goram, N Spackman, D Robertson, R Gough, D McPherson, J Brown, I Durrant, I Ferguson, A McCoist, G McSwegan, (T Steven), P Huistra. Sub: A Mikhailitchenko
Scorers: R Gough, A McCoist, P Huistra

Heart of Midlothian 1, Celtic 2

Heart of Midlothian: H Smith, G Hogg, T McKinlay, (G Snodin), C Levein, G Mackay, P Van De Ven, J Robertson, D Ferguson, S Crabbe, A Mauchlen, (N Berry), W Foster
Scorer: G Mackay
Celtic: G Marshall, T Boyd, D Wdowczyk, P Grant, A Mowbray, M Galloway, B O'Neil, P McStay, G Creaney, A Payton, (S Slater), J Collins. Sub: M McNally
Scorers: G Creaney, A Payton

Falkirk 1, Aberdeen 4

Falkirk: I Westwater, N Oliver, (R Cadette), T McQueen, C Duffy, J Hughes, B Rice, K McAllister, E May, K Drinkell, C Baptie, P Smith, (I McCall)
Scorer: T McQueen
Aberdeen: T Snelders, S McKimmie, S Wright, R Aitken, B Irvine, G Smith, P Mason, J Bett, (S Thomson), E Jess, D Shearer, D Winnie. Sub: P Kane
Scorers: B Irvine, D Shearer (3)

SEMI-FINALS

Tuesday, 22nd September, 1992
Hampden Park, Glasgow

St Johnstone 1, Rangers 3

St Johnstone: A Rhodes, K McGowne, (M Treanor), I Redford, G McGinnis, J Inglis, J McClelland, A Moore, (S Maskrey), T Turner, P Wright, V Arkins, H Curran
Scorer: P Wright
Rangers: A Goram, S McCall, D Robertson, R Gough, (S Nisbet), D McPherson, J Brown, I Durrant, I Ferguson, A McCoist, M Hateley, P Huistra. Sub: A Mikhailitchenko
Scorer: A McCoist (3)

Wednesday, 23rd September, 1992
Hampden Park, Glasgow

Celtic 0, Aberdeen 1

Celtic: P Bonner, T Boyd, D Wdowczyk, (J Miller), P Grant, M Galloway, G Gillespie, (M McNally), S Slater, P McStay, A Payton, G Creaney, J Collins
Aberdeen: T Snelders, S Wright, D Winnie, B Grant, A McLeish, G Smith, P Mason, R Aitken, E Jess, D Shearer, (L Richardson), M-M Paatelainen. Sub: T Ten Caat
Scorer: E Jess

FINAL

Sunday, 25th October, 1992
Hampden Park, Glasgow

Rangers 2, Aberdeen 1
(A.E.T.) 1-1 after 90 minutes

Rangers: A Goram, S McCall, D Robertson, R Gough, (A Mikhailitchenko), D McPherson, J Brown, T Steven, (D Gordon), I Ferguson, A McCoist, M Hateley, I Durrant
Scorers: S McCall, G Smith (o.g.)
Aberdeen: T Snelders, S Wright, D Winnie, B Grant, A McLeish, G Smith, R Aitken, (L Richardson), J Bett, (S Booth), E Jess, D Shearer, M-M Paatelainen
Scorer: D Shearer

Referee: D D Hope (Erskine)
Attendance: 45,298

Skol Cup celebrations for Rangers

SEASON 1946/47

th April, 1947 at Hampden Park;
ttendance 82,584;
eferee: Mr R Calder (Rutherglen)

RANGERS 4   ABERDEEN 0
Gillick, Williamson,
Duncanson (2)

RANGERS: R Brown, G Young, J Shaw,
McColl, W Woodburn, W Rae, E Rutherford,
Gillick, W Williamson, W Thornton,
Duncanson.
ABERDEEN: G Johnstone, W Cooper,
McKenna, J McLaughlin, F Dunlop, G Taylor,
R Harris, G Hamilton, A Williams, A Baird,
W McCall.

SEASON 1947/48

5th October, 1947 at Hampden Park;
ttendance 52,781;
eferee: Mr P Craigmyle (Aberdeen)

EAST FIFE 0   FALKIRK 0
(After Extra-Time)

EAST FIFE: J Niven, W Laird, S Stewart, J Philp,
F Finlay, G Aitken, T Adams, D Davidson,
Morris, J Davidson, D Duncan.
FALKIRK: J Dawson, J Whyte, J McPhie, R Bolt,
Henderson, J Whitelaw, J Fiddes, C Fleck,
Aikman, J Henderson, K Dawson.

Replay

st November, 1947 at Hampden Park;
ttendance 30,664;
eferee: Mr P Craigmyle (Aberdeen)

EAST FIFE 4   FALKIRK 1
Duncan 3, Adams   Aikman

EAST FIFE: J Niven, W Laird, S Stewart, J Philp,
F Finlay, G Aitken, T Adams, D Davidson,
Morris, J Davidson, D Duncan.
FALKIRK: J Dawson, J Whyte, J McPhie, R Bolt,
Henderson, J Gallacher, J Fiddes, J Alison,
Aikman, J Henderson, K Dawson.

SEASON 1948/49

2th March, 1949 at Hampden Park;
ttendance 53,359;
eferee: Mr W G Livingstone (Glasgow)

RANGERS 2   RAITH ROVERS 0
Gillick, Paton

RANGERS: R Brown, G Young, J Shaw,
McColl, W Woodburn, S Cox, T Gillick,
F Paton, W Thornton, J Duncanson,
Rutherford.
RAITH ROVERS: D Westland, M McLure,
McNaught, A Young, H Colville, A Leigh,
Maule, A Collins, W Penman, T Brady,
Joyner.

SEASON 1949/50

29th October, 1949 at Hampden Park;
Attendance 38,897;
Referee: Mr W Webb (Glasgow)

EAST FIFE 3 DUNFERMLINE ATHLETIC 0
Fleming, Duncan, Morris

EAST FIFE: J McGarrity, W Laird, S Stewart,
J Philp, W Finlay, G Aitken, R Black, C Fleming,
H Morris, A Brown, D Duncan.
DUNFERMLINE ATHLETIC: G Johnstone, R Kirk,
A McLean, J McCall, J Clarkson, A Whyte,
G Mays, J Cannon, G Henderson, T McGairy,
S Smith.

SEASON 1950/51

28th October, 1950 at Hampden Park;
Attendance 63,074;
Referee: Mr J A Mowat (Glasgow)

MOTHERWELL 3   HIBERNIAN 0
Kelly, Forrest, Watters

MOTHERWELL: J Johnstone, W Kilmarnock,
A Shaw, D MacLeod, A Paton, W Redpath,
W Watters, J Forrest, A Kelly, J Watson,
J Aitkenhead.
HIBERNIAN: T Younger, J Govan, J Ogilvie,
A Buchanan, J Paterson, R Combe, G Smith,
R Johnstone, L Reilly, W Ormond, J Bradley.

SEASON 1951/52

27th October, 1951 at Hampden Park;
Attendance 91,075;
Referee: Mr J A Mowat (Glasgow)

DUNDEE 3   RANGERS 2
Flavell, Pattillo, Boyd   Findlay, Thornton

DUNDEE: J Brown, G Follon, J Cowan,
T Gallacher, A Cowie, A Boyd, J Toner,
J Pattillo, R Flavell, W Steel, G Christie.
RANGERS: R Brown, G Young, R Little,
J McColl, W Woodburn, S Cox, W Waddell,
W Findlay, W Thornton, J Johnson,
E Rutherford.

SEASON 1952/53

25th October, 1952 at Hampden Park;
Attendance 51,830;
Referee: Mr J A Mowat (Glasgow)

DUNDEE 2   KILMARNOCK 0
Flavell (2)

DUNDEE: R Henderson, G Follon, G Frew,
K Zeising, A Boyd, D Cowie, J Toner,
A Henderson, R Flavell, W Steel, G Christie.
KILMARNOCK: J Niven, R Collins, J Hood,
J Russell, R Thyne, J Middlemass, T Henaughan,
W Harvey, G Mays, W Jack, M Murray.

SEASON 1953/54

24th October, 1953 at Hampden Park;
Attendance 88,529;
Referee: Mr J S Cox (Rutherglen)

EAST FIFE 3   PARTICK THISTLE 2
Gardiner, Fleming,   Walker, McKenzie
Christie

EAST FIFE: J Curran, D Emery, S Stewart,
F Christie, W Finlay, D McLennan, J Stewart,
C Fleming, J Bonthrone, J Gardiner,
A Matthew.
PARTICK THISTLE: T Ledgerwood, J McGowan,
R Gibb, W Crawford, J Davidson, A Kerr,
J McKenzie, R Howitt, W Sharp, A Wright,
J Walker.

SEASON 1954/55

23rd October, 1954 at Hampden Park;
Attendance 55,640;
Referee: Mr J A Mowat (Glasgow)

HEART OF MIDLOTHIAN 4
Bauld 3, Wardhaugh
MOTHERWELL 2 Redpath (pen), Bain

HEART OF MIDLOTHIAN: W Duff, R Parker,
T Mackenzie, D Mackay, F Glidden,
J Cumming, J Souness, A Conn, W Bauld,
J Wardhaugh, J Urquhart.
MOTHERWELL: S Weir, W Kilmarnock,
W McSeveney, C Cox, A Paton, W Redpath,
R Hunter, C Aitken, A Bain, W Humphries,
A Williams.

SEASON 1955/56

22nd October, 1955 at Hampden Park;
Attendance 44,103;
Referee: Mr H Phillips (Wishaw)

ABERDEEN 2   ST MIRREN 1
Mallan (o.g.), Leggat   Holmes

ABERDEEN: F Martin, J Mitchell, D Caldwell,
R Wilson, J Clunie, A Glen, G Leggat,
H Yorston, P Buckley, R Wishart, J Hather.
ST MIRREN: J Lornie, D Lapsley, J Mallan,
W Neilson, W Telfer, R Holmes, J Rodger,
D Laird, J Brown, T Gemmell, C Callan.

SEASON 1956/57

27th October, 1956 at Hampden Park;
Attendance 58,973;
Referee: Mr J A Mowat (Glasgow)

CELTIC 0   PARTICK THISTLE 0

CELTIC: R Beattie, M Haughney, J Fallon,
R Evans, J Jack, R Peacock, C Walsh, R Collins,
W McPhail, C Tully, W Fernie.
PARTICK THISTLE: T Ledgerwood, A Kerr,
R Gibb, P Collins, J Davidson, D Mathers,
J McKenzie, G Smith, J Hogan, A Wright,
T Ewing.

Replay

31st October, 1956 at Hampden Park;
Attendance 31,126;
Referee: Mr J A Mowat (Glasgow)

CELTIC 3   PARTICK THISTLE 0
McPhail (2), Collins

CELTIC: R Beattie, M Haughney, J Fallon,
R Evans, J Jack, R Peacock, C Tully, R Collins,
W McPhail, W Fernie, N Mochan.
PARTICK THISTLE: T Ledgerwood, A Kerr,
R Gibb, P Collins, W Crawford, D Mathers,
J McKenzie, A Wright, J Hogan, D McParland,
T Ewing.

SEASON 1957/58

19th October, 1957 at Hampden Park;
Attendance 82,293;
Referee: Mr J A Mowat (Glasgow)

CELTIC 7   RANGERS 1
Mochan (2), Wilson,   Simpson
McPhail (3), Fernie (pen)

CELTIC: R Beattie, J Donnelly, J Fallon,
W Fernie, R Evans, R Peacock, C Tully,
R Collins, W McPhail, S Wilson, N Mochan.
RANGERS: G Niven, R Shearer, E Caldow,
I McColl, J Valentine, H Davis, A Scott,
W Simpson, M Murray, S Baird, J Hubbard.

SEASON 1958/59

25th October, 1958 at Hampden Park;
Attendance 59,960;
Referee: Mr R H Davidson (Airdrie)

HEART OF MIDLOTHIAN 5
Murray (2), Bauld (2), Hamilton
PARTICK THISTLE 1
Smith

HEART OF MIDLOTHIAN: G Marshall, R Kirk,
G Thomson, D Mackay, F Glidden, J Cumming,
J Hamilton, J Murray, W Bauld, J Wardhaugh,
J Crawford.
PARTICK THISTLE: T Ledgerwood, J Hogan,
F Donlevy, D Mathers, J Davidson, A Wright,
J McKenzie, R Thomson, G Smith,
D McParland, T Ewing.

SEASON 1959/60

24th October, 1959 at Hampden Park;
Attendance 57,974;
Referee: Mr R H Davidson (Airdrie)

HEART OF MIDLOTHIAN 2
Hamilton, Young
THIRD LANARK 1 Gray

HEART OF MIDLOTHIAN: G Marshall, R Kirk,
G Thomson, A Bowman, J Cumming,
W Higgins, G Smith, J Crawford, A Young,
R Blackwood, J Hamilton.
THIRD LANARK: J Robertson, W Lewis, J Brown,
J Reilly, G McCallum, W Cunningham,
J McInnes, R Craig, D Hilley, M Gray, I Hilley.

SEASON 1960/61

29th October, 1960 at Hampden Park;
Attendance 82,063;
Referee: Mr T Wharton (Glasgow)

RANGERS 2   KILMARNOCK 0
Brand, Scott

RANGERS: G Niven, R Shearer, E Caldow,
H Davis, W Paterson, J Baxter, A Scott,
J McMillan, J Millar, R Brand, D Wilson.
KILMARNOCK: J Brown, J Richmond,
M Watson, F Beattie, W Toner, R Kennedy,
H Brown, J McInally, A Kerr, R Black, W Muir.

SEASON 1961/62

28th October, 1961 at Hampden Park;
Attendance 88,635;
Referee: Mr R H Davidson (Airdrie)

RANGERS 1 Millar
HEART OF MIDLOTHIAN 1
Cumming (pen)

RANGERS: W Ritchie, R Shearer, E Caldow,
H Davis, W Paterson, J Baxter, A Scott,
J McMillan, J Millar, R Brand, D Wilson.
HEART OF MIDLOTHIAN: G Marshall, R Kirk,
D Holt, J Cumming, W Polland, W Higgins,
D Ferguson, M Elliott, W Wallace, A Gordon,
J Hamilton.

Replay

18th December, 1961 at Hampden Park;
Attendance 47,552;
Referee: Mr R H Davidson (Airdrie)

RANGERS 3 HEART OF MIDLOTHIAN 1
Millar, Brand   Davidson
McMillan

RANGERS: W Ritchie, R Shearer, E Caldow,
H Davis, D Baillie, J Baxter, A Scott, J McMillan,
J Millar, R Brand, D Wilson.
HEART OF MIDLOTHIAN:J Cruikshank, R Kirk,
D Holt, J Cumming, W Polland, W Higgins,
D Ferguson, N Davidson, W Bauld,
R Blackwood, J Hamilton.

SEASON 1962/63

27th October, 1962 at Hampden Park;
Attendance 51,280;
Referee: Mr T Wharton (Glasgow)

HEART OF MIDLOTHIAN 1
Davidson
KILMARNOCK 0

HEART OF MIDLOTHIAN: G Marshall,
W Polland, D Holt, J Cumming, R Barry,
W Higgins, W Wallace, R Paton, N Davidson,
W Hamilton, J Hamilton.
KILMARNOCK: A McLaughlin, J Richmond,
M Watson, P O'Connor, J McGrory, F Beattie,
H Brown, R Black, A Kerr, J McInally, J McIlroy.

SEASON 1963/64

26th October, 1963 at Hampden Park;
Attendance 105,907;
Referee: Mr H Phillips (Wishaw)

RANGERS 5   MORTON 0
Forrest (4), Willoughby

RANGERS: W Ritchie, R Shearer, D Provan,
J Greig, R McKinnon, J Baxter, W Henderson,
A Willoughby, J Forrest, R Brand, D Wilson.
MORTON: A Brown, J Boyd, J Mallan, J Reilly,
J Keirman, H Strachan, R Adamson,
R Campbell, M Stevenson, A McGraw,
J Wilson.

SEASON 1964/65

24th October, 1964 at Hampden Park;
Attendance 91,000;
Referee: Mr H Phillips (Wishaw)

RANGERS 2   CELTIC 1
Forrest (2)   Johnstone

RANGERS: W Ritchie, D Provan, E Caldow,
J Greig, R McKinnon, W Wood, R Brand,
J Millar, J Forrest, J Baxter, W Johnston.
CELTIC: J Fallon, J Young, T Gemmell, J Clark,
J Cushley, J Kennedy, J Johnstone, R Murdoch,
S Chalmers, J Divers, J Hughes.

SEASON 1965/66

23rd October, 1965 at Hampden Park;
Attendance 107,609;
Referee: Mr H Phillips (Wishaw)

CELTIC 2   RANGERS 1
Hughes 2 (2 pen)   Young (og)

CELTIC: R Simpson, J Young, T Gemmell,
R Murdoch, W McNeill, J Clark, J Johnstone,
C Gallagher, J McBride, R Lennox, J Hughes.
RANGERS: W Ritchie, K Johansen, D Provan,
W Wood, R McKinnon, J Greig, W Henderson,
A Willoughby, J Forrest, D Wilson, W Johnston.

SEASON 1966/67

29th October, 1966 at Hampden Park;
Attendance 94,532;
Referee: Mr T Wharton (Glasgow)

CELTIC 1   RANGERS 0
Lennox

CELTIC: R Simpson, T Gemmell, W O'Neill,
R Murdoch, W McNeill, J Clark, J Johnstone,
R Lennox, J McBride, R Auld, J Hughes
(S Chalmers).
RANGERS: W Martin, K Johansen, D Provan,
J Greig, R McKinnon, D Smith, W Henderson,
R Watson, G McLean, A Smith, W Johnston.

SEASON 1967/68

18th October, 1967 at Hampden Park;
Attendance 66,660;
Referee: Mr R H Davidson (Airdrie)

CELTIC 5   DUNDEE 3
Chalmers (2), Hughes,   McLean G (2),
Wallace, Lennox   McLean J)

CELTIC: R Simpson, J Craig, T Gemmell,
R Murdoch, W McNeill, J Clark, S Chalmers,
R Lennox, W Wallace, R Auld, (W O'Neill),
J Hughes.
DUNDEE: J Arrol, R Wilson, D Houston,
G Murray, G Stewart, A Stuart, W Campbell,
J McLean, S Wilson, G McLean, A Bryce.

SEASON 1968/69

5th April, 1969 at Hampden Park;
Attendance 74,000;
Referee: Mr W M M Syme (Airdrie)

CELTIC 6   HIBERNIAN 2
Lennox (3), Wallace,   O'Rourke, Stevenson
Auld, Craig

CELTIC: J Fallon, J Craig, T Gemmell, (J Clark),
R Murdoch, W McNeill, J Brogan, J Johnstone,
W Wallace, S Chalmers, R Auld, R Lennox.
HIBERNIAN: T Allan, A Shevlane, J Davis,
J Stanton, J Madsen, J Blackley, P Marinello,
P Quinn, P Cormack, J O'Rourke, E Stevenson.

SEASON 1969/70

25th October, 1969 at Hampden Park;
Attendance 73,067;
Referee: Mr J W Paterson (Bothwell)

CELTIC 1   ST JOHNSTONE 0
Auld

CELTIC: J Fallon, J Craig, D Hay, R Murdoch,
W McNeill, J Brogan, T Callaghan, H Hood,
J Hughes, S Chalmers, (J Johnstone), R Auld.
ST JOHNSTONE: J Donaldson, J Lambie,
J Coburn, H Gordon, B Rooney, I McPhee,
J Aird, J Hall, W McCarry, (G Whitelaw),
J Connolly, F Aitken.

SEASON 1970/71

24th October, 1970 at Hampden Park;
Attendance 106,263;
Referee: Mr T Wharton (Glasgow)

RANGERS 1   CELTIC 0
Johnstone

RANGERS: P McCloy, W Jardine, A Miller,
J Conn, R McKinnon, C Jackson,
A Henderson, A MacDonald, D Johnstone,
C Stein, W Johnston.
CELTIC: E Williams, J Craig, J Quinn,
R Murdoch, W McNeill, D Hay, J Johnstone,
G Connolly, W Wallace, H Hood (R Lennox),
L Macari.

SEASON 1971/72

23rd October, 1971 at Hampden Park;
Attendance 62,740;
Referee: Mr W J Mullan (Dalkeith)

PARTICK THISTLE 4   CELTIC 1
Rae, Lawrie, McQuade,   Dalglish
Bone

PARTICK THISTLE: A Rough, J Hansen,
A Forsyth, R Glavin (J Gibson), J Campbell,
H Strachan, D McQuade, F Coulston, J Bone,
A Rae, R Lawrie.
CELTIC: E Williams, D Hay, T Gemmell,
R Murdoch, G Connelly, J Brogan, J Johnstone,
(J Craig), K Dalglish, H Hood, T Callaghan,
L Macari.

SEASON 1972/73

9th December, 1972 at Hampden Park;
Attendance 71,696;
Referee: Mr A MacKenzie (Larbert)

HIBERNIAN 2   CELTIC 1
Stanton, O'Rourke   Dalglish

HIBERNIAN: J Herriot, J Brownlie, E Schaedler,
P Stanton, J Black, J Blackley, A Edwards,
J O'Rourke, A Gordon, A Cropley, A Duncan.
CELTIC: E Williams, D McGrain, J Brogan,
P McCluskey, W McNeill, D Hay, J Johnstone
(T Callaghan), G Connelly, K Dalglish, H Hood,
L Macari.

SEASON 1973/74

15th December, 1973 at Hampden Park;
Attendance 27,974;
Referee: Mr R H Davidson (Airdrie)

DUNDEE 1   CELTIC 0
Wallace

DUNDEE: T Allan, R Wilson, T Gemmell,
R Ford, G Stewart, I Phillip, J Duncan,
R Robinson, G Wallace, J Scott, D Lambie.
CELTIC: A Hunter, D McGrain, J Brogan,
P McCluskey, W McNeill, S Murray, H Hood
(J Johnstone), D Hay (G Connelly), P Wilson,
T Callaghan, K Dalglish.

SEASON 1974/75

26th October, 1974 at Hampden Park;
Attendance 53,848;
Referee: Mr J R P Gordon (Newport on Tay)

CELTIC 6   HIBERNIAN 3
Johnstone, Deans (3),   Harper (3)
Wilson, Murray

CELTIC: A Hunter, D McGrain, J Brogan,
S Murray, W McNeill, P McCluskey,
J Johnstone, K Dalglish, J Deans, H Hood,
P Wilson.
HIBERNIAN: J McArthur, J Brownlie (R Smith),
D Bremner, P Stanton, D Spalding, J Blackley,
A Edwards, A Cropley, J Harper, I Munro,
A Duncan (W Murray)

SEASON 1975/76

25th October, 1975 at Hampden Park;
Attendance 58,806;
Referee: Mr W Anderson (East Kilbride)

RANGERS 1   CELTIC 0
MacDonald

RANGERS: S Kennedy, W Jardine, J Greig,
T Forsyth, C Jackson, A MacDonald, T McLean,
C Stein, D Parlane, D Johnstone, Q Young.
CELTIC: P Latchford, D McGrain, A Lynch,
P McCluskey, R MacDonald, J Edvaldsson,
H Hood (J McNamara), K Dalglish, P Wilson,
(R Glavin), T Callaghan, R Lennox.

SEASON 1976/77

6th November, 1976 at Hampden Park;
Attendance 69,268;
Referee Mr J W Paterson (Bothwell)

ABERDEEN 2   CELTIC 1 (After Extra-Time)
Jarvie, Robb   Dalglish (pen)

ABERDEEN: R Clark, R S Kennedy,
W Williamson, J Smith, W Garner, W Miller,
D Sullivan, J Scott, J Harper, A Jarvie (D Robb),
A Graham.
CELTIC: P Latchford, D McGrain, A Lynch,
J Edvaldsson, R MacDonald, R Aitken, J Doyle,
R Glavin, K Dalglish, T Burns (R Lennox),
P Wilson.

SEASON 1977/78

18th March, 1978 at Hampden Park;
Attendance 60,168;
Referee: Mr D F T Syme (Rutherglen)

RANGERS 2   CELTIC 1 (After Extra-Time)
Cooper, Smith   Edvaldsson

RANGERS: S Kennedy, W Jardine, J Greig,
T Forsyth, C Jackson, A MacDonald, T McLean,
J Hamilton, (A Miller), D Johnstone, G Smith,
D Cooper (D Parlane).
CELTIC: P Latchford, A Sneddon, A Lynch
(P Wilson), F Munro, R MacDonald, J Dowie,
R Glavin (J Doyle), J Edvaldsson, G McCluskey,
R Aitken, T Burns.

SEASON 1978/79

31st March, 1979 at Hampden Park;
Attendance 54,000;
Referee: Mr I M D Foote (Glasgow)

RANGERS 2   ABERDEEN 1
McMaster (o.g.),   Davidson
Jackson

RANGERS: P McCloy, W Jardine, A Dawson,
D Johnstone, C Jackson, A MacDonald,
T McLean, R Russell, W Urquhart (A Miller),
G Smith (D Parlane), D Cooper.
ABERDEEN: R Clark, R S Kennedy, C McLelland,
J McMaster, D Rougvie, W Miller, G Strachan,
S Archibald, J Harper, A Jarvie (A McLeish),
D Davidson.

103

Trevor Francis and Graham Roberts celebrate Rangers' League Cup triumph in 1987/88 when Aberdeen were beaten on penalties after a thrilling 3-3 draw.

SEASON 1979/80 - BELL'S LEAGUE CUP

8th December, 1979 at Hampden Park;
Attendance 27,299;
Referee: Mr B R McGinlay (Balfron)

DUNDEE UNITED 0 ABERDEEN 0
(After Extra-Time)

DUNDEE UNITED: H McAlpine, D Stark, F Kopel, I Phillip (G Fleming), P Hegarty, D Narey, E Bannon, P Sturrock, W Pettigrew, J Holt, G Payne (S Murray).
ABERDEEN: R Clark, R S Kennedy, D Rougvie, A McLeish, W Garner, W Miller, G Strachan, S Archibald, M McGhee (A Jarvie), J McMaster (D Hamilton), J Scanlon.

REPLAY

12th December at Dens Park;
Attendance 28,984;
Referee: Mr B R McGinlay (Balfron)

DUNDEE UNITED 3 ABERDEEN 0
Pettigrew (2), Sturrock

DUNDEE UNITED: H McAlpine, D Stark, F Kopel, G Fleming, P Hegarty, D Narey, E Bannon, P Sturrock, W Pettigrew, J Holt, W Kirkwood.
ABERDEEN: R Clark, R S Kennedy, D Rougvie, A McLeish, W Garner, W Miller, G Strachan, S Archibald, M McGhee (A Jarvie), J McMaster, J Scanlon (D Hamilton).

SEASON 1980/81 BELL'S LEAGUE CUP

6th December, 1980 at Dens Park;
Attendance 24,466;
Referee: Mr R B Valentine (Dundee)

DUNDEE UNITED 3 DUNDEE 0
Dodds, Sturrock (2)

DUNDEE UNITED: H McAlpine, J Holt, F Kopel, I Phillip, P Hegarty, D Narey, E Bannon, G Payne, W Pettigrew, P Sturrock, D Dodds.

DUNDEE: R Geddes, L Barr, E Schaedler, C Fraser, R Glennie, G McGeachie, P Mackie, R Stephen, E Sinclair, W Williamson, A Geddes

SEASON 1981/82

28th November, 1981 at Hampden Park;
Attendance 53,795;
Referee: Mr E H Pringle (Edinburgh)

RANGERS 2 DUNDEE UNITED
Cooper, Redford   Milne

RANGERS: J Stewart, W Jardine, A Miller, G Stevens, C Jackson, J Bett, D Cooper, D Johnstone, R Russell, J MacDonald, G Dalzie (I Redford).
DUNDEE UNITED: H McAlpine, J Holt, D Star, D Narey, P Hegarty, I Phillip, E Bannon, R Milne, W Kirkwood, P Sturrock, D Dodds.

SEASON 1982/83

4th December, 1982 at Hampden Park;
Attendance 55,372;
Referee: Mr K J Hope (Clarkston)

CELTIC 2   RANGERS 1
Nicholas, MacLeod   Bett

CELTIC: P Bonner, D McGrain, G Sinclair,
R Aitken, T McAdam, M MacLeod, D Provan,
P McStay (M Reid), F McGarvey, T Burns,
C Nicholas.
RANGERS: J Stewart, D MacKinnon, I Redford,
J McClelland, C Paterson, J Bett, D Cooper,
R Prytz (A Dawson), D Johnstone, R Russell
(J MacDonald), G Smith.

SEASON 1983/84

25th March, 1984 at Hampden Park;
Attendance 66,369;
Referee: Mr R B Valentine (Dundee)

RANGERS 3   CELTIC 2
McCoist (3) (1 pen)   McClair, Reid (pen)

RANGERS: P McCloy, J Nicholl, A Dawson,
J McClelland, C Paterson, D McPherson,
R Russell, A McCoist, A Clark (C McAdam),
J MacDonald (H Burns), D Cooper.
CELTIC: P Bonner, D McGrain, M Reid,
R Aitken, T McAdam, M MacLeod, D Provan
(G Sinclair), P McStay, F McGarvey (J Melrose),
T Burns, B McClair.

SEASON 1984/85 - SKOL CUP

28th October, 1984 at Hampden Park;
Attendance 44,698;
Referee: Mr B R McGinlay (Balfron)

RANGERS 1   DUNDEE UNITED 0
Ferguson

RANGERS: P McCloy, A Dawson, J McClelland,
C Fraser, C Paterson, D McPherson, R Russell,
R Prytz, A McCoist, I Ferguson (D Mitchell),
I Redford, D Cooper.
DUNDEE UNITED: H McAlpine, J Holt (J Clark),
M Malpas, R Gough, P Hegarty, D Narey,
J Bannon, R Milne (S Beedie), W Kirkwood,
P Sturrock, D Dodds.

SEASON 1985/86 - SKOL CUP

27th October, 1985 at Hampden Park;
Attendance 40,065;
Referee: Mr R B Valentine (Dundee)

ABERDEEN 3   HIBERNIAN 0
Black (2), Stark

ABERDEEN: J Leighton, S McKimmie,
T Mitchell, W Stark, A McLeish, W Miller,
J Black (S Gray), N Simpson, F McDougall,
J Cooper, J Hewitt.
HIBERNIAN: A Rough, A Sneddon, I Munro,
A Brazil (C Harris), M Fulton, G Hunter, P Kane,
G Chisholm, S Cowan, G Durie, J McBride
(Collins).

SEASON 1986/87 - SKOL CUP

26th October, 1986 at Hampden Park;
Attendance 74,219;
Referee: Mr D F T Syme (Rutherglen)

RANGERS 2   CELTIC 1
Durrant, Cooper (pen) McClair

RANGERS: C Woods, J Nicholl, S Munro,
C Fraser (D MacFarlane), A Dawson, T Butcher,
D Ferguson, K McMinn, A McCoist (R Fleck),
I Durrant, D Cooper.
CELTIC: P Bonner, P Grant, M MacLeod,
R Aitken, D Whyte, M McGhee
(O Archdeacon), B McClair, P McStay,
M Johnston, A Shepherd, A McInally.

SEASON 1987/88 - SKOL CUP

25th October 1987 at Hampden Park;
Attendance 71,961;
Referee: Mr R B Valentine (Dundee)

RANGERS 3   ABERDEEN 3 (After Extra-Time)
Cooper,   Bett, Falconer, Hewitt
Durrant, Fleck

Rangers won 5-3 on Kicks from the Penalty
Mark

RANGERS: J N Walker, J Nicholl, S Munro,
G Roberts, D Ferguson (T Francis) R Gough,
J McGregor (A Cohen), R Fleck, A McCoist,
I Durrant, D Cooper.
ABERDEEN: J Leighton, S McKimmie,
R Connor, N Simpson (P Weir), A McLeish,
W Miller, J Hewitt, J Bett, J Miller, P Nicholas,
W Falconer.

SEASON 1988/89 - SKOL CUP

23rd October, 1988 at Hampden Park;
Attendance 72,122;
Referee: Mr G B Smith (Edinburgh)

RANGERS 3   ABERDEEN 2
McCoist (2),   Dodds (2)
I Ferguson

RANGERS C Woods, G Stevens, J Brown,
R Gough, R Wilkins, T Butcher, K Drinkell,
I Ferguson, A McCoist, N Cooper, M Walters.
ABERDEEN: T Snelders, S McKimmie,
D Robertson, N Simpson, (B Irvine), A McLeish,
W Miller, C Nicholas, J Bett, D Dodds,
R Connor, J Hewitt.

SEASON 1989/90 - SKOL CUP

22nd October, 1989 at Hampden Park;
Attendance 61,190;
Referee: Mr G B Smith (Edinburgh)

ABERDEEN 2 RANGERS 1 (After Extra-Time)
Mason (2)   Walters (pen)

ABERDEEN: T Snelders, S McKimmie,
D Robertson, B Grant, (W Van Der Ark),
A McLeish, W Miller, C Nicholas, J Bett,
P Mason, R Connor, E Jess, (B Irvine).
RANGERS: C Woods, G Stevens, S Munro,
R Gough, R Wilkins, T Butcher, T Steven,
I Ferguson, A McCoist, M Johnston, M Walters,
(I McCall)

SEASON 1990/91 - SKOL CUP

28th October, 1990 at Hampden Park;
Attendance 62,817;
Referee: Mr J McCluskey (Stewarton)

RANGERS 2   CELTIC 1
Walters, Gough   Elliott

RANGERS: C Woods, G Stevens, S Munro,
R Gough, N Spackman, J Brown, T Steven,
T Hurlock,(P Huistra), A McCoist, (I Ferguson),
M Hateley, M Walters.
CELTIC: P Bonner, P Grant, D Wdowczyk,
S Fulton, (J Hewitt), P Elliott, A Rogan, J Miller,
(C Morris), P McStay, D Dziekanowski,
G Creaney, J Collins.

SEASON 1991/92 - SKOL CUP

27th October, 1991 at Hampden Park;
Attendance 40,377;
Referee: Mr B R McGinlay (Balfron)

HIBERNIAN 2   DUNFERMLINE ATHLETIC 0
McIntyre (pen),
Wright

HIBERNIAN: J Burridge, W Miller, G Mitchell,
G Hunter, T McIntyre, M MacLeod, M Weir,
B Hamilton, K Wright, G Evans, P McGinlay
DUNFERMLINE ATHLETIC: A Rhodes, T Wilson,
R Sharp (E Cunnington), N McCathie,
D Moyes, C Robertson, D McWilliams,
I Kozma, S Leitch, W Davies, C Sinclair
(I McCall)

SEASON 1992/93 - SKOL CUP

25th October, 1992 at Hampden Park;
Attendance 45,298;
Referee: Mr D D Hope (Erskine)

RANGERS 2   ABERDEEN 1 (After Extra-Time)
McCall, Smith (og)   Shearer

RANGERS: A Goram, S McCall, D Robertson,
R Gough, (A Mikhailitchenko), D McPherson,
J Brown, T Steven (D Gordon), I Ferguson,
A McCoist, M Hateley, I Durrant.
ABERDEEN: T Snelders, S Wright, D Winnie,
B Grant, A McLeish, G Smith, R Aitken,
(L Richardson), J Bett, (S Booth), E Jess,
D Shearer, M-M Paatelainen.

League Cup Winners at a glance	
RANGERS	18
CELTIC	9
ABERDEEN	4
HEART OF MIDLOTHIAN	4
DUNDEE	3
EAST FIFE	3
DUNDEE UNITED	2
HIBERNIAN	2
MOTHERWELL	1
PARTICK THISTLE	1

TREBLE JOY FOR RANGERS

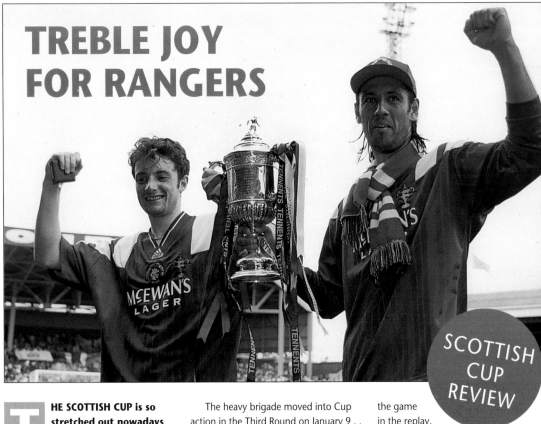

THE SCOTTISH CUP is so stretched out nowadays that it has to start the year before it finishes.

The First Round began on December 5, 1992. The Final was played on May 29, 1993. Talk about a long-running affair!

Young Jamie McCarron of Clyde had a double distinction. Scorer of the FIRST goal of the competition... the one and only one in the 21st minute against Queen's Park at Hampden. And scorer of the ONLY Cup goal to be netted at the National Stadium in that season since refurbishment work began right after the tie.

Brian Thomson bagged the first hat-trick of the competition in the 4-2 win for Huntly over Stranraer and before the Bells had been toasted there had been 13 ties played in December.

Unlucky for some, including Stranraer, Civil Service Strollers, Spartans, Queen's Park, Peterhead, Albion Rovers, Brechin, Montrose, Inverness Thistle, Stenhousemuir, Alloa, Gala Fairydean and Vale of Leithen who were all out of the Cup before the turn of the year.

The heavy brigade moved into Cup action in the Third Round on January 9 . . . and straight away Aberdeen laid out their intentions with a four-goal salvo against Hamilton Accies at Pittodrie, helped by a hat-trick from Scotland Under-21 captain Scott Booth.

The Edinburgh rivals Hearts and Hibs were just capital . . . both at home on the same day and making Auld Reekie ring to a goal barrage: Hearts beating Huntly 6-0 and Hibs thrashing St. Mirren 5-2. Other big winners were St. Johnstone (6-0 v Forfar) and Killie who obliterated First Division top-table rivals Raith Rovers 5-0, with the help of a treble from Bobby Williamson.

Cup holders Rangers eased their way through the first test of their defence of the trophy with a 2-0 victory over Motherwell at Fir Park with both goals coming from . . . yes, you guessed it, Ally McCoist.

But the Third Round also provided stutters and shocks.

Celtic faltered in a goalless meeting with Clyde, before putting that right thanks to Tommy Coyne's only goal of the game in the replay.

Two goals from Ken Eadie saw Clydebank through their replay against Premier club Airdrie.

But the shock of the round came . . . where else . . . but Firhill where lowly Cowdenbeath went through thanks to a Nicky Henderson penalty converted just one minute after the interval.

As you would anticipate, goals were more scarce and draws more prevalent when the Fourth Round ties were fought out in February. Three of the eight ties needed replays, and no side could manage victory by more than a two goal margin.

And it was two goals from Falkirk which supplied the stunner of the day . . Falkirk's 2-0 success over a struggling Celtic side. Neil Duffy just before the break and then Eddie May late in the game did the damage, leaving Celts to look over the wreckage of a dismal season.

The inevitable McCoist was on the mark again for Rangers as they eased aside Ayr in another 2-0 away victory.

Cowdenbeath, conquerors of Firhill, performed nobly again . . . holding Hibs to a goalless draw at Central Park and only going down to a sole strike from Pat McGinlay in the replay at Easter Road.

Eoin Jess was a two-goal hero for Aberdeen in their 2-0 win over Dundee United . . . but when the Quarter-Finals came around in March, the competition dealt a severe blow to the Scotland Under-21 star. The tie against Clydebank was only four minutes old when he had to be carted off with a broken ankle. Insult was added to injury when Bankies scored a late equaliser with a ferocious 25 yard free kick.

Jess-less Dons then turned to another of their young lions, Scott Booth, for salvation and he duly obliged with a double in the 4-3 replay victory.

Hearts and Hibs, again occupying Edinburgh on the same afternoon, produced identical 2-0 results against Falkirk and St. Johnstone respectively. And once again Rangers cruised through an away tie . . . 3-0 winners over Arbroath. Before you ask, yes, McCoist scored again!

With the National Stadium at Hampden still under refurbishment, the Semi-Finals were taken to Tynecastle and Celtic Park on March 16.

And on the day when there were amazing scenes in the shambolic Grand National at Aintree when the tapes failed . . . amazingly Ally McCoist didn't! He netted his 52nd goal of the season in the 73rd minute against Hearts to ease his side through 2-1. Allan Preston had given the Edinburgh side the lead in 58 minutes with a stunning header, which was cancelled out by a Dave McPherson equaliser 10 minutes later.

Meanwhile over at Hearts' home ground at Tynecastle, young Scott Booth stayed hot on the Cup goal trail to notch his sixth of the competition and take Dons through 1-0 against Hibs to set up the forecasted Rangers-Aberdeen Final.

Which EVENTUALLY came about. Families were reared and sent to school in the time between the semis and the Final. O.K,. there was only an eight week gap, but for the fans it seemed a lifetime.

The Great Day was May 29, not far from Midsummers Day it seemed. And it was at Celtic Park, with Rangers playing in their 42nd Final and Dons appearing for the 14th time.

In the end, there was no stopping Rangers from retaining the trophy and completing a domestic grand slam . . . even though by this time there was no contribution from Ally McCoist, out of action nursing a broken leg received while playing for Scotland in Portugal.

Goals from Neil Murray . . . with the help of a wicked deflection off Brian Irvine . . . and a superb Mark Hateley strike set up the victory, although Englishman Lee Richardson set up a pulsating finish with a cracking 25 yarder 13 minutes from time.

So that was it. Six months after it all began the Scottish Cup was back where it started in 92-93. At Ibrox.

DIXON BLACKSTOCK
(Sunday Mail)

Action from the Aberdeen-Hibs Semi-Final involving Alex McLeish and Pat McGinlay (above) and Roy Aitken and Murdo MacLeod (inset).

FIRST ROUND

5th December, 1992

Huntly 4, Stranraer 2

Huntly: Gardiner, Walker K, McGinlay, Murphy, Rougvie, Selbie, Stewart, Copeland, (De Barros), Thomson, Whyte, (Walker C), Dunsire
Scorers:Thomson(3), Copeland
Stranraer: Ross, McIntyre, (Diver), Hughes, Duncan, Brannigan, McCann, Grant, Sloan, Fraser, McLean, Cody, (Spittal)
Scorers: Duncan, Cody

Inverness Thistle 3, Civil Service Strollers 1

Inverness Thistle: Calder, MacDonald S, Stevenson, Wilson, Milroy, Murphy, MacDonald A, MacDonald T, Polworth, Bell, MacLean
Scorers: T MacDonald (2), Bell
Civil Service Strollers: Mackintosh, Leslie, McKinlay, (Davies), Wood, Chambers, Burns, Scott, Temple, (McPhee), Keenan, McGhee, Givven
Scorer: Givven

Queen of the South 3, Spartans 0

Queen of the South: Hoy, Dickson, Sim, McKeown, Rowe, McFarlane, Sermanni, Fraser, Thomson, McGuire J, Henderson
Scorers: Rowe (2), Henderson
Spartans: Houston F, Finlay, Lynch, Carrick, Lennox, McKeating, Smith, (McDaide), Thomson, Govan, Houston T, (Galbraith), McKinnon

Queen's Park 0, Clyde 1

Queen's Park: Chalmers, Sneddon, Stevenson, Elder, Mackay, Orr G, Jackson, Graham, (Kerr), Rodden, Caven, Crooks, (Devlin)
Clyde: Howie, McFarlane, Tennant, McAulay, (Thomson J), Knox, Mitchell, (Quinn), Thompson D, McCheyne, McGarvey, McCarron, Strain
Scorer: McCarron

8th December 1992

Cove Rangers 2 Peterhead 0

Cove Rangers: MacLean, Forbes, Whyte, Morland, Paterson, Cormack, Yule, Baxter, Stephen, Murphy, Megginson
Scorer: Stephen (2)
Peterhead: Tait, Watson, King, (Brown), Madden, McCarron, Gerrard, Campbell, (Fraser), Emslie, McGachie, Wilson, Mackintosh

Forfar Athletic 5, Albion Rovers 0

Forfar Athletic: Thomson, Mearns, McPhee, Morris, Mann, Byrne, McKenna, McIntyre, Petrie, (Smith), Hamill, (Cameron), Heddle
Scorers: Mearns, McKenna, Petrie, Cadden (o.g.), Heddle
Albion Rovers: McConnachie, Millar, Gallagher, McKeown, Kelly, (Archer), Gaughan, McBride, (McCoy), Cadden, Moore, Ferguson, Hendry

SECOND ROUND

19th December, 1992

Clyde 3, Brechin City 1

Clyde: Howie, McFarlane, Tennant, McAulay, Knox, Thomson J, Dickson, Mitchell, (Morrison), McGarvey, McCarron, Strain, (Quinn)
Scorers: Thomson, McCarron, Dickson
Brechin City: Allan, McLaren, Cairney, Brown, Paterson, Lorimer, Lees, Scott, Ross, Miller, Brand, (Fisher)
Scorer: Lees

Cove Rangers 2 Montrose 0

Cove Rangers: MacLean, Forbes, Whyte, Morland, Paterson, Cormack, (Park), Yule, Baxter, Stephen, (Lavelle), Murphy, Megginson
Scorers: Stephen, Cormack
Montrose: Moffat, Morrison, Robertson, Craib M, Fraser, Fleming, Maver, (Craib S), Irvine, Grant, Logan, (Allan), Yeats

East Fife 1, Alloa 1

East Fife: Charles, Bell, Beaton, Allan, (Skelligan), Burgess, Taylor, Brown, Hope, Scott, Sludden, McBride
Scorer: Hope
Alloa: Butter, Newbigging, (Russell), Bennett, Wilcox, McCulloch, Campbell, Gibson, McNiven, McCormick, (Smith), Moffat, McAvoy
Scorer: Moffat

Gala Fairydean 1, Arbroath 1

Gala Fairydean: Cairns, Henry, Main, Jones, Frizzel, Neil Collins, (Potts), Whitehead, Norman Collins, Lothian, Kerr, (Hunter), D'Acrosa
Scorer: Lothian
Arbroath: Harkness, Tindal, Martin, Mitchell, Boyd, Farnan, Will, Hamilton, McNaughton, Tosh, (Macdonald), Sorbie
Scorer: McNaughton

Vale of Leithen 2, East Stirlingshire 2

Vale of Leithen: McDermott, Finlayson, Ross, Shearer, McNaughton, Nisbet, (Rathie), Thorpe, Mitchell, Hogarth, Gray, (Brown), Selkirk

Scorers: Hogarth, Ross
East Stirlingshire: Watson, Ross, Friar, Houston, Woods, Thomson, McKinnon, Kemp, Barclay, Walker, Geraghty
Scorers: McKinnon, Walker

26th December, 1992

Inverness Thistle 0, Berwick Rangers 1

Inverness Thistle: Calder, Wilson, (Murphy), Stevenson, Sweeney, Milroy, Masson, (Bremner), MacDonald A, MacDonald T, Polworth, Bell, MacLean
Berwick Rangers: Massie, Hendrie, Valentine, Davidson, Anderson, Richardson, Irvine, Hall, Scott, Cunningham, Graham
Scorer: Anderson

28th December, 1992

Stenhousemuir 2, Forfar Athletic 3

Stenhousemuir: Barnstaple, Aitken, Hallford, Armstrong, Godfrey, Fisher, Logan, Clouston, (McLafferty), Mathieson, Lytwyn, Haddow
Scorers: Lytwyn, Hallford (pen)
Forfar Athletic: Thomson, Mearns, McPhee, Morris, Mann, Winter, Bingham, McIntyre, (McCafferty), McKenna, (Smith), Hamill, Heddle
Scorers: McIntyre, Heddle (2)

4th January, 1993

Huntly 2, Queen of the South 1

Huntly: Gardiner, Walker K, Grant, Murphy, Rougvie, Selbie, Walker C, (De Barros), Copeland, Thomson, Whyte, (Paterson), Dunsire
Scorers: Copeland, Rougvie
Queen of the South: Hoy, Dickson, Sim, Rowe, McGhie, Fraser, (Templeton), Sermanni, McFarlane, McGuire J, (Gordon), Henderson, Robertson
Scorer: Henderson

SECOND ROUND REPLAYS

28th December, 1992

Alloa 1, East Fife 1

(A.E.T.) East Fife won 6-5 on Kicks from the Penalty Mark

Alloa: Butter, Russell, (Newbigging), Bennett, Wilcox, McCulloch, Campbell, Gibson, McNiven, McCormick, (Tait), Moffat, McAvoy
Scorer: McAvoy
East Fife: Charles, Bell, Allan, (Andrew), Beaton, Burgess, Taylor, Hope, Burns, Brown, Sludden, McBride, (Elliott)
Scorer: Brown

Arbroath 2, Gala Fairydean 0

Arbroath: Harkness, Tindal, Martin, Mitchell, Boyd, Farnan, Will, Hamilton, McNaughton, (Tosh), Macdonald, Sorbie
Scorers: Macdonald, Tindal

Neil Murray scores for Rangers first goal in the Final with Aberdeen at Celtic Park.

Gala Fairydean: Cairns, Henry, Loughran, Jones, Frizzel, Hunter, Kerr, (Notman), Neil Collins, Whitehead, (Main), Norman Collins, Lothian

East Stirlingshire 3, Vale of Leithen 2
(A.E.T.)

East Stirlingshire: Watson, Ross, Kemp, Barclay, Woods, Thomson, (Friar), McKinnon, Houston, Roberts, Walker, (Tierney), Geraghty
Scorers: Roberts (2), Geraghty
Vale of Leithen: McDermott, Finlayson, Ross, Shearer, (Brown), McNaughton, Nisbet, Thorpe, Rathie, (McCulloch), Hogarth, Gray, Selkirk
Scorers: Hogarth, Selkirk

THIRD ROUND

9th January, 1993

Aberdeen 4, Hamilton Academical 1

Aberdeen: Snelders, Wright, Winnie, (Smith), Grant, Irvine, McLeish, Richardson, Bett, (Mason), Jess, Booth, Paatelainen
Scorers: Booth (3), Irvine
Hamilton Academical: Ferguson, Hillcoat, Miller, Millen, Weir, Napier, (Cramb), Ward, Reid, Harris, Clark, McDonald
Scorer: Reid

Airdrieonians 0, Clydebank 0

Airdrieonians: Martin, Kidd, Stewart, Sandison, Caesar, Black, Boyle, Balfour (Kirkwood), Watson, (Smith), Coyle, Jack
Clydebank: Woods, Murdoch, Hay, Barron, Sweeney, Jack, Harvey, Henry, Eadie, Flannigan C,Wilson, (McIntosh)

Arbroath 3, Morton 0

Arbroath: Harkness, Tindal, Martin, Mitchell, Boyd, Farnan, Will, Florence, Adam, Macdonald, Sorbie
Scorer: Sorbie (3)
Morton: Wylie, Collins, Pickering, Rafferty, McCahill, Johnstone, Mathie, Tolmie, (McDonald), Alexander, (Fowler), McInnes, Gahagan

Clyde 0, Celtic 0

Clyde: Howie, McFarlane, Tennant, McAulay, Knox, Thomson J, Dickson, (Quinn), Morrison, (McCheyne), McGarvey, McCarron, Strain
Celtic: Bonner, Grant, Boyd, Wdowczyk, (Coyne), McNally, Galloway, O'Neil, (Miller), McStay, Creaney, Slater, Collins

Cove Rangers 2, East Stirlingshire 2

Cove Rangers: MacLean, Park, Whyte, Morland, Paterson, Cormack, (McLennan), Yule, Baxter, Stephen, (Lavelle), Murphy, Megginson
Scorers: Megginson, Lavelle
East Stirlingshire: Watson, Woods, Ross, Barclay, Yates, Kemp, (Friar), McKinnon, Houston, Geraghty, Walker, Thomson
Scorers: Thomson, Barclay

Dundee United 3, Meadowbank Thistle 1

Dundee United: Main, Perry, Malpas, McInally, Van Der Hoorn, Welsh, McLaren, (Cleland), McKinlay, Crabbe, (Connolly), Ferguson, O'Neil J
Scorers: McKinlay, Welsh, Ferguson
Meadowbank Thistle: Ellison, Murray, Elder, (Roseburgh), Williamson, Rae, Banks, Little, Wilson, Rutherford, McLeod, Bailey, (Coyle)
Scorer: Rutherford

Dunfermline Athletic 1, Ayr United 2

Dunfermline Athletic: Hamilton, Shannon, Cunnington, (Grant), McCathie, Moyes, Williamson, French, Leitch, (McWilliams), Robertson, Davies, Chalmers
Scorer: Chalmers
Ayr United: Duncan, Burley, Robertson S, Shotton, Howard, George, Robertson G, (Kennedy), Walker, Graham, (McTurk), Traynor, Mair
Scorers: Mair (pen), Walker

Heart of Midlothian 6, Huntly 0

Heart of Midlothian: Walker, McLaren, Snodin, Levein, Mackay, Van De Ven, Robertson, Ferguson D, (Boothroyd), Baird, Mauchlen, Preston, (Foster)
Scorers: Baird, Ferguson D, Snodin, Robertson, Boothroyd (2)
Huntly: Gardiner, Walker K, (Grant), McGinlay, Murphy, Rougvie, Selbie, Stewart, Copeland, Thomson, Whyte, (Walker C), De Barros

Hibernian 5, St. Mirren 2

Hibernian: Reid, Orr, Mitchell, Hunter, McIntyre, MacLeod, Weir, (Fellenger), Hamilton, Wright, Jackson, (Evans), McGinlay
Scorers: Jackson, McGinlay, Weir (2), Wright
St. Mirren: Fridge, Manley, (Elliot), Broddle, McWhirter, Baillie, Fullarton, Gallagher, Lambert, McIntyre, Hewitt, Farrell, (Lavety)
Scorers: Lavety, Gallagher

Kilmarnock 5, Raith Rovers 0

Kilmarnock: Geddes, Wilson, McSkimming, Montgomerie, Skilling, Burns T, (Crainie), Porteous, MacPherson, McCluskey, Stark, Williamson, (Campbell)
Scorers: Williamson (3), McCluskey, MacPherson
Raith Rovers: Carson, (Crawford), McStay, MacLeod, Coyle, (Raeside), Sinclair, McGeachie, Mackenzie, Dalziel, Hetherston, Brewster, Thomson

Motherwell 0, Rangers 2

Motherwell: Dykstra, Nijholt, McKinnon, (Angus), Martin, Philliben, McCart, Kirk, (Ferguson), Simpson, Arnott, Kromheer, Cooper
Rangers: Goram, Nisbet, Robertson D, Gordon, McPherson, Brown, Steven, McCall, McCoist, Hateley, Mikhailitchenko
Scorer: McCoist (2)

Partick Thistle 0, Cowdenbeath 1

Partick Thistle: Nelson, Law, McVicar, (English), McLaughlin, Jamieson, Kinnaird, Shaw, Johnston, (Cameron), Britton, Irons, Magee
Cowdenbeath: Lamont W, Watt, Robertson, McGovern, Douglas, Herd, Henderson, Petrie, Callaghan, Maratea, Condie, (Wright)
Scorer: Henderson (pen)

St. Johnstone 6, Forfar Athletic 0

St. Johnstone: Rhodes, McGowne, Deas, McClelland, (Maskrey), Inglis, Baltacha, (McGinnis), Davies, Cherry, Wright, Arkins, Curran
Scorers: Wright (2), Cherry, Arkins (2), Maskrey
Forfar Athletic: Thomson, Mearns, McPhee, Morris, (McIntyre), Mann, Winter, Bingham, McKenna, (Smith), Petrie, Hamill, Heddle

Stirling Albion 1, East Fife 2

Stirling Albion: McGeown, McCormack, Watson, Tait, Lawrie, Mitchell, Reilly, McInnes, McKenna, (McCallum), Callaghan, (Docherty A), Armstrong
Scorer: McInnes
East Fife: Charles, Bell, Spence, Skelligan, Burgess, (Andrew), Taylor, Burns, Hope, Brown, Sludden, (Scott), Allan
Scorer: Skelligan (2)

10th January, 1993

Dundee 2, Dumbarton 0

Dundee: Mathers, McQuillan, Pittman, Wieghorst, Duffy, (McGowan), Dow, Bain, Vrto, Stainrod, Dodds, Campbell D, (Den Bieman)
Scorers: Wieghorst, Dodds (pen)

Dumbarton: MacFarlane, Marsland, Boyd, (McConville), Melvin, Martin, Gow, McQuade, Boag, (Meechan), Mooney, Nelson, McAnenay

27th January, 1993

Falkirk 5, Berwick Rangers 2

Falkirk: Parks, Wishart, McQueen, Duffy, Weir, May, (Rice), McAllister, Drinkell, (Lennox), Cadette, McCall, Sloan
Scorers: Sloan (2), McCall, May, Cadette
Berwick Rangers: Massie, Hendrie, (Hutchinson), Valentine, Davidson, Anderson, Richardson, Irvine, Hall, Scott, (Waldie), Cunningham, Graham
Scorers: Richardson, Hall

THIRD ROUND REPLAYS

19th January, 1993

Clydebank 2, Airdrieonians 0

Clydebank: Woods, Barron, Hay, Murdoch, Sweeney, Jack, Harvey, Henry, Eadie, Flannigan C, Wilson
Scorer: Eadie (2)
Airdrieonians: Martin, Boyle, Jack, Sandison, Honor, (Watson), Reid, Kirkwood, Balfour, Smith, Coyle, Lawrence, (Conn)

20th January, 1993

Celtic 1, Clyde 0

Celtic: Bonner, McNally, Boyd, Slater, Galloway, Gillespie, Miller, (Grant), McStay, Payton, (Creaney), Coyne, Collins
Scorer: Coyne
Clyde: Howie, McFarlane, Tennant, McAulay, Knox, Thomson J, Quinn, (McCheyne), Morrison, McGarvey, (Dickson), McCarron, Strain

25th January, 1993

East Stirlingshire 2, Cove Rangers 1

East Stirlingshire: Watson, O'Sullivan, Kemp, Ross, Barclay, Yates, Friar, McKinnon, Houston, Walker, (Tierney), Geraghty
Scorers: McKinnon, Morland (o.g.)
Cove Rangers: MacLean, Baxter, Whyte, Morland, Paterson, Cormack, Megginson, Yule, Stephen, (McLennan), Murphy, Lavelle
Scorer: Stephen (pen)

FOURTH ROUND

6th February, 1993

Arbroath 0, East Fife 0

Arbroath: Harkness, Tindal, (Tosh), Martin, Martin, Mitchell, Boyd, Farnan, Hamilton, Florence, Will, Macdonald, (Buckley), Sorbie
East Fife: Charles, Bell, Allan, (Elliott), Skelligan, Burgess, Taylor, Burns, Hope, Andrew, (Scott), Sludden, Beaton

Ayr United 0, Rangers 2

Ayr United: Duncan, Burley, Robertson, Shotton, Traynor, (Howard), George, Kennedy, McGivern, Graham, Russell, Mair
Rangers: Goram, Stevens, Robertson D, Gordon, Nisbet, Brown, Steven, McCall, McCoist, Hateley, Mikhailitchenko, (Huistra)
Scorers: McCoist, Gordon

Cowdenbeath 0, Hibernian 0

Cowdenbeath: Lamont, Watt, Robertson, McGovern, Archibald E, Douglas, Henderson, Petrie, (Herd), Callaghan, Scott, Condie, (Wright)
Hibernian: Reid, Orr, Mitchell, Hunter, McIntyre, MacLeod, (Miller), Weir, Hamilton, Wright, Jackson, McGinlay

Falkirk 2, Celtic 0

Falkirk: Parks, Wishart, Johnston, Duffy, Weir, Hughes, McAllister, (Sloan), Drinkell, Cadette, McCall, May
Scorers: Duffy, May
Celtic: Bonner, McNally, Boyd, Vata, (Grant), Wdowczyk, Galloway, Slater, McStay, McAvennie, (Payton), Coyne, Collins

Heart of Midlothian 2, Dundee 0

Heart of Midlothian: Walker, McLaren, McKinlay, Levein, Mackay, Van De Ven, Robertson, Ferguson D, Baird, Bannon, Mauchlen, Ferguson I, (Boothroyd)
Scorers: Baird, Robertson
Dundee: Mathers, McQuillan, Pittman, (Kiwomya), Dinnie, (Den Bieman), Duffy, McGowan, Bain, Vrto, Paterson, Dodds, West

Kilmarnock 0, St. Johnstone 0

Kilmarnock: Geddes, Wilson, McSkimming, Montgomerie, Skilling, Burns T, Porteous, (Campbell), MacPherson, Crainie, (Mitchell), Stark, Williamson
St. Johnstone: Rhodes, McGowne, Deas, Cherry, Inglis, McClelland, Davies, Curran, Wright, Arkins, Moore, (Maskrey)

7th February, 1993

Aberdeen 2, Dundee United 0

Aberdeen: Snelders, Wright, Smith, Grant, Irvine, McLeish, Richardson, Mason, (Booth), Jess, Shearer, (Aitken), Paatelainen
Scorer: Jess (2)
Dundee United: Main, Clark, Malpas, Bowman, Perry, Narey, McKinlay, Johnson, (Connolly), Dailly, Crabbe, Bollan

East Stirlingshire 1, Clydebank 2

East Stirlingshire: Watson, Woods, (McMillan), Kemp, Ross, Yates, Barclay, Friar, McKinnon, Houston, Roberts, Geraghty, (Tierney)
Scorer: Geraghty
Clydebank: Woods, Maher, Crawford, Murdoch, Sweeney, Hay, Harvey, Jack, Eadie, Flannigan C, Wilson, (Lansdowne)
Scorers: Eadie, Flannigan C

FOURTH ROUND REPLAYS

10th February, 1993

Hibernian 1, Cowdenbeath 0

Hibernian: Reid, Orr, Mitchell, Hunter, McIntyre, MacLeod, Weir, Hamilton, Wright, Evans, McGinlay

Scorer: McGinlay
Cowdenbeath: Lamont W, Watt, (Petrie),
Robertson, McGovern, Archibald E, Douglas,
Henderson, (Condie), Herd, Callaghan, Scott,
Wright

St. Johnstone 1, Kilmarnock 0 (A.E.T.)

St. Johnstone: Rhodes, McGowne, Deas,
Cherry, (McGinnis), Inglis, McClelland, Davies,
Curran, Wright, Arkins, Moore, (Maskrey)
Scorer: Davies
Kilmarnock: Geddes, Wilson, McSkimming,
Montgomerie, Skilling, Burns T, Porteous,
MacPherson, McCluskey, (Mitchell), Stark,
Williamson

16th February, 1993

East Fife 1, Arbroath 4

East Fife: Charles, Bell, (Elliott), Spence, Burns,
Burgess, Taylor, Hope, Beaton, Scott,
(Andrew), Sludden, McBride
Scorer: Sludden
Arbroath: Harkness, Tindall, Martin, Mitchell,
Boyd, Farnan, Hamilton, (Will), Florence,
Macdonald, (McNaughton), Tosh, Sorbie
Scorers: Tosh(2), Martin (2)

QUARTER-FINALS

5th March, 1993

Aberdeen 1, Clydebank 1

Aberdeen: Snelders, Wright, Smith, Grant,
Irvine, McLeish, Richardson, Aitken, Jess,
(Booth), Shearer, (Ten Caat), Paatelainen
Scorer: Shearer (pen)

Clydebank: Woods, Maher, Hay, (Crawford),
Murdoch, Sweeney, McIntosh, Harvey, Henry,
(Lansdowne), Eadie, Flannigan C, Jack
Scorer: McIntosh

Arbroath 0, Rangers 3

Arbroath: Harkness, Tindal, (Will), Martin,
Mitchell, Boyd, Farnan, Hamilton, Florence,
Macdonald, (Buckley), Adam, Sorbie
Rangers: Maxwell, Nisbet, Robertson D,
Murray, McPherson, Brown, Mikhailitchenko,
(Durrant), McCall, McCoist, Hateley, Huistra,
(McSwegan)
Scorers: Hateley, Murray, McCoist (pen)

Heart of Midlothian 2, Falkirk 0

Heart of Midlothian: Walker, McLaren,
McKinlay, Berry, Mackay, Wright, Robertson,
(Thomas), Ferguson D, Baird, Mauchlen,
(Bannon), Preston
Scorers: Preston, Robertson (pen)
Falkirk: Westwater, Oliver, McQueen, Duffy,
Weir, Rice, McAllister, Lennox, Drinkell, May,
Sloan, (Taggart)

Hibernian 2, St. Johnstone 0

Hibernian: Burridge, Orr, Mitchell, Hunter,
Tweed, MacLeod, Lennon, Hamilton, Wright,
Jackson, (Evans), McGinlay
Scorers: Tweed, Wright
St. Johnstone: Rhodes, McGowne, (Moore),
Sweeney, (McGinnis), Deas, Redford,
McClelland, Davies, Inglis, Wright, Arkins,
Turner

*Below: Aberdeen's
Theo Snelders
makes a fine save
in the Final*

QUARTER-FINAL REPLAY

16th March, 1993

Clydebank 3, Aberdeen 4

Clydebank: Woods, Maher, Hay, Murdoch,
Sweeney, McIntosh, Harvey, Henry, Eadie,
Flannigan C, Jack
Scorers: Eadie, Maher, Henry
Aberdeen: Snelders, Wright, McKimmie, Grant,
Irvine, McLeish, Kane, Aitken, Booth, Ten Caat,
Paatelainen
Scorers: Irvine, Paatelainen, Booth (2)

SEMI-FINALS

3rd April, 1993

Tynecastle Park, Edinburgh

Hibernian 0, Aberdeen 1

Hibernian: Burridge, Miller, Mitchell, Hunter,
Tweed, MacLeod, (Evans), Lennon, Hamilton,
(Orr), Wright, Jackson, McGinlay
Aberdeen: Snelders, McKimmie, Smith, Aitken,
(Ten Caat), Irvine, McLeish, Richardson,
Mason, Booth, (Shearer), Kane, Paatelainen
Scorer: Booth

Celtic Park, Glasgow

Rangers 2, Heart of Midlothian 1

Rangers: Goram, McCall, Robertson D, Gough,
McPherson, Brown, Steven, Ferguson,
McCoist, Hateley, Hagen, (Durrant)
Scorers: McPherson, McCoist
Heart of Midlothian: Walker, McLaren,
McKinlay, Levein, Mackay, Van De Ven,
Robertson, Ferguson D, (Snodin), Baird, Millar,
Preston, (Ferguson I)
Scorer: Preston

FINAL

29th May, 1993
Celtic Park, Glasgow

Rangers 2, Aberdeen 1

Rangers: Goram, McCall, Robertson D, Gough, McPherson, Brown,
Murray, Ferguson, Durrant, Hateley, Huistra; (Pressley)
Sub not used: McSwegan
Scorers: Murray, Hateley
Aberdeen: Snelders, McKimmie, Wright, (Smith), Grant, Irvine,
McLeish, Richardson, Mason, Booth, Shearer, (Jess), Paatelainen
Scorer: Richardson
Referee: J. McCluskey (Stewarton)
Attendance: 50,715

SEASON 1919/20

17th April, 1920 at Hampden Park;
Attendance 95,000;
Referee: Mr W Bell (Hamilton)

KILMARNOCK 3   ALBION ROVERS 2
Culley, Shortt,   Watson, Hillhouse
Smith J

KILMARNOCK: T Blair, T Hamilton, D Gibson,
J Bagan, M Shortt, R Neave, J McNaught,
M Smith, J R Smith, W Culley, M McPhail.
ALBION ROVERS: J Short, R Penman, J Bell,
J Wilson, J Black, A Ford, W Ribchester, James
White, John White, G Watson, W Hillhouse.

SEASON 1920/21

16th April, 1921 at Celtic Park;
Attendance 28,294;
Referee: Mr H Humphreys (Greenock)

PARTICK THISTLE 1   RANGERS 0
Blair

PARTICK THISTLE: K Campbell, T Crichton,
W Bulloch, J Harris, M Wilson, W Borthwick,
J Blair, J Kinloch, D B Johnstone, J McMenemy,
W Salisbury.
RANGERS: W Robb, R Manderson,
W McCandless, D D Meiklejohn, A Dixon,
J Bowie, A Archibald, A Cunningham,
G D Henderson, T Cairns, A L Morton.

SEASON 1921/22

15th April, 1922 at Hampden Park;
Attendance 75,000;
Referee: Mr T Dougray (Bellshill)

MORTON 1   RANGERS 0
Gourlay

MORTON: M Edwàrds, J McIntyre, R Brown,
J Gourlay, J S Wright, R McGregor, A McNab,
R McKay, J Buchanan, A Brown, J H McMinn.
RANGERS: W Robb, R Manderson,
W McCandless, D D Meiklejohn, A Dixon,
T Muirhead, A Archibald, A Cunningham,
G D Henderson, T Cairns, A L Morton.

SEASON1922/23

31st March, 1923 at Hampden Park;
Attendance 80,100;
Referee: Mr T Dougray (Bellshill)

CELTIC 1   HIBERNIAN 0
Cassidy

CELTIC: C Shaw, A McNair, W McStay,
J McStay, W Cringan, J MacFarlane, A McAtee,
P Gallacher, J Cassidy, A McLean, P Connolly.
HIBERNIAN: W Harper, W McGinnigle,
W Dornan, P Kerr, W Miller, H Shaw, H Ritchie,
J Dunn, J McColl, J Halligan, J Walker.

SEASON1923/24

19th April, 1924 at Ibrox Stadium;
Attendance 59,218;
Referee: Mr T Dougray (Bellshill)

AIRDRIEONIANS 2 HIBERNIAN 0
Russell 2

AIRDRIEONIANS: J Ewart, A Dick, G McQueen,
T Preston, J McDougall, R Bennie, J Reid,
W Russell, H Gallacher, R L McPhail,
J Somerville.
HIBERNIAN: W Harper W McGinnigle,
W Dornan, P Kerr, W Miller, H Shaw, H Ritchie,
J Dunn, J McColl, J Halligan, J Walker.

SEASON 1924/25

11th April, 1925 at Hampden Park;
Attendance 75,137;
Referee: Mr T Dougray (Bellshill)

CELTIC 2   DUNDEE 1
Gallacher, McGrory   McLean

CELTIC: P Shevlin, W. McStay, H Hilley,
P Wilson, J McStay, J Macfarlane, P Connolly,
P Gallacher, J McGrory, A Thomson, A McLean.
DUNDEE: J Britton, J F Brown, J R Thomson,
J B Ross, W Rankin, S Irving, C S Duncan,
D McLean, D Halliday, J Rankin, J Gilmour.

SEASON 1925/26

10th April, 1926 at Hampden Park;
Attendance 98,620;
Referee: Mr P Craigmyle (Aberdeen)

ST MIRREN 2   CELTIC 0
McCrae, Howieson

ST MIRREN: J Bradford, A Findlay,
W Newbiggin, T Morrison, W Summers,
J McDonald, M Morgan, A Gebbie, D McCrae,
J Howieson, J Thomson.
CELTIC: P Shevlin, W McStay, H Hilley,
P Wilson, J McStay, J Macfarlane, P Connolly,
A Thomson, J McGrory, T B McInally, W Leitch.

SEASON 1926/27

16th April, 1927 at Hampden Park;
Attendance 79,500;
Referee: Mr T Dougray (Bellshill)

CELTIC 3   EAST FIFE 1
Robertson (o.g.),   Wood
McLean, Connolly

CELTIC: J Thomson, W McStay, H Hilley,
P Wilson, J McStay, J Macfarlane, P Connolly,
A Thomson, T B McInally, J McMenemy,
A McLean.
EAST FIFE: R Gilfillan, S Robertson, W Gillespie,
J Hope, J Brown, R Russell, P Weir, G Paterson,
J Wood, P Barrett, D Edgar.

SEASON 1927/28

14th April, 1928 at Hampden Park;
Attendance 118,115;
Referee: Mr W Bell (Motherwell)

RANGERS 4   CELTIC 0
Meiklejohn (pen),
McPhail, Archibald (2)

RANGERS: T Hamilton, D Gray, R Hamilton,
J Buchanan, D D Meiklejohn, T Craig,
A Archibald, A Cunningham, J Fleming,
R L McPhail, A L Morton.
CELTIC: J Thomson, W McStay, J Donoghue,
P Wilson, J McStay, J Macfarlane, P Connolly,
A Thomson, J McGrory, T B McInally,
A McLean.

SEASON 1928/29

6th April, 1929 at Hampden Park;
Attendance 114,708;
Referee: Mr T Dougray (Bellshill)

KILMARNOCK 2   RANGERS 0
Aitken, Williamson

KILMARNOCK: S T Clemie, T G Robertson,
J Nibloe, H A Morton, H McLaren, J McEwan,
W Connell, M Smith, H Cunningham,
J Williamson, J Aitken.
RANGERS: T Hamilton, D Gray, R Hamilton,
J Buchanan, D D Meiklejohn, T Craig,
A Archibald, T Muirhead, J Fleming,
R L McPhail, A L Morton.

SEASON 1929/30

12th April, 1930 at Hampden Park;
Attendance 107,475;
Referee: Mr W Bell (Motherwell)

RANGERS 0   PARTICK THISTLE 0

RANGERS: T Hamilton, D Gray, R Hamilton,
J Buchanan, D D Meiklejohn, T Craig,
A Archibald, J Marshall, J Fleming, R L McPhail,
W Nicholson.
PARTICK THISTLE: J Jackson, S Calderwood,
J Rae, A C Elliot, A Lambie, E McLeod, D Ness,
R Grove, G Boardman, J Ballantyne, J M Torbet.

Replay

16th April,1930 at Hampden Park;
Attendance 90,000;
Referee: Mr W Bell (Motherwell)

RANGERS 2   PARTICK THISTLE 1
Marshall, Craig   Torbet

RANGERS: T Hamilton, D Gray, R Hamilton,
R L McDonald, D D Meiklejohn, T Craig,
A Archibald, J Marshall, J Fleming, R L McPhail,
A L Morton.
PARTICK THISTLE: J Jackson, S Calderwood,
J Rae, A C Elliot, A Lambie, E McLeod, D Ness,
R Grove, G Boardman, J Ballantyne, J M Torbet.

SEASON 1930/31

11th April, 1931 at Hampden Park;
Attendance 104,803;
Referee: Mr P Craigmyle (Aberdeen)

CELTIC 2   MOTHERWELL 2
McGrory, Craig (o.g.) Stevenson, McMenemy

CELTIC: J Thomson, W Cooke, W McGonigle,
P Wilson, J McStay, C Geatons, R Thomson,
A Thomson, J McGrory, P Scarffe, C E Napier.
MOTHERWELL: A McClory, J Johnman,
A Hunter, H Wales, A Craig, W Telfer,
J Murdoch, J McMenemy, W McFadyen,
G Stevenson, R Ferrier.

Replay

15th April, 1931 at Hampden Park;
Attendance 98,579;
Referee: Mr P Craigmyle (Aberdeen)

CELTIC 4   MOTHERWELL 2
Thomson R. (2)   Murdoch, Stevenson
McGrory (2)

CELTIC: J Thomson, W Cooke, W McGonigle,
P Wilson, J McStay, C Geatons, R Thomson,
A Thomson, J McGrory, P Scarffe, C E Napier.
MOTHERWELL: A McClory, J Johnman,
A Hunter, H Wales, A Craig, W Telfer,
J Murdoch, J McMenemy, W McFadyen,
G Stevenson, R Ferrier.

SEASON 1931/32

16th April, 1932 at Hampden Park;
Attendance 111,982;
Referee: Mr P Craigmyle (Aberdeen)

RANGERS 1   KILMARNOCK 1
McPhail   Maxwell

RANGERS: T Hamilton, D Gray, R MacAulay,
D D Meiklejohn, J Simpson, G C P Brown,
A Archibald, J Marshall, S English, R L McPhail,
A L Morton.
KILMARNOCK: W Bell, J Leslie, J Nibloe,
H A Morton, T Smith, J McEwan, W Connell,
S Muir, J Maxwell, J Duncan, J Aitken.

Replay

20th April, 1932 at Hampden Park;
Attendance 110,695;
Referee: Mr P Craigmyle (Aberdeen)

RANGERS 3   KILMARNOCK 0
Fleming, McPhail, English

RANGERS: T Hamilton, D Gray, R MacAulay,
D D Meiklejohn, J Simpson, G C P Brown,
A Archibald, J Marshall, S English, R L McPhail,
Fleming.
KILMARNOCK: W Bell, J Leslie, J Nibloe,
H A Morton, T Smith, J McEwan, W Connell,
S Muir, J Maxwell, J Duncan, J Aitken.

SEASON 1932/33

15th April, 1933 at Hampden Park;
Attendance 102,339;
Referee: Mr T Dougray (Bellshill)

CELTIC 1   MOTHERWELL 0
McGrory

CELTIC: J Kennaway, R Hogg, W McGonigle,
P Wilson, J McStay, C Geatons, R Thomson,
A Thomson, J McGrory, C E Napier,
H O'Donnell.
MOTHERWELL: A McClory, J Crapnell, B Ellis,
H Wales, J Blair, T Mackenzie, J Murdoch,
J McMenemy, W McFadyen, G Stevenson,
R Ferrier.

SEASON 1933/34

21st April, 1934 at Hampden Park;
Attendance 113,430;
Referee: Mr M C Hutton (Glasgow)

RANGERS 5   ST MIRREN 0
Nicholson (2), McPhail,
Main, Smith

RANGERS: T Hamilton, D Gray, R McDonald,
D D Meiklejohn, J Simpson, G C P Brown,
R Main, J Marshall, J Smith, R L McPhail,
W G Nicholson.
ST MIRREN: J McCloy, W Hay, R F D Ancell,
A A Gebbie, T F Wilson, J Miller, J P Knox,
J Latimer, J G McGregor, J McCabe, J Phillips.

SEASON 1934/35

20th April, 1935 at Hampden Park;
Attendance 87,286;
Referee: Mr H Watson (Glasgow)

RANGERS 2   HAMILTON ACADEMICAL 1
Smith (2)   Harrison

RANGERS: J Dawson, D Gray, R McDonald,
J Kennedy, J Simpson, G C P Brown, R Main,
A Venters, J Smith, R L McPhail, T Gillick.
HAMILTON ACADEMICAL: J Morgan,
R Wallace, J Bulloch, J Cox, J McStay, J Murray,
J King, W McLaren, D Wilson, R G Harrison,
R Reid.

SEASON 1935/36

18th April, 1936 at Hampden Park;
Attendance 88,859;
Referee: Mr J M Martin (Ladybank)

RANGERS 1   THIRD LANARK 0
McPhail

RANGERS: J Dawson, D Gray, W A Cheyne,
D D Meiklejohn, J Simpson, G C P Brown,
J Fiddes, A Venters, J Smith, R L McPhail,
J Turnbull.
THIRD LANARK: R Muir, J Carabine, R Hamilton,
J Blair, J Denmark, J S McInnes, R Howe,
P Gallacher, G Hay, R Kennedy, A Kinnaird.

SEASON 1936/37

24th April, 1937 at Hampden Park;
Attendance 147,365;
Referee: Mr M C Hutton (Glasgow)

CELTIC 2   ABERDEEN 1
Crum, Buchan   Armstrong

CELTIC: J Kennaway, R Hogg, J Morrison,
C Geatons, W Lyon, G Paterson, J Delaney,
W Buchan, J McGrory, J Crum, F Murphy.
ABERDEEN: G Johnstone, W Cooper, R Temple,
F Dunlop, E Falloon, G Thomson, J Benyon,
J McKenzie, M Armstrong, W Mills, W Lang.

SEASON 1937/38

23rd April, 1938 at Hampden Park;
Attendance 80,091;
Referee: Mr H Watson (Glasgow)

EAST FIFE 1   KILMARNOCK 1
McLeod   McAvoy

EAST FIFE: J D Milton, W Laird, R Tait,
D Russell, J Sneddon, A C Herd, T Adams,
E McLeod, R McCartney, D Miller, D McKerrell.
KILMARNOCK: J Hunter, A Fyfe, F Milloy,
G Robertson, J Stewart, S Y Ross, B Thomson,
G Reid, A Collins, D H McAvoy, F McGrogan.

Replay

27th April, 1938 at Hampden Park;
Attendance 92,716;
Referee: Mr H Watson (Glasgow)

EAST FIFE 4   KILMARNOCK 2
McKerrell 2,   Thomson (pen),
McLeod, Miller   McGrogan
After extra-time.

EAST FIFE: J D Milton, W Laird, R Tait,
D Russell, J Sneddon, J Harvey, T Adams,
E McLeod, R McCartney, D Miller, D McKerrell.
KILMARNOCK: J Hunter, A Fyfe, F Milloy,
G Robertson, J Stewart, S Y Ross, B Thomson,
G Reid, A Collins, D H McAvoy, F McGrogan.

SEASON 1938/39

22nd April, 1939 at Hampden Park;
Attendance 94,770;
Referee: Mr W Webb (Glasgow)

CLYDE 4   MOTHERWELL 0
Wallace, Martin (2),
Noble

CLYDE: J Brown, J Kirk, J Hickie, H Beaton,
E Falloon, E Weir, T Robertson, D H Wallace,
W Martin, D S Noble, J C Gillies.
MOTHERWELL: A Murray, H Wales, B Ellis,
T Mackenzie, J Blair, W Telfer, J Ogilvie,
T H Bremner, D Mathie, G Stevenson,
J McCulloch

SEASON 1946/47

19th April, 1947 at Hampden Park;
Attendance 82,140;
Referee: Mr R Calder (Glasgow)

ABERDEEN 2   HIBERNIAN 1
Hamilton, Williams   Cuthbertson

ABERDEEN: G Johnstone, P McKenna, G Taylor,
J McLaughlin, F Dunlop, W Waddell, J R Harris,
G Hamilton, A Williams, A M Baird, W McCall.
HIBERNIAN: J Kerr, J Govan, D Shaw, H Howie,
P Aird, S Kean, G Smith, W G Finnigan,
J G Cuthbertson, E Turnbull, W Ormond.

SEASON 1947/48

17th April, 1948 at Hampden Park;
Attendance 129,176;
Referee: Mr J M Martin (Blairgowrie)

RANGERS 1 MORTON 1 (After Extra Time)
Gillick   Whyte

RANGERS: R Brown, G Young, J Shaw,
J McColl, W Woodburn, S Cox, E Rutherford,
T Gillick, W Thornton, W Findlay, J Duncanson.
MORTON: J Cowan, G Mitchell, J E Whigham,
W Campbell, A Miller, J Whyte, J Hepburn,
E Murphy, D Cupples, T Orr, C M Liddell.

Replay

21st April, 1948 at Hampden Park;
Attendance 131,975;
Referee: Mr J M Martin (Blairgowrie)

RANGERS 1 MORTON 0 (After Extra Time)
Williamson

RANGERS: R Brown, G Young, J Shaw,
J McColl, W Woodburn, S Cox, E Rutherford,
W Thornton, W M Williamson, J Duncanson,
T Gillick.
MORTON: J Cowan, G Mitchell, J E Whigham,
W Campbell, A Miller, J Whyte, J Hepburn,
E Murphy, D Cupples, T Orr, C M Liddell.

SEASON 1948/49

23rd April, 1949 at Hampden Park;
Attendance 108,435;
Referee: Mr R G Benzie (Irvine)

RANGERS 4   CLYDE 1
Young 2 (2 pens),   Galletly
Williamson, Duncanson

RANGERS: R Brown, G Young, J Shaw,
J McColl, W Woodburn, S Cox, W Waddell,
J Duncanson, W Thornton, W M Williamson,
E Rutherford.
CLYDE: S Gullan, A Gibson, F Mennie,
J Campbell, R Milligan, H Long, R Davies,
A Wright, A Linwood, P Galletly, C Bootland.

SEASON 1949/50

22nd April, 1950 at Hampden Park;
Attendance 118,262;
Referee: Mr J A Mowat (Burnside)

RANGERS 3   EAST FIFE 0
Findlay, Thornton 2

RANGERS: R Brown, G Young, J Shaw,
J McColl, W Woodburn, S Cox, E Rutherford,
W Findlay, W Thornton, J Duncanson, W Rae.
EAST FIFE: J G Easson, W Laird, I M Stewart,
J M Philip, W G Finlay, G G Aitken, R Black,
C Fleming, H M Morris, A D Brown,
D M Duncan.

SEASON 1950/51

21st April, 1951 at Hampden Park;
Attendance 131,943;
Referee: Mr J A Mowat (Burnside)

CELTIC 1   MOTHERWELL 0
McPhail

CELTIC: G Hunter, J Fallon, A Rollo, R Evans,
A Boden, J Baillie, J Weir, R Collins, J McPhail,
R Peacock, C Tully.
MOTHERWELL: J Johnston, W Kilmarnock,
A Shaw, D MacLeod, A Paton, W Redpath,
W W Humphries, J Forrest, A Kelly, J Watson,
J Aitkenhead.

SEASON 1951/52

19th April, 1952 at Hampden Park;
Attendance 136,304;
Referee: Mr J A Mowat (Burnside)

MOTHERWELL 4   DUNDEE 0
Watson, Redpath,
Humphries, Kelly

MOTHERWELL: J Johnston, W Kilmarnock,
A Shaw, C Cox, A Paton, W Redpath, T Sloan,
W W Humphries, A Kelly, J Watson,
J Aitkenhead.
DUNDEE:R Henderson, G Follon, J L Cowan,
T Gallacher, D Cowie, A Boyd, J R Hill,
J T Patillo, R Flavell, W Steel, G Christie.

SEASON 1952/53

25th April, 1953 at Hampden Park;
Attendance 129,861;
Referee: Mr J A Mowat (Burnside)

RANGERS 1   ABERDEEN 1
Prentice   Yorston

RANGERS: G Niven, G Young, R J Little,
J M McColl, D Stanners, J Pryde, W Waddell,
D Grierson, W Paton, J W Prentice,
J G Hubbard.
ABERDEEN: F Martin, J Mitchell, D Shaw,
J R Harris, A Young, J Allister, J Rodger,
H Yorston, P Buckley, G Hamilton, J Hather.

Replay

29th April, 1953 at Hampden Park;
Attendance 112,619;
Referee: Mr J A Mowat (Burnside)

RANGERS 1   ABERDEEN 0
Simpson

RANGERS: G Niven, G Young, R J Little,
J M McColl, W Woodburn, J Pryde,
W Waddell, D Grierson, W Simpson, W Paton,
J G Hubbard.
ABERDEEN: F Martin, J Mitchell, D Shaw,
J R Harris, A Young, J Allister, J Rodger,
H Yorston, P Buckley, G Hamilton, J Hather.

SEASON 1953/54

24th April, 1954 at Hampden Park;
Attendance 129,926;
Referee: Mr C E Faultless (Giffnock)

CELTIC 2   ABERDEEN 1
Young (o.g.), Fallon   Buckley

CELTIC: J Bonnar, M A Haughney, F Meechan,
R Evans, J Stein, R Peacock, J Higgins, W Fernie,
J Fallon, C Tully, N Mochan.

ABERDEEN: F Martin, J Mitchell, D L Caldwell,
J Allister, A Young, A Glen, G Leggat,
G Hamilton, P Buckley, J R Clunie, J Hather.

SEASON 1954/55

23rd April, 1955 at Hampden Park;
Attendance 106,111;
Referee: Mr C E Faultless (Giffnock)

CLYDE 1   CELTIC 1
Robertson   Walsh

CLYDE: K Hewkins, A Murphy, H Haddock,
R Granville, T Anderson, D Laing, T Divers,
A Robertson, A Hill, G Brown, T Ring.
CELTIC: J Bonnar, M A Haughney, F Meechan,
R Evans, J Stein, R Peacock, R Collins, W Fernie,
J McPhail, J Walsh, C Tully.

Replay

27th April, 1955 at Hampden Park;
Attendance 68,735;
Referee: Mr C E Faultless (Giffnock)

CLYDE 1   CELTIC 0
Ring

CLYDE: K Hewkins, A Murphy, H Haddock,
R Granville, T Anderson, D Laing, T Divers,
A Robertson, A Hill, G Brown, T Ring.
CELTIC: J Bonnar, M A Haughney, F Meechan,
R Evans, J Stein, R Peacock, J Walsh, W Fernie,
J Fallon, J McPhail, C Tully.

SEASON 1955/56

21st April, 1956 at Hampden Park;
Attendance 133,399;
Referee: Mr R H Davidson (Airdrie)

HEART OF MIDLOTHIAN 3 CELTIC 1
Crawford 2, Conn   Haughney

HEART OF MIDLOTHIAN: W Duff, R Kirk,
T F Mackenzie, F MacKay, F Glidden,
J Cumming, A Young, A Conn, W Bauld,
J Wardhaugh, J Crawford.
CELTIC: R Beattie, F Meechan, J Fallon,
J E Smith, R Evans, R Peacock, W Craig,
M A Haughney, N Mochan, W Fernie, C Tully.

SEASON 1956/57

20th April, 1957 at Hampden Park;
Attendance 81,057;
Referee: Mr J A Mowat (Burnside)

FALKIRK 1   KILMARNOCK 1
Prentice (pen)   Curlett

FALKIRK: R Slater, A Parker, I J Rae, A M Wright,
A Irvine, J W Prentice, T Murray, D Grierson,
G Merchant, D Moran, A E O'Hara.
KILMARNOCK: J Brown, R Collins, J Stewart,
R Stewart, W Toner, A Mackay, G Mays,
W Harvey, D Curlett, R Black, D Burns.

Replay

24th April, 1957 at Hampden Park;
Attendance 79,785;
Referee: Mr J A Mowat (Burnside)

FALKIRK 2 KILMARNOCK 1 (After Extra Time)
Merchant,   Curlett
Moran

FALKIRK: R Slater, A Parker, I J Rae, A M Wright,
 Irvine, J W Prentice, T Murray, D Grierson,
G Merchant, D Moran, A E O'Hara.
KILMARNOCK: J Brown, R Collins, J Stewart,
 Stewart, W Toner, A Mackay, G Mays,
W Harvey, D Curlett, R Black, D Burns.

SEASON 1957/58

26th April, 1958 at Hampden Park;
Attendance 95, 123;
Referee: Mr J A Mowat (Burnside)

CLYDE 1   HIBERNIAN 0
Coyle

CLYDE: T McCulloch, A Murphy, H Haddock,
 Walters, W Finlay, M Clinton, G Herd,
 Currie, J Coyle, A Robertson, T Ring.
HIBERNIAN: L Leslie, J Grant, J McClelland,
 Turnbull, J Plenderleith, J Baxter, J Fraser,
 Aitken, J Baker, T Preston, W Ormond.

SEASON 1958/59

25th April, 1959 at Hampden Park;
Attendance 108,951;
Referee: Mr J A Mowat (Burnside)

ST MIRREN 3   ABERDEEN 1
Bryceland, Miller,   Baird
Baker

ST MIRREN: D Walker, D Lapsley, J Wilson,
 Neilson, J McGugan, T Leishman, J Rodger,
 Bryceland, G Baker, T Gemmell, A Miller.
ABERDEEN: F Martin, D Caldwell, J Hogg,
 Brownlie, J Clunie, A Glen, R Ewan,
 Davidson, H Baird, R Wishart, J Hather.

SEASON 1959/60

23rd April, 1960 at Hampden Park;
Attendance 108,017;
Referee: Mr R H Davidson (Airdrie)

RANGERS 2   KILMARNOCK 0
Millar 2

RANGERS: G Niven, E Caldow, J Little,
 M McColl, W Paterson, W Stevenson, A Scott,
 R McMillan, J Millar, S Baird, D Wilson.
KILMARNOCK: J Brown, J Richmond,
 Watson, F Beattie, W Toner, R Kennedy,
 Stewart, J McInally, A Kerr, R Black, W Muir.

SEASON 1960/61

22 April, 1961 at Hampden Park;
Attendance 113,618;
Referee: Mr H Phillips (Wishaw)

DUNFERMLINE ATHLETIC 0 CELTIC 0

DUNFERMLINE: E Connachan, J C Fraser,
 W Cunningham, R Mailer, J Williamson,
 G Miller, G Peebles, D Smith, C Dickson,
 D McLindon, H Melrose.
CELTIC: F Haffey, D McKay, J Kennedy,
 P Crerand, W McNeill, J Clark, C Gallacher,
 W Fernie, J Hughes, S Chalmers, A Byrne.

Replay

26th April, 1961 at Hampden Park;
Attendance 87,866;
Referee: Mr H Phillips (Wishaw)

DUNFERMLINE ATHLETIC 2 CELTIC 0
Thomson, Dickson

DUNFERMLINE: E Connachan, J C Fraser,
 W Cunningham, R Mailer, G Miller,
 G Sweeney, G Peebles, D Smith, D Thomson,
 C Dickson, H Melrose.
CELTIC: F Haffey, D McKay, W O'Neill,
 P Crerand, W McNeill, J Clark, C Gallacher,
 W Fernie, J Hughes, S Chalmers, A Byrne.

SEASON 1961/62

21st April, 1962 at Hampden Park;
Attendance 126,930;
Referee: Mr T Wharton (Clarkston)

RANGERS 2   ST MIRREN 0
Brand, Wilson

RANGERS: W Ritchie, R Shearer, E Caldow,
 H Davis, R McKinnon, J Baxter, W Henderson,
 J R McMillan, J Millar, R Brand, D Wilson.
ST MIRREN: R Williamson, R Campbell,
 J Wilson, R Stewart, J R Clunie, G McLean,
 A W Henderson, T Bryceland, D Kerrigan,
 W Fernie, T Beck.

SEASON 1962/63

4th May, 1963 at Hampden Park;
Attendance 129,527;
Referee: Mr T Wharton (Clarkston)

RANGERS 1   CELTIC 1
Brand   Murdoch

RANGERS: W Ritchie, R Shearer, D Provan,
 J Greig, R McKinnon, J Baxter, W Henderson,
 G McLean, J Millar, R Brand, D Wilson.
CELTIC: F Haffey, D McKay, J Kennedy,
 J McNamee, W McNeill, W Price, J Johnstone,
 R Murdoch, J Hughes, J Divers, J Brogan.

Replay

15th May, 1963 at Hampden Park;
Attendance 120,263;
Referee: Mr T Wharton (Clarkston)

RANGERS 3   CELTIC 0
Brand 2, Wilson

RANGERS: W Ritchie, R Shearer, D Provan,
 J Greig, R McKinnon, J Baxter, W Henderson,
 J R McMillan, J Millar, R Brand, D Wilson.
CELTIC: F Haffey, D McKay, J Kennedy,
 J McNamee, W McNeill, W Price, R Craig,
 R Murdoch, J Divers, S Chalmers, J Hughes.

SEASON 1963/64

25th April, 1964 at Hampden Park;
Attendance 120,982;
Referee Mr H Phillips (Wishaw)

RANGERS 3   DUNDEE 1
Millar 2, Brand   Cameron

RANGERS: W Ritchie, R Shearer, D Provan,
 J Greig, R McKinnon, J Baxter, W Henderson,
 G McLean, J Millar, R Brand, D Wilson.
DUNDEE: R Slater, A Hamilton, R Cox, R Seith,
 G Ryden, A Stuart, A Penman, A Cousin,
 K Cameron, A Gilzean, H Robertson.

SEASON 1964/65

24th April, 1965 at Hampden Park;
Attendance 108,800;
Referee: Mr H Phillips (Wishaw)

CELTIC 3 DUNFERMLINE ATHLETIC 2
Auld 2,   Melrose, McLaughlin
McNeill

CELTIC: J J Fallon, J Young, T Gemmell,
 R Murdoch, W McNeill, J Clark, S Chalmers,
 C Gallacher, J Hughes, R Lennox, R Auld.
DUNFERMLINE: J Herriot, W Callaghan, J Lunn,
 J Thomson, J MacLean, T Callaghan,
 A Edwards, A Smith, J McLaughlin, H Melrose,
 J Sinclair.

SEASON 1965/66

23rd April, 1966 at Hampden Park;
Attendance 126,559;
Referee: Mr T Wharton (Clarkston)

RANGERS 0   CELTIC 0

RANGERS: W Ritchie, K Johansen, D Provan,
 J Greig, R McKinnon, J Millar, D Wilson,
 R Watson, J Forrest, W Johnston, W Henderson.
CELTIC: R Simpson, J Young, T Gemmell,
 R Murdoch, W McNeill, J Clark, J Johnstone,
 J McBride, S Chalmers, C Gallacher, J Hughes.

Replay

27th April, 1966 at Hampden Park;
Attendance 96,862;
Referee: Mr T Wharton (Clarkston)

RANGERS 1   CELTIC 0
Johansen

RANGERS: W Ritchie, K Johansen, D Provan,
 J Greig, R McKinnon, J Millar, W Henderson,
 R Watson, G McLean, W Johnston, D Wilson.
CELTIC: R Simpson, J P Craig, T Gemmell,
 R Murdoch, W McNeill, J Clark, J Johnstone,
 J McBride, S Chalmers, R Auld, J Hughes.

SEASON 1966/67

29th April, 1967 at Hampden Park;
Attendance 127,117;
Referee: Mr W M M Syme (Glasgow)

CELTIC 2   **ABERDEEN 0**
Wallace 2

CELTIC: R Simpson, J P Craig, T Gemmell,
R Murdoch, W McNeill, J Clark, J Johnstone,
W Wallace, S Chalmers, R Auld, R Lennox.
ABERDEEN: R Clark, J B Whyte, A J Shewan,
F Munro, T McMillan, J Peterson, J Wilson,
J Smith, J Storrie, H Melrose, D L Johnston.

SEASON 1967/68

27th April, 1968 at Hampden Park;
Attendance 56,365;
Referee: Mr W Anderson (East Kilbride)

DUNFERMLINE ATHLETIC 3
Gardner 2, Lister (pen)
HEART OF MIDLOTHIAN 1
Lunn (o.g)

DUNFERMLINE: B Martin, W Callaghan, J Lunn,
J McGarty, R Barry, T Callaghan, I Lister,
R Paton, P Gardner, H Robertson, A Edwards.
HEART OF MIDLOTHIAN: J Cruikshank,
J W Sneddon, A F Mann, A Anderson,
E Thomson, G Miller, R Jensen (*R Moller),
J Townsend, D Ford, J Irvine, T Traynor.
* First use of substitute in 1968.

SEASON 1968/69

26th April, 1969 at Hampden Park;
Attendance 132,870;
Referee: Mr J Callaghan (Glasgow)

CELTIC 4   **RANGERS 0**
McNeill, Lennox,
Connelly, Chalmers

CELTIC: J J Fallon, J P Craig, T Gemmell,
R Murdoch, W McNeill, J Brogan, (J Clark),
G Connelly, S Chalmers, W Wallace, R Lennox,
R Auld.
RANGERS: N Martin, K Johansen,
W Mathieson, J Greig, R McKinnon, D Smith,
W Henderson, A Penman, A Ferguson,
W Johnston, O Persson.

SEASON 1969/70

11th April, 1970 at Hampden Park;
Attendance 108,434;
Referee: Mr R H Davidson (Airdrie)

ABERDEEN 3   **CELTIC 1**
Harper (pen),   Lennox
McKay 2

ABERDEEN: R Clark, H Boel, G Murray,
J Hermiston, T McMillan, M Buchan, D McKay,
D Robb, J Forrest, J Harper, A Graham.
CELTIC: E Williams, D Hay, T Gemmell,
R Murdoch, W McNeill, J Brogan, J Johnstone,
W Wallace, G Connelly, R Lennox, J Hughes,
(R Auld).

SEASON 1970/71

8th May, 1971 at Hampden Park;
Attendance 120,092;
Referee: Mr T Wharton (Glasgow)

CELTIC 1   **RANGERS 1**
Lennox   D Johnstone

CELTIC: E Williams, J P Craig, J Brogan,
G Connelly, W McNeill, J Johnstone,
R Lennox, W Wallace, T Callaghan, H Hood.
RANGERS: P McCloy, A Miller, W Mathieson,
J Greig, R McKinnon, C Jackson, W Henderson,
A Penman, (D Johnstone), C Stein,
A MacDonald, W Johnston.

Replay

12th May, 1971 at Hampden Park;
Attendance 103,332;
Referee: Mr T Wharton (Glasgow)

CELTIC 2   **RANGERS 1**
Macari, Hood (pen)   Craig (o.g)

CELTIC: E Williams, J P Craig, J Brogan,
G Connelly, W McNeill, D Hay, J Johnstone,
L Macari, H Hood, (W Wallace), T Callaghan,
R Lennox.
RANGERS: P McCloy, J Denny, W Mathieson,
J Greig, R McKinnon, C Jackson, W Henderson,
A Penman, (D Johnstone), C Stein,
A MacDonald, W Johnston.

SEASON 1971/72

6th May, 1972 at Hampden Park;
Attendance 106,102;
Referee: Mr A MacKenzie (Larbert)

CELTIC 6   **HIBERNIAN 1**
McNeill, Deans 3,   Gordon
Macari 2

CELTIC: E Williams, J P Craig, J Brogan,
R Murdoch, W McNeill, G Connelly,
J Johnstone, J Deans, L Macari, K Dalglish,
T Callaghan.
HIBERNIAN: J Herriot, J Brownlie, E Schaedler,
P Stanton, J Black, J Blackley, A Edwards,
J Hazel, A Gordon, J O'Rourke, A Duncan,
(R Auld).

SEASON 1972/73

5th May, 1973 at Hampden Park;
Attendance 122,714;
Referee: Mr J R P Gordon (Newport-on-Tay)

RANGERS 3   **CELTIC 2**
Parlane, Conn,   Dalglish, Connelly (pen)
Forsyth

RANGERS: P McCloy, W Jardine, W Mathieson,
J Greig, D Johnstone, A MacDonald, T McLean,
T Forsyth, D Parlane, A Conn, Q Young.
CELTIC: A Hunter, D McGrain, J Brogan,
(R Lennox), R Murdoch, W McNeill,
G Connelly, J Johnstone, J Deans, K Dalglish,
D Hay, T Callaghan.

SEASON 1973/74

4th May, 1974 at Hampden Park;
Attendance 75,959;
Referee: Mr W S Black (Glasgow)

CELTIC 3   **DUNDEE UNITED 0**
Hood, Murray, Deans

CELTIC: D Connaghan, D McGrain,
(T Callaghan), J Brogan, S Murray, W McNeill,
P McCluskey, J Johnstone, H Hood, J Deans,
D Hay, K Dalglish.
DUNDEE UNITED: A Davie, P Gardner, F Kopel,
J Copland, D Smith, (T Traynor), W Smith,
G Payne, (A Rolland), A Knox, A Gray,
G Fleming, D Houston.

SEASON 1974/75

3rd May, 1975 at Hampden Park;
Attendance 75,457;
Referee: Mr I M D Foote (Glasgow)

CELTIC 3   **AIRDRIEONIANS 1**
Wilson 2,   McCann
McCluskey (pen)

CELTIC: P Latchford, D McGrain, A Lynch,
S Murray, W McNeill, P McCluskey, H Hood,
R Glavin, K Dalglish, R Lennox, P Wilson.
AIRDRIEONIANS: D McWilliams, P Jonquin,
M Cowan, J Menzies, J Black, D Whiteford,
K McCann, T Walker, W McCulloch, (J March),
J Lapsley, (T Reynolds), W Wilson.

SEASON 1975/76

1st May, 1976 at Hampden Park;
Attendance 85,354;
Referee: Mr R H Davidson (Airdrie)

RANGERS 3 HEART OF MIDLOTHIAN 1
Johnstone 2,   Shaw
MacDonald

RANGERS: P McCloy, A Miller, J Greig,
T Forsyth, C Jackson, A MacDonald, R McKean,
J Hamilton, (W Jardine), M Henderson,
T McLean, D Johnstone.
HEART OF MIDLOTHIAN: J Cruikshank,
J Brown, A Burrell, (K Aird), J Jefferies,
J Gallacher, R Kay, W Gibson, (D Park),
A Busby, G Shaw, R Callachan, R Prentice.

SEASON 1976/77

7th May, 1977 at Hampden Park;
Attendance 54,252;
Referee: Mr R B Valentine (Dundee)

CELTIC 1   **RANGERS 0**
Lynch (pen)

CELTIC: P Latchford, D McGrain, A Lynch,
P Stanton, R MacDonald, R Aitken, K Dalglish,
J Edvaldsson, J Craig, A Conn, P Wilson.
RANGERS: S Kennedy, W Jardine, J Greig,
T Forsyth, C Jackson, K Watson, (C Robertson),
T McLean, J Hamilton, D Parlane,
A MacDonald, D Johnstone.

SEASON 1977/78

6th May, 1978 at Hampden Park;
Attendance 61,563;
Referee: Mr B R McGinlay (Glasgow)

RANGERS 2   ABERDEEN 1
MacDonald,   Ritchie
Johnstone

RANGERS: P McCloy, W Jardine, J Greig,
T Forsyth, C Jackson, A MacDonald, T McLean,
R Russell, D Johnstone, G Smith, D Cooper
(K Watson).
ABERDEEN: R Clark, S Kennedy, S Ritchie,
J McMaster, W Garner, W Miller, D Sullivan,
J Fleming (J Scanlon), J Harper, A Jarvie,
D Davidson.

SEASON 1978/79

12th May, 1979 at Hampden Park;
Attendance 50,610;
Referee: Mr B R McGinlay (Glasgow)

RANGERS 0   HIBERNIAN 0

RANGERS: P McCloy, W Jardine, A Dawson,
D Johnstone, C Jackson, A MacDonald,
(A Miller), T McLean, R Russell, D Parlane,
G Smith, D Cooper.
HIBERNIAN: J McArthur, A Brazil, A Duncan,
D Bremner, G Stewart, J McNamara,
R Hutchinson, (G Rae), A MacLeod,
C Campbell, R Callachan, A Higgins.

Replay

16th May, 1979 at Hampden Park;
Attendance 33,504;
Referee: Mr B R McGinlay (Glasgow)

RANGERS 0 HIBERNIAN 0 (After Extra Time)

RANGERS: P McCloy, W Jardine, A Dawson,
D Johnstone, C Jackson, A MacDonald,
T McLean (A Miller), R Russell, D Parlane,
G Smith, D Cooper.
HIBERNIAN: J McArthur, A Brazil, A Duncan,
D Bremner, G Stewart, J McNamara, G Rae,
A McLeod, C Campbell, R Callachan,
A Higgins, (S Brown).

Second Replay

28th May, 1979 at Hampden Park;
Attendance 30,602;
Referee: Mr I M D Foote (Glasgow)

RANGERS 3 HIBERNIAN 2 (After Extra Time)
Johnstone 2,   Higgins, MacLeod (pen)
Duncan (o.g.)

RANGERS: P McCloy, W Jardine, A Dawson,
D Johnstone, C Jackson, K Watson, (A Miller),
T McLean, (G Smith), R Russell, D Parlane,
A MacDonald, D Cooper.
HIBERNIAN: J McArthur, A Brazil, A Duncan,
D Bremner, G Stewart, J McNamara, G Rae,
A MacLeod, C Campbell, R Callachan,
(S Brown), A Higgins, (R Hutchinson).

SEASON 1979/80

10th May, 1980 at Hampden Park;
Attendance 70,303;
Referee: Mr G B Smith (Edinburgh)

CELTIC 1 RANGERS 0 (After Extra Time)
McCluskey

CELTIC: P Latchford, A Sneddon, D McGrain,
R Aitken, M Conroy, M MacLeod, D Provan,
J Doyle, (R Lennox), G McCluskey, T Burns,
F McGarvey.
RANGERS: P McCloy, W Jardine, A Dawson,
T Forsyth, (A Miller), C Jackson, G Stevens,
D Cooper, R Russell, D Johnstone, G Smith,
J MacDonald, (T McLean).

SEASON 1980/81

9th May, 1981 at Hampden Park;
Attendance 53,000;
Referee: Mr I M D Foote (Glasgow)

RANGERS 0   DUNDEE UNITED 0
(After Extra Time)

RANGERS: J Stewart, W Jardine, A Dawson,
G Stevens, T Forsyth, J Bett, T McLean,
R Russell, C McAdam (D Cooper), I Redford,
W Johnston (J MacDonald).
DUNDEE UNITED: H McAlpine, J Holt, F Kopel,
I Phillip, (D Stark), P Hegarty, D Narey,
E Bannon, R Milne (W Pettigrew), W Kirkwood,
P Sturrock, D Dodds.

Replay

12th May, 1981 at Hampden Park;
Attendance 43,099;
Referee: Mr I M D Foote (Glasgow)

RANGERS 4   DUNDEE UNITED 1
Cooper, Russell,   Dodds
MacDonald 2

RANGERS: J Stewart, W Jardine, A Dawson,
G Stevens, T Forsyth, J Bett, D Cooper,
R Russell, D Johnstone, I Redford, J MacDonald.
DUNDEE UNITED: H McAlpine, J Holt, F Kopel,
I Phillip, (D Stark), P Hegarty, D Narey,
E Bannon, R Milne, W Kirkwood, P Sturrock,
D Dodds.

SEASON 1981/82

22nd May, 1982 at Hampden Park;
Attendance 53,788;
Referee: Mr B R McGinlay (Balfron)

ABERDEEN 4 RANGERS 1 (After Extra Time)
McLeish,   MacDonald
McGhee,
Strachan, Cooper

ABERDEEN: J Leighton, S Kennedy, D Rougvie,
J McMaster, (D Bell), A McLeish, W Miller,
G Strachan, N Cooper, M McGhee,
N Simpson, J Hewitt, (E Black).
RANGERS: J Stewart, W Jardine, (C McAdam),
A Dawson, J McClelland, C Jackson, J Bett,
D Cooper, R Russell, G Dalziel, (T McLean),
A Miller, J MacDonald.

SEASON 1982/83

21st May, 1983 at Hampden Park;
Attendance 62,979;
Referee: Mr D F T Syme (Rutherglen)

ABERDEEN 1 RANGERS 0 (After Extra Time)
Black

ABERDEEN: J Leighton, D Rougvie, (A Watson),
J McMaster, N Cooper, A McLeish, W Miller,
G Strachan, N Simpson, M McGhee, E Black,
P Weir, (J Hewitt).
RANGERS: P McCloy, A Dawson, J McClelland,
D McPherson, C Paterson, J Bett, D Cooper,
(W Davies), D MacKinnon, A Clark, R Russell,
J MacDonald, (G Dalziel).

SEASON 1983/84

19th May, 1984 at Hampden Park;
Attendance 58,900;
Referee: Mr R B Valentine (Dundee)

ABERDEEN 2 CELTIC 1 (After Extra Time)
Black,   McStay P
McGhee

ABERDEEN: J Leighton, S McKimmie,
D Rougvie, (W Stark), N Cooper, A McLeish,
W Miller, G Strachan, N Simpson, M McGhee,
E Black, P Weir, (D Bell).
CELTIC: P Bonner, D McGrain, M Reid,
(J Melrose), R Aitken, W McStay, M MacLeod,
D Provan, P McStay, F McGarvey, T Burns,
B McClair, (G Sinclair).

SEASON 1984/85

18th May, 1985 at Hampden Park;
Attendance 60,346;
Referee: Mr B R McGinlay (Balfron)

CELTIC 2   DUNDEE UNITED 1
Provan, McGarvey   Beedie

CELTIC: P Bonner, W McStay, D McGrain,
R Aitken, T McAdam, M MacLeod, D Provan,
P McStay, (P O'Leary), J Johnston, T Burns,
(B McClair), F McGarvey.
DUNDEE UNITED: H McAlpine, M Malpas,
S Beedie, (J Holt), R Gough, P Hegarty,
D Narey, E Bannon, R Milne, W Kirkwood,
P Sturrock, D Dodds.

SEASON 1985/86

10th May, 1986 at Hampden Park;
Attendance 62,841;
Referee: Mr H Alexander (Irvine)

ABERDEEN 3 HEART OF MIDLOTHIAN 0
Hewitt 2, Stark

ABERDEEN: J Leighton, S McKimmie,
T McQueen, J McMaster, (W Stark), A McLeish,
W Miller, J Hewitt, (J Miller), N Cooper,
F McDougall, J Bett, P Weir.
HEART OF MIDLOTHIAN: H Smith, W Kidd,
B Whittaker, W Jardine, N Berry, C Levein,
J Colquhoun, K Black, A Clark, G Mackay,
J Robertson.

SEASON 1986/87

16th May, 1987 at Hampden Park;
Attendance 51,782;
Referee: Mr K J Hope (Clarkston)

ST MIRREN 1   DUNDEE UNITED 0
Ferguson   (After Extra Time)

ST MIRREN: C Money, T Wilson, D Hamilton,
W Abercromby, D Winnie, N Cooper,
F McGarvey, I Ferguson, K McDowall,
(I Cameron), B Hamilton, P Lambert,
(A Fitzpatrick).
DUNDEE UNITED: W Thomson, J Holt,
M Malpas, J McInally, J Clark, D Narey,
I Ferguson, D Bowman, E Bannon, P Sturrock,
(K Gallacher), I Redford, (P Hegarty).

SEASON 1987/88

14th May, 1988 at Hampden Park;
Attendance 74,000;
Referee: Mr G B Smith (Edinburgh)

CELTIC 2   DUNDEE UNITED 1
McAvennie 2   Gallacher

CELTIC: A McKnight, C Morris, A Rogan,
R Aitken, M McCarthy, D Whyte, (W Stark),
J Miller, P McStay, F McAvennie, A Walker
(M McGhee), T Burns.
DUNDEE UNITED: W Thomson, D Bowman,
M Malpas, J McInally, P Hegarty, D Narey,
E Bannon, K Gallacher, P Paatelainen, (J Clark),
I Ferguson, W McKinlay.

SEASON 1988/89

20th May, 1989 at Hampden Park;
Attendance 72,069;
Referee: Mr R B Valentine (Dundee)

CELTIC 1   RANGERS 0
Miller

CELTIC: P Bonner, C Morris, A Rogan, R Aitken,
M McCarthy, D Whyte, P Grant, P McStay,
J Miller, M McGhee, T Burns.
RANGERS: C Woods, G Stevens, S Munro,
(G Souness), R Gough, M Sterland,
(D Cooper), T Butcher, K Drinkell, I Ferguson,
A McCoist, J Brown, M Walters.

SEASON 1989/90

12th May, 1990 at Hampden Park;
Attendance 60,493;
Referee: Mr G B Smith (Edinburgh)

ABERDEEN 0   CELTIC 0 (After Extra Time)
(Aberdeen won 9-8 on Kicks from the Penalty
Mark)

ABERDEEN: T Snelders, S McKimmie,
D Robertson, B Grant, A McLeish, B Irvine,
C Nicholas, J Bett, P Mason, (G Watson),
R Connor, H Gillhaus.
CELTIC: P Bonner, D Wdowcyzk, A Rogan,
P Grant, P Elliott, D Whyte, W Stark,
(M Galloway), P McStay, D Dziekanowski,
A Walker, (T Coyne), J Miller.

SEASON 1990/91

18th May, 1991 at Hampden Park;
Attendance 57,319;
Referee: Mr D F T Syme (Rutherglen)

MOTHERWELL 4   DUNDEE UNITED 3
Ferguson, O'Donnell,   Bowman, O'Neil,
Angus, Kirk   Jackson
(After Extra Time)

MOTHERWELL: A Maxwell, L Nijholt, T Boyd,
J Griffin, C Paterson, C McCart, D Arnott,
I Angus, I Ferguson, (S Kirk), P O'Donnell,
D Cooper, (C O'Neill).
DUNDEE UNITED: A Main, J Clark, M Malpas,
J McInally, M Krivokapic, D Bowman, F Van der
Hoorn, R McKinnon, (W McKinlay), H French,
D Ferguson, (J O'Neil), D Jackson.

SEASON 1991/92

9th May, 1992 at Hampden Park;
Attendance 44,045;
Referee: Mr D D Hope (Erskine)

RANGERS 2   AIRDRIEONIANS 1
Hateley, McCoist,   Smith

RANGERS: A Goram, G Stevens, D Robertson,
R Gough, N Spackman, J Brown, I Durrant
(D Gordon), S McCall, A McCoist, M Hateley,
A Mikhailitchenko.
AIRDRIEONIANS: J Martin, W Kidd, A Stewart,
C Honor, G Caesar, P Jack, J Boyle,
E Balfour, A Lawrence (A Smith),
O Coyle, D Kirkwood (W Reid).

SEASON 1992/93

29th May, 1993 at Celtic Park;
Attendance 50,715;
Referee: Mr J. McCluskey (Stewarton)

RANGERS 2   ABERDEEN 1
Murray, Hateley,   Richardson

RANGERS: A Goram, S McCall, D Robertson,
R Gough, D McPherson, J Brown, N Murray,
I Ferguson, I Durrant, M Hateley, P Huistra,
(S Pressley).
ABERDEEN: T Snelders, S McKimmie, S Wright,
(G Smith), B Grant, B Irvine, A McLeish,
L Richardson, P Mason, S Booth, D Shearer,
(E Jess), M-M Paatelainen.

Rangers - Tennents Scottish Cup Winners 1993

FIRST ROUND

Tuesday, 29th September, 1992

Berwick Rangers 2, East Stirlingshire 2
(A.E.T.) 1-1 after 90 minutes. Berwick Rangers won 5-4 on Kicks from the Penalty Mark

BERWICK: D Neilson, T Hendrie, J Robertson, G Davidson, A Hall, M Cass, I Hutchinson, (D Kerr), C Valentine, D Scott, C Cunningham, (I Waldie), T Graham
Scorers: G Davidson, C Cunningham
EAST STIRLINGSHIRE: P Imrie, T Woods, B Kemp, B Ross, D Craig, C McKinnon, S Thomson, P Friar, P Houston, D Walker, M Geraghty. Subs not used: P Roberts, C McMillan
Scorer: M Geraghty (2)

Forfar Athletic 2, Morton 5
FORFAR: S Thomson, D Cameron, (J Byrne), A Hamill, R Morris, R Mann, G Winter, G Mearns, I McPhee, (A McAulay), S Petrie, McKenna, I Heddle
Scorers: G Winter, G Mearns
MORTON: D Wylie, D Collins, S McArthur, M Pickering, M Doak, D Johnstone, A Mathie, (D Lilley), A Mahood, R Alexander, D McInnes, McDonald, (J Fowler)
Scorers: A Mathie (3), A Mahood, R Alexander

Stenhousemuir 2, Cowdenbeath 4
STENHOUSEMUIR: K Barnstaple, B Clouston, Hallford, R Barr, J Clarke, (S Prior), N Aitken, Fisher, D Bell, M Mathieson, T Steel, S Dickov, Irvine)
Scorers: D Bell, M Mathieson
COWDENBEATH: W Lamont, D Watt, Robertson, (W Syme), W Herd, E Archibald, H Henderson, J Wright, G Malone, T Condie, Lee, W Callaghan, (G Buckley)
Scorers: G Malone, I Lee, W Callaghan, G Buckley

Queen's Park 2, Montrose 3
(A.E.T.) 2-2 after 90 minutes

QUEEN'S PARK: J Chalmers, S Sneddon, (G Millar), D Graham, G Elder, M Mackay, R Callan, R Caven, D Jackson, S McCormick, Mackenzie, (D Greig), G Crooks
Scorers: D Jackson, S McCormick
MONTROSE: D Larter, S Forsyth, J Fleming, M Craib, J Smith, I Robertson, G Fraser, Yeats, M Kelly, A Logan, N Irvine. Subs not used: M Garden, G Houghton
Scorers: C Fraser (2), M Kelly

Kilmarnock 2, Clyde 1
KILMARNOCK: R Geddes, A MacPherson, M Reilly, R Montgomerie, M Skilling, M Roberts, A Mitchell, I Porteous, Williamson, G McCluskey, (C Campbell), McSkimming. Sub not used: D Reid
Scorers: A Mitchell, G McCluskey
CLYDE: S Howie, R McFarlane, G McCheyne,

G Wylde, (P Ronald), B Strain, J Thomson, D Thompson, J Mitchell, J Dickson, S Clarke, (S Morrison), J McCarron
Scorer: G McCheyne

Dumbarton 0, Hamilton Academical 3
DUMBARTON: I MacFarlane, J Marsland, (J Cowell), A Foster, (A Willock), D McDonald, P Martin, M Melvin, J McQuade, M Nelson, C Gibson, J Meechan, R Docherty
HAMILTON: A Ferguson, C Hillcoat, C Miller, A Millen, J Weir, C Napier, G Clark, W Reid, C Harris, (C Cramb), T Smith, (K Ward), P McDonald
Scorers: G Clark, W Reid, P McDonald

Ayr United 2, St Mirren 1
AYR UNITED: C Duncan, G Burley, G McVie, M Shotton, N Howard, D Kennedy, G Robertson, T Walker, A Graham, J Traynor, G Mair, (A McTurk). Sub not used: P McLean
Scorer: T Walker (2)
ST MIRREN: L Fridge, S Farrell, M Baker, R Manley, (R Dawson), W A Baillie, R Fabiani, K Gillies, P Lambert, (J Charnley), D McGill, J Hewitt, D Elliot
Scorer: J Charnley

Stranraer: 3, Alloa 2
STRANRAER: S Ross, S McIntyre, J Hughes, I Spittal, K Brannigan, G Duncan, (A Gallagher), T Sloan, A Grant, D Diver, S Cody, (S Evans), J Love
Scorers: S McIntyre, T Sloan, D Diver
ALLOA: N Binnie, W Newbigging, N Bennett, D Wilcox, K McCulloch, J McNiven, P Sheerin, J Mackay, (G Russell), B Moffat, S Smith, M Hendry. Sub not used: K Campbell
Scorers: D Wilcox, J McNiven

Tuesday, 6th October, 1992

Arbroath 3, Dunfermline Athletic 0
ARBROATH: M Harkness, B Mitchell, C Martin, K Tindal, P Godfrey, W Boyd, C Farnan, P Tosh, K Macdonald, S Florence, S Sorbie. Subs not used: W Holmes, C Adam
Scorers: P Tosh, K Macdonald, S Sorbie
DUNFERMLINE ATHLETIC: L Hamilton, M Bowes, E Cunnington, N McCathie, C Robertson, (N Kelly), A Williamson, J McNamara, P Chalmers, (D Laing), H French, S Leitch, C Sinclair.

Wednesday, 7th October, 1992

Meadowbank Thistle 1, East Fife 0
(A.E.T.)

MEADOWBANK: S Ellison, A Nicol, A Banks, G Armstrong, G McLeod, S Williamson, S Wilson, S Elder, (S Logan), J Young, I Little, (W McNeill), D Roseburgh
Scorer: S Logan
EAST FIFE: R Charles, P H Taylor, (D Elliott), D Beaton, G Allan, S Burgess, (R Skelligan), W Burns, J McBride, W Brown, R Scott, J Sludden, D Hope

SECOND ROUND

Tuesday, 20th October, 1992

Stranraer 0, Queen of the South 2
STRANRAER: S Ross, J Hughes, J Love, G Duncan, K Brannigan, A Gallagher, T Sloan, A Grant, D Diver, S Evans, P Kelly. Subs not used: T Watson, B Duffy
QUEEN OF THE SOUTH: D Hoy, S Gordon, A McFarlane, G Rowe, J Dickson, B McKeown, P Sermanni, A Bell, A Thomson, (H Templeton), D McGuire, J Robertson. Sub not used: G Fraser
Scorers: G Rowe, H Templeton

Raith Rovers 0, Meadowbank Thistle 0
(A.E.T.) Meadowbank Thistle won 4-3 on Kicks from the Penalty Mark

RAITH: G Arthur, J McStay, I MacLeod, J Nicholl, M Herrick, R Coyle, (D Young), T Williamson, C Cameron, (S Crawford), A MacKenzie, C Brewster, J Dair
MEADOWBANK: J McQueen, A Nicol, M Murray, S Williamson, S Elder, (D Roseburgh), A Banks, I Little, S Wilson, P Rutherford, G McLeod, K Kane, (L Bailey)

Kilmarnock 1, Ayr United 0
KILMARNOCK: R Geddes, A MacPherson, M Reilly, R Montgomerie, C Paterson, T Burns, A Mitchell, M Skilling, R Williamson, G McCluskey, (C Campbell), S McSkimming. Sub not used: R Jack
Scorer: G McCluskey
AYR UNITED: C Duncan, G Burley, G Agnew, M Shotton, N Howard, D George, G Robertson, T Walker, A Graham, J Traynor, A Fraser, (J Carse). Sub not used: G McVie

Cowdenbeath 0, Montrose 4
COWDENBEATH: S O'Hanlon, D Watt, A Robertson, D McGovern, E Archibald, H Douglas, N Henderson, G Malone, P Lamont, (T Condie), I Lee, (W Herd), W Callaghan
MONTROSE: D Larter, S Forsyth, J Fleming, G Forbes, J Smith, M Craib, (M Allan), C Fraser, C Maver, D Grant, A Logan, N Irvine. Sub not used: C Yeats
Scorers: D Grant (2), A Logan, M Allan

Stirling Albion 2, Clydebank 1
STIRLING ALBION: M McGeown, D Shanks, P Watson, T Callaghan, D Lawrie, C Mitchell, I McInnes, (A Docherty), V Moore, W Watters, (I Brown), A McKenna, P Armstrong
Scorers: V Moore, W Watters
CLYDEBANK: S Woods, J Maher, G Hay, (J Crawford), D Barron, S Sweeney, M McIntosh, P Harvey, (A Lansdowne), J Henry, K Eadie, C Flannigan, S Jack
Scorer: C Flannigan

Albion Rovers 0, Hamilton Academical 2

ALBION ROVERS: M Guidi, R Walsh, D McKeown, N Armour, (D Seggie), J McCaffrey, S Cadden, M McBride, M Gaughan, S Kerrigan, M Scott, S Archer. Sub not used: D Kiernan
HAMILTON: A Ferguson, K McKee, C Hillcoat, A Millen, J Weir, C Napier, G Clark, S McEntegart, C Harris, (P McKenzie), T Smith, (K Ward), P McDonald
Scorers: T Smith, P McDonald

Berwick Rangers 1, Arbroath 0

BERWICK: D Neilson, T Hendrie, I Hutchinson, J Robertson, A Hall, M Cass, W Fisher, W Irvine, D Scott, C Cunningham, T Graham. Subs not used: D Kerr, C Valentine
Scorer: D Scott
ARBROATH: M Harkness, B Mitchell, C Martin, K Tindal, P Godfrey, W Holmes, (P Tosh), C Farnan, (W Boyd), J Hamilton, K Macdonald, S Florence, S Sorbie

Brechin City 1, Morton 2

BRECHIN: R Allan, P McLaren, H Cairney, R Brown, A McKillop, R Lorimer, (G Hutt), G Lees, W D Scott, A Ross, M Miller, R Brand, (A Heggie)
Scorer: R Lorimer
MORTON: D Wylie, D Collins, M Pickering, S Rafferty, M Doak, D Johnstone, A Mathie, A Mahood, J Tolmie, (D Lilley), J Fowler, (I McDonald), S McArthur
Scorers: A Mathie, J Tolmie

THIRD ROUND

Tuesday, 27th October, 1992

Stirling Albion 0, Montrose 1

STIRLING ALBION: S Robertson, D Shanks, P Watson, I McInnes, (T Callaghan), D Lawrie, C Mitchell, A McKenna, V Moore, W Watters, S Robertson, P Armstrong. Sub not used: I Brown
MONTROSE: D Larter, S Forsyth, J Fleming, M Craib, G Forbes, J Smith, C Fraser, (C Yeats), C Maver, D Grant, A Logan, (M Allan), N Irvine
Scorer: D Grant

Wednesday, 28th October, 1992

Kilmarnock 1, Morton 2

KILMARNOCK: R Geddes, A MacPherson, M Reilly, R Montgomerie, W Furphy, T Burns, A Mitchell, M Skilling, R Williamson, G McCluskey, S McSkimming, (R Jack). Sub not used: M Roberts
Scorer: T Burns
MORTON: D Wylie, D Collins, M Pickering, S Rafferty, M Doak, D Johnstone, A Mathie, A Mahood, J Tolmie, (J Fowler), D McInnes, D Lilley. Sub not used: I McDonald
Scorers: A Mathie, D Lilley

Hamilton Academical 5, Berwick Rangers 2

HAMILTON: A Ferguson, K McKee, C Hillcoat, A Millen, J Weir, S McEntegart, K Ward, W Reid, (M Waters), C Harris, (T Smith), G Clark, P McDonald
Scorers: J Weir, K Ward, G Clark (2), T Smith
BERWICK: D Neilson, T Hendrie, I Hutchinson, G Davidson, A Hall, M Cass, W Irvine, J Robertson, (C Valentine), D Scott, C Cunningham, (L Malone), T Graham
Scorers: G Davidson, W Irvine

Meadowbank Thistle 3, Queen of the South 2

MEADOWBANK: J McQueen, J Coughlin, M Murray, G McLeod, A Nicol, A Banks, I Little, (M Duthie), S Wilson, P Rutherford, D Roseburgh, K Kane. Sub not used: T Graham
Scorers: S Wilson, D Roseburgh, K Kane
QUEEN OF THE SOUTH: D Hoy, S Gordon, (B Wright), A McFarlane, G Rowe, J Dickson, B McKeown, P Sermanni, (H Templeton), A Bell, A Thomson, D Henderson, D McQuire
Scorers: G Rowe, A Thomson

SEMI-FINALS

Tuesday, 10th November, 1992

Morton 3, Montrose 1

(A.E.T.) 1-1 after 90 minutes

MORTON: D Wylie, D Collins, M Pickering, S Rafferty, M Doak, D Johnstone, A Mathie, A Mahood, D Lilley, (R Alexander), D McInnes, J Tolmie, (I McDonald)
Scorers: A Mathie (2), R Alexander
MONTROSE: D Larter, B Morrison, J Fleming, (G Houghton), S Forsyth, G Forbes, M Craib, C Maver, N Irvine, D Grant, C Yeats, A Logan, (M Kelly)
Scorer: S Forsyth

Hamilton Academical 1, Meadowbank Thistle 1 (A.E.T.)

1-1 after 90 minutes. Hamilton Academical won 2-1 on Kicks from the Penalty Mark

HAMILTON: A Ferguson, C Hillcoat, C Napier, A Millen, J Weir, W Reid, K Ward, G Clark, C Harris, T Smith, P McDonald. Subs not used: P McKenzie, S McEntegart
Scorer: P McDonald
MEADOWBANK: S Ellison, J Coughlin, M Murray, A Nicol, T Graham, (S Elder), A Banks, G McLeod, S Wilson, P Rutherford, D Roseburgh, L Bailey, (I Little)
Scorer: S Wilson

FINAL

Sunday, 13th December, 1992
St Mirren Park, Paisley

Morton 2, Hamilton Academical 3

MORTON: D Wylie, D Collins, M Pickering, S Rafferty, M Doak, D Johnstone, A Mathie, A Mahood, (J Gahagan), R Alexander, D McInnes, J Tolmie. Sub not used: I McDonald
Scorer: R Alexander (2)
HAMILTON: A Ferguson, C Hillcoat, C Miller, A Millen, J Weir, C Napier, M Waters, (P McKenzie), C Harris, C Cramb, (K Ward), G Clark, P McDonald
Scorers: C Hillcoat, G Clark (2)
Referee: J J Timmons (Kilwinning)
Attendance: 7,391

Below: Chris Hillcoat's long-range shot hits the ne[t] for Hamilton's winning goal in the Final with Morto[n]

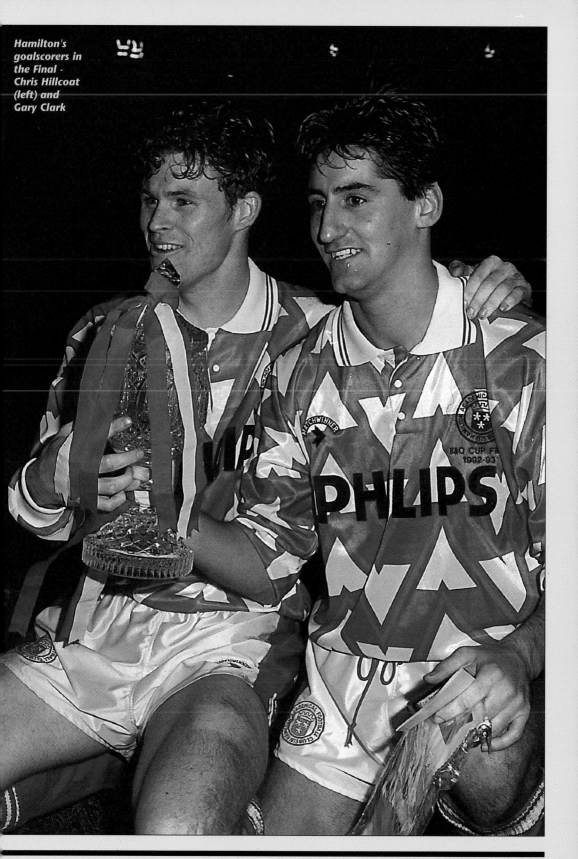

Hamilton's goalscorers in the Final - Chris Hillcoat (left) and Gary Clark

PREMIER DIVISION

■ ABERDEEN
WILLIE MILLER, M.B.E.
Player: Aberdeen and Scotland
Manager: Aberdeen

■ DUNDEE
JAMES DUFFY
Player: Celtic, Morton, Dundee, Partick Thistle, Dundee
Manager: Falkirk, Dundee

■ DUNDEE UNITED
IVAN GOLAC
Player: Partizan Belgrade, Southampton, Bournemouth, Portsmouth, Manchester City and Yugoslavia
Manager: Macva, Partizan Belgrade (both Yugoslavia), Torquay, Macva, Dundee United

■ HEART OF MIDLOTHIAN
SANDY CLARK
Player: Airdrieonians, West Ham United, Rangers, Heart of Midlothian, Partick Thistle, Dunfermline Athletic, Heart of Midlothian
Manager: Partick Thistle, Heart of Midlothian

■ HIBERNIAN
ALEX MILLER
Player: Rangers, Morton
Manager: Morton, St. Mirren, Hibernian

■ KILMARNOCK
TOMMY BURNS
Player: Celtic, Kilmarnock and Scotland
Manager: Kilmarnock

■ MOTHERWELL
TOMMY McLEAN
Player: Kilmarnock, Rangers and Scotland
Manager: Morton, Motherwell

■ PARTICK THISTLE
JOHN LAMBIE
Player: Falkirk, St. Johnstone
Manager: Hamilton Academical, Partick Thistle, Hamilton Academical, Partick Thistle

■ RAITH ROVERS
JIMMY NICHOLL
Player: Manchester United, Toronto Blizzards, Sunderland, West Bromwich Albion, Rangers (Twice), Dunfermline Athletic, Raith Rovers and Northern Ireland
Manager: Raith Rovers

■ RANGERS
WALTER SMITH
Player: Dundee United, Dumbarton, Dundee United
Manager: Rangers

■ ST. JOHNSTONE
JOHN McCLELLAND
Player: Portadown, Cardiff City, Bangor, Mansfield Town, Rangers, Watford, Leeds United, Watford, Notts County, St. Johnstone and Northern Ireland
Manager: St. Johnstone

FIRST DIVISION

■ AIRDRIEONIANS
ALEX MACDONALD
Player: St. Johnstone, Rangers, Heart of Midlothian and Scotland
Manager: Heart of Midlothian, Airdrieonians

■ AYR UNITED
GEORGE BURLEY
Player: Ipswich Town, Sunderland, Gillingham, Motherwell, Ayr United and Scotland
Manager: Ayr United

■ BRECHIN CITY
IAN REDFORD
Player: Dundee, Rangers, Dundee United, Ipswich Town, St. Johnstone, Brechin City
Manager: Brechin City

■ CLYDE
ALEX SMITH
Player: Stirling Albion, East Stirlingshire, Albion Rovers, Stenhousemuir
Manager: Stenhousemuir, Stirling Albion, St. Mirren, Aberdeen, Clyde

■ CLYDEBANK
BRIAN WRIGHT
Player: Hamilton Academical, Motherwell, Clydebank, Partick Thistle, Clydebank, Queen of the South, Clydebank
Coach: Clydebank

■ DUNFERMLINE ATHLETIC
BERT PATON
Player: Leeds United, Dunfermline Athletic
Manager: Cowdenbeath, Raith Rovers, Dunfermline Athletic

■ DUMBARTON
MURDO MACLEOD
Player: Dumbarton, Celtic, Borussia Dortmund (Germany), Hibernian, Dumbarton and Scotland
Manager: Dumbarton

■ FALKIRK
JIM JEFFERIES
Player: Heart of Midlothian, Berwick Rangers
Manager: Berwick Rangers, Falkirk

■ GREENOCK MORTON
ALLAN McGRAW
Player: Greenock Morton, Hibernian
Manager: Greenock Morton

■ HAMILTON ACADEMICAL
IAIN MUNRO
Player: St. Mirren, Hibernian, Rangers, St. Mirren, Stoke City, Sunderland, Dundee United, Hibernian and Scotland

Manager: Dunfermline Athletic,
Dundee, Hamilton Academical

■ ST. MIRREN
JIMMY BONE
Player: Partick Thistle, Norwich City,
Sheffield United, Celtic,
Arbroath, St. Mirren, Hong Kong
Rangers, Heart of Midlothian,
Arbroath and Scotland
Manager: Arbroath, Airdrieonians,
Power Dynamos (Zambia), St. Mirren

■ STIRLING ALBION
JOHN BROGAN
Player: Albion Rovers, St. Johnstone,
Hibernian, Hamilton Academical,
Stirling Albion
Manager: Stirling Albion

SECOND DIVISION

■ ALBION ROVERS
TOMMY GEMMELL
Player: Celtic, Nottingham Forest,
Dundee and Scotland
Manager: Dundee, Albion Rovers
(Twice)

■ ALLOA
BILLY LAMONT
Player: Albion Rovers, Hamilton
Academical
Manager: East Stirlingshire, Falkirk,
Partick Thistle, Falkirk, Dumbarton,
Alloa

■ ARBROATH
DANNY McGRAIN
Player: Celtic, Hamilton Academical
and Scotland
Manager: Arbroath

■ BERWICK RANGERS
JIMMY CREASE
Player: Berwick Rangers
Manager: Berwick Rangers

■ COWDENBEATH

■ EAST FIFE
ALEX TOTTEN
Player: Liverpool, Dundee,
Dunfermline Athletic, Falkirk, Queen
of the South, Alloa

Manager: Alloa, Falkirk, Dumbarton,
St. Johnstone, East Fife

■ EAST STIRLINGSHIRE
BILLY LITTLE
Player: Aberdeen, Falkirk, Stirling
Albion, East Stirlingshire
Manager: Falkirk, Queen of the
South, East Stirlingshire (Twice)

■ FORFAR ATHLETIC
TOM CAMPBELL
Player: Did not Play at Senior Level
Manager: Forfar Athletic

■ MEADOWBANK THISTLE
DONALD PARK
Player: Heart of Midlothian, Partick
Thistle, Heart of Midlothian,
Brechin City, Meadowbank Thistle
Manager: Meadowbank Thistle

■ MONTROSE
JOHN HOLT
Player: Dundee United, Dunfermline
Athletic, Dundee, Forfar Athletic
Manager: Montrose

■ QUEEN OF THE SOUTH
BILLY McLAREN
Player: Queen of the South (Twice),
Morton (Twice), East Fife,
Cowdenbeath, Dunfermline Athletic,
Hibernian, Partick Thistle
Manager: Queen of the South,
Hamilton Academical, Albion Rovers,
Queen of the South

■ QUEEN'S PARK
EDDIE HUNTER
Player: Queen's Park
Coach: Queen's Park

■ STENHOUSEMUIR
TERRY CHRISTIE
Player: Dundee, Raith Rovers, Stirling
Albion
Manager: Meadowbank Thistle,
Stenhousemuir

■ STRANRAER
ALEX McANESPIE
Player: Ayr United
Manager: Stranraer

INFORMATION COMPILED BY
JIM JEFFREY

OFFICIAL LIST OF
CLASS 1 REFEREES
1993/94

T. Brown (Edinburgh)
K.W. Clark (Paisley)
M.A. Clark (Edinburgh)
G.T. Clyde (Bearsden)
W.N.M. Crombie (Edinburgh)
H. Dallas (Bonkle)
S. Dougal (Burnside)
G.M. Dunbar (East Kilbride)
G.A. Evans (Bishopbriggs)
A. Freeland (Aberdeen)
J.A. Herald (Newton Mearns)
D.D. Hope (Erskine)
A.N. Huett (Edinburgh)
W. Innes (Glasgow)
J. Kelly (East Kilbride)
J. McCluskey (Stewarton)
T.M. McCurry (Glasgow)
J.F. McGilvray (Edinburgh)
D. T. McVicar (Carluke)
E. Martindale (Glasgow)
W.R. Morrison (Carluke)
L.W. Mottram (Forth)
J.C. O'Hare (Glenboig)
R. Orr (Kilbarchan)
M.F. Pocock (Aberdeen)
J. Rowbotham (Kirkcaldy)
A.M. Roy (Aberdeen)
G.H. Simpson (Peterhead)
J.D.K. Smith (Troon)
D.F.T. Syme (Rutherglen)
R. Tait (East Kilbride)
I. Taylor (Edinburgh)
L.B. Thow (Ayr)
J.J. Timmons (Kilwinning)
G.A. Tran (Kirkcaldy)
A.W. Waddell (Edinburgh)
H.F. Williamson (Renfrew)
W.S.G. Young (Clarkston)

SCOTTISH PROFESSIONAL FOOTBALLERS' ASSOCIATION

1977/78
Premier Division · **Derek Johnstone** Rangers
First Division · **Billy Pirie** Dundee
Second Division · **Dave Smith** Berwick Rangers
Young Player of the Year · **Graeme Payne** Dundee United

1978/79
Premier Division · **Paul Hegarty** Dundee United
First Division · **Brian McLaughlin** Ayr United
Second Division · **Michael Leonard** Dunfermline Athletic
Young Player of the Year · **Raymond Stewart** Dundee United

1979/80
Premier Division · **Davie Provan** Celtic
First Division · **Sandy Clark** Airdrieonians
Second Division · **Paul Leetion** Falkirk
Young Player of the Year · **John MacDonald** Rangers

1980/81
Premier Division · **Mark McGhee** Aberdeen
First Division · **Eric Sinclair** Dundee
Second Division · **Jimmy Robertson** Queen of the South
Young Player of the Year · **Charlie Nicholas** Celtic

1981/82
Premier Division · **Sandy Clark** Airdrieonians
First Division · **Brian McLaughlin** Motherwell
Second Division · **Pat Nevin** Clyde
Young Player of the Year · **Frank McAvennie** St Mirren

1982/83
Premier Division · **Charlie Nicholas** Celtic
First Division · **Gerry McCabe** Clydebank
Second Division · **John Colquhoun** Stirling Albion
Young Player of the Year · **Paul McStay** Celtic

1983/84
Premier Division · **Willie Miller** Aberdeen
First Division · **Gerry McCabe** Clydebank
Second Division · **Jim Liddle** Forfar Athletic
Young Player of the Year · **John Robertson** Heart of Midlothian

1984/85
Premier Division · **Jim Duffy** Morton
First Division · **Gerry McCabe** Clydebank
Second Division · **Bernie Slaven** Albion Rovers
Young Player of the Year · **Craig Levein** Heart of Midlothian

1985/86
Premier Division · **Richard Gough** Dundee United
First Division · **John Brogan** Hamilton Academical
Second Division · **Mark Smith** Queen's Park
Young Player of the Year · **Craig Levein** Heart of Midlothian

1986/87
Premier Division · **Brian McClair** Celtic
First Division · **Jim Holmes** Morton
Second Division · **John Sludden** Ayr United
Young Player of the Year · **Robert Fleck** Rangers

1987/88
Premier Division · **Paul McStay** Celtic
First Division · **Alex Taylor** Hamilton Academical
Second Division · **Henry Templeton** Ayr United
Young Player of the Year · **John Collins** Hibernian

1988/89
Premier Division · **Theo Snelders** Aberdeen
First Division · **Ross Jack** Dunfermline Athletic
Second Division · **Paul Hunter** East Fife
Young Player of the Year · **Billy McKinlay** Dundee United

1989/90
Premier Division · **Jim Bett** Aberdeen
First Division · **Ken Eadie** Clydebank
Second Division · **Willie Watters** Kilmarnock
Young Player of the Year · **Scott Crabbe** Heart of Midlothian

1990/91
Premier Division · **Paul Elliott** Celtic
First Division · **Simon Stainrod** Falkirk
Second Division · **Kevin Todd** Berwick Rangers
Young Player of the Year · **Eoin Jess** Aberdeen

1991/92
Premier Division · **Ally McCoist** Rangers
First Division · **Gordon Dalziel** Raith Rovers
Second Division · **Andy Thomson** Queen of the South
Young Player of the Year · **Phil O'Donnell** Motherwell

1992/93
Premier Division · **Andy Goram** Rangers
First Division · **Gordon Dalziel** Raith Rovers
Second Division · **Sandy Ross** Brechin City
Young Player of the Year · **Eoin Jess** Aberdeen

THE SCOTTISH FOOTBALL WRITERS' ASSOCIATION

1965 **Billy McNeill** Celtic
1966 **John Greig** Rangers
1967 **Ronnie Simpson** Celtic
1968 **Gordon Wallace** Raith Rovers
1969 **Bobby Murdoch** Celtic
1970 **Pat Stanton** Hibernian
1971 **Martin Buchan** Aberdeen
1972 **Dave Smith** Rangers
1973 **George Connelly** Celtic
1974 **World Cup Squad**
1975 **Sandy Jardine** Rangers
1976 **John Greig** Rangers
1977 **Danny McGrain** Celtic
1978 **Derek Johnstone** Rangers
1979 **Andy Ritchie** Morton
1980 **Gordon Strachan** Aberdeen
1981 **Alan Rough** Partick Thistle
1982 **Paul Sturrock** Dundee United
1983 **Charlie Nicholas** Celtic
1984 **Willie Miller** Aberdeen
1985 **Hamish McAlpine** Dundee United
1986 **Sandy Jardine** Heart of Midlothian
1987 **Brian McClair** Celtic
1988 **Paul McStay** Celtic
1989 **Richard Gough** Rangers
1990 **Alex McLeish** Aberdeen
1991 **Maurice Malpas** Dundee United
1992 **Ally McCoist** Rangers
1993 **Andy Goram** Rangers

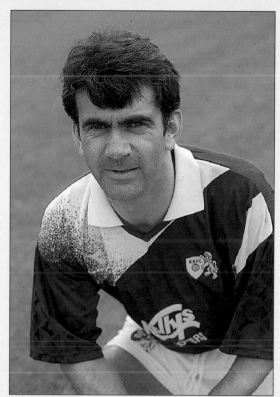

Premier Division Player of the Year **ANDY GORAM**

First Division Player of the Year **GORDON DALZIEL**

Second Division Player of the Year **SANDY ROSS**

Young Player of the Year **EOIN JESS**

AUGUST 1993

Sun 1	
Mon 2	
Tue 3	LEAGUE CUP 1ST ROUND
Wed 4	LEAGUE CUP 1ST ROUND
Thu 5	
Fri 6	
Sat 7	
Sun 8	
Mon 9	
Tue 10	LEAGUE CUP 2ND ROUND
Wed 11	LEAGUE CUP 2ND ROUND
Thu 12	
Fri 13	
Sat 14	
Sun 15	
Mon 16	
Tue 17	
Wed 18	
Thu 19	
Fri 20	
Sat 21	
Sun 22	
Mon 23	
Tue 24	LEAGUE CUP 3RD ROUND
Wed 25	LEAGUE CUP 3RD ROUND
Thu 26	
Fri 27	
Sat 28	
Sun 29	
Mon 30	
Tue 31	LEAGUE CUP 4TH ROUND

SEPTEMBER 1993

Wed 1	LEAGUE CUP 4TH ROUND
Thu 2	
Fri 3	
Sat 4	
Sun 5	
Mon 6	
Tue 7	SCOTLAND v SWITZERLAND (UEFA U21)
Wed 8	**SCOTLAND v SWITZERLAND (WCQ)**
Thu 9	
Fri 10	
Sat 11	
Sun 12	
Mon 13	
Tue 14	
Wed 15	EC/ECWC/UEFA CUP 1ST RND 1ST LEG
Thu 16	
Fri 17	
Sat 18	
Sun 19	
Mon 20	
Tue 21	LEAGUE CUP SEMI-FINAL
Wed 22	LEAGUE CUP SEMI-FINAL
Thu 23	
Fri 24	
Sat 25	
Sun 26	
Mon 27	
Tue 28	
Wed 29	EC/ECWC/UEFA CUP 1ST RND 2ND LEG
Thu 30	

OCTOBER 1993

Fri 1	
Sat 2	
Sun 3	
Mon 4	
Tue 5	
Wed 6	B & Q CUP 1ST ROUND
Thu 7	
Fri 8	
Sat 9	
Sun 10	
Mon 11	
Tue 12	
Wed 13	ITALY v SCOTLAND (UEFA U21) **and**
Thu 14	**ITALY v SCOTLAND (WCQ)**
Fri 15	
Sat 16	
Sun 17	
Mon 18	
Tue 19	
Wed 20	B & Q CUP 2ND ROUND **and**
Thu 21	EC/ECWC/UEFA CUP 2ND RND 1ST LEG
Fri 22	
Sat 23	
Sun 24	LEAGUE CUP FINAL
Mon 25	
Tue 26	
Wed 27	B & Q CUP 3RD ROUND
Thu 28	
Fri 29	
Sat 30	
Sun 31	

NOVEMBER 1993

Mon 1	
Tue 2	B & Q CUP SEMI-FINALS
Wed 3	EC/ECWC/UEFA CUP 2ND RND 2ND LEG
Thu 4	
Fri 5	
Sat 6	
Sun 7	
Mon 8	
Tue 9	
Wed 10	
Thu 11	
Fri 12	
Sat 13	
Sun 14	
Mon 15	
Tue 16	MALTA v SCOTLAND (UEFA U21)
Wed 17	**MALTA v SCOTLAND (WCQ)**
Thu 18	
Fri 19	
Sat 20	
Sun 21	
Mon 22	
Tue 23	
Wed 24	EC GROUP MATCHES/UEFA CUP 3RD
Thu 25	RND 1ST LEG
Fri 26	
Sat 27	
Sun 28	
Mon 29	
Tue 30	

DECEMBER 1993

Wed 1	
Thu 2	
Fri 3	
Sat 4	
Sun 5	B & Q CUP FINAL
Mon 6	
Tue 7	
Wed 8	EC GROUP MATCHES/UEFA CUP 3RD
Thu 9	RND 2ND LEG
Fri 10	
Sat 11	TENNENTS SCOTTISH CUP 1ST ROUND
Sun 12	
Mon 13	
Tue 14	
Wed 15	
Thu 16	
Fri 17	
Sat 18	
Sun 19	
Mon 20	
Tue 21	
Wed 22	
Thu 23	
Fri 24	
Sat 25	
Sun 26	
Mon 27	
Tue 28	
Wed 29	
Thu 30	
Fri 31	

JANUARY 1994

Sat 1	
Sun 2	
Mon 3	
Tue 4	
Wed 5	
Thu 6	
Fri 7	
Sat 8	TENNENTS SCOTTISH CUP 2ND ROUND
Sun 9	
Mon 10	
Tue 11	
Wed 12	
Thu 13	
Fri 14	
Sat 15	
Sun 16	
Mon 17	
Tue 18	
Wed 19	
Thu 20	
Fri 21	
Sat 22	
Sun 23	
Mon 24	
Tue 25	
Wed 26	
Thu 27	
Fri 28	
Sat 29	TENNENTS SCOTTISH CUP 3RD ROUND
Sun 30	
Mon 31	

FEBRUARY 1994

Tue 1	
Wed 2	
Thu 3	
Fri 4	
Sat 5	
Sun 6	
Mon 7	
Tue 8	
Wed 9	
Thu 10	
Fri 11	
Sat 12	
Sun 13	
Mon14	
Tue 15	
Wed16	
Thu 17	
Fri 18	
Sat 19	TENNENTS SCOTTISH CUP 4TH ROUND
Sun 20	
Mon21	
Tue 22	
Wed23	
Thu 24	
Fri 25	
Sat 26	
Sun 27	
Mon28	

MARCH 1994

Tue 1	
Wed 2	EC GROUP MATCHES/ECWC/UEFA CUP — QF 1ST LEG
Thu 3	
Fri 4	
Sat 5	
Sun 6	
Mon 7	
Tue 8	
Wed 9	
Thu 10	
Fri 11	
Sat 12	TENNENTS SCOTTISH CUP 5TH ROUND
Sun 13	
Mon14	
Tue 15	
Wed16	EC GROUP MATCHES/ECWC/UEFA CUP — QF 2ND LEG
Thu 17	
Fri 18	
Sat 19	
Sun 20	
Mon21	
Tue 22	
Wed23	
Thu 24	
Fri 25	
Sat 26	
Sun 27	
Mon28	
Tue 29	
Wed30	EC GROUP MATCHES/ECWC/UEFA CUP — SF 1ST LEG
Thu 31	

APRIL 1994

Fri 1	
Sat 2	
Sun 3	
Mon 4	
Tue 5	
Wed 6	
Thu 7	
Fri 8	
Sat 9	TENNENTS SCOTTISH CUP SEMI-FINALS
Sun 10	
Mon11	
Tue 12	
Wed13	EC GROUP MATCHES/ECWC/UEFA CUP — SF 2ND LEG
Thu 14	
Fri 15	
Sat 16	
Sun 17	
Mon18	
Tue 19	AUSTRIA v SCOTLAND (U21)
Wed20	AUSTRIA v SCOTLAND
Thu 21	
Fri 22	
Sat 23	
Sun 24	
Mon25	
Tue 26	
Wed27	EC SF/UEFA CUP FINAL 1ST LEG
Thu 28	
Fri 29	
Sat 30	

MAY 1994

Sun 1	
Mon 2	
Tue 3	
Wed 4	ECWC FINAL
Thu 5	
Fri 6	
Sat 7	
Sun 8	
Mon 9	
Tue 10	
Wed11	UEFA CUP FINAL 2ND LEG
Thu 12	
Fri 13	
Sat 14	
Sun 15	
Mon16	
Tue 17	
Wed18	EUROPEAN CHAMPIONS' CUP FINAL
Thu 19	
Fri 20	
Sat 21	TENNENTS SCOTTISH CUP FINAL
Sun 22	
Mon23	
Tue 24	
Wed25	
Thu 26	
Fri 27	
Sat 28	
Sun 29	
Mon30	
Tue 31	

JUNE 1994

Wed 1	
Thu 2	
Fri 3	
Sat 4	
Sun 5	
Mon 6	
Tue 7	
Wed 8	
Thu 9	
Fri 10	
Sat 11	
Sun 12	
Mon13	
Tue 14	
Wed15	
Thu 16	
Fri 17	WORLD CUP - U.S.A. '94
Sat 18	WORLD CUP - U.S.A. '94
Sun 19	WORLD CUP - U.S.A. '94
Mon20	WORLD CUP - U.S.A. '94
Tue 21	WORLD CUP - U.S.A. '94
Wed22	WORLD CUP - U.S.A. '94
Thu 23	WORLD CUP - U.S.A. '94
Fri 24	WORLD CUP - U.S.A. '94
Sat 25	WORLD CUP - U.S.A. '94
Sun 26	WORLD CUP - U.S.A. '94
Mon27	WORLD CUP - U.S.A. '94
Tue 28	WORLD CUP - U.S.A. '94
Wed29	WORLD CUP - U.S.A. '94
Thu 30	WORLD CUP - U.S.A. '94

JULY 1994

Fri 1	
Sat 2	WORLD CUP - U.S.A. '94
Sun 3	WORLD CUP - U.S.A. '94
Mon 4	WORLD CUP - U.S.A. '94
Tue 5	WORLD CUP - U.S.A. '94
Wed 6	
Thu 7	
Fri 8	WORLD CUP - U.S.A. '94
Sat 9	WORLD CUP - U.S.A. '94
Sun 10	WORLD CUP - U.S.A. '94
Mon11	
Tue 12	WORLD CUP - U.S.A. '94
Wed13	WORLD CUP - U.S.A. '94
Thu 14	
Fri 15	
Sat 16	WORLD CUP - U.S.A. '94
Sun 17	WORLD CUP - U.S.A. '94
Mon18	
Tue 19	
Wed20	
Thu 21	
Fri 22	
Sat 23	
Sun 24	
Mon25	
Tue 26	
Wed27	
Thu 28	
Fri 29	
Sat 30	
Sun 31	

Above: Kevin Gallacher celebrates his goal against Estonia in Tallinn.
Below: Pat Nevin nets against Malta at Ibrox.

WORLD CUP QUALIFYING GAMES

9th September, 1992 in Berne
Switzerland 3 Scotland 1
Scorer: McCoist

14th October, 1992 at Ibrox Stadium
Scotland 0 Portugal 0

18th November, 1992 at Ibrox Stadium
Scotland 0 Italy 0

17th February, 1993 at Ibrox Stadium
Scotland 3 Malta 0
Scorers: McCoist (2), Nevin

28th April, 1993 in Lisbon
Portugal 5 Scotland 0

19th May, 1993 in Tallinn
Estonia 0 Scotland 3
Scorers: Gallacher, Collins, Booth

2nd June, 1993 at Pittodrie Stadium
Scotland 3 Estonia 1
Scorers: Nevin (2, 1 pen), McClair

CHALLENGE MATCH

24th March, 1993 at Ibrox Stadium
Scotland 0 Germany 1